What if
everything you knew
about education was
wrong?

David Didau

Forewords by
Robert A. Bjork and Dylan Wiliam

© David Didau, 2015

The list on page 49 has been adapted with permission of Andrew Old.

The extract on page 95 is used with permission of Laura McInerney.

The extract on page 124 is used with permission of Dorothy Bishop.

The list on pages 134–135 has been adapted with permission of Daniel Willingham.

The list on page 155 and the extract on pages 298–299 are used with permission of Robert Coe.

The extract on page 193 is used with permission of Gerald Haigh.

The extracts on page 215 and page 254 are used with permission of Robert A. Bjork.

The extract on page 236 has been adapted with permission of Harry Fletcher-Wood.

Table 17.1 on page 252 is used with permission of Solution Tree Press.

The extracts on pages 266–267, pages 284–287 and pages 287–288 are used with permission of Dylan Wiliam.

Figure 22.1 on page 322 is used with permission of Greg Ashman.

Table 24.1 on page 339 is used with permission of David Thomas.

Quotes from Ofsted documents used in this publication have been approved under an Open Government Licence. Please visit http://www.nationalarchives.gov.uk/doc/open-government-licence/version/3/.

Megaphone image © aeroking - Fotolia.com

Images page 19 © Les Evans

This edition of **What if everything you knew about education was wrong?** is published by arrangement with Crown House Publishing Limited.

1641 Worthington Road, Suite 210
West Palm Beach, FL 33401
724.459.2100
email: pub@learningsciences.com
learningsciences.com

22 21 20 19 18   1 2 3 4 5

Names: Didau, David, author.
Title: What if everything you knew about education was wrong / David Didau.

West Palm Beach, FL : Learning Sciences, 2019. | Also available in ebook format.

Identifiers:
ISBN 978-1-943920-81-5 (paperback)
ISBN 978-1-943920-83-9 (ebook)

Subjects: LCSH: Educational leadership. | Education--Aims and objectives. | Teacher effectiveness. | BISAC: EDUCATION / Professional Development. | EDUCATION / Aims & Objectives. | EDUCATION / Leadership.

For my father

We think our fathers fools, so wise we grow;
Our wiser sons, no doubt will think us so.
Alexander Pope

Foreword by
Robert A. Bjork

Using various versions of the title, "How We Learn versus How We Think We Learn", I have given talks to different audiences on the surprising discrepancy that exists between what research has revealed about how humans learn and remember versus how people tend to think they learn and remember. The discrepancy is surprising because one might expect that as lifelong users of our memories and learning capabilities, coupled with the "trials and errors of everyday living and learning",[1] we would have come to understand how to optimize not only our own learning, but also the learning of those we are responsible for teaching, whether at home, in schools or in the workplace. The discrepancy is important, too, because as David Didau documents and illustrates so well in this book, optimizing the effectiveness of our teaching and our own learning depends on incorporating methods and activities that mesh with how we actually learn versus how we think we learn.

That we tend to have a faulty mental model of how we learn and remember has been a source of continuing fascination to me. Why are we misled? I have speculated that one factor is that the functional architecture of how we learn, remember and forget is unlike the corresponding processes in man-made devices.[2] We tend not, of course, to understand the engineering details of how information is stored, added, lost or overwritten in man-made devices, such as video recorders or the memory in a computer, but the functional architecture of such devices is simpler and easier to understand than the complex architecture of human learning and memory. If we do think of ourselves as working like such devices, we become susceptible to thinking, explicitly or implicitly, that exposing ourselves to information and procedures will lead to their being stored in our memories – that they will write themselves on our brains – which could not be further from the truth.

Also, to the extent that we think of ourselves as some kind of recording device, we are unlikely to realize how using our memories shapes our memories. That is, we can fail to appreciate the extent to which retrieving information from our memories increases subsequent access to that information and reduces access to competing information. Retrieving information from a compact disc or computer memory leaves that information and related information unchanged, but that is far from the case with respect to human memory. More globally, to the extent that we think of ourselves as recording devices, we may fail to appreciate the volatility that characterizes access to information from our memories as conditions change, events intervene and new learning happens. Information that is readily accessible in one context at one point in time may be completely inaccessible at another point in time in a different context – and vice versa.

We can also be led astray by oversimplifying what it means to have stronger or weaker memories. We may think, for example, that memory traces in our brains are like footprints in the sand that can be shallower or deeper and, hence, more or less resistant to the effects of forgetting. In fact, how memories are represented in our brains is multidimensional: some memory A, for example, may appear stronger than some other memory B by one measure, such as recognition or the subjective sense of familiarity, whereas memory B may appear stronger by some other measure, such as free or cued recall. Basically, by intuition or experience alone, we can never come to realize the amazing array of interactions of encoding conditions and test conditions that have been shown in controlled experiments to affect our ability to retain and recall to-be-learned information. We may have a general idea, even an accurate idea, that some learning activities produce better retention than others, but appreciating fully the complex interactions of encoding conditions, retention interval, type of later test and what cues will or will not be available at the time of the final test requires a whole different level of understanding.

To make things even more challenging for us as learners and/or teachers, conditions of instruction or practice that appear to result in rapid progress and learning can fail to produce good long-term retention of skills and knowledge, or transfer of such skills or knowledge to new situations where they are relevant, whereas other conditions that pose challenges for the learner – and appear to slow the learning process – can enhance such long-term retention and transfer. Conditions of the latter type, which I have labelled "desirable difficulties",[3] include spacing, rather than massing, repeated study opportunities; interleaving, rather than blocking, instruction or practice on the separate components of a given task; providing intermittent, rather than continuous, feedback to learners; varying the conditions of learning, rather than keeping them constant and predictable; and using tests, rather than re-presentations, as learning opportunities.

The key point – one that David Didau emphasizes and one that readers of this book should be sure to take away – is that there is a critical distinction in research on learning, one that dates back decades: namely, the distinction between learning and performance. What we can observe and measure during instruction is performance; whereas learning, as reflected by the long-term retention and transfer of skills and knowledge, must be inferred, and, importantly, current performance can be a highly unreliable guide to whether learning has happened. In short, we are at risk of being fooled by current performance, which can lead us, as teachers or instructors, to choose less effective conditions of learning over more effective conditions, and can lead us, as learners ourselves, to prefer poorer conditions of instruction over better conditions of instruction.

Several aspects of this book make it especially valuable. One is that David Didau has not only explained and illustrated the research findings to which I have alluded, as well as other key findings from social psychology and cognitive psychology, but he has also done so in terms of their relevance to real world schools and education. He has also discussed such findings and their implications with respect to historical trends and ideas that have guided, and sometimes misled, educational practices. Finally, and critically, he is able to discuss research findings and their implications for real world teaching from the standpoint of somebody who has been in the trenches, as it were. His career as a teacher and as an administrator in pre-college settings provides a perspective that is lacked by those of us who have spent our careers doing research and teaching in the ivory tower.

Notes

1   Robert A. Bjork, Assessing Our Own Competence: Heuristics and Illusions, in D. Gopher and A. Koriat (eds), *Attention and Performance XVII. Cognitive Regulation of Performance: Interaction of Theory and Application* (Cambridge, MA: MIT Press, 1999), pp. 435–459.
2   Robert A. Bjork, On the Symbiosis of Learning, Remembering, and Forgetting, in A. S. Benjamin (ed.), *Successful Remembering and Successful Forgetting: A Festschrift in Honor of Robert A. Bjork* (London: Psychology Press, 2011), pp. 1–22.
3   Robert A. Bjork, Memory and Metamemory Considerations in the Training of Human Beings, in J. Metcalfe and A. Shimamura (eds), *Metacognition: Knowing About Knowing* (Cambridge, MA: MIT Press, 1994), pp. 185–205.

Foreword by
Dylan Wiliam

Education has always had a rather uneasy relationship with psychology. As Ellen Condliffe Lagemann describes in her account of "the troubling history of education research", for many years, it was thought that psychology could provide a disciplinary foundation for the practice of education.[1] Indeed, for a while, many of those engaged in teacher education behaved as if education was really just applied psychology. Psychologists would determine the optimal conditions for learning, and teachers would then create those conditions in their classrooms. As a result, in the 1960s and 1970s, courses on the psychology of learning featured prominently in most, if not all, pre-service teacher education programs.

However, even the staunchest proponents of the relevance of psychology to teacher education would hesitate to claim that these courses were successful. Initial teacher education students regarded the courses as irrelevant to what they saw as the task at hand. Perhaps, most importantly, it was clear that the available research was of little use in telling teachers what to do, whether this was in terms of the best way to explain concepts to children or how to get them to behave.

In the education research community, this led many researchers to look to sociology and social anthropology as sources of insights on how to understand classrooms, and, predictably, in many universities, courses on the sociology of education were added to pre-service programs. But, again, trainee teachers found these courses of limited relevance to their own practice.

Beginning in the 1980s, partly as a response to government initiatives, there was a shift in the way that pre-service teacher education courses were designed. The four-year bachelor of education programs fell out of favor, and, for secondary teachers at least, the most common route into the profession was a three-year undergraduate degree in a specialist subject, followed by a one-year post-graduate certificate in education (PGCE) program. Furthermore, because many politicians saw university departments of education as hotbeds of radical left-wing thought (which is bizarre because they *really* weren't), they sought to reduce the role of universities in teacher education. First came the idea that 24 weeks of a 36-week PGCE program had to be spent in schools, and this was quickly followed by specifications of what students should be learning on PGCEs, together with inspections of these program, with funded student numbers tied to the results of these inspections.

Predictably, PGCE programs concentrated on ensuring that teachers mastered hundreds of 'competencies' on the practicalities of teaching, and any systematic exposure to the 'foundation disciplines' of psychology or sociology was at best marginalized and in many cases dropped entirely. By 1990 it was common to find that a university department of education did not have a single card-carrying psychologist on its faculty (by which I mean someone who would have been eligible for membership, if not actually a member, of the British Psychological Society).

As a card-carrying psychologist myself, I hadn't realized how profoundly teacher training had moved away from psychology until, in the late 1990s, Paul Black and I started working with teachers to help them develop their practice of formative assessment. What surprised us most was that every group of teachers with whom we worked asked us, typically about three months into a project, for some formal input on the psychology of learning. Our emphasis on questioning as a way of eliciting evidence about student learning, and feedback that would be useful to students, required the teachers to use mental models of what was happening in their students' heads. Most of the teachers with whom we were working, including many who were perceived as highly effective, had no such models. It turned out that it was possible to be regarded as a highly effective teacher with no idea what was happening in the minds of students.

The irony in all this is that, just as university departments of education began to dispense with the psychology of education as a key input into teacher training, psychologists were producing insights into learning in real, as opposed to laboratory settings, that had relatively straightforward applications to practice.

Now, of course, it is unlikely that the psychology of learning will ever be developed to the point where psychology will tell teachers what to do. To build a bridge, you need to know about the behavior of steel and stone when compressed and stretched, but knowing all this will never tell you what the bridge should look like. In the same way, psychology will never tell teachers how to teach, but there are now clear principles emerging about how we learn best; principles that teachers can use to make teaching more effective, such as the fact that spaced practice is better than massed practice and the benefits of frequent classroom testing for long-term retention.

This is what makes the book you have in your hands so important and exciting. There are many excellent accounts of recent work in cognitive science (most of which are listed in the bibliography at the end of this book), and some of them also do a good job of drawing out the implications of this research for learning. However, to my knowledge, this is the first book that gets the cognitive science right and at the same time is written from a profound understanding of the reality of classrooms.

The title of this book, *What If Everything You Knew About Education Was Wrong?*, says it all really. This book does not claim that everything we know about education is, in fact, incorrect. Rather it is an invitation to reflect on our beliefs about teaching and learning, and to examine in detail whether our assumptions are as well-founded as we would like them to be. You will see that David and I have debated a number of issues, and, in particular, the evidence for the usefulness of what has, in the UK at least, become known as Assessment for Learning. Engaging in this debate has forced me to clarify some of my ideas and modify others, and I have also become clearer about how to communicate them to others. I suspect that David and I still disagree about some of these issues, but being open to the idea that we might be wrong allows us both to continue to develop our thinking about how to harness the power of education to transform lives.

In short, this is my new favorite book on education. I read it from cover to cover before writing this foreword, and I plan to revisit it regularly. If I was still running a PGCE program it would be required reading for my students, and I can think of no better choice for a book-study for experienced teachers. Anyone seriously interested in education should read this book.

Notes

1   Ellen Condliffe Lagemann, *An Elusive Science: The Troubling History of Education Research* (Chicago, IL: Chicago University Press, 2000), p. 282.

Acknowledgements

This book has lived in my head for some years, and without the help and guidance of a great many people that's where it would have stayed. Instrumental in the process of getting it down on paper have been the education community on Twitter. I struggle to bring to mind everyone whose thinking, advice and support have helped me along the way, but chief among them are Martin Robinson (@SurrealAnarchy) for some cracking quotes and avuncular advice; Carl Hendrick (@CarlHendrick) for telling me about negative capability; James Theobold (@jamestheo) for letting me steal some of his best ideas; Glen Gilchrist (@mrgpg) for explaining the difference between causation and correlation; Gerald Haigh (@geraldhaigh1) for the anecdote about forgetting in music; David Thomas (@dmthomas90) for attempting to explain game theory; Andrew Smith (@OldAndrewUK) for providing so many examples of poor school leadership and showing me the error of my ways; Laura McInerney (@miss_mcinerney) for also asking what might happen if everything we knew about education was wrong; Nick Rose (@turnfordblog) for being "the angriest man in education" as well as one of the most sensible; Kris Boulton (@Kris_Boulton) for making me *really* think about retrieval-induced forgetting; Sam Freedman (@samfr) for letting me pick his considerable brain; Rob Coe (@ProfCoe) for giving up his time to patiently explain things to me; Cristina Milos (@sureallyno) for challenging and supporting in equal measure; Stuart Lock (@StuartLock) for travelling the same path; Harry Fletcher-Wood (@HFletcherWood) for spotting mistakes and providing clarifications; Daniel T. Willingham (@DTWillingham) for writing such consistently thought-provoking articles and books; Pedro De Bruyckere (@thebandb) for exposing me to so much fascinating research; Greg Ashman (@greg_ashman) for saying the same thing enough times that I started to understand it; Dan Brinton (@dan_brinton) for blowing all that smoke and Phil Beadle (@PhilBeadle) for all the al fresco wine consumption.

Of those I need to single out, Bob Bjork is the foremost. His decades' worth of research and thinking has formed the basis of my ideas. Quite literally, without his theory of memory, the observation that performance and learning need to be disassociated and the concept of 'desirable difficulties', there would have been no book. Any weaknesses in my presentation of his work are wholly due to my limited understanding.

I also need to publically acknowledge the huge debt owed to Dylan Wiliam (@dylanwiliam), not only for allowing me to reproduce his comments on my blog posts critiquing his work, but also for being consistently wise, generous and clear sighted. The time he has given to debating with me has greatly enhanced both my thinking and the content of this book.

Nothing really compares to the approval of one's heroes and to say that I'm grateful to Bob and Dylan for contributing such enthusiastic forewords is something of an understatement. Both are giants in their respected fields and I am both proud and humbled to have stood on their shoulders.

Then there are those who have directly contributed their words to the book. Their contributions show other ways in which we can be wrong in education. Jack Marwood's (@Jack_Marwood) magisterial demolition of the way we use data in schools (Appendix 1) and Andrew Sabisky's (@andrewsabisky) elegant unpicking of how the nature vs. nurture debate should inform our thinking on 'closing the gap' (Appendix 2) have both added significantly to my thesis and expanded it into fields of which I am lamentably ignorant. I must also thank Joe Kirby (@Joe_Kirby) for allowing me to use material from his excellent blog, *Pragmatic Education*. These additions have made Chapter 24 so much better than it would otherwise have been.

As well as thanking Caroline Lenton, Emma Tuck, Bev Randell, Rosalie Williams and all the usual suspects at Crown House for working their magic behind the scenes, I need to pay tribute to the contribution of my editor, Peter Young. Despite our battles and my stubborn and short-sighted refusal to accept his wisdom on several points, his ferocious insight, extensive knowledge, attention to detail and willingness to read absolutely everything I've read in order to pull me up on sloppy interpretations has been the making of this book. Without him it would have been a much poorer effort.

Thanks also to Graham, my father, for reading through my drafts, spotting so many errors and making so many useful suggestions.

And, finally, Rosie – for putting up with so much nonsense.

Contents

Figures and tables

The ideas of economists and political philosophers, both when they are right and when they are wrong, are more powerful than is commonly understood. Indeed, the world is ruled by little else. Practical men, who believe themselves to be quite exempt from any intellectual influence, are usually the slaves of some defunct economist.

John Maynard Keynes

If God held enclosed in his right hand all truth, and in his left hand the ever-striving drive for truth, even with the corollary of erring forever and ever, and were to say to me: Choose! – I would humbly fall down at his left hand and say: "Father, give! Pure truth is indeed only for you alone."

G. E. Lessing

If human nature were not base, but thoroughly honorable, we should in every debate have no other aim than the discovery of truth; we should not in the least care whether the truth proved to be in favor of the opinion which we had begun by expressing, or of the opinion of our adversary. That we should regard as a matter of no moment, or, at any rate, of very secondary consequence; but, as things are, it is the main concern. Our innate vanity, which is particularly sensitive in reference to our intellectual powers, will not suffer us to allow that our first position was wrong and our adversary's right. The way out of this difficulty would be simply to take the trouble always to form a correct judgment. For this a man would have to think before he spoke. But, with most men, innate vanity is accompanied by loquacity and innate dishonesty. They speak before they think; and even though they may afterwards perceive that they are wrong, and that what they assert is false, they want it to seem the contrary. The interest in truth, which may be presumed to have been their only motive when they stated the proposition alleged to be true, now gives way to the interests of vanity: and so, for the sake of vanity, what is true must seem false, and what is false must seem true.

Arthur Schopenhauer

While people are entitled to their illusions, they are not entitled to a limitless enjoyment of them and they are not entitled to impose them upon others.

Christopher Hitchens

Believe those who are seeking the truth; doubt those who find it.

André Gide

I don't necessarily agree with everything I say.

Marshall McLuhan

Introduction

I beseech you, in the bowels of Christ, think it possible you may be mistaken.

Oliver Cromwell

This is a book about teaching, but it is not a manual on how to teach. It is a book about ideas, but not, I hope, ideological. It is a book about thinking and questioning and challenging, but it also attempts some possible answers.

By training and inclination I'm a teacher. The ideas in this book are therefore viewed through the prism of my experience of working in schools, but they should be equally applicable to every other area where people want, or are required, to learn. The intention is to help you to develop the healthy skepticism needed to spot bad ideas masquerading as common sense. In so doing, I hope this will provide a better appreciation both of what 'learning' might mean and how we might get better at it.

If you feel a bit angry at the presumption of some lout daring to suggest everything you know about education might be wrong, please take it with a grain of salt. It's just a title. Of course, you probably think a great many things that aren't wrong. The question refers to education in the widest as well as the most narrow senses. Although I'm explicitly critical of certain policies and practices, what I'm really criticizing is certainty. My hope is that you will consider the implications of being wrong and consider what you would do differently if your most cherished beliefs about education turned out not to be true.

Naturally, there are countless things that you do, day in, day out, which you take completely for granted and that work just fine. By the same token, there are probably very many other things that might be wrong with education but which fall outside the scope of this book. I've chosen to write about those beliefs and certainties that I've found most confounding in my career as a teacher. These are often concepts and ideas that we accept so unquestioningly that we've stopped thinking *about* them because we think *with* them.

To that end, I have identified certain ideas and ways of thinking which you may well find challenging or troublesome. These are the *threshold concepts** of the book:

- Seeing shouldn't always result in believing (Chapter 1).

- We are all victims of cognitive bias (Chapter 2).

- Compromise doesn't always result in effective solutions (Chapter 4).

- Evidence is not the same as proof (Chapter 5).

- Progress is a gradual, non-linear process (Chapters 6 and 7).

- Learning is invisible (Chapter 8).

- Current performance is not only a poor indication of learning, it actually seems to prevent it (Chapters 8 and 9).

- Forgetting aids learning (Chapter 9).

- Experts and novices learn differently (Chapter 10).

- Making learning more difficult can make it more durable (Chapter 11).

The main thing I think we're wrong about is the belief that we can see learning. This conviction has probably been around for as long as there have been teachers and students. It is so deeply embedded in the way we see the world that we don't even think about it: it is a self-evident truth. Almost everything teachers are asked to do is predicated on this simple idea. We teach, children learn. This is the input/output myth. We may have an inkling that things aren't quite this straightforward, but we act as if they are. Pretty much every lesson taught by every teacher in every school depends on the idea that we can see learning happen.

---

*   If you're desperate to find out what on earth a threshold concept might be, feel free to skip ahead to Chapter 7.

If we're wrong about this, what else might we be wrong about? If it's true that learning is invisible, where does that leave Assessment for Learning (Formative Assessment), lesson observation and the whole concept of 'outstanding' teaching? Up a particularly filthy creek in a paper canoe, that's where!

Education has become like the woman in the gospels who 'suffered under many doctors'. Everyone is happy to prescribe their own favorite medicine. And how do they know it works? Because it 'feels right'. But often what has the greatest impact on students' learning is deeply and bafflingly counter-intuitive. In Part 1 we will dismantle the flaws in our thinking on which the edifice of belief depends. We'll survey the tangle of assumptions that have grown up around the education debate and hack through the current vogue for research and evidence in our attempt to find some solutions.

You see, there are some things in which we might be able to place our trust. These are not magic beans – they're the product of rigorous, repeatable scientific research, and they're free! For over a century, researchers have been investigating how we learn and remember. Nowadays, this gets called cognitive science, but investigations into these areas go back at least as far as Plato. They picked up speed in the 19th century with such thinkers as William James and Hermann Ebbinghaus, and an explosion of research in the latter half of the 20th century started to indicate that what we thought we knew about learning was widely misunderstood and that the facts were deeply surprising. This will be the focus of Part 2.

One man who has had a very particular influence on the field of cognitive psychology, especially in the area of learning, memory and forgetting, but is little known within education circles, is Professor Robert A. Bjork of UCLA. Despite spending much of the past five decades amassing a trove of fascinating insights on remembering, forgetting and learning, his research – and that of other cognitive psychologists – has, until very recently, received little attention in the secret garden of education. Why this is I'm not sure. But one of my hopes in writing this book is that teachers and policy makers are made more aware of this hidden body of knowledge. Because curriculum time is always limited, we need to decide which is more important: teaching or learning. Do we want to make sure we teach as much as possible or that students learn as much as possible? Do we want students to perform well in a lesson or in the future? Do we want them to learn quickly or do we want that learning to last? You can't necessarily have both, so in Part 3 we'll take a look at some of Bjork's ideas about making learning harder.

Then, in Part 4, we'll look at how we can rethink some of the classroom practices we take for granted and consider whether we might benefit from doing them differently. Although we could pick on all sorts of sacred calves, the ones we will concentrate on are formative assessment, lesson observation, differentiation, character, praise, motivation and creativity.

You might find this book provocative. It's meant to be. My hope is that we have enough in common to discuss our beliefs about education without anyone getting too upset. Obviously, there are no guarantees that this will play out as I intend. Misunderstandings will occur; mistakes will be made, and you may need to adjust your views to some degree.*

Of course, I acknowledge that I have no idea of the best way to teach your subject to your students. That is (or should be) your area of expertise. I don't intend to make sweeping assumptions or assertions about what you should be doing, just speculations on what you could be doing. As far as I'm concerned, teachers can teach standing up, sitting down, hopping on one leg, wearing flip-flops or with a bag over their heads. I'm not interested in how students are seated, what techniques are used in classrooms or what resources are produced. I'm broadly keen on grading books, but I don't much care whether teachers use green or red pen, pencil, invisible ink or human blood. I'm in favor of having high expectations for every student, but it should be up to individuals what this looks like. I'm a fan of hard work and suspicious of fun for fun's sake, but that's just me; you should do what you deem best. It really doesn't matter *what* you do, as long as it's effective.

And that's the problem. An awful lot of what teachers think of as 'effective' only seems so because it works for them; the alarming truth is that this doesn't mean it works for their students – judging your impact is a little more complicated than that.

....

* Ideally this readjustment would be a two-way process with your experiences coloring my perceptions as mine color yours, but because you're reading a book it's hard to participate. Rather than just dismissing me as a fool and a charlatan, if you do feel compelled to set me straight on anything, please do visit my website and offer your criticism and raise your concerns: www.learningspy.co.uk.

I want to make it very clear here, right at the outset, that I offer no guarantees and no assurances that what I suggest will 'work'. There is no template you can simply adopt to solve the problems you face. Regrettably, life – and especially education – is rarely that simple. Anyone who makes such an offer is not to be trusted. Your experiences will be different to mine; you will have worked in different contexts, with different students and you may well have different values and aspirations. But whatever our differences, being prepared to subject your beliefs to a fearless examination will, if nothing else, make you a more thoughtful educator. The offer I make is that if you've given sufficient thought to what you believe and actively looked for errors in your thinking, all will probably be well. Just as, if you do anything simply because someone told you to, it will probably fail. In the words of Shakespeare's Hamlet, "There is nothing either good or bad, but thinking makes it so."

So, if you disagree with any or all of the points I make, that's fine. Really. I'm not trying to convince you of anything, except that you are sometimes wrong. What you do with that information is entirely up to you. You see, we're all wrong at times. Naturally no one sets out to be wrong. No one ever at any point in history pursued a course of action firm in the belief that they were wrong to do so. Everything we do, we do in the belief that we are right. But believing that we are right necessarily means that there must be times when others are wrong. I'm going to spend some time explaining all this in Chapters 1 and 2, but for now, just try to entertain the uncomfortable possibility that you may be wrong. Or, if it makes you feel better, blame someone else.

The aim of this book is to help you 'murder your darlings'. We will question your most deeply held assumptions about teaching and learning, expose them to the fiery eye of reason and see if they can still walk in a straight line after the experience. It seems reasonable to suggest that only if a theory or approach can withstand the fiercest scrutiny should it be encouraged in classrooms. I make no apologies for this; why wouldn't you be skeptical of what you're told and what you think you know? As educated professionals, we ought to strive to assemble a more accurate, informed or at least considered understanding of the world around us.

To that end, I will share with you some tools to help you question your assumptions and assist you in picking through what you believe. We will stew findings from the shiny white laboratories of cognitive psychology, stir in a generous dash of classroom research and serve up a side order of experience and observation. Whether you spit it out or lap it up matters not. If you come out the other end having vigorously and violently disagreed with me, you'll at least have had to think hard about what you believe.

And I'll be happy with that.

Part 1
Why we're wrong

Part 1
Why we're wrong

Before we get started, have a go at answering the following questions:

1. Have you ever been wrong?

2. Might you ever be wrong?

3. List five things you've been told about education which you think might possibly be wrong:

    _____

    _____

    _____

    _____

    _____

4. Have you ever acted on any of this information or anything else about which you weren't positive?

5. If so, why?

Now, check your answers below.

....

If you've answered yes to questions 1 and 2, well done. You can skip Part 1 if you like and pass straight through the threshold. If you answered no, I'm going to attempt to persuade you that you might be wrong. Read on.

If you managed to list one or more items in response to question 3, well done. There are undoubtedly more. If you weren't able to think of anything, stick around.

If you answered yes to question 4, I congratulate you on your ability to face the uncomfortable truth. If you answered no, you're either a very superior being or just plain wrong.

And if you answered 'I don't know' to question 5, welcome to my world. This is exactly where I found myself before I began the process of thinking about the content of this book. I hope my journey is of some use to you.

Chapter 1
Don't trust your gut

Man prefers to believe what he prefers to be true.

Francis Bacon

Nobody wants to be wrong – it feels terrible. In order to protect ourselves from acknowledging our mistakes, we have developed a sophisticated array of techniques that prevent us from having to accept such an awful reality. In this way we maintain our feeling of being right. This isn't me being smug by the way. Obviously, I'm as susceptible to self-deception as anyone else; as they say, denial ain't just a river in Egypt.

There are two very good reasons for most of the mistakes we make. Firstly, we don't make decisions based on what we *know*. Our decisions are based on what feels right. We're influenced by the times and places in which we live, the information most readily available and which we've heard most recently, peer pressure and social norms, and the carrots and sticks of those in authority. We base our decisions both on our selfish perceptions of current needs and wants and on more benevolent desires to positively affect change. And all of this is distilled by the judgements we make of the current situation. But our values and our sense of what's right and wrong can lead us into making some very dubious decisions.

Secondly, we're deplorable at admitting we don't know. Because of the way we're judged, it's far less risky to be wrong than it is to admit ignorance. If we're confident enough, people assume we must know what we're talking about. Most of us would prefer a clear answer, even if it turns out to be wrong, than an admission that someone is unsure. Because no one likes a procrastinator, certainty has become a proxy for competence. Added to this, very often we don't know that we don't know.

Feeling uncertain is uncomfortable, so when we're asked a hard question we very often substitute that question for an easier one. If we're asked, "Will this year's exam classes achieve their target grades?", how could we know? It's impossible to answer this question honestly. But no one wants to hear, "I don't know," so we switch it for an easier question like, "How do I feel about these students?" This is much easier to answer – we make our prediction without ever realizing we're not actually answering the question we were asked.

Despite it being relatively easy to spot other people making mistakes, it's devilishly difficult to set them straight. Early in my career as an English teacher, I noticed that children would arrive in secondary school with a clear and set belief that a comma is placed where you take a breath. This is obviously untrue: what if you suffered from asthma? So how has this become an accepted fact? Well, mainly because many teachers believe it to be true. This piece of homespun wisdom has been passed down from teacher to student as sure and certain knowledge, probably for centuries. If you do enough digging, it turns out punctuation marks were originally notation for actors on how to read scripts. It's still fairly useful advice that you might *take* a breath where you *see* a comma, but it's a staggeringly unhelpful rule on how to use them.*

I've spent many years howling this tiny nugget of truth at the moon, but it remains utterly predictable that every year children arrive at secondary school with no idea how to use commas. Teaching correct comma use depends on a good deal of basic grammatical knowledge. It's a lot easier to teach a proxy which is sort of true. Although the 'take a breath' rule allows students to mimic how writing should work, it prevents a proper understanding of the process. And so the misunderstanding remains. As is often observed, a lie can travel halfway around the world before the truth has had time to find its boots, let alone tug them on.

This kind of 'wrongness' is easy to see. It's much more difficult when what we believe validates who we are. Many of our beliefs define us; a

---

* In case you're interested, the only times you use commas are to separate items or adjectives in a list, before (never after) a coordinating conjunction, after a subordinate clause (if it begins a sentence), to separate direct speech from other elements of a sentence or to separate elements in a sentence that express contrast. All other uses, such as parenthetical commas and the serial comma, are mere variants of these instances.

challenge to our beliefs is a challenge to our sense of self. No surprise then that we resist such challenges. Here are some things which defined me and which I used to believe were certain:

- Good lessons involve children learning in groups with minimal intervention from the teacher.

- Teachers should minimize the time they spend talking in class and particularly avoid whole-class teaching.

- Children should be active; passivity is a sure sign they're not learning.

- Children should make rapid and sustained progress every lesson.

- Lessons should be fun, relevant to children's experiences and differentiated so that no one is forced to struggle with a difficult concept.

- Children are naturally good and any misbehavior on their part must be my fault.

- Teaching children facts is a fascistic attempt to impose middle class values and beliefs.

These are all things I was either explicitly taught as part of my training to be a teacher or that I picked up tacitly as being self-evidently true. Maybe you believe some or all of these things to be true too. It's not so much that I think these statements are definitively wrong, more that the processes by which I came to believe them were deeply flawed. In education (as in many other areas I'm sure), it would appear to be standard practice to present ideological positions as facts. Like many teachers, I had no idea how deeply certain ideas are contested as I was only offered one side of the debate.

I'll unpick how and why I now think these ideas are wrong in Chapter 3, but before that I need to soften you up a bit. If the rest of the book is going to work, I need you to accept the possibility that you might sometimes be wrong, even if we quibble about the specifics of exactly *what* you might be wrong about. You see, we're all wrong, all the time, about almost everything. Look around: everyone you've ever met is regularly wrong. To err is human.

In our culture, everyone is a critic. We delight in other people's errors, yet are reluctant to acknowledge our own. Perhaps your friends or family members have benefited from you pointing out their mistakes? Funny how they fail to appreciate your efforts, isn't it? No matter how obvious it is to you that they're absolutely and spectacularly wrong, they just don't seem able to see it. And that's true of us all. We can almost never see when we ourselves are wrong. Wittgenstein got it dead right when he pointed out: "If there were a verb meaning 'to believe falsely', it would not have any significant first person, present indicative."[1] That is to say, saying "I believe falsely" is a logical impossibility – if we believe it, how could we think of it as false? Once we know a thing to be false we no longer believe it.* This makes it hard to recognize when we are lying to ourselves or even acknowledge we're wrong after the fact. Even when confronted with irrefutable evidence, we can still doubt what is staring us in the face and find ways of keeping our beliefs intact.

Part of the problem is perceptual. We're prone to blind spots; there are things we, quite literally, cannot see. We all have a physiological blind spot: due to the way the optic nerve connects to our eyes, there are no rods or cones to detect light where it joins the back of the eye, which means there is an area of our vision – about six degrees of visual angle – that is not perceived. You might think we would notice a great patch of nothingness in our field of vision but we don't. We infer what's in the blind spot based on surrounding detail and information from our other eye, and our brain fills in the blank. So, whatever the scene, whether a static landscape or rush hour traffic, our brain copies details from the surrounding images and pastes in what it thinks should be there. For the most part our brains get it right, but occasionally they paste in a bit of empty highway when what's actually there is a motorcycle.

---

* This is the liar paradox. The statement negates itself and means nothing. Ironically, the problem of self-reference undermined much of Wittgenstein's thinking (and a good deal of the rest of 20th century philosophy).

Maybe you're unconvinced? Fortunately there's a very simple blind spot test:

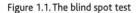

Figure 1.1. The blind spot test

Close your right eye and focus your left eye on the cross. Hold the page about 25 cm in front of you and gradually bring it closer. At some point the left-hand spot will disappear. If you do this with your right eye focused on the cross, at some point the right-hand spot will disappear.

So, how can we trust when our perception is accurate and when it's not? Worryingly, we can't. But the problem goes further. French philosopher Henri Bergson observed, "The eye sees only what the mind is prepared to comprehend." Quite literally, what we are able to perceive is restricted to what our brain thinks is there.

Further, Belgian psychologist Albert Michotte demonstrated that we 'see' causality where it doesn't exist. We know from our experience of the world that if we kick a ball, the ball will move. Our foot making contact is the cause. We then extrapolate from this to infer causal connections where there are none. Michotte designed a series of illustrations to demonstrate this phenomenon. If one object speeds across a screen, appears to make contact with a second object and that object then moves, it *looks* like the first object's momentum is the cause of the second object's movement. But it's just an illusion – the 'illusion of causality'. He showed that with a delay of a second, we no longer *see* this cause and effect. If a large circle moves quickly across the screen preceded by a small circle, it *looks* like the large circle is chasing the small circle.* We attribute causality depending on speed, timing, direction and many other factors. All we

* Describing these illustrations is frustratingly inadequate – you'd do much better to watch the online animation of Michotte's ideas here: http://cogweb.ucla.edu/Discourse/Narrative/michotte-demo.swf.

physically see is movement, but there's more to perception than meets the eye. Consider how we infer causes to complex events: if we see a teacher teach two lessons we consider inadequate, we infer that they're an inadequate teacher.

This leads us to naive realism – the belief that our senses provide us with an objective and reliable awareness of the world. We tend to believe that we see objects as they really are, when in fact what we see is just our own internal representation of the world. And why wouldn't we? If an interactive whiteboard falls on our head, it'll hurt! But while we may agree that the world is made of matter, which can be perceived, matter exists independently of our observations: the whiteboard will still be smashed on the floor even if no one was there to see it fall. Mostly this doesn't signify; what we see tends to be similar enough to what others see as to make no difference. But sometimes the perceptual differences are such that we do not agree on the meaning and therefore on the action to be taken.

The existence of optical illusions proves not only that our senses can be mistaken, but more importantly they also demonstrate how the unconscious processes we use to construct an internal reality from raw sense data can go awry.

Figure 1.2. Checker shadow illusion
Source: http://web.mit.edu/persci/people/adelson/checkershadow_illusion.html.

In Edward H. Adelson's checker shadow illusion (Figure 1.2), the squares labeled A and B are the exact same shades of grey. No really. The shadow cast by the cylinder makes B as dark as A, but because the squares sur-rounding B are also darker you may not believe it.

Here's a second version of the illusion:

Figure 1.3. Checker shadow illusion version 2
Source: http://persci.mit.edu/gallery/checkershadow/proof.

We *know* A is a dark square and B is a light square. Seeing the squares as the same shade is rejected by our brain as unhelpful. We are unable to see what is right there in front of us. This neatly proves that there cannot be a simple, direct correspondence between what we perceive as being out there and what's *actually* out there. Our brains edit our perceptions so that we literally see something that isn't there. When I first saw this I couldn't accept that the evidence of my eyes could be so wrong. I had to print out a copy, cut out the squares and position them side by side in order to see the truth. Illusions like this are "a gateway drug to humil-ity".[2] They teach us what it is like to confront the fact we're wrong in a relatively non-threatening way.

Here's another example. Log on to the internet and watch this video before reading further: http://goo.gl/ZXEGQ7.*

....

*   For those who can't be bothered to watch the clip, it shows two teams of basketball
     players, one team in white, the other in black. You are asked to focus on the white
     shirted players and count the number of completed passes they make but to ignore
     the players in black. Midway through the film, a man in a gorilla costume takes the
     stage, beats his chest and walks off.

The research of Daniel Simons and Christopher Chabris into 'inattention blindness' reveals a similar capacity for wrongness.[3] Their experiment, the Invisible Gorilla, has become famous – if you've not seen it before, it can be startling: between 40–50 percent of people fail to see the gorilla. And if you have seen it before, did you notice one of the black T-shirted players leave the stage? You did? Did you also see the curtain change from red to gold? Vanishingly few people see all these things. And practically no one sees all these changes and still manages to count the passes! Intuitively, we don't believe that almost half the people who first see that clip would fail to see someone in a gorilla suit walk on stage and beat his chest for a full nine seconds. But we are wrong.

So is it never OK to believe the evidence of our own eyes? Of course there are times when we absolutely should accept the evidence of our own eyes over what we're told. If you had read some research which stated that children are safe in nurseries and were then to visit a nursery and see a child being slapped, it would be ludicrous to deny the evidence of what you'd seen over the research that refuted it. But we would be foolish indeed to draw any conclusion about all nurseries, or all children, based merely on the evidence of our own eyes. For the most part 'anecdotal evidence' is an oxymoron. We're always guessing and predicting several steps beyond the available evidence.

Cognitive illusions can be as profound as perceptual illusions

Should we place our trust in research, or can we rely on our own experiences? Of course first-hand observations can sometimes be trusted. Often, if it walks like a duck and sounds like a duck, we should accept that it's a duck. But it's possible to be so eager to accept we're right and others are wrong that we start seeing ducks where they don't exist. It's essential for anyone interested in what might be true, rather than what they might prefer to be true, to take the view that the more complicated the situation, the more likely we are to have missed something.

Sometimes when it looks like a duck it's actually a rabbit.

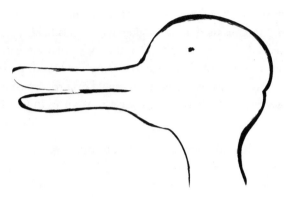

Figure 1.4. Jastrow's duck/rabbit illusion

The philosopher Ludwig Wittgenstein records his confusion with the seeming impossibility that the same image could contain multiple contrary meanings and asked: "But how is it possible to see an object according to an interpretation? – The question represents it as a queer fact, as if something were being forced into a form it did not really fit. But no squeezing, no forcing took place here."[4]

We cannot hold both perceptions in mind simultaneously. Once we become aware that both forms can be inferred from the lines on the paper we can see either duck or rabbit at will, but we can't see them both *at the same time*. Our mind flips from one perception to the other, but the *possibility* of seeing both duck and rabbit remains constant. When we persuade ourselves and others that what we see is what must be there, could we be missing what else might be there?

Possibly though 'truth' is relative. How could we ever hope to divine objective truth when all we have at our disposal are perception, logic and faith? Some things we decide are true based on the evidence of our senses. This might work for small, common truths, but I'm not sure it works for anything much beyond this. And as we've seen, we cannot trust the evidence of our own eyes.

Logic enables us to make inferences based on what we already know. For example, dogs can't fly. I don't have to see every dog to know a particular dog will be flightless. While this may be true, it is also limited to our actual experience. Logic is a notoriously poor predictor of exceptions

– the black swans that force us to change our beliefs. The existence of black swans* teaches us that our logic must be 'falsifiable'** – that is to say, we must be able to conceive of a theory as being incorrect. If we cannot, then it is an unhelpful way of seeing the world; nothing could reasonably convince us we might be wrong. For a theory to be logically coherent, we must be able to agree the circumstances in which it would be wrong.

And finally faith. Although we can obtain documentary evidence, we take our birthdate on faith; we've no actual way of knowing for sure that what we're told is correct. Whenever we accept the authority of others we act on faith. For example, we take the fact that the Battle of Hastings took place in 1066 on faith. But perhaps that's no surprise; the psychologist Daniel Gilbert suggests we are predisposed to take pretty much anything, even obviously nonsensical or ludicrous things, on faith. He submits that in order to try to understand a statement we must first believe it. Only when we have worked out what it would mean for the statement to be true can we choose *not* to believe it.[5] So although certain beliefs are contested, I'm willing to accept, for instance, that the Holocaust occurred, that Neil Armstrong walked on the moon and that Elvis didn't. Others may not be so eager to accept these articles of faith, but in order not to do so they must first believe them.

The point of this apparent digression is that there are all too many 'truths' about education that I've been prepared to take on faith, which, as we will see, have turned out to be plain wrong. Truth *as such* is more slippery than all that. Can contradictory truths coexist? Or can truth sometimes be subjective? Can a thing just be true for me? Sadly, a belief in subjective truth is incoherent. Subjectivism states that no claims about reality can be objectively true or false, but this itself is an objective claim about reality. That doesn't prove it's false, just that it's incoherent. No rational person can truly believe in a subjective reality. But why then is it such a popular misconception? Well, some things (like taste) really are subjective. More

---

*   Before Europeans discovered Australia it was believed that all swans were white because every swan that had been encountered up to that point was, undeniably, white. Such anomalies may well be highly improbable, but their possibility is an important reminder of the limits of logic based on observation. I can recommend Nassim Taleb's *The Black Swan* for a lively and lengthy development of this point.

**   The concept of falsifiability is one of Karl Popper's most important contributions to the philosophy of science.

importantly, subjectivism appeals to us because it seems like the only alternative that captures the idea that our perspective matters. We may each look at the same situation and come to different conclusions, and we might all be right. Clearly it's possible to have different viewpoints, so it seems truth can be conditional or provisional within an objective framework. But this is confusing and clashes with the equally powerful belief that there must be some things which are always true.

The fusion of these beliefs is *enactivism*: there really is an objective reality out there, but we cannot perceive it directly. Instead we share in the generation of meaning; we don't just exchange information and ideas, we change the world by our participation in it. We take the evidence of our senses and construct our own individual models of the world. But because we start with the same objective reality, our individual constructed realities have lots of points of contact. Although we all perceive education differently, usually we're all talking about more or less the same thing.

Objective reality is just stuff that happens. Meaning and purpose only exist as we construct reality. Because we're constantly interacting with each other, individual realities are permeable. When others interact with us we often have to adjust our view of reality. In this way we cooperate in the creation of a shared, constructed reality. We can encounter the same manifestations of reality but have a profoundly different experience of it. The psychologist Daniel Kahneman calls this effect What You See Is All There Is[6] – if we're not aware of a thing it fails to exist. For example, when we plan a lesson it exists only in our own imagination; as soon as we get in front of the class and teach the lesson every student will interpret it differently in order to make it real for them. Their experience is all there is, and they will only remember that experience. Our hope is that we have enough in common for students to think about and remember the ideas we want them to learn about.

As well as faulty perceptual systems, we are also at the mercy of faulty thinking, far more than most of us would believe possible. A good deal of what we believe to be right is based on emotional feedback. We are predisposed to fall for a comforting lie rather than wrestle with an inconvenient truth. And we tend to be comforted by what's familiar rather than what makes logical sense. We go with what 'feels right' and allow our preferences to inform our beliefs. If we're asked to explain these beliefs, we post-rationalize them; we layer on a sensible logical structure and bury the emotional roots because we instinctively know that it's not OK to say, "Because it just *feels right*."*

Most of the time this doesn't matter. When we're dealing with stuff that fits with our world view, or just seems sensible, we're pretty accommodating; we accept working assumptions without questioning them. But when a cognitive clash occurs, when our beliefs are challenged, then rationality is trumped by self-perception and vested interest.

In the 1950s, psychologist Leon Festinger proposed the theory of *cognitive dissonance* which suggests that we are programmed to hold our attitudes and beliefs in harmony, or as Festinger put it, *cognitive consistency*.[7] Attempting to hold two contradictory thoughts or beliefs (cognitions) in our heads at the same time results in us experiencing a deeply uncomfortable sense of dissonance. This leads us to take one of the following actions:

1.   Change our beliefs to fit the new evidence.

2.   Seek out new evidence which confirms the belief we'd prefer to hold.

3.   Reduce the importance of disconfirming evidence.

So, for instance, if we're told that good teachers grade frequently, and we believe ourselves to be a good teacher and yet we can never seem to make headway into that teetering pile of books, we will experience cognitive dissonance. This feeling is so unpleasant that we will justify our beliefs in such a way that we can make these apparently opposing ideas fit neatly into our world view and self-image. We either excuse ourselves: *I'm ridiculously overworked; it's almost the holidays, I'll do it then; they did this work so long ago it's not worth grading it now.* Or we dismiss the idea that grading is important: *I'd be better off spending my time planning; the only reason I'm asked to grade is for accountability purposes, it has no real impact on my students; I'd rather give them verbal feedback, that's a much*

----

*   The realm of the emotions is known by psychologists as the *affective domain*; the part of the brain that deals with thinking is called the *cognitive domain*. When errors are based on feelings they are affective biases, whereas mistakes that stem from faulty thinking are cognitive biases. For convenience, I use the term cognitive bias to refer to both.

more effective way to let them know how to make progress. In this way our mental harmony is restored.

Cognitive dissonance has a dramatic impact on how we react when confronted with folk who disagree with our most fervently held beliefs. We tend to assume they must be ignorant, stupid or evil. When we're critical of anything that someone else holds dear, the standard response is for our opponent to point out that we clearly don't understand their position. When we present the incontestable evidence that we do understand, opponents often treat us as if we're a bit silly: only an idiot could believe anything so ludicrous and patently untrue. When they finally accept that our counter-arguments are sufficiently cogent that we prove ourselves to possess at least a modicum of intelligence, there are only two remaining propositions: either we are evil or they are wrong. Of these, it is far easier, and massively less damaging to the sense of self, to assume that we must be unscrupulous villains seeking to poison children's life chances. But after enough time and enough repetition, any old dogma can be accepted as true. The philosopher Arthur Schopenhauer may have observed, "All truth passes through three stages. First, it is ridiculed. Second, it is violently opposed. Third, it is accepted as being self-evident."*

The passage from ridicule to acceptance is, in large part, due to *cognitive ease*. Our brains are well-practiced at protecting us from the uncomfortable sensation of being wrong. Unfamiliar ideas make us wary and suspicious, but when an idea becomes familiar it induces a sense of recognition and ease: it's not a threat. As well as repeating ourselves, we can make ideas more believable by writing them more legibly.

Writing a statement like this makes it more believable. Honest!

Using high quality paper, printing in bright red or blue, straightforward vocabulary, rhyming and quoting sources with easy to pronounce names also produce a sense of cognitive ease and are therefore less threatening.[8]

It's hard to accept that we're so easily taken in; it's deeply shocking that our beliefs are based on emotional responses of which we're largely unaware, even though the advertising industry has been taking advantage of these findings for decades. Frustratingly, it's not usually so simple

---

* It may be that Schopenhauer didn't exactly, or even actually, say this. But someone did. And it sounds good. You can read about the attribution dispute here: http://en.wikiquote.org/wiki/Arthur_Schopenhauer#Disputed.

to spot where we go wrong as it is when looking at pictures of checkerboards or watching gorillas playing basketball. This is illustrated by the following anecdote which comes from a secondary science teacher who we will call Mr. Garvery.*

Most teachers are concerned about the gender gap, specifically boys' underachievement. Science teacher, Mr. Garvery and his colleagues were presented with data showing a difference in the mean scores for average GCSE (General Certificate of Secondary Education) points – with girls achieving a higher mean than boys. The obvious conclusion drawn was that this difference mattered and something needed to be done. Urgently. No 'proper' statistics were used to quantify the significance of this difference.** So Mr. Garvery went back to the raw data and performed a factor analysis of the impact of the following variables:

- Gender

- Free school meals (FSM)

- Originating primary school

- Key Stage 2 English/math/science results

- Key Stage 3 English/math/science results

- Reading age

- Student attendance

- Teacher attendance

- Special educational needs (SEN)

- English as a foreign language (EAL)

---

*   This is a true story – the names have been changed to protect the innocent.

**   Significance actually means something quite different to statisticians than it does to us ordinary folk. Surprisingly, it doesn't mean 'important', rather it refers to the likelihood that an occurrence is not due to chance. So, if you take a random sample of a population and find its mean, you would expect it to be slightly different to the mean of another sample of the same population, but it would be broadly similar. If the variance is greater than might be accounted for by simply chance, this is 'significant'. Significance tests suggest that where two means are very different, they may be from different populations and any variance is unlikely to be simply a matter of chance.

All had an impact 'on average',* but the most significant factors were:

- Teacher attendance

- Students' attendance

- Key Stage 2 English results

Of those factors measured, gender and free school meals were the least significant.

So armed, Mr. Garvery returned to his Principal and explained that he wouldn't be putting into place a scheme to address gender differentials in science as other factors were more important. The principal's response was to explain that this was not a request and the instruction came from the director of education at the local authority. Resigned, Mr. Garvery returned to his desk, wrote up his findings and sent them to the director of education who, perhaps unsurprisingly, declined to reply.

Time moved on and the whole school gender 'issue' gathered momentum, this time supported by 'evidence' from a professor no less. Perturbed, Mr. Garvery contacted the professor to express his concerns. The professor agreed his data had been taken out of context and that he had never prescribed anything so draconian. Sensibly, he suggested that teachers should act only if the evidence in their school showed that an intervention was necessary. Sadly, this had been lost in translation and schools were mandated to 'have a gender differential policy'.

Why has the story of boys' underachievement become such a widely accepted and compelling narrative? The problem is that we see graphs with girls' performance clearly ahead of boys', so the cause *must* be due to gender.

We are natural pattern seekers, but when noticing a pattern we need to be extremely wary of attributing a causal relationship. Correlation by

....

*   Likewise, this is the mathematical definition of average: an average is a measure of central tendency of a range of variables. The mean (the technical term for average) is calculated by adding all the individual values together and dividing the total by the number of values. The assumption is that it's possible to best represent a range of values with a single number. That average has an 'everyday' meaning as well as a mathematical meaning leads to some hilarious blunders, such as when the then secretary of state for education, Michael Gove, announced that he wanted all schools to be 'above average'.

itself does not imply causation. There are many amusing examples of this, but Figure 1.5 is one of my favorites:

Piracy and global warming over the years

Figure 1.5. Piracy and global warming

As the number of pirates active on the high seas has decreased, so average global temperatures have increased. Clearly, if we want to reduce global warming we need to increase piracy. Except that this example is obviously ridiculous: we feel certain there is unlikely to be any kind of causal link between piracy and global temperatures. But when such correlations seem likely to be linked it's much harder to avoid being trapped into believing that one set of variables causes the other. This is what Michael Shermer calls "patternicity": the tendency to find meaningful patterns in random noise.[9] The way information is presented makes it appear that gender is the biggest factor underlying students' achievement, but the data makes it clear that attendance and prior achievement correlate much more closely.

Our inability to think statistically causes us to routinely misinterpret what data tells us. In a survey of school results in Pennsylvania, many of the top performing schools were very small. Intuitively this makes sense – in a small school teachers will better know their students and will be able to give much more tailored support. This finding encouraged the Bill and Melinda Gates Foundation to make a $1.7 billion investment in founding a string of small schools. Sadly the project was a failure. The finding that smaller schools do better was a confound; the worst schools in the Pennsylvania survey were also small schools. Statistically small schools are not better. In fact, larger schools tend to produce better results due to the diversity of curriculum options they can offer.[10] Our desire to find patterns and explanations trips us up. We ignore the statistical fact that small populations tend to yield more extreme results than larger populations, and we focus instead on causes and narratives.

This 'pattern' of boys' underachievement is compelling because of the way we think about gender: girls are quiet, hard-working and sensible; boys are immature, unruly and easily bored. But as any teacher and every parent could tell you, these are stereotypes – a shorthand that saves us from having to think about reality. But, as ever, reality is a little bit more complicated than that. Recent research into achievement and gender differences has found that school behavior is much more likely to be a decisive factor for achievement than gender. Hard-working students achieve good grades while badly behaved students perform more poorly and get worse grades. The distribution of boisterous students among the two genders is much the same – about 40 percent are girls.[11]

At the start of the following academic year, Mr. Garvery's science department had conclusive evidence that gender difference was among the least important factors impacting their students' performance. Nevertheless, they were compelled to discuss how to implement a solution to this non-existent problem. Meanwhile, Mr. Garvery continued his data exploration and surveyed all Key Stage 4 students for gender, as well as whether they lived in houses with an odd or even house number, whether they owned a games console and whether they were left-handed or right-handed.

As anticipated, when considered as averages, all four factors had an impact on the outcomes of Key Stage 4 results. In order of significance they were:

1. Odd/even house number

2. Games console ownership

3. Left-handed or right-handed

4. Gender

So, living in an odd numbered house had greater impact on GCSE results than a student's gender! He wrote up these new findings and presented them to the school's leadership team. It was treated as a 'bit of fun'. One leadership team member looked a bit worried and asked, "You're not seriously expecting us to buy all our students a PlayStation are you?"

Inspection was looming and the school needed to demonstrate effective monitoring of data. Mr. Garvery was told to 'wind his neck in' and 'play ball'. So, in order to show that the school was 'research-based' and was 'putting in place appropriate interventions', he conceived the following experiment.

The 7th grade class was made up of mixed ability group classes. All classes were taught the same curriculum topics at the same time and following the same schemes of work. In addition, the same teachers taught classes 1 and 3 and classes 2 and 4. So that teaching could be kept as consistent as possible, classes 1 and 3 were selected for the 'intervention' and classes 2 and 4 were selected to be 'controls' with no intervention.

The intervention consisted of informing the classes that they were 'part of an experiment to try out new teaching ideas' and that 'they would be monitored closely'. A letter was sent to parents informing them that their child's class had been selected to trial a new science scheme of work and that teachers would be updating parents at the end of the study. That was it. Nothing else changed between the classes. The only intervention was telling students that there was an intervention.

You will, of course, be aware of the placebo effect – the phenomenon that a placebo triggers a psychological response, which in turn impacts on a patient's health.* Sometimes a patient's symptoms may improve, but equally they may suffer what appear to be side effects from the treatment. Research on the placebo effect has focused on the relationship between mind and body. One of the most common theories is that it may be due to our expectations: if we expect a pill to do something, then it's possible that our body's chemistry can trigger effects similar to those the medication might have caused. It seems reasonable to suggest that a student's belief about their learning might be influenced in a similar way.

Less well-known is the Hawthorne effect. This is the name given to the tendency to work harder and perform better when we know that we're taking part in an experiment. It seems we change our behavior due to the attention we receive from researchers rather than because of any manipulation of independent variables.

Henry A. Landsberger first described the effect in the 1950s in his analysis of experiments conducted during the 1920s and 1930s at the Hawthorne Works electric company to determine if there was a relationship between productivity and work environment. The focus of the studies was to determine if the amount of light workers received had an effect on their productivity. Productivity seemed to increase due to the changes, but then decreased when the experiment was over. Researchers suggested that productivity increased due to attention from the research team and not because of changes to the experimental variables. Landsberger defined the Hawthorne effect as a short-term improvement in performance caused by observing workers.

We should also be aware of the Pygmalion effect. According to ancient Greek legend, Pygmalion invested so much love and care in sculpting a statue of the most beautiful and inspiring woman he could imagine that he fell in love with it. Too ashamed to admit he'd fallen for a statue, he prayed to the goddess Aphrodite for a bride who would be a living likeness of his impossibly beautiful sculpture. His wish was granted and the statue was transformed into a living woman.

Pygmalion's impossibly high expectations for the woman of his desires resulted in him getting what he wanted. Likewise, teachers' expectations

---

* In medicine, a placebo is any treatment which appears to be a real medical treatment but isn't. Placebos are usually an inert substance which contain no active ingredients that might affect a patient's health.

are often a self-fulfilling prophecy. Our beliefs about students have a tremendous impact on their progress and attainment. The self-defeating corollary of the Pygmalion effect is the Golem effect – that negative beliefs lead to a decrease in performance. In 1968, Rosenthal and Jacobson ran a landmark experiment which demonstrated that if teachers were led to expect enhanced performance from children, then their performance was indeed enhanced.[12] Students were given a disguised IQ test at the beginning of the study. Teachers were told that some of their students (about 20 percent of the school chosen at random) would likely be 'spurters' that year, doing better than expected in comparison to their classmates. At the end of the study, all students were retested and showed statistically significant gains favoring the experimental group. This led to the conclusion that teacher expectations influence student achievement.

To return to Mr. Garvery, all the 7th grade students were assessed before and after the intervention. Students in the classes who received the pseudo intervention achieved on average 2 sub-levels of progress* whereas the control classes only achieved 1.5 sub-levels.** Importantly, this intervention was more significant than the gender split teachers were expected to 'do something about'.

Any measure where students are split into two groups will always produce a difference between the two groups when you look at the average of the data set. Only by analyzing *variance* between groups and significance is it possible to determine whether it's worth acting on any differences. Even obviously meaningless splits such as left/right-handed, odd/even houses or fake strategies will show a difference on average.

Telling students they were part of an experiment – that they were special and were receiving some extra attention – produced an impact. So, armed with this wealth of data and interesting evidence, Mr. Garvery and his colleagues began the next school year full of vim and vinegar.

....

*   Sub-levels are the incremental differences between national curriculum levels. Generally they are denoted as a, b and c. So, for instance, a low level 4 is a 4c, a middling level 4 is a 4b and a high level 4 is a 4a. They are entirely made up and a perversion of how national curriculum levels were intended to be applied.

**   This was significant to $p = 0.005$. The p-value is a function of the observed sample results used for testing a statistical hypothesis. Before performing a test, a threshold value is chosen – the significance level – traditionally 5 percent or 1 percent. A p-value of 0.005 tells us there is only a 0.5 percent chance of the result occurring due to chance and is therefore statistically significant.

But did it make a difference to school priorities? No. The school contin-ued to mount expensive, time consuming interventions that focused on gender, free school meals and students' levels of literacy and numeracy.

It's a sad reflection on schools and their relationship with data that this exercise could probably be repeated pretty much anywhere and would likely get similar results. But why? Showing someone – particularly someone as educated and high powered as an education director or a principal – compelling evidence that they might be wrong should make *some* sort of difference, but they might have been threatened by a more powerful body even less susceptible to statistical logic. Whatever the case, our minds are staggeringly skilled at maintaining our existing world view.

We depend on our intuition and routinely disregard uncomfortable evidence. Relying on intuition will lead us into unconsciously using heu-ristics and falling into a range of cognitive traps and biases. In order to escape some of the grossest errors of judgement, we must mistrust the illusion of certainty and seek to avoid entirely predictable cognitive bias-es.* These biases are the subject of the next chapter.

Notes

1   Ludwig Wittgenstein, *Philosophical Investigations*, tr. G. E. M. Anscombe (Oxford: Basil Blackwell, 1953), p. 190.
2   Kathryn Schulz, *Being Wrong: Adventures in the Margin of Error* (London: Portobello Books, 2010), p. 65.
3   Christopher Chabris and Daniel Simons, *The Invisible Gorilla* (London: HarperCollins, 2010).
4   Wittgenstein, *Philosophical Investigations*, p. 200.
5   Daniel T. Gilbert, George S. Krull and Patrick S. Malone, Unbelieving the Unbelievable: Some Problems in the Rejection of False Information, *Journal of Personality and Social Psychology* 59 (1990): 601–613.
6   Daniel Kahneman, *Thinking, Fast and Slow* (London: Penguin, 2012).
7   Leon Festinger, *A Theory of Cognitive Dissonance* (Stanford, CA: Stanford University Press, 1957).

....

*   In his book *Influence: The Psychology of Persuasion*, Robert Cialdini suggests that sometimes the only way out of a cognitive trap is to consult our 'heart of hearts'. He says the only reliable way of doing this is to notice the flash of cognitive dissonance we feel before it's rationalized away. This 'consultation' is intuitive and takes place in the blink of an eye.

8   Kahneman, *Thinking, Fast and Slow*, pp. 63–64.

9   Michael Shermer, *The Believing Brain* (London: Robinson, 2011).

10 Howard Wainer and Harris L. Zwerling, Evidence That Smaller Schools Do Not Improve Pupils' Achievement, *Phi Delta Kappan* 88 (2006): 300–303.

11 Elin Borg, Beyond a Dual Understanding of Gender Differences in School Achievement: A Study of the Gender Gap Among Youth in Oslo Secondary Schools, PhD thesis, University of Oslo, 2014, quoted in Ida Irene Bergstrøm, All Boys Are Not Poor School Achievers, And All Girls Are Not Smart Pupils, *KILDEN* (15 December 2014). Available at: http://eng.kilden.forskningsradet.no/c52778/nyhet/vis.html?tid=89729.

12 Robert Rosenthal and Lenore Jacobson, Pygmalion in the Classroom, *The Urban Review* (September 1968): 16–20. Available at: https://www.uni-muenster.de/imperia/md/content/psyifp/aeechterhoff/sommersemester2012/schluesselstudiendersozialpsychologiea/rosenthal_jacobson_pygmalionclassroom_urbrev1968.pdf.

Chapter 2
Traps and biases

Life is not governed by will or intention. Life is a question of nerves, and fibres, and slowly built-up cells in which thought hides itself, and passion has its dreams.

Oscar Wilde, *The Picture of Dorian Grey*

A study of cognitive bias, the ways we routinely fool ourselves, would be useful to almost anyone but especially so for those entrusted with educating the next generation. These biases often stem from mental shortcuts or rules of thumb that allow us to form judgements and make decisions when we are uncertain. These heuristics* can be useful. Without them we would very likely fall into inertia, but relying on heuristics leads us to make very predictable mistakes. Here follows an all too brief digest of some of our most common biases filtered through the prism of teaching and education.

Fundamental attribution error

You know that boy in 9th grade who gives you constant grief? He's a manipulative little jerk and he hates you. And that lovely, hard-working girl in 11th grade? She's such a warm, kind-hearted soul – what a privilege it is to teach her.

---

* Fascinatingly, *heuristic* comes from the same Greek root as *eureka*! Maybe when we think we've 'got it' we're using a lazy shortcut instead of thinking deeply.

As we trudge from day to weary day, we are each the hero of our own story; others we meet are merely bit players. But no matter the size of their part, we see everyone as a fragment of our unfolding narrative. As such, we tend to mistakenly assume that other people's behavior is attributable to their character. And so it may be, but more often than not behavior has as much to do with circumstance as it does with character. How often have we said of a difficult student that he or she is perfectly pleasant when we interact with them in a different environment? What's more likely – that their character has changed, or that their behavior is dependent on the context in which we encounter them? Although we know the behavior of others is a tug of war between their character and their circumstances, we are seduced by the power of narrative as we struggle to make sense of the world.

Remember Michotte's 'illusion of causality' we discussed on page 15? We appear to be predisposed to attribute causes and make up personality traits where none exist. Back in 1992, psychologists investigated attitudes towards Soviet citizens defecting to the United States and vice versa. Most people believed defection to the United States would be explained by the hardships Soviet citizens experienced, but if Americans defected to the USSR, this must be due to fundamental disloyalty and a fault in their character. It was easier to blame such defections on shortcomings in American citizens' personalities and on endemic problems with the Soviet system.[1]

In another experiment, researchers asked male subjects to be interviewed by a female actress. They were then shown either positive or negative reports she had written about their meeting. When the researchers told the indignant subjects that the actress had been *forced* to write the negative reports as part of the experiment, they nodded sagely and agreed this was a reasonable explanation. But when told positive reports were similarly invented, they continued to believe the actress had liked them despite the evidence to the contrary.[2]

In our attempts to make sense of the world we seek causal relationships. As Mr. Garvery found, people want to understand why things happen: is it because of who we are, something we did or believed, our character? Or was it pure chance, a random combination of events: 'such things happen'? Our need for understanding extends to how we interpret other people's behavior, and this is especially true in the classroom. We see children behaving in various ways, and in trying to attribute cause, bias creeps into our 'explanation'.

These ways of ascribing causality are examples of the fundamental attribution error. That is, when making sense of other people, we put greater emphasis on what we assume are their character traits and under-value contextual factors. We see a student obviously bored and switched off, and assume that they are a 'low achiever', rather than noticing the room has become rather stuffy after lunch. But we don't make that assumption about ourselves; we have excellent explanations of *our* drowsiness.

We instinctively take the credit when things go well – it seems obvious that our success is due to our talents and efforts. But when something goes badly, we're inclined to look for external causes and explanations. Conversely, we can be guilty of assuming that when things go well it's just down to luck, but when we do poorly we wallow in self-recrimination and reproach. Each approach is guilty of the fundamental attribution error. When it comes to interpreting other people's behavior, we invariably make the mistake of overestimating the importance of fundamental character traits and underestimating the importance of the situation and context. We will always reach for a 'dispositional' explanation for events, as opposed to a contextual explanation.

Schools do this every year when exam results come in. Should we congratulate ourselves on increases, or are these due to natural variation or wide-scale dumbing down? When results are poorer than expected, should we wring our hands and search for what went wrong, or should we blame the year group, the exam board or the government of the day?

We view the world from within our own internalized context where it appears that we determine everything we do. In situations where we have no control over events, we attribute causes to an outside agent. These agents fill in the gaps in our knowledge, allowing us to 'understand' a complex and sometimes incomprehensible world.

As teachers, finding ourselves in a situation where we utilize a certain teaching approach, and find it doesn't work, we have a tendency to blame our students: they didn't listen, they didn't try hard enough, they are too dumb to learn. It's their fault – their personal choices, behaviors, disposition and actions.

School leaders might be guilty of making similarly flawed judgements of teachers. We like to believe we're objective and reasonable in the way that we treat others, but it's incredibly difficult to evaluate teachers' performance in a way that is both valid and reliable. It's so much easier to go with our gut and assume we 'just know' who is 'good' and who 'requires improvement'.

Labeling teachers as effective or ineffective is another way to make the fundamental attribution error. Stereotyping is a seductively simple shortcut to explaining the world. We don't have to think further – events are caused by character traits. But the way we act is at least as dependent on the circumstances we're in as the people we are. Is a teacher effective because they feel supported, or are they hard-working and talented? Might a teacher be ineffective because they feel under threat, or are they weak and unprofessional? It's relatively easy to do well when everyone around you is supportive and believes in you. Success breeds success, and it becomes easier to think of some teachers as 'outstanding' than to honestly scrutinize their performance. Likewise, reputations can be easily crushed. If a member of staff is perceived as underperforming, how do we react? Do we give them our trust and support, or do we put them on notice?

Likewise with students: is Sean doing badly in math because he's stupid or because his mother has lung cancer? Might Clara be excelling in English because of her prodigious natural gifts or because she sits next to Jonathan who is doing even better? To really know, we need to apply statistical reasoning rather than inferring inappropriate causal thinking. Rather than trying to make the data fit with a view of the world, Mr. Garvery derived his conclusions from the data. He observed the strongest correlations and came up with a theory that fitted the facts.*

Thinking about where people are in a process, rather than who they are, might help us to avoid making this kind of error in our thinking. Mr. Garvery's story might have unfolded quite differently if his colleagues had been able to think in terms of context and statistics rather than personalizations and narratives.

....

* Clearly, statistical reasoning is as open to abuse as any other way of thinking, but it does help us step away from thinking about the world in terms of simple cause and effect.

The confirmation bias

Probably the most well-known and widely documented of our cognitive oddities is the confirmation bias: the tendency to seek out only that which confirms what we already believe and to ignore that which contradicts these beliefs. Bertrand Russell resignedly observed, "If a man is offered a fact which goes against his instincts, he will scrutinize closely, and unless the evidence is overwhelming, he will refuse to believe it. If, on the other hand, he is offered something which affords a reason for acting in accordance to his instincts, he will accept it even on the slightest evidence."[3] (In case you're wondering, I'm fairly sure this applies equally to women.)

Now, this isn't necessarily a deliberate or partisan avoidance of contrary evidence; it's just a state of mind to which it's almost impossible not to fall victim. Let's imagine, just for a moment, that you think math is boring. If you're told that learning math is pointless, because most people get by using the calculators on their phones, you're likely to accept it without question. If, on the other hand, you're shown a report detailing the need for math in high status jobs and calling for compulsory math education until the age of 18, you're likely to find yourself questioning the quality of the jobs, the accuracy of the report's findings and the author's motives. If we find confirming examples – and we generally can – we are predisposed to accept what we're told as being true. As a rule, we want to think and feel positively about ourselves. We overestimate our standing on most positive characteristics, engage in self-serving thinking and project our futures as likely to be brighter than those of our peers. When evidence threatens these cheerful fictions, we find ways to ignore, discredit or minimize the significance of threatening information.

The confirmation bias is at work in every facet of the way we see the world. If you become pregnant, suddenly every other person you meet is also pregnant or has just had a baby. If you buy a vintage VW Camper van, without warning the road is full of Camper van drivers cheerfully hooting and flashing their lights. Our brains are programmed to recognize patterns and connections; the familiar and humdrum goes unnoticed and unremarked. We ignore anything that does not support our current view of the world. More importantly, though, this causes us to act foolishly and blindly. Despite knowing I'm overweight, I'd rather not get on the scales and discover the extent of the problem. Far easier to delude myself and devour another cream cake if I continue in happy ignorance.

For example, what must Mr. Garvery's head teacher have believed in order to continue supporting expensive interventions aimed at closing the gender gap in the face of evidence that this gap was an irrelevant distraction? When scanning the results of every test, looking for some kind of differentiation, you only notice those results that show the difference you're looking for and dismiss the others as being unrepresentative or a fluke.

In the same way, schools adopt various classroom strategies that are seen to work – for example, Popsicle sticks, traffic lights and other trendy trappings of apparent 'best practice'.* It might well appear that these interventions 'work', but what effect are they actually having? If we're content to merely raise students' current performance then we'll see plenty of evidence to support our beliefs. And when we don't see the evidence we expect, we're happy to ignore these occasions as an 'off day', or worse, evidence that a teacher isn't up to snuff if they can't teach using the latest gimmickry. When a teacher's practice is held up as a model of 'best practice', we tend to cherry-pick those bits we're comfortable with, or already know something about, and ignore anything unfamiliar, difficult or strange.

This leads to teachers who teach in the preferred style being rewarded and promoted. Those who don't, undergo scrutiny and risk being fired. We're constantly having our belief that there must be a right way to teach confirmed by the messages we receive from outside evaluators, school leaders and colleagues. It takes unusual willfulness to dissent from what is 'obviously right'.

Wilfulness of the sort possessed by math teacher Jaime Escalante. Escalante taught for 12 years in Bolivia before emigrating to the United States. He was shocked at how badly his students had been taught and

---

* The rationale for using Popsicle sticks is that each student in a class has their name written on a stick and these sticks are then drawn at random whenever a teacher asks a question to ensure all students contribute. Traffic lights are a means of students displaying their understanding of material covered in a lesson: displaying a red card would signal they have little or no understanding, yellow indicates some understanding and green suggests they are good to go.

resolved to make a difference. He had sky-high expectations for what his students could achieve and decided to teach them advanced calculus. This was a controversial decision and the school administration opposed Escalante frequently during his first few years. He was threatened with dismissal for coming in too early, leaving too late and failing to get permission to raise funds to pay for his students' tests. Not to be deterred, Escalante came into the spotlight when 18 of his students passed the challenging Advanced Placement (AP) calculus exam. Suspicions were raised because identical errors were made on several questions and the students were asked to retake the exam. They passed again. In subsequent years, the number of students enrolling and passing the AP calculus test more than doubled, and in 1987, 73 students passed.

A happy ending? Well, not quite. Over the next few years, Escalante's calculus program continued to grow but not without its own price. Tensions that had simmered since the beginning of his career boiled over. Escalante's math enrichment program had grown to over 400 students and class sizes had increased to over 50 students, way over the 35 student limit set by the teachers' union, which in turn escalated the criticism of Escalante's work. In 1991, the number of students taking advanced placement examinations in math and other subjects jumped to 570. That same year, citing faculty politics and petty jealousies, Escalante quit.

Class size is a predictable cause of confirmation bias, and I can well understand how Escalante might have fallen foul of critics who I'm sure believed themselves to be well-intentioned, despite the evidence of Escalante's success. Everyone likes the idea of smaller class sizes; politicians, parents and teachers are all seduced by the blindingly obvious certainty that the fewer students there are in a class, the more teacher time can be lavished on each. But this isn't supported by the evidence. And when such evidence butts up against common sense, we ignore it in favor of the evidence of our own experience. Of course, smaller classes are better because we find it easier to give everyone individual feedback, it's quicker to grade a class set of books and the chances for misbehavior are minimized. In short, small classes are better because they *feel* better. And if it feels so right, how could it be wrong?

Well, what we often fail to consider is that what's good for teachers is not necessarily good for students. Unless a reduction in class size is sufficient to allow us to change our approach to teaching – and whether, as a result, students change their approach to learning – any benefits will be so trivial as to be meaningless. If no change occurs then learning is unlikely to improve. Some studies suggest that significant change is only likely to occur if class size is reduced to about 15–17 students. Even then, the benefits may be marginal. And what benefits there are will be outweighed by the costs of employing additional teachers.[4] But how many schools plough money into reducing class sizes to, say, 25 students when the evidence is clear that the money could be much better spent elsewhere? As Peter Blatchford, Professor in Psychology and Education at London's Institute of Education, says, "just reducing class sizes and hoping for the best is not likely to be effective and it's little surprise if some class size reduction efforts have led to little or no discernible impact on students".[5]

Interestingly, in his book *David and Goliath*, Malcolm Gladwell proposes a happy medium.[6] Clearly no one wants huge classes, but there might be some disadvantages to having too few students in a class. He suggests that there's an inverted U effect in operation (see Figure 2.1): as class sizes are reduced, learning improves until the optimum class size is reached. If class size drops below the optimum, learning declines. Gladwell suggests this optimum class size is between 16 and 24 students.

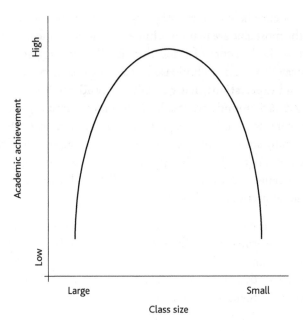

Figure 2.1. Class size – inverted U

I'm not for a moment saying that class size doesn't matter – clearly too many students would completely overwhelm a teacher – but we should think carefully before ignoring evidence which is at odds with our own experience.*

Another example of education policy where we ignore what the evidence actually says in favor of what feels right is on the issue of setting. The overwhelming majority of schools employ some kind of mechanism for separating out students according to their ability and then teaching them within sets or streams – the assumption being that when there is a narrower range of ability in a class, it's easier to teach more effectively.

....

*   I should point out that at practically the last possible moment before going to press, I read Pedro De Bruyckere, Paul A. Kirschner and Casper D. Hulshof's *Urban Myths about Learning and Education* in which they suggest everything I've just argued is correlational nonsense (pp. 171–174). They cite several studies which actually show considerable benefits for students taught in smaller classes. So feel free to dig a little deeper and come to your own conclusions – sometimes a soupçon of confirmation bias might just be helpful.

But the evidence here is stark: 30 years of research has shown the benefits for the most able are marginal, but everyone else suffers. Blatchford's colleague at the Institute of Education, Ed Baines, suggests we should "move away from an ability-based class organization, to avoid the labeling and expectations that go with it".[7] Students from various disadvantaged backgrounds are less likely to make it into top sets and are therefore consigned to lower expectations and attainment. On average, lower attaining students' progress is delayed by a couple of months every year when they're taught in ability groups.[8] But we routinely ignore this evidence because it doesn't fit with our beliefs and it isn't confirmed by our wholly subjective experiences.

The classic example of confirmation bias in education is the enduring popularity of learning styles. Despite the overwhelming lack of evidence that they have any effect on outcomes, apparently almost 90 percent of teachers believe that different people have different learning styles, and that if we want them to learn a thing we have to present it in the way they learn best.[9] I'm sure you've come across VAK – the idea that we're all either visual, auditory or kinaesthetic learners – and we can only really be expected to learn when instruction is tailored to these specific needs. Although we may well have a preference for seeing, listening or doing, if we believe that the best way to learn the shape of a map of Australia is to listen to a description of it, or that the best way to learn how to sight read music is just to randomly bash away at a piano, or that we might become a great tennis player merely by watching Wimbledon, then we're very clearly wrong.

The field of cognitive psychology relies on us being more similar than we are different. Despite our beguilingly different abilities, everyone will best learn what the route between Bristol and London looks like by being shown a map, just as everyone best understands data by being shown a visual representation. No one best learns to sight read music through unguided experimentation; it helps everyone to be taught the principles of musical notation and then to practice performing set pieces. There may be some gifted individuals who pick up the basics of a sport by watching others perform, but everyone benefits from having movements and techniques deconstructed and modeled. And, more controversially, there may be several methods for teaching children to read, but the evidence that systematic synthetic phonics is most effective in the majority of cases is overwhelming.*

Convincing evidence for the existence of learning styles would need to show that people who prefer to learn either visually, aurally or kinaesthetically would learn better when taught in the way they prefer, and a different group with different learning styles should learn the same material better when taught according to their preferences. But no such evidence exists. Despite the thorough debunking of the idea that pandering to students' preferred learning style is in any way useful, the theory shambles on.** But why? Because our brains work in very similar ways, we all have the tendency to fall victim to the same cognitive biases. Possibly, part of the appeal is that we want to believe our failure to learn is due to teachers failing to teach us effectively – if only they could be bothered to understand the way in which we learn, all would be well. But I also think that we cling to ideas like learning styles because we want to believe our differences matter more than our similarities.

The alternative is bleak. Professor of Philosophy of Education John White says, "Putting children into boxes that have been proved not to exist may end up restricting the education they receive, leading teachers to overly rigid views of individual students' potentialities, and, what is worse, a new type of stereotyping."[10] And Scott Lilienfeld and colleagues point out that even if learning styles did exist, they would still be harmful as teachers are encouraged "to teach to students' intellectual strengths rather than their weaknesses ... students need to correct and compensate for their shortcomings, not avoid them".[11]

....

*   This is a can of worms. There isn't the scope to deal comprehensively with the reading wars in this book, but for those who are interested I can recommend Diane McGuiness' *Early Reading Instruction* for a very thorough, expert and ideologically neutral grounding.

**   As always there are doubters, but the research evidence against the efficacy of learning styles in general, and VAK specifically, really is overwhelming. If Pashler, McDaniel, Rohrer and Bjork's 'Learning Styles: Concepts and Evidence', doesn't persuade then I'll be forced to order an exorcism. You can find the paper here: http://www.psychologicalscience.org/journals/pspi/PSPI_9_3.pdf. Also read Frank Coffield's contribution to Philip Adey and Justin Dillon's *Bad Education: Debunking Myths in Education*. If you still believe I'm wrong, please get in touch with Will Thalheimer who for the last seven years has offered a cash prize for anyone who can provide acceptable evidence of the existence of learning styles.

The belief that achievement is primarily due to gender is closely linked to the notion that boys and girls have different learning styles. There is already plenty of unhelpful gender stereotyping without adding more. The tendency to overinflate our differences also makes the need to differentiate teaching for the needs of all students seductive. Sociologist Richard Sennett argues that "inflating small differences in degree into large differences in kind legitimates the system of privilege".[12] Instead, he contends that we would do better to foster a belief that all students are capable of good work. Maybe we should accept that, despite their differences, students learn and forget in fairly predictable ways.

The sunk cost fallacy

We have an irrational response to having wasted time, effort or money: I've committed this much, so I must continue or it will have been a waste. I spent all this time training my students to work in groups, so they're damn well going to work in groups, and hang the evidence! If you've ever paid for a movie ticket only to realize, five minutes in, that the film will be dreadful and then opted to watch it anyway, you have fallen victim to the sunk cost fallacy. Sitting through something tedious may feel worthy but you're essentially throwing good money after bad; your continued investment in the film makes no logical sense. The money you've spent is gone and you can never get it back. You could, however, save 90 minutes of your precious time.

Imagine this scenario. A school leadership team is faced with a difficult decision: the previous principal had been a passionate advocate of one-to-one devices and believed that the best way to transform students' experience of education was for everyone to have their own wireless tablet. Protests from parents and staff had been swept aside and the school outlaid a huge sum to create a wireless network which would be sufficient to support over a thousand devices at any one time. The future was bright, shiny and encased in brushed aluminium.

Then the principal left. No one else on the leadership team believed in the project, but all the discussions were about how to roll it out in the least damaging and intrusive way. When one member of the team suggested that maybe the best decision would be to cut their losses and abandon the whole thing, they were shouted down. The new principal made it clear that things had progressed too far, that too much money and credibility had been invested to simply pull the plug. So, even though no one thought it was the right choice, the juggernaut rolled on. Parents were asked to lease tablets for their children and students in receipt of free school meals had a device paid for by the school. Teachers were trained in how to use various apps in lessons and further resources were committed to ensuring the project was a success.

And the result? Because no one really believed in the efficacy of tablet devices to transform education they became merely a distraction from teaching, and students were often instructed to keep them in their bags in order for lessons to proceed. Staff members became cynical and parents were resigned, but the students were for the most part delighted with their new toys.

Now, I'm not saying that handheld devices could never be used effectively in schools – I'm sure they can – but not if nobody believes in them. This can become a hugely expensive distraction with no discernibly positive effects on outcomes. If this can happen with something as bloated and expensive as handheld devices, just think of the more subtle distorting effects the sunk cost fallacy can have on the way we teach. Are we doing what we do simply because we've already invested many years in training and practice, and now feel we can't afford to change course?

Because there is always a cost. If it's not sunk cost, it's an opportunity cost. What else could you be doing instead? This is especially pressing in education where everything can be claimed to work to some extent. And even if our preferred teaching method is roundly debunked by research, we can always assert that whatever it is we're doing 'works for me'. And who can say it doesn't? How you choose to spend your time depends on your priorities, your values and the perceived needs of the job. But you can't do everything – you have to make choices. So time spent developing strategy x is time that cannot also be spent on developing strategy y. And if the scientific consensus is that y would get better results, is it immoral to continue investing in x?

And with every decision and judgement you make, you will descend further down what Tavris and Aronson call, the pyramid of choice.[13] At the apex of the pyramid, how we feel about our beliefs is relatively neutral, but with each choice we make we become more invested in our beliefs, and so justify our choices by seeing our own actions as sensible and honorable and those of others as silly and despicable. We find a way to reconcile our preference for x over y in the face of contrary evidence. Our view of people who've made different choices becomes less flattering: they are ignorant, stupid or evil. Our descent down one or other side of the pyramid leads to us categorizing others into 'them' and 'us'.

In Mr. Garvery's case, his attempt to get people who had invested time, resources and credibility in the notion that gender is a determining factor in achievement came up against the immoveable wall of the sunk cost fallacy. The incurred cost may well have prevented his colleagues from being able to entertain the thought that they had made a mistake.

Group biases

If everyone around us believes a thing, we generally decide it must be true. We readily accept that what everyone else is doing must be the correct way of behaving in a given situation because we assume, wrongly, that everyone else knows something we don't. This accounts for the emperor's new clothes: everyone could see he was in the nuddy, but pointing out the apparently obvious would have been a terrible gaff because what if everyone else was in the know? If we're the only one to notice something, maybe it's because we're defective. It took a child with no appreciation of social norms to point out the obvious.

Less well-known is the Chinese proverb, "Three men make a tiger". A vizier asked his king whether he would believe a citizen's report that he'd seen a tiger roaming the markets. The king said no, of course he wouldn't. The vizier then asked what if two people reported they'd seen a tiger in the busy markets, and the king said he'd begin to wonder. But when asked his reaction if three people reported seeing the tiger, the king said he would believe it. The vizier pointed out that the likelihood of a tiger wandering a crowded market was absurd, and it reflected poorly on the king that he was credulous enough to believe something so improbable simply because it was repeated often enough. But the king is no different from the rest of us: what is repeated becomes normal. Bertrand Russell cautioned, "Even when the experts all agree, they may well be mistaken."[14] For all their expertise, experts are little different from kings or anyone else.

There are lots of individually identified biases and cultural prejudices relating to social grouping: social proof, groupthink, social loafing, bystander apathy and many others. Basically, as social animals we're prone to herd mentality; dissenting from a prevailing belief or acting contrary to those around us is socially awkward. But is it just as straightforward as not caring what other people think?

Maybe not. Back in 1935, social psychologist Muzafer Sherif placed subjects in a dark room and asked them to focus on a dot of light about 15 feet away. The light was entirely static, but to observers it appeared to be moving. Subjects were then asked how much the dot of light was moving. A few days later, subjects were grouped in threes and asked to estimate how much the light was moving out loud. Even though the subjects had previously given different estimates, groups would come to a common estimate. But maybe they just didn't want to look silly in front of their peers? To rule out this possibility, Sherif had the subjects judge the lights again by themselves. Weirdly, they maintained the group's judgement. Because the movement of the light was ambiguous, participants were relying on each other to define reality.[15]

One particularly worrying result of the social proof phenomenon is that anyone who's been made redundant may struggle to find new employment because prospective employers are prone to assume that unemployment is proof of personal inadequacy rather than the result of circumstance. Likewise, if you're perceived to be in high demand, you will attract additional job offers; if others think you're great, you must be great. But, as the novelist Anatole France said, "If fifty million people say something foolish, it's still foolish."[16]

How much of what goes on in schools and classrooms is done merely because everyone else does it like that, or because enough people repeat the same piece of homespun wisdom? Or do people just follow the herd because they think that everyone else must have got it sorted? This is certainly the message of the Abilene paradox. A family decide to drive 53 miles from their home to eat at a restaurant in Abilene, Texas. Despite a few reservations, they all agree it sounds like a wonderful idea. But after a long, hot, dusty drive, the food they're served is terrible. They arrive back home four hours later exhausted. When they discuss their decision to drive to Abilene they all admit that none of them actually wanted to go but merely went along to please each other.[17]

Often groups not only have problems managing disagreements, but also there may be real problems with what they actually agree on. Almost every teacher agrees that boys' underachievement is a huge concern, so when someone like Mr. Garvery comes along and tells us it isn't, he's fighting against powerful group biases. Stepping out of line and being socially 'disagreeable' is uncomfortable, but it's the Mr. Garverys of the world who force us to accept uncomfortable truths.*

The illusion of asymmetric insight

We have a unique insight into our own minds. We are aware of the complex and nuanced nature of our thoughts and decisions. The philosopher Daniel Dennett suggests problems may be caused precisely *because* we spend so much time in our own heads. If our capacity for introspection and self-observation is less reliable than we assume then we're in trouble:

> Ever since Descartes and his '*cogito ergo sum*,' this capacity of ours has been seen as somehow immune from error; we have privileged access to our own thoughts and feelings, an access guaranteed to be better than the access of any outsider.[18]

No one can tell us we're wrong about what we think or feel. We're guaranteed either to be right or at least impossible to correct. What we believe makes sense to us. We think we have the same awareness of others because we're conscious of thinking about them. By watching how they behave and listening to what they say we come to well-reasoned and sensible conclusions. Although we believe our perceptions of others are accurate and insightful, their perceptions of *us* are shallow and illogical. The logic goes: I know myself better than you do, but I also know you better than you do.

This asymmetry becomes starker when augmented by group biases: we progressives see clearly the flaws in traditionalist arguments, but they,

---

* Malcolm Gladwell's book *David and Goliath* contains some excellent examples of how being disagreeable serves an essential social function.

poor saps, are incapable of understanding the sophistication of *our* arguments. If any dare to disagree they are, by their opposition, living proof that others do not share our sophistication and distinction. If others agree, well then, they must be almost as clear sighted as we are. This asymmetry makes us fiercely tribal and viciously inflexible.

Think of the damage that can be wrought when we're deceived by this illusion. It can lead us to observe another teacher and, through the fundamental attribution error, assume that we know why they've done what they've done. That, in turn, could lead to all kinds of dreadful management and unthinking leadership, resulting in teachers being 'supported' out of the profession.

Veteran education blogger Old Andrew (as he likes to be known) provides an extensive list of management behavior and beliefs which can wreck schools, ruin careers and destroy students' life chances.[19] Here are a few of my favorites:

- Lesson observations are needlessly stressful, especially if they are held early in the year.

- Grading and homework policies that no full-time teacher could ever hope to follow are introduced with little or no consultation.

- School leaders are isolated in their offices, particularly during lesson changeover, and teachers are expected to monitor the corridors and settle their classes at the same time.

- Excuses are made for poor behavior and results, particularly based on poverty, special educational needs or blaming teachers.

- Teachers are criticized for enforcing the rules or enacting punishments, with the assumption being that if teachers are using sanctions then they must have a poor relationship with students.

- New initiatives that needlessly add to workload are introduced and then abandoned without anyone being told.

Maybe you've fallen victim to some of these. Maybe you've even been guilty of some of them. The point is that the illusion of asymmetric insight leads to a 'them and us' situation in which it's easy for leaders to become isolated from the experiences of teachers. Similarly, it could also easily lead to school leaders being caricatured as irrational idiots with no understanding or compassion.

In Mr. Garvery's case, he became one of 'them' – not a team player. It's so much easier to dismiss people when we can caricature them as having interests which are contrary to our own. We stereotype the out-group and dismiss them with crude generalizations. Consider the way elementary and secondary teachers view each other. Elementary teachers are a bit simple; secondary teachers are uncaring brutes. Or maybe the way progressive and traditional factions in education characterize each other: progs patiently encourage children's whims to bloom in whatever direction their fancy should wander; trads drone on to serried ranks bored past witlessness. From these caricatures it all becomes so much easier to despise and condemn those who appear not to be aligned with us.

The backfire effect

When confirmation bias, the sunk cost fallacy and group bias combine, sometimes we experience the backfire effect. When we are confronted with evidence contrary to our beliefs, we can become even more certain that we are right. If we have sunk sufficient time, effort and credibility into the belief, such evidence forces us to rationalize our mistakes even more strongly. In such cases, we look to others for cues as to how we should react – if we're part of an in-group, we'll get all the social proof we need that our position is coherent. Our erroneous logic can appear unassailable even though to those on the outside it's a house of cards.

Why does the evidence on learning styles have so little impact on teachers' beliefs? Because it doesn't fit with what we want to believe, we dismiss it as irrelevant and continue planning lessons using VAK questionnaires and feeling guilty for not doing enough kinaesthetic activities. After all, if everyone you know believes something then it's socially awkward to dissent.

Arguing with teachers who have a vested interest in being right about a particular ideological view of education is like presenting fundamentalist Christians with the incontrovertible evidence of evolution. It just bounces off them and makes them even more convinced that they are right and you are wrong. We desperately scramble to reduce dissonance by justifying beliefs in the face of disconfirming evidence and often dismiss it as the exception that proves the rule. Leon Festinger's research into doomsday cults is a fascinating insight into the self-deception and ease with which we ignore troubling evidence. Specifically, he wanted to find out why cult members continued to believe despite the most disconfirming piece of evidence possible: the world doesn't end.[20]

Like many others before and since, American housewife Dorothy Martin prophesied the end of world. Martin had urged her group of believers to leave their jobs, colleges and spouses. Many had given away money and possessions to prepare for their departure on a flying saucer which was to rescue the group of true believers. She claimed to have received a message from a fictional planet named Clarion whose inhabitants had revealed that the world would end in a great flood before dawn on December 21, 1954.

After the failure of the prediction, Martin's followers were understandably devastated. She shortly received a new message from the space aliens telling her the group's faith had averted disaster, but further and greater acts of faith would be required to keep the threat at bay. With renewed fervor, Martin and her disciples contacted the press to spread the good news and recruit more followers.

Festinger states that in order for evidence to backfire, five conditions must be met:

1. Not only must we be convinced of belief but also it must have some impact on our behavior.

2. There must be an investment of some kind in the belief – the greater the investment, the stronger our commitment to the belief (see the sunk cost fallacy).

3. The belief must be specific enough that it's possible for evidence to unequivocally refute it.

4. We have to be aware of incontrovertible evidence that our belief is mistaken.

5. We need the support of a group. On our own we quickly accept disconfirming evidence, but if we're part of a group able to support

one another, the belief may be maintained (see the illusion of asymmetric insight).

How often are these conditions met in education? A lot of what we believe governs our day-to-day behavior and this, in turn, will lead to an investment of credibility and time in a course of action. The third condition is trickier, but the weight of evidence in favor of phonics and against learning styles would seem sufficiently undeniable for most reasonable people not in the grip of cognitive dissonance. The fourth condition is also interesting. It's easy to see that the world hasn't ended; it's harder to stumble across disconfirming academic research when we're busy teaching. The final condition is one we meet in spades.

Despite what we may think, most of our beliefs are founded on faith not logic. We have faith in what we believe *because* it's what we believe. To have our most deeply held convictions attacked is intolerable and it forces us into a corner. You cannot sway someone's faith with evidence and we rarely win arguments with logic.

The anchoring effect

Many of our beliefs and decisions are 'anchored' on extraneous information. The anchoring effect reveals how suggestible we are. Amazingly, we base our decisions and beliefs on what we have been told, even when what we're told is completely irrelevant or patently absurd. We want to believe that our evaluations are fair, but are they?

In the *Horizon* television program, 'How You Really Make Decisions', passers-by were asked to estimate the price of a bottle of vintage champagne. But before they made their guess, they were asked to draw a ball, eyes closed, from a bag of table tennis balls. Each ball had a number written on it. Participants were told the number was random but in fact the first group of people in the experiment all chose a ball with the number 10 written on it. A second group had number 65 on their balls. When the participants were then asked how much the bottle of champagne costs, the first group estimated about £10, whereas the second group guessed around £65. Although the number on the ball had no connection to the champagne, it still anchored the passers-by who based their estimate on it.[21]

This seems almost magical. Why should our judgements be affected by something so obviously unrelated? Before I attempt an explanation, let's try an experiment. Answer the following questions and jot down your answers:

> Is the number of medical students who are privately educated higher or lower than 86 percent? Estimate the percentage of medical students who are privately educated.*
>
> Answer: _____
>
> The average working vocabulary for graduate professionals is about 20,000 words. A recent study estimated that 16-year-olds use an average of how many words a day?**
>
> Answer: _____

Evidence suggests that we're susceptible to having our decision anchored by the information we're given. In their landmark study, 'Judgment under Uncertainty', psychologists Amos Tversky and Daniel Kahneman demonstrated that the answers given to questions like these could be anchored by the statistic given on a rigged wheel of fortune which stopped only at the numbers 10 and 65.[22] When we don't have enough information to make a clear judgement, or when we make decisions concerning something too complex to fully grasp, instead of backing off and admitting our ignorance, we rush to any available information to make our decision. If your answers to the questions above were close to the anchoring information in the question, you may well have fallen victim to this subtle bias.

This may seem trivial; it doesn't much matter if we estimate wrongly in this instance. But what about when our decision really matters? Another study asked trial judges with more than 15 years of experience to consider sentencing demands made by non-experts before sentencing. One set of judges was given the recommendation of a 34 month sentence, whereas a second group was asked to consider a recommendation of 12 months. Guess what? The judges, despite their experience and the fact

....

*   It's actually 51 percent – still shockingly high!

**   According to Jean Gross, England's first Communication Champion for Children, 1 in 12 16-year-olds use an average of only 800 words a day.

53

that the crimes in question were identical, were influenced by the recommendations. Judges who considered the high demand of 34 months prior to their decision gave final sentences that were almost eight months longer than judges who considered a low demand of 12 months.[23]

Why does this happen? When making a decision we consider what we already know about a particular topic and compare this to whatever information is immediately available. For example, if we see a stranger in a suit carrying a clipboard walking down the corridor outside our classroom, we might assume that they were some sort of evaluator. Our assumptions about clipboard carrying, suit wearing strangers in school corridors are based on previous experiences. This kind of stereotyping is known as top-down processing (as opposed to bottom-up or data-driven processing). Top-down processing is easier and requires fewer mental resources, but it can lead us into error.

Unlikely as it may seem, competitive hotdog eating may help to shed some light on the power of the anchoring effect. Eating contests are a big deal in the United States. The most prestigious of these events is Nathan's Hot Dog Eating Contest. In 1979, the winner ate 19 hotdogs in 12 minutes, and by 2001, the record stood at 25⅛ HDB (hotdogs and buns).

Typically, aspiring champions are big men who prepare by gorging themselves on as many hotdogs as they can wolf down. So, when a mild-mannered 23-year-old, 126-pound Japanese man called Takeru Kobayashi made his debut nobody could have expected what would happen: Kobayashi consumed a staggering 50 HDB, nearly doubling the previous record, and went on to win the $10,000 prize for the next five years.

How was this possible? Many of his competitors assumed there must have been some kind of trick, but the solution was far simpler than that. Other competitive eaters thought about eating 26 hotdogs. Kobayashi thought about eating one. That is, he thought about how he could eat one as quickly as possible. He wasn't interested in beating a target; he just set about getting better at what he was doing. The current record was an artificial barrier. By disregarding it he was able to establish a new record.

Consider also the case of Australian farmer Cliff Young. In 1983, the 61-year-old won the inaugural Westfield Sydney to Melbourne

Ultramarathon, a distance of 544 miles. He trailed way behind the leaders for most of the first day. After that first day, most of the athletes underwent a strict regime of physiotherapy and nutrition, before going to sleep on special orthopaedic beds. But no one told Cliff to stop. By running while the others slept, he took the lead on the first night and maintained it for the remainder of the race, eventually winning by 10 hours.

Before running the race, he told the press that he had previously run for two to three days straight in wellies rounding up sheep. The Westfield run took him five days, fifteen hours and four minutes, almost two days faster than the previous record for any run between Sydney and Melbourne. Most of us are anchored by what has gone before. The idea of running for five days straight simply hadn't occurred to anyone else.

Can we learn anything from Takeru Kobayashi and Cliff Young? Presumably you're not reading this book for tips on marathon running or hotdog eating, but maybe their stories can cast some light as to what we're anchored to as teachers.

Think about the way we give students target grades. Teachers and students inevitably become anchored to these fictions and we start trying to solve the wrong problems. Kobayashi's example tells us that target grades may be holding students back. When we grade students' work, we see their name and immediately have an expectation of what grade it's going to be. If we're told a student has a D grade target, they lose all chance of being treated like an A-grade student. And if teachers fall victim so easily to this bias, what effect might it have on students? Do they also anchor themselves to their target grade, not realizing that their potential stretches further than the available data says is probable?

Could we perhaps try a different approach to target setting? Could we set targets on how best to eat hotdogs rather than on how many we should be eating? Rather than setting targets for what students should achieve by the end of an assessment period, targets could instead reflect what they need to achieve next. When a target is achieved, should they set their sights on the next target? If you are working at a D grade, your target is to work at a C grade. When you break through that C grade target, your target then becomes a B. Is setting a target actually accepting a limit? Can we learn a lesson from Kobayashi – a lesson that is about refusing to accept limits and to see targets as false barriers? Would students work harder knowing that their next target is actually within reach? Maybe the momentum of achievement might carry students to realize potential beyond the targets that would normally be set for them.[24]

As Mr. Garvery's experience shows, if we're not anchored by irrelevancies, we make decisions based on the easiest, most readily available explanation. If it makes sense, why look for another cause?

As we'll see in Chapter 24, we can make positive uses of the anchoring effect, but we also need to be mindful of how this powerful bias can cause us to make faulty judgements. Numbers seem to have a particularly powerful effect and are particularly hard to resist. Deliberately thinking the opposite of what you've been told and trying to falsify statements can help to prevent anchors from taking root in our minds.

The availability bias

What's more likely to kill you, a shark or a bathtub?* We've all heard stories of killer sharks, but as yet Spielberg hasn't made a thriller about killer plumbing. Our reasoning is based on the information most readily available to us. We assume that the risk of dying in a plane crash is greater than the risk of dying on our sofa because plane crashes are so much more dramatic and newsworthy. But we're wrong.

If we only read what everyone else is reading, we will only have access to a very limited pool of ideas. If everyone writing about education only reads as far as Hattie, Willingham and Lemov and then stops, their thinking stops with them. This is the availability bias. We want to know the likelihood of something happening, but we have only limited data. Therefore we make decisions based on the information most readily available in the belief that *because* it's readily available, it's more likely to be true.

If there has been a recent plane crash we cancel our tickets, even though there is a greater chance of dying in a car crash on the way to the airport

---

* Sharks kill an average of 10 people a year whereas about 35 people a year drown in the bath.

than being killed mid-air. Anything that has a strong emotional component dominates our thinking. In the classroom, suppose you start grading some work and realize after the first few papers that the exact same mistake is being made. Cheating alert! You're now actively looking for the same error in every other paper you grade. It may just have been chance, but you have jumped to a conclusion and that has affected your judgement for the rest of your grading. Sometimes the information we can draw to mind might be accurate, but sometimes it's not. Ignorance isn't bliss; it's scary. We are often most terrified by the unknown. But if something feels familiar, no matter how bad it is, we can cope. We prefer erroneous information to no information at all.

The ease with which we recall things affects how we feel. Struggling to bring things to mind is uncomfortable. Weirdly, the more examples of a category people are asked to come up with, the less certain they'll feel about their knowledge of the subject. We become less confident of a decision the more reasons we're asked to come up with to support it. The more incidences of our expertise we're asked to recall, the less we're inclined to trust our ability.

In a study, participants were asked to recall either six or twelve examples of their assertive or very unassertive behavior. Participants were later asked to rate their own assertiveness. Although it was possible to come up with twelve examples, it wasn't easy. Participants rated themselves as more assertive after describing six examples of assertiveness, but less assertive after describing twelve examples of assertiveness.[25] Intuitively, you'd expect that coming up with more examples would be more persuasive, but because finding six examples is easier than finding twelve, the way we feel about making effort tricks us into believing something that isn't true.

One way of making ourselves feel like we know what we're doing is to collect data. We assign numbers to things such as performance measures or evaluate something on a scale of 1–10. But although this may provide a superficial sense of accuracy, there is little guarantee that the data has much bearing on reality. Data is uniquely comforting because it's just so quantifiable; turning something into a percentage or a bar graph gives it the appearance of being objectively true. The problem is, it's all too easy to assign numbers with little justification or simply to make up data to support our beliefs – the old confirmation bias again. Such activity leads us to do all kinds of foolish things in schools.

Consider this scenario: a school leadership group is considering moving away from grading individual lesson observations in the light of a landslide of disconfirming evidence.* They accept that lesson grading is invalid and unreliable, and that taking a lesson study approach is more likely to support the professional development of teachers. But, and it's a big but, how can we hold ourselves to account without numbers?

Numbers assigned to graded lesson observations are entirely and utterly subjective, but they are so comforting because they provide the illusion of hard data. As Robert Coe, professor of education at Durham University, and colleagues observe:

> If we were to use the best classroom observation ratings, for example, to identify teachers as 'above' or 'below' average and compare this to their impact on student learning we would get it right about 60% of the time, compared with the 50% we would get by just tossing a coin.[26]

Many school leaders have been seduced into the easy certainties of grading lesson observations, aggregating the grades and then proudly declaring that teaching in their school is 80 percent good or better. But this is meaningless; there is no objective standard with which to compare this. Assigning numerical values to our preferences and biases gives them the power of data, but they're still just made up.

We tumble into the same bear pits when setting students' targets. We hand these to students as if they are cast iron certainties. But while they may not be simply plucked from the air like lesson observation grades, they're based on statistical probabilities that may have some validity when applied to large classes but are reduced to meaningless drivel when applied to individuals. Possibly, the most useful thing we can do is to subvert these targets to harness the power of the growth mindset. (See Chapter 21 for further explanation of the growth mindset.)

Data cannot be intrinsically bad. Just as guns don't kill people, data doesn't distort the curriculum or warp decisions about what to teach: we do that. We are comforted by the illusion of knowing, but we really don't know. Any accountability system that allows people to either lazily pluck

---

* It really is a landslide. See Chapter 20 for details.

the most readily available numbers from their brains or wrestle data into meaning something it was never intended to mean is doomed to fail. But what's worse is that many schools, teachers, parents and children aren't even aware of the failure.

Next time someone shows you a spreadsheet, try asking the following questions:

- If these data are the solution, what's the problem?

- Is there a different way of interpreting the data?

- How can I verify the quality of the data I'm being shown, and what are the margins for error?

- What are the limitations of these data – what don't they show?

- How are these data likely to affect my decision making? What would I do differently if I didn't have these data?

- How were these data acquired, and are they valid?

In this way maybe, just maybe, we can avoid some of the potential pitfalls associated with availability bias.

The halo effect

As we've seen, despite our ignorance we often make decisions based on irrelevant and available information. The halo effect is another form of confirmation bias which prevents us from becoming aware of the uncertainty we really ought to feel.

The term was first coined by educational psychologist Edward Thorndike back in the 1920s, and has since been thoroughly established as a real and powerful bias. In one study designed to test how people reacted when given information that made no apparent sense, business school students were grouped into threes. Each group was asked to estimate the sales and earnings per share for a company based on its financial reports from the previous five years.

Researchers told the business students they had previously analyzed the performance of groups of five people on this task, and were now keen to see how smaller groups would perform. When the students were told they had performed very well, they attributed that success to things like great communication, group cohesion, openness to change, competence, a lack of conflict and so on. Groups told that they'd performed very poorly did just the opposite. They explained their poor results as a lack of communication, differences in ability, closed mindedness, sparks of conflict and a variety of other confounding variables. In truth, neither group was able to explain their performance as the results had been rigged. Regardless of how well they performed, each group were randomly told either that they had done extremely well or spectacularly badly. In an effort to explain the unexplainable, they resorted to plucking causes from the air.[27]

How often might this desperate hunt for reasons be enacted to explain unexpected exam performance? When we are uncertain, our brains use a heuristic and then cover up the evidence so we won't notice that we had no idea what we were doing. 'Communication skills' are too vague to quantify, so when the business school students were asked to rate their communication skills, they looked for something more concrete to go on. In this case it was the randomly assigned rating. That rating then became a halo whose light affected the way they were able to see their experiences. This might have worked except that the rating was a lie, and consequently so were their explanations. When target grades are applied to individual students, instead of classes, they are also a lie.

In his book *Thinking, Fast and Slow*, Daniel Kahneman relates how the halo effect led him to systematically mis-grade students' essays. Quite reasonably, if a students' first essay was awarded a high score, mistakes in later essays were ignored or excused. But Kahneman noticed a problem:

> If a student had written two essays, one strong one weak, I would end up with different final grades depending on which essay I read first. I had told students that the two essays had equal weight but this was not true: the first one had a much greater impact on the final grade than the second.[28]

You might think we could pick up these sorts of mistakes through a process of introspectively retracing our mental steps back to the original mistake, but you'd be wrong. Research into the halo effect suggests this sort of thing happens all the time. In a study into the way students make judgements about their lecturers, students were told the experimenters were interested in whether judgements varied depending on the amount of exposure students had to a particular lecturer. This was another of those pesky lies psychology researchers tell their participants. The American students were divided into two groups to watch two different videos of the same lecturer, who happened to have a thick Belgian accent. In one video the professor was cold and distant, in the other he was warm and approachable. Both groups of students were asked to rate his appearance, mannerisms and accent. As you're no doubt expecting, the students who'd seen a warm, friendly professor rated him as more attractive and his accent as more pleasant, while those who'd seen an unfriendly professor rated him as unattractive and his accent as distracting.[29]

It probably comes as no surprise to know we make decisions about people's intelligence and competence based on our perception of their attractiveness, but the extent to which we do this is terrifying. In studies where teachers were told that a student had a learning disability, they rated that student's performance as weaker than did other teachers who were told nothing at all about the student before the assessment began.[30] The fact that we treat students according to the halo cast by superficial traits is well-known. We assume that "well-behaved students are also bright, diligent, and engaged".[31]

And the same thing is likely to happen when school leaders evaluate teachers' performance. It's easy to be swayed by traits, such as enthusiasm, into arriving at a flawed judgement. Even if we lack the competence to perform our job successfully, if we seem suitably keen, we may very well end up with a higher performance rating than is justified by our knowledge or ability.[32]

Just like the availability bias and the anchoring effect, the halo effect covers up our lack of insight and changes uncertainty into pseudo-certainty.* We use irrelevant, superficial details to make assumptions about things we don't really understand. While we might be able to agree that there's little that is certain in life, our awareness of how we make decisions is appallingly limited. We have no idea why we react as we do.

....

* In *Rush Limbaugh is a Big Fat Idiot*, US senator Al Franken used the term 'pseudo-certainty' to describe the behavior displayed by those pundits and politicians who use 'common sense' as the basis for confident assertions, without actually backing them up with bothersome research and facts. Franken suggests we describe this phenomenon using the refreshingly blunt, "being a fucking moron".

To the extent that girls do seem to achieve better than boys, how much of this might be due to the halo effect? Are boys and girls treated differently in school and in wider society? Gender is socially constructed, not biological. We expect girls to be made of sugar and spice and all things nice, whereas boys are unwashed louts. Might we be making it easier for girls to achieve in schools because of the expectation we have of them?

Overconfidence bias

Although we all suffer from cognitive bias, the more certain we are, the greater the probability that we may be mistaken. The philosopher Bertrand Russell pointed out, "in the modern world the stupid are cocksure while the intelligent are full of doubt".[33] Is this just more bias? Well, apparently not. Research seems to indicate Russell was right. Certainty appears to indicate a lack of nuance and sophistication in our thinking. The Dunning–Kruger effect is the finding that the poorest performers are the least aware of their own incompetence. Or put more crudely: stupid people are too stupid to recognize their own stupidity.

Psychologists David Dunning and Justin Kruger were inspired to conduct research in this area after reading the sorry tale of incompetent criminal McArthur Wheeler, a man who robbed two banks in the absurdly mistaken belief that, as lemon juice can be used as invisible ink, covering his face with it would somehow prevent his features from being identified on surveillance recordings.[34]

After comparing participants' tests results with their self-assessment of their performance in such diverse fields as sense of humor, grammar and logic, Dunning and Kruger proposed that, for a given skill, the incompetent not only fail to recognize their own lack of skill but also fail to recognize genuine skill in others. Encouragingly, they also found that if incompetents are given training in an area in which they are identified as being unskilled, they are able to recognize and acknowledge their own previous lack of skill.[35] As Dunning observes, "If you're incompetent, you can't know you're incompetent ... the skills you need to produce a right answer are exactly the skills you need to recognize what a right answer is."[36]

The reverse of this effect, the imposter syndrome, is also at work. Those with genuine skill tend to underestimate their ability and see themselves as less competent than others. From our reading of the halo effect, it's not hard to see how the loudest, most confident people are often promoted well beyond their ability.

As we know, a little knowledge can be a dangerous thing, leading us to fall victim to the anchoring effect and availability bias. When we know something about a problem we can be misled into believing we're an expert. We rarely admit our ignorance – we just rely on heuristics and go with the easiest possible answer. As we'll see in Part 2, expertise is acquired slowly as the result of grappling with and internalizing troublesome knowledge. As Charles Darwin noted in *The Descent of Man*, "Ignorance more frequently begets confidence than does knowledge." Although there's no shortcut to expertise, the Dunning–Kruger effect suggests that we often think there is. I began writing this book in the belief that I knew and understood enough to explain the consequences of the mistakes we make in education. It's only as I've read and researched that I've realized just how little I know. Maybe beginning to realize the extent of our ignorance allows us to be more humble. If so, I probably still have some way to go.

I certainly don't want to suggest that readers are incompetent; rather I'm suggesting that certainty can sometimes be an indicator of our ignorance. This leads to pseudo-certainty, defensiveness and the backfire effect. Conversely, doubt enables us to more easily accept new ideas. Ask yourself: what is it I believe most strongly? Those areas may well be where the gold is, if only you're prepared to dig.

Overconfidence certainly isn't just caused by stupidity. Often, otherwise very sensible people are led astray because they're unable to think outside their own experience. Sometimes we're overconfident because we recognize our own talents and the strength of the people around us and assume that this will always be enough to make things a success. We're blind to the role of chance and almost never calculate the role of bad luck, unpredictable change and the effects of time. If we want to overcome the pernicious effects of overconfidence, we should think ourselves into the following scenario. Imagine you are one year down the line from introducing the new policy or project and it has gone spectacularly and horribly wrong. Spend five minutes detailing all the things that contributed to the project's failure. This process unleashes our imaginations to work exactly where it should: on the uncontrollable and the external.

Perverse incentives

In our efforts to get others to do the 'right thing', we have an unwitting tendency to create perverse incentives. Back in the good old days, when the great unwashed could simply be shipped off to the colonies with nary a second thought, transportation of convicts was in the hands of private enterprises. These companies were compensated based on the number of prisoners shipped. As long as they were signed and sealed, no one cared over much if they were delivered, and a depressing percentage of prisoners perished on-board these dreadful hulks. Eventually the government, realizing they were being short-changed and running the risk of running out of forced laborers, changed the metric from prisoners shipped to the number who arrived still living.

In the former Soviet Union, glass plant managers were rewarded according to the tonnage of sheet glass they produced. Inevitably, plants churned out sheet glass so thick as to be useless. Right, thought the apparatchiks, we'll sort out you bourgeois shirkers! and changed the rules so that square metreage of glass produced was rewarded instead. How did our entrepreneurial factory managers respond? Yep, you guessed it – they produced glass so thin and fragile it would shatter as soon as you looked sternly at it.

Often, our response to a perceived difficulty is to offer incentives. Students misbehaving and not working hard enough? Vivo Miles!* Teachers not working their fingers down to the bone? Performance related pay!

If no suitable enticement is offered we're in the terrifying position of simply relying on altruism. But if people are properly incentivized, the reasoning goes, they will act with motivation, determination and efficiency. Generally speaking, most teachers do want to do the right thing.

---

*   Vivo Miles is a commercial rewards system intended to work a little like air miles. Students gain rewards for good behavior, and you know what points make? That's right. Prizes.

We're nice like that. Rare indeed is the teacher who chooses education as a shortcut to fame and fortune. Although we want to be adequately remunerated for our efforts, we teach because we want to teach. There aren't many teachers holding on to exciting new methods for teaching spelling or oxbow lakes until somebody offers to pay them a little bit more.

Unavoidably, schools always want to take a little bit more and given the chance will suck the soul out of teachers. This isn't the fault of unscrupulous leaders, more the result of being a faceless cog in an institutional system: the bigger the school, the easier it is to make impersonal demands. In the best cases, teachers are spurred to work through shared values and vision, but nothing beats the simplicity of the carrot and stick. And as soon as an incentive is offered, people change. We tend, unerringly, to respond by doing what is in our best interests. We respond to the letter of the initiatives rather than their spirit; we ignore the intention and focus solely on the incentive.

Sometimes the perverse ways in which we're encouraged to behave are fairly obvious – for example, education can seem plagued with cheating. A quick internet search unearths countless tales of shady practice, with schools and teachers bending the rules in order to meet perverse incentives. Sometimes, though, the inducements are less obvious.

Consider the way schools are held accountable for 'closing the attainment gap' between the most disadvantaged and the most privileged students. In England, schools are given extra funding for children in receipt of free school meals in order to close the gap. It makes complete sense to scrutinize what public money is being spent on; we can't have schools simply squandering it on whatever shiny baubles are offered for sale by the sharp suited consultant class. But because we're unwilling to trust that schools will do the right thing we create perverse incentives. It's not enough for less advantaged students to be doing better than the national average, or even better than every other school's figures for disadvantaged students' attainment. You have to ensure that there is no gap between different classes of students within your own school.

Now, I'm sure no school would be so cynical, but if the goal is for schools to narrow the gap, the obvious solution is to reduce the attainment of non-student premium students. Obviously this is undesirable, but it would be a logical, self-interested solution to a perverse incentive.

Economist Rolf Dobelli offers this advice: "Good incentive systems comprise both intent and reward."[37] Clearly this is sage counsel, but how so to do? When managing change, we tend to focus on problems. We look at what is preventing people from behaving in the way we want them to behave rather than focusing on those instances of success. Often, the best way to change behavior is to focus on these positives instead of all the frustratingly negative, er … negatives. Most of us willingly tread the path of least resistance, so if we're offered enticements that make it easy to replicate these successes, we might get more of the changes we want.

Here's a process we could use to interrogate whether our incentive system is likely to do what we actually want:

- What is the behavior you want to change, and how exactly do you want to change it? Be specific.

- Remember the fundamental attribution error: to what extent might the behavior be caused by the situation rather than the people?

- Incentives work best when they affect emotions. How do people feel now, and how do you want them to feel?

- What can you take away to ensure that people are not too exhausted to make the desired change, to consciously opt out of old initiatives?

- What examples can you find of the behavior you want to encourage, and how can you make others aware of them?

- How could you use the anchoring effect to make this behavior the new norm?

- Is your incentive working? How do you know? What unexpected changes have occurred?

Dobelli suggests, "If a person's or an organization's behavior confounds you, ask yourself what incentive might lie behind it. I guarantee you'll be able to explain 90% of the cases that way. What makes up the remaining 10%? Passion, idiocy, psychosis or malice."[38]

....

These few examples of the confounding ways we fool ourselves merely scratch the surface of the self-deception to which we are so depressingly prone. Knowing about these weaknesses in our ability to reason is, you'd think, half the battle. Surely, if you knew you were being biased you'd be able to stop yourself, right?

Well, maybe not. Once you know about these biases you'll become excellent at recognizing specks in others' eyes, but still be a bit bad at spotting the plank in your own. The bias blind spot predicts that even when we know we're engaging in an explicitly biased strategy, we'll still respond in a biased way but claim we're behaving objectively.[39] We appear to have psychological blind spots every bit as unavoidable as our physiological ones.

All this makes it very difficult to change our mind about our views on education without fear of being pilloried. Astronomer and science writer Carl Sagan had this to say about changing one's mind: "In science it often happens that scientists say, 'You know that's a really good argument; my position is mistaken,' and then they would actually change their minds and you never hear that old view from them again. They really do it."[40] Even within science this doesn't happen as often as it should, because we're all human and change is painful. But it happens even less in politics and religion. And it's pretty rare in education too. In contrast, as philosopher Maurice Arthus points out most people "shut their ears so as not to hear the crying facts, and they shut their eyes so as not to see the glaring facts, in order to remain faithful to their theories in spite of all and everything".[41]

Maybe it's impossible for us always to head off poor decisions and flawed thinking; *knowing* is very different to *doing*. I'm just as prone to error as I ever was, but by learning about cognitive bias I've become much better at examining my thoughts, decisions and actions after the fact. At least by being aware of the biases to which we routinely fall prey, and our inherent need to justify our beliefs to ourselves, maybe we can stay open to the possibility that some of what we believe is likely to be wrong some of the time.

The checklist solution

There is perhaps one possible solution to our very predictable fallibility. In his book, *The Checklist Manifesto*, surgeon Atul Gawande puts forward the humble checklist as a way of coping with the terrifying complexity of the intensive care unit.[42] He argues that medicine has become so specialized that no one, no matter how experienced and expert, can hope to anticipate every possible permutation of biology and technology. If we rely on expertise, we will fail.

I'm not for a moment arguing that education is the same as medicine. The decisions that teachers and school leaders make might affect students' life chances, but they're not life and death. If we make a poor decision in the classroom no one is likely to die. Education professor Lee S. Shulman sees classroom teaching as "perhaps the most complex, most challenging, and most demanding, subtle, nuanced, and frightening activity that our species has ever invented".[43]

Even though what we do is unlikely to kill people if we get it wrong, it's still fiendishly complex. Could a checklist be designed to help us avoid some of the lazy, unthinking decisions we make when planning, teaching and grading?* Although if used to make judgements checklists can easily become an inflexible tool for evil, we could use a checklist of cognitive biases to avoid some of our worst excesses when planning professional development activities, writing policies and conducting appraisals.

According to Gawande, a good checklist should be no more than seven items long, fit into a 90 second 'pause point' when it's convenient and it makes sense to make a check, and all decision makers should get to discuss the items on the list.

Here are some suggestions of items which might usefully appear on such a checklist:

- Have you considered the real root cause of the problem you're trying to solve?

- Have you considered other possible reasons for the problem?

---

* Harry Fletcher-Wood suggests some very useful ideas for designing a checklist to plan lessons in his blog post, 'So Simple, It Doesn't Seem Worth Doing. So Potent, It's A Must: How Can Checklists Improve Teaching?'

- Have you sought out sources and evidence which contradict your beliefs?

- Have you allowed for dissenting opinions to be voiced and considered?

- Have you considered the weight of time, resources and credibility you or others have already sunk into this course of action?

- Is there any asymmetry in your thinking?

- How might groupthink and social proof be influencing your decisions?

- Have you encouraged others to criticize and suggest problems with your plans?

- How far is your decision based on your opinion of the individuals concerned?

- To what extent are your decisions anchored by possibly irrelevant information?

- Do you really understand the data you're using to inform decision making?

- What perverse incentives might you be creating?

- Often certainty blinds us to alternatives. How confident are you that your decision is correct?

- What would be the consequences of *not* taking this course of action?

- Have any other schools tried this course of action? How many were still doing it three years later? What were the results?

- Who else could you ask to spot the biases in your thinking?

This is by no means an exhaustive list, but it might serve to give you some insight into the errors to which we are all prone and which you will no doubt be influenced by whenever you have a decision or judgement to make. Other suggestions to help us slow down and avoid predictable pitfalls include:

- Falsify your belief – what conditions would cause it to be untrue?

- Make direct comparisons – it's much harder to miss errors of thinking when making comparisons between two outcomes.

- Construct hierarchies – order outcomes from most to least desirable.

- Use the language of heuristics and biases to diagnose and discuss the errors we are all prone to make.

Notes

1   Constantine Sedikides and Craig Anderson, Causal Explanations of Defection: A Knowledge Structure Approach, *Personality and Social Psychology Bulletin* 18 (1992): 420–429.
2   Geoffrey D. Munro and Peter H. Ditto, Biased Assimilation, Attitude Polarization, and Affect in the Processing of Stereotype-Relevant Scientific Information, *Personality and Social Psychology Bulletin* 23 (1997): 636–653.
3   Bertrand Russell, *Proposed Roads to Freedom: Socialism, Anarchism and Syndicalism* (New York: H. Holt, 1919), p. 147.
4   Matthew M. Chingos and Grover J. 'Russ' Whitehurst, *Class Size: What Research Says and What It Means for State Policy* (Brown Center on Education Policy at Brookings, 2011). Available at: http://www.brookings.edu/research/papers/2011/05/11-class-size-whitehurst-chingos.
5   Peter Blatchford, Class Size: Is Small Better?, in Philip Adey and Justin Dillon (eds), *Bad Education: Debunking Myths in Education* (Buckingham: Open University Press, 2012), pp. 57–76 at p. 72.
6   Malcolm Gladwell, *David and Goliath: Misfits and the Art of Battling Giants* (London: Penguin, 2013).
7   Ed Baines, Grouping Pupils By Ability In Schools, in Philip Adey and Justin Dillon (eds), *Bad Education: Debunking Myths in Education* (Buckingham: Open University Press, 2012), pp. 37–55 at p. 52.
8   See http://educationendowmentfoundation.org.uk/toolkit/toolkit-a-z/ability-grouping/.
9   Robert Coe, Cesare Aloisi, Steve Higgins and Lee Elliot Major, *What Makes Great Teaching? Review of the Underpinning Research* (London: Sutton Trust, 2014). Available at: http://www.suttontrust.com/wp-content/uploads/2014/10/What-makes-great-teaching-FINAL-4.11.14.pdf.
10 John White, *Howard Gardner: The Myth of Multiple Intelligences* (London: Institute of Education, University of London, 2005), p. 9.
11 Scott O. Lilienfeld, Steven J. Lynn, John Ruscio and Barry L. Beyerstein, *50 Great Myths of Popular Psychology* (Oxford: Wiley-Blackwell), p. 96.
12 Richard Sennett, *The Craftsman* (London: Penguin, 2009), p. 285.
13 Carol Tavris and Elliot Aronson, *Mistakes Were Made (But Not By Me): Why We Justify Foolish Beliefs, Bad Decisions and Hurtful Acts* (Orlando, FL: Harcourt Books, 2007), pp. 32–37.

14 Bertrand Russell, *On the Value of Scepticism*, in *The Will to Doubt* (New York: Philosophical Library, 1958). Available at: http://www.positiveatheism.org/hist/russell4.htm.

15 Muzafer Sherif, A Study of Some Social Factors in Perception, *Archives of Psychology* 27(187) (1935): 17–22.

16 As quoted in Ralph G. Nichols and Thomas R. Lewis, *Listening and Speaking: A Guide to Effective Oral Communication* (Dubuque, IA: W.C. Brown, 1954), p. 74.

17 Jerry B. Harvey, *The Abilene Paradox and Other Meditations on Management* (San Francisco, CA: Jossey-Bass, 1996).

18 Daniel Dennett, *Consciousness Explained* (London: Penguin, 1993), p. 67.

19 Andrew Old, How To Be Bad SMT, *Scenes from the Battleground* (19 October 2013). Available at: http://teachingbattleground.wordpress.com/2013/10/19/how-to-be-bad-smt/.

20 Leon Festinger, Henry Riecken and Stanley Schachter, *When Prophecy Fails: A Social and Psychological Study of a Modern Group That Predicted the Destruction of the World* (Eastford, CT: Martino Fine Books, 2009).

21 BBC Two, How You Really Make Decisions, *Horizon* [video] (3 April 2014).

22 Amos Tversky and Daniel Kahneman, Judgment under Uncertainty: Heuristics and Biases, *Science, New Series* 185(4157) (1974): 1124–1131.

23 Thomas Mussweiler and Fritz Strack, The Semantics of Anchoring, *Organizational Behaviour and Human Decision Processes* 86 (2001): 234–255.

24 This example comes from English teacher James Theobald's wonderful blog post: How to Eat 50 Hot Dogs in 12 Minutes (and Why Setting Targets Might Hold Back Progress), *Othmar's Trombone* (18 July 2014). Available at: https://othmarstrombone.wordpress.com/2014/07/18/how-to-eat-50-hot-dogs-in-12-minutes-and-why-setting-targets-may-hold-back-progress/.

25 Norbert Schwarz, Herbert Bless, Fritz Strack, Gisela Klumpp, Helga Rittenauer-Schatka and Annette Simons, Ease of Retrieval as Information: Another Look at the Availability Heuristic, *Journal of Personality and Social Psychology* 61(2) (1991): 195–202.

26 Coe et al., *What Makes Great Teaching?*, p. 3.

27 Barry Staw, Attribution of the 'Causes' of Performance: A General Alternative Interpretation of Cross-Sectional Research on Organizations, *Organization Behaviour and Human Performance* 13 (1975): 414–432.

28 Kahneman, *Thinking, Fast and Slow*, p. 83.

29 Richard E. Nisbett and Timothy D. Wilson, The Halo Effect: Evidence for Unconscious Alteration of Judgments, *Journal of Personality and Social Psychology* 35(4) (1977): 250–256.

30 Howard Abikoff, Mary Courtney, William E. Pelham and Harold S. Koplewicz, Teachers' Ratings of Disruptive Behaviors: The Influence of Halo Effects, *Journal of Abnormal Child Psychology* 21(5) (1993): 519–533.

31 Neil J. Salkind and Kristin Rasmussen (eds), *Encyclopedia of Educational Psychology*, Vol. 1 (Thousand Oaks, CA: Sage, 2008).

32 Frank Schneider, Jamie Gruman and Larry Coutts, *Applied Social Psychology*, 2nd edn (Thousand Oaks, CA: Sage, 2012).

33 Bertrand Russell, The Triumph of Stupidity, in *Mortals and Others, Vol. II: American Essays, 1931–1935* (New York: Psychology Press, 1998), p. 28. Available at: http://russell-j.com/0583TS.HTM.

34 New York Post, Why Losers Have Delusions of Grandeur (23 May 2010). Available at: http://nypost.com/2010/05/23/why-losers-have-delusions-of-grandeur/.

35 Justin Kruger and David Dunning, Unskilled and Unaware Of It: How Difficulties in Recognizing One's Own Incompetence Lead to Inflated Self-Assessments, *Journal of Personality and Social Psychology* 77(6) (1999): 1121–1134.

36 Interview with David Dunning, *New York Times* (20 June 2010).

37 Rolf Dobelli, *The Art of Thinking Clearly: Better Thinking, Better Decisions* (London: Sceptre, 2014), p. 57.

38 Dobelli, *The Art of Thinking Clearly*, p. 58.

39 Emily Pronin, Daniel Lin and Lee Ross, *The Bias Blind Spot: Perceptions of Bias in Self Versus Others*, *Personality and Social Psychology Bulletin* 28 (2013): 369–381.

40 Carl Sagan, keynote address at the Committee for the Scientific Investigation of Claims of the Paranormal (CSICOP) conference, Pasadena, 3–4 April 1987, as quoted in Judson Poling, *Do Science and the Bible Conflict?* (Great Rapids, MI: Zondervan, 2003), p. 30.

41 Maurice Arthus, *Philosophy of Scientific Investigation* (Baltimore, MD: Johns Hopkins Press, 1943), p. 16.

42 Atul Gawande, *The Checklist Manifesto: How to Get Things Right* (London: Profile Books, 2011).

43 Lee S. Shulman, *The Wisdom of Practice: Essays on Teaching, Learning, and Learning to Teach* (San Francisco, CA: Jossey-Bass, 2004), p. 504.

Chapter 3
Challenging assumptions

Rational discussion is useful only when there is a significant base of shared assumptions.

Noam Chomsky

You know what they say about assuming?* The trouble is, we can't help leaping to conclusions. We are judgement making machines. As we saw in the previous two chapters, we all assume our decisions are for the best. Why else would we make them? Without these assumptions we'd have to do a lot more thinking than is efficient. So we use heuristics and take shortcuts. Shared assumptions can be very useful; without them we'd be unable to communicate. When I use terms like 'student', 'lesson' or 'school', I assume your understanding is broadly similar to mine. And by and large it is. Sometimes, though, we collude in assumptions that are just plain wrong.

These can be minor. I was once observed teaching a class of 11-year-olds Tennyson's ballad 'The Lady of Shalott'. During the post-lesson feedback, the observer told me the lesson hadn't been sufficiently challenging because some of the children said they had previously studied the poem in elementary school. The assumption was that the poem was too easy for secondary school students. I pointed out that I was also studying the same poem with my A level group. Just because we've encountered something before doesn't mean we can't discover new depth and meaning in it.

. . . .

*   Oh, come on! Everyone knows this, right? When we assume we make an ASS out of U and ME. Sorry.

But then, I'm as guilty of making these sorts of assumptions as anyone else. Once, when observing another teacher's lesson, I noticed a student wearing earphones. Naturally, I assumed he was avoiding work and interpreted his subsequent actions in this light. Afterwards I asked the teacher if she'd noticed. "Oh, yes," she said. "He always wears earphones after I've finished explaining a task so that he can block out chatter and get on with his work." I wasn't convinced. Surely listening to music is every bit as distracting – hadn't she allowed herself to be fooled? She pointed out that the earphones weren't plugged in – they were just being used as ear plugs. Although I felt a bit foolish, I was really glad I'd asked rather than leaving with the assumption that this teacher was either unobservant or overly tolerant.

That experience made me reflect on another boy I taught. Karl (not his real name) was lazy. He spent every lesson building little towers out of erasers. Whatever I did, he refused to work. I spent months battling with him: I invited his parents in to discuss his lack of effort; I put him in detention every day; I sent him out of lessons. Nothing worked. I spoke to other teachers who reported similar difficulties and were similarly stumped. How, I wondered, would he pass his exams? I notably failed to solve this problem, wrote him off as impossible and prepared myself for his inevitable failure. He got an A*. When I approached him on results day to express my astonishment and ask him to account for his extraordinary success, he shrugged and said, "Just because I never did anything didn't mean I wasn't listening."

With these experiences in mind, let's look again at some of the beliefs about education I held and filter them through the cognitive biases we've explored:

1. Good lessons involve children learning in groups with minimal intervention from the teacher.

2. Teachers should minimize the time they spend talking in class and particularly avoid whole-class teaching.

3. Children should be active; passivity is a sure sign they're not learning.

4. Children should make rapid and sustained progress every lesson.

5.   Lessons should be fun, relevant to children's experiences and differentiated so that no one is forced to struggle with a difficult concept.

6.   Children are naturally good and any misbehavior on their part must be my fault.

7.   Teaching children facts is a fascistic attempt to impose middle class values and beliefs.

On the face of it, these beliefs may not sound particularly startling. They seem reasonable because they contain a kernel of truth. But often, and certainly in my experience, this kernel was interred beneath layers of assumption. Let me unpick each of these to see if there are any gleaming nuggets among the accretions of received wisdom, bias and logical fallacy.

1. Good lessons involve children learning in groups with minimal intervention from the teacher

Firstly, let me state that I see nothing inherently wrong with students working collaboratively. Like any method of working, it has its time and place – the idea of sports or drama devoid of teamwork is absurd. But I was led to believe that unless a lesson contained an element of group-work it could not be a good lesson. It's not enough to claim that 'no one really believes this'. I did. This is due to a mix of the availability bias – it's all I knew – and the sunk cost fallacy – the more I tried to make it work, the more determined I was to see my efforts rewarded. I come from a generation of teachers raised to believe groupwork is inherently good and for that reason alone it deserved to be questioned, prodded and poked.

It's easy to poke fun at groupwork (just Google "groupwork + funny"), but let's consider what the problems might actually be.

Way back in 1913, French agricultural engineer Maximilien Ringelmann discovered something rather surprising: the productivity of a group decreases as its size increases. If we pull a rope all by ourselves we tend to pull our hardest, but as soon as others pop up to help us out we slacken off. Even though they are likely to be unaware of this slackening of effort, everyone pulls a bit less hard. The bigger the group, the greater the tendency for social loafing.

The Ringelmann effect suggests that when we're part of a group we believe every other member is doing the hard work. We can take it easy because our lack of effort won't be exposed. Unconsciously, we rely on those around us to pull out the stops to get the job done. This phenomenon is well-known to teachers. It ought to be reasonable to expect a group of four students to produce four times as much work collectively as they would produce alone. In fact they tend to produce less together than they might alone.

Not only that, working in groups actually makes us less creative. In particular, 'brain-storming' (or 'thought-showering' if you prefer the more politically correct synonym) actually limits our capacity to come up with interesting ideas.[1]

Add to that the fact that groupwork is devilishly difficult to implement. Bad groupwork can be worse than almost any other classroom sin, ending in the tyranny of the strong and the persecution of the weak. Enormous effort and expertise must be applied to get groups working functionally. It requires teachers' relationships with students to be rock solid. For groups to work effectively, Robert Slavin says two conditions must be met: collaborative goals and individual accountability.[2] The first is relatively straightforward but the second is far trickier. If you put enough effort into it, you can condition students to perform quite efficiently as part of a team, but for the vast majority of lessons I'm not convinced they would really learn any more. Unless resources are expended in training teachers how to do it well, groupwork rarely works. And if we spend time training teachers how to conduct groupwork, what other, potentially more useful, areas of professional development might be neglected?

Considerations of opportunity cost should also be applied to students – how are they spending their time when working in groups? Puzzling things out with peers is more time consuming than listening to an expert explanation. Curriculum time is limited and we should be aware that some activities are less efficient than others. Getting students to discuss ideas and puzzle out alternatives might be worthwhile if they already know enough about a subject, but it is much more limiting if they haven't learned anything about it yet.

So why do we bother? Why have students work together at all?

Russian psychologist Lev Vygotsky believed that students performed at higher intellectual levels when asked to work in collaborative situations.[3] Advocates for groupwork – or collaborative learning as it's often referred to in academic circles – claim it develops skills which, in turn, lead to better performance in schools. Groupwork has been averred to improve learning, develop students' social skills, develop empathy and altruism, deepen learning, improve test scores and retention, help students to develop complex learning strategies, create the conditions for independent learning and encourage a habit of lifelong learning.[4] These claims are either founded on assumptions and wish fulfilment, are unfalsifiable or are based on studies so small and poorly constructed as to be worth very little.

But will the experience of groupwork give students a much needed edge in the world of work? If we learn how to work well in teams, won't we acquire the soft skills so valued by employers? This reasoning rests on the same fallacy which suggests that doing 'independent learning' will result in independence. But in order to perform like experts, we must first *be* experts. Rushing students into situations where they are expected to behave like experts misses the fact that they don't yet know enough to do so. Simply making students work in groups will not create better workers.

So *is* there a point to groupwork?

We've all encountered students who struggle to answer questions and come up with ideas. Left to their own devices they sit, head on desk, and dream of being somewhere better. We know that simply getting them to discuss some possibilities with the student sitting next to them can be sufficient to jolly them along. Maybe they haven't become more creative, and maybe this just gives them less of an excuse for doing nothing. Who cares: *it gets them working.* I'm sure we can all cite thousands of examples from our own lives of occasions where a simple conversation with a friend or colleague opened up new possibilities or pointed us in previously unexplored directions. This is what the philosopher Michael Oakeshott calls "the conversation of mankind".[5] The point of collaboration is that it opens us up to the ideas of others. But so does reading books.

A useful rule of thumb might be to have students working in groups when it suits the subject they are studying. Drama or PE without group-work would be a poor thing, and there are times in other curriculum areas when it makes sense for students to collaborate on aspects of their study. Also consider what they already know – might it be more effective to teach them something *before* asking them to share ideas?

Feel free to have your students work in groups if you must, but don't pretend there is sufficient evidence out there to support your preferences being imposed on others.

2. Teachers should minimze the time they spend talking in class and particularly avoid whole-class teaching

One of the reasons often given for having children work in groups is that the alternative would mean teachers delivering lectures. The unspoken narrative is that teachers are dull and it's both cruel and pointless to ask children to listen to them drone on. But talking is the most efficient and effective means of communicating; there is no quicker way to transfer an idea from one mind to another. Asking teachers not to talk is madness. If it is the case that teachers are dull, shouldn't we be asking how we could improve their ability to explain the tricky underpinning concepts of their subjects rather than finding increasingly bizarre ways to mini-mize teacher talk?

Back in 2008, after an observed lesson, I was told I talked too much. This judgement was based on a body of thinking that assumed teachers are boring and being forced to listen to a bore drone on about some-thing is unlikely to result in learning. Teachers have had carte blanche to bang on in whatever tedious manner they decided was appropriate for far too long and maybe it was right and proper that this practice should be challenged. Every boring teacher added to the confirmation bias that all teachers are boring. Predictably, as soon as it became acceptable to critique the concept of 'teacher talk', this began to be interpreted as a preference for minimizing the time teachers spend talking.

One of the roots of this problem is that the concept of adult authority is anathema to many educators. Teachers talking is seen as teachers dominating. But there's no getting away from the fact that, on the whole, the teacher will be the most expert, knowledgeable person in the room. Expecting them not to share their knowledge and expertise is just silly.

If students are actually going to learn anything worthwhile, teachers absolutely *must* talk. The trick is to make that talk as clear, relevant and memorable as possible. The attack against teacher talk has had a toxic effect. Students' academic success depends on their ability to think in academic language. If you want to change the way someone thinks, then change the way they speak. Many students are unlikely to encounter this kind of language outside the classroom. Hearing academic language used and – even more importantly – being expected to use it in discussions is a powerful lever for cognitive change. Effective modeling is impossible if teachers are afraid to speak. Instead of trying to shut teachers up, maybe we should be training them in improving the quality of their talk.*

3. Children should always be active; being passive is a sure sign they're not learning

The assumption here is that passivity means sitting still and listening. Because we can't *see* anything happening, we assume nothing *is* happening. But listening is a highly active skill that requires focus and attention. In our misguided desire to demonstrate what great teachers we are, we get students running around, massaging their brain buttons and slapping sticky notes on every available surface. 'Active learning' is reduced to a caricature.

When working with a group of middle leaders on the need to reclaim teacher talk from the wastebasket of pedagogy, a teacher stopped me to say, "That's all very well, but our kids just can't pay attention for more than five minutes." Superficially, this makes a certain kind of sense, but what if you were to say, "The trouble with 'our kids' is that they can't read

---

* If you're interested in a lengthy exposition on the links between speech and thought, and how we might go about improving teachers' talk, please see my book, *The Secret of Literacy*, pp. 90–95.

so we don't give them any books"? Or, "'Our kids' can't behave so we just let them chuck chairs about"? This would be clearly unacceptable if not downright negligent. If 'our kids' can't pay attention for more than five minutes then we damn well need to teach them to do so! Pandering to their inability to pay attention is terrifying. Paying attention for extended periods is a crucial ability for anyone who is likely to flourish. It is much too important to be left to chance.

The word 'passive' implies a lack of purposeful learning. Daydreaming might be passive, but it might be that ideas are gestating, ready to pop out later. Going to sleep might be passive, but then sleeping on a problem can lead to greater clarity on awakening. Not listening is entirely passive. But listening is active and requires our complete attention. As I found with Karl (he who made the towers of erasers), we cannot see what is going on in the minds of others. Assuming we can is an example of the illusion of asymmetric insight. Claiming that students ought to be able to wander about in order to learn is just foolish.

4. Children should make rapid and sustained progress every lesson

This belief led to the practice of expecting teachers to demonstrate students' progress every 20 minutes. In turn, this led to the inexorable (and execrable) rise of the mini-lesson. If teachers are judged on whether students make progress in 20 minutes, then that progress will be inevitably shallow – the perverse but predictable incentive is that teachers are encouraged to make it as easy as possible for children to succeed.

I have taught lessons which have been buzzing and everyone is excited about 'the learning'. I explain what I intend to be learned, I set up conditions where children are exposed to a new concept or have to apply a skill, and then I employ a range of pedagogic techniques to ascertain whether students are on track. They troop out happy and secure in the knowledge that they have made progress. I might do a spot of grading and pick up some misapprehensions, maybe make a hasty revision to next lesson's plan, but basically we're good. Then, next week, they file back in with absolutely no idea what we did last lesson. Has that ever happened to you? What was going on? Was that really progress?

I've also taught lessons of which I have been ashamed. I've overestimated what my class could do and left them baffled and frustrated. By the end of the lesson it's clear that no one really gets it and they shamble out shaking their heads and muttering imprecations. I hang my head and go back to the drawing board. Then, much to everyone's surprise, they showed up next week having 'got it'. Somehow, after the lesson was over, they seem to have snuck in a bit of illicit learning. Is this progress?

We all know which of those lessons would feel better to teach. I'm not advocating chaotic lessons, but learning, it turns out, is a lot more complicated and messy than we've been led to believe. It happens inside children's heads and, lacking telepathic abilities, we can't see it taking place. All we can ever see is what they can do *now*. We mistake this for learning at our peril. Learning does not proceed in an orderly, predictable fashion; at times we appear to be learning nothing and then some sudden insight surprises and hijacks us. But its suddenness is a trick – new insights depend on slow accretions of knowledge. Attempts to map the way we learn can never adequately describe the complexity of human thought, but that's not to say we can't make some fairly accurate predictions about what sorts of things might grease the mind's wheels.

Spending time proving something has been learned is time that could be better spent learning stuff. Expecting students to do something really quickly and for it to last for a long time is silly. Happily, official sanction for this practice is in decline, but there is still a desperate need of inoculation against it in many schools. We will discuss the myth of progress further in Chapter 6.

5. Lessons should be fun, relevant to children's experiences and differentiated so that no one is forced to struggle with a difficult concept

Some years ago, I took part in a department meeting where we were asked to prioritize those qualities we most valued about teaching. We came up with all the tiresomely worthy answers you might expect, but, somewhat controversially, I insisted on including 'fun'. The case I made went something like this: I don't teach for the money, I do it because I enjoy it. So, having fun must be at the center of what I do in the classroom. It wasn't even (or just) about the kids having fun: it was all about me. And, to an extent, I can still just about follow this tortured logic. I mean, who doesn't like having fun?

On reflection, though, there's a bit of a problem with fun for fun's sake, and it's this: what are students doing while they're having all this fun? If they're enjoying the challenge of mastering a difficult concept or new skill, then fine. But when students decide they've worked just about hard enough for one day and ask, full of pathetic hope, for a 'fun lesson', they're not wanting to be challenged, they're wanting to be entertained. And if they're being entertained by my fun packed lesson then they're probably not going to be paying sufficient attention to whatever it is I want them to learn. Why? Because we remember what we think about. If we're not careful, students will be too busy thinking about all the fun they're having to remember any of what they're supposed to be learning.

The priority for any lesson planning is to consider what the students will be thinking *about*. There's nothing wrong with thinking about icing cakes or making sock puppets as long as that's what you want them to learn. But if they're actually a cunningly devised 'fun' disguise for the real topic of the lesson, then they won't be thinking about *why* they're doing those things. I once watched a lesson in which the teacher wanted the class to learn what life was like for Irish peasants during the Great Potato Famine. She decided to do this by hiding potatoes around the classroom. Students were highly engaged from the word go and had great fun. They learned loads about the likely hiding places for a potato in a classroom, but they failed to remember anything about the life of Irish peasants.

It's also worth remembering that most kids don't really know what they're going to enjoy. They might *think* they want to fritter away lessons watching films but they'll quickly tire of it. Often students find enjoyment in the most unexpected places: grammar for instance. I'm regularly surprised at just how much they seem to enjoy grasping some tricky syntactical point and then going off to apply what they've learned. But, despite this, they never ask for more grammar. Kids don't know what they'll enjoy because they haven't experienced all that much of the world yet. It's up to us to expose them to things they're unlikely to choose to do in their own time to expand their cultural horizons and knowledge of the world.

As in every school, a reputation gathers around the best teachers. This is the halo effect – students' impression of a teacher influences their feelings and thoughts about that teacher's character and qualities. Students want to be in these teachers' lessons, and consequently there are rarely behavior issues to deal with. Other students will often help to manage difficult behavior because students want to be there. These teachers are hard-working, often to the extent that other colleagues wonder how they can possibly manage. Although they're highly professional, they often only get mediocre results. (However, achieving mediocre results in a school that gets terrible results is great.) Engaging teachers probably do about the best possible for children in bad schools. Learning is secondary to fun.

In a school with poor behavior management systems, these teachers are held up as examples of what other staff should aspire to. Inevitably this leads to teachers feeling guilt and inadequacy, and to a culture in which lessons are more about fun than learning. And fun can be the enemy of learning.

As we'll see in Part 2, struggle is, I think, an essential component of learning. By being overly concerned with what students cannot do *now*, we risk losing sight of the direction we could be taking them in. By making lessons easier, we run the not inconsiderable risk of making it more difficult to retain or apply the knowledge and skills we intend students to learn.

If students achieve beyond expectation then criticism of a teacher's efforts to differentiate must be irrelevant. Yes, of course, we should be aware of the differences between students, but shouldn't we have the same high expectations for all?

A teacher's role is to get their students transcending their current limitations rather than comfortably meeting the low expectations of their current ability. If differentiation is reduced to a set of practices or techniques that teachers can 'do' in a lesson, then we will inevitably lower our expectations in line with what it appears students are able to do during the lesson. Instead, we might think of differentiation as the need to vary our explanations and the support we give to enable students to cope with the challenge of having to struggle with new concepts. Rather than consigning students to what they are merely able to do, we might instead think about what they could do. Maybe then we would stand a better chance of having them learn these concepts rather than merely respond to classroom cues and prompts.

6. Children are naturally good and any misbehavior on their part must be my fault

Children are not naturally good. As the playwright Aphra Behn put it, "There is no sinner like a young saint." They can be as mean spirited, spiteful and selfish as, well, anyone else. Children, like adults, pursue the course of action which leads to the most reward for the least effort. If behaving well requires less effort and produces greater rewards, they'll behave. But if it seems easier and more socially acceptable to fiddle around, then they probably will. Children's poor behavior is a choice, and telling them otherwise just undermines their ability to get on in life.

The Romantic meta-belief that children are all little angels corrupted by the adult world is a dangerous but powerful anchor. It leads us to make two mistakes:

1.   We don't see children as they truly are.

2.   We feel guilty if they're not good.

Much better if we saw children honestly as the complex but immature beings they are – full of soaring beauty and ugly failings. Golding's *Lord of the Flies* suggests that without adult guidance and authority children will revert to barbarity (although adult authority can be every bit as savage). I've seen enough cruelty and cynicism from children to inure me against the belief that being 'good' and 'kind' is in any way natural.

And much better too if we acknowledge that children's misbehavior is not the teacher's fault. Yes, we are responsible for dealing with it when they step out of line, but we don't cause it.

Some years ago I taught a boy, let's call him Ben, who had a diagnosis of attention deficit hyperactivity disorder (ADHD). He behaved perfectly in my lessons but was hell on wheels for various other teachers.

In particular, his relationship with his French teacher had descended to a running feud; his behavior towards her was appalling. The school decided to confront his outrageous shenanigans by offering him a mentor. And because I got on with him, Ben nominated me as the teacher he most wanted as his guide. After one particularly horrific low I confronted him about his behavior:

Ben: It's not me, sir, it's my ADHD.

Me: But how come you don't have ADHD in my lessons?

Ben: That's 'cos you're alright, sir.

Ben was exercising a choice. He chose when and where to behave and pay attention. The school's expectation of him was incredibly low, but in the end he was permanently excluded after committing one atrocity too many. If, on the other hand, the expectation was for him to jolly well do as he was told, I'm sure we would have done him a far kinder service. At the very least he'd have had an early lesson about consequences and had more time to settle in to a new school.

One of the most damaging and appalling lies circulating around many schools and teacher training institutions is this: if you plan your lessons well children will behave. And the corollary: if your lessons are not 'fun and engaging' they won't. This patent untruth has crushed the spirit of many a bright young teacher, and it needs to be challenged.

The primary responsibility for behavior rests with the school, not the teacher. And before you start frothing uncontrollably, please note the word 'primary'. Of course teachers must bear some of the responsibility for the behavior of students in their lessons. Of course having a well-planned lesson helps. But without watertight systems classroom teachers are put in an untenable position. Blaming teachers for the failure of a school to implement and stick to a robust behavior system is morally reprehensible.

But if new teachers are to survive they must be told that bad behavior is not their fault. It just isn't. No matter our age or circumstances, we choose the way we behave. Yes, there will be *reasons* why students choose to act up – and, as we discussed in the previous chapter, self-control can be hard to master – but this should never be accepted as an excuse.

In schools where poor choices are tolerated, new teachers are up against it. Your best recourse will be to follow the school rules, whatever they are, even if you don't always agree with them. Set your expectations early: what you accept on day one will haunt you for the rest of the year. Anything you allow becomes established as allowed; anything you challenge is established as unacceptable. At any point, if you are not happy with the behavior in your lessons, you have to address it explicitly.

But in a good school, effective systems and good leadership mean that poor behavior is unusual. Here teachers can concentrate on teaching their subjects and building relationships. Here students will think hard about subject content, not about who can run fastest to the answer or whether their teacher might come in fancy dress to the next lesson.

This is not about passing the buck. There's a sacred covenant at work in good schools: just as the school has a responsibility to ensure teachers don't have to put up with abuse and can get on with the business of making kids cleverer, teachers have the equally weighty responsibility to uphold even the most trivial and inconsequential of school rules. These rules are there for everyone's protection. Students need to know that the rules will be upheld consistently. I'd much rather set the bar at doing up top buttons than at not throwing chairs. Teachers who are too cool for these rules actively undermine their colleagues. If you 'can't be bothered' to enforce uniform rules because you don't see how a pair of sneakers can affect learning, Beelzebub has a devil put aside for you. Every time you decide to let a school rule slide, you are actively undermining your colleagues. Yes! This means you, trendy, leather-jacketed drama teacher!

7. Teaching children facts is a fascistic attempt to impose middle class values and beliefs

Are there some facts *everyone* should know? French sociologist Pierre Bourdieu extended the idea of capital to encompass knowledge of culture. He argued that, while we all occupy a position within society, we are not defined only by membership of a social class. More important is the 'capital' we can amass through social relations. Needless to say, this can, and often does, result in inequality.

What constitutes cultural capital is not subjective, or at least, not very subjective. It's based on the body of knowledge which collectively and over time we, as a culture, have decided is worthwhile. Personal preference doesn't come into it. There are those who claim it is elitist and the preserve of posh kids in private schools, and that 'kids like these' should be given a more 'relevant' diet because that is what is most suited to their foreshortened little lives. I understand the thinking that learning should be made relevant to students' experiences, but that kind of thinking is what leads teachers to say, "Right, the World Cup is on so we must have World Cup themed lessons." Or, "*Grand Theft Auto 6* is out soon – how will I get *that* into my lesson?"

This is unbelievably patronizing, selfish and short-sighted. If we allow cultural capital to be the preserve of the elite, we ought to be ashamed of ourselves. To the extent that it's elitist, let's reclaim it. The canon is not mine or yours and it's certainly not theirs: it's ours. And we should damn well appreciate it!

Knowing what is considered to be useful and important is powerful. This view is often attacked on the grounds that teaching students to revere the works of Dead White Men is reactionary and bound to burden them with thoughts and ideas that are irrelevant to their lives and circumstances. And so, perhaps, it would be if that were what I was advocating. But knowledge is power. The more you know, the better equipped you are to think. Students should be encouraged to critique what we teach, but to do that we have to first teach them.

Unless children from disadvantaged backgrounds are given the opportunity to study an academic curriculum, they'll never be able to be anything other than disadvantaged. Having children of my own focused my thinking on this. If it's not good enough for my children, then it's not good enough for anyone else's.

....

These, then, are a few instances where I have changed my beliefs. A more recent belief that has gained widespread approval is that a growth mindset is necessarily good and a fixed mindset is necessarily bad. I think this assumption deserves interrogation; we will take a closer look at it in Chapter 21.

Depending on your own beliefs and assumptions, you may be nodding in agreement or shaking your head in resigned pity. It doesn't matter so much who's right; either way, we must stay aware of the biases we use to reduce the cognitive dissonance we feel. If your beliefs won't bear up under close critical evaluation then maybe, just maybe, you believe something silly. We should question everything and always be prepared to murder our darlings.

If you're undecided then this is a fascinating place to be. Right now, your beliefs about education and the way you feel about these beliefs may be broadly similar to those of many other people. But remember the pyramid of choice: you will justify every choice you make until, by the time you reach the bottom of the pyramid, your "ambivalence will have morphed into certainty".[6]

And as we become more certain of our beliefs, they are more likely to cast a halo over the rest of our thoughts, and it seems that those who get angry about being challenged are much more likely to be mistaken. Our ability to learn from each other through debate rapidly erodes. If we could stand the cognitive dissonance of doubting what we feel *must* be true then we're taking a real risk. This kind of skepticism threatens our sense of self. But when we allow ourselves to doubt, we put ourselves in the position where we are most likely to learn.

Here are some questions to ponder in the wee small hours:

- So, what are you absolutely sure of?

- What is the evidence for these beliefs?

- What would you stand to lose if it turned out you were wrong?

One area on which most of us will have some fairly settled views is the purpose of education, and *that* is why we find it so hard to agree.

Notes

1   Brian Mullen, Craig Johnson and Eduardo Salas, Productivity Loss in Brainstorming Groups: A Meta-Analytic Integration, *Basic and Applied Social Psychology* 12 (1991): 3–23.
2   Robert Slavin, Eric Hurley and Anne Chamberlain, Cooperative Learning and Achievement, in William M. Reynolds and Gloria J. Miller (eds), *Handbook of Psychology*, Vol. 7: *Educational Psychology* (Hoboken, NJ: Wiley, 2003), pp. 177–198.
3   Lev Semenovich Vygotsky, *Mind in Society: The Development of Higher Psychological Processes*, ed. Michael Cole (Cambridge, MA: Harvard University Press, 1978).
4   Sources include: Robert Slavin, *Educational Psychology: Theory and Practice*, 8th edn (Boston, MA: Pearson/Allen & Bacon, 2006); Robert Slavin, Eric Hurley and Anne Chamberlain, Cooperative Learning and Achievement: Theory and Research, in William M. Reynolds and Gloria E. Miller (eds), *Handbook of Psychology*, Vol. 7: *Educational Psychology* (Hoboken, NJ: Wiley, 2003), pp. 177–198; and Maurice Galton and Linda Hargreaves, Group Work: Still a Neglected Art?, *Cambridge Journal of Education* 39 (2009): 1–6.
5   Michael Oakeshott, The Voice of Poetry in the Conversation of Mankind, in *Rationalism in Politics and Other Essays* (London: Methuen, 1962), pp. 197–247.
6   Carol Tavris and Elliot Aronson, *Mistakes Were Made (But Not By Me): Why We Justify Foolish Beliefs, Bad Decisions and Hurtful Acts* (Orlando, FL: Harcourt Books), p. 33.

Chapter 4

Why we disagree and how we might agree

But most of us are apt to settle within ourselves that the man who blocks our way is odious, and not to mind causing him a little of the disgust which his personality excites in ourselves.

George Eliot, *Middlemarch*

Education is as hotly contested and ideologically riven as any other field of human endeavor, probably more than most. Sadly, the debate seldom moves beyond knee-jerk reaction and participants fail to embrace the dissonant possibility that another human being could, at the same time, disagree with them and not be some sort of child hating monster.

No one goes into education to make a fast buck or to bathe in the warm glow of society's esteem. Teachers teach because they think it's important. On application forms, we're disposed to spout platitudes about life chances, the joy of learning, passion, creativity and fun tempered on the anvil of hard work and rigor. What's missing in the debate is a clear understanding of what education is actually for. As long as we disagree about the purpose of education, we will never agree on how to improve it.

I started writing this book with the idea that, as well as hacking at the roots of some of the more abject ideas that choke our understanding of education, I might attempt also to present some wisdom about how we should think instead. But the deeper I've dug, the less sure I've become. As Einstein may have said, "Education is the progressive realization of our ignorance."* This journey into ignorance is one every seeker after truth follows, and I'm afraid I have little in the way of certainty to offer you.

When I started my career as a teacher I was bad. Really. Those early years are nought but a source of shame. I failed often and hugely. If I'd qualified in the current climate, I'd probably have been drummed out of the profession in short order. But, for some strange quixotic reason, I persevered and became a little less appalling. The turning point came when I joined a school which promptly failed an external inspection (a coincidence, I assure you). In the process, I learned a huge amount, some of it even useful, and became a better teacher. However, given my ignorance about the profession, I hitched my wagon to every passing fad and gimmick as if my job depended on it. This was a successful strategy. My teaching was lauded as 'outstanding'; I was promoted and led a very successful English department before joining the ranks of senior leadership. But I still knew astonishingly little about education.

As we saw in Chapter 3, I've been forced to confront that some of what I unquestioningly believed was probably wrong and that some of the things I unthinkingly did as a teacher might actually have been unhelpful. This stemmed from the fact that I had little sense of the theories and ideologies that bubble under the surface of education. All I knew was what I was told: this is what a teacher should know about teaching. I was not expected to critically analyze this knowledge; I was simply to accept and apply it. I've come to understand that the way I was taught to approach teaching was based on a set of contested assumptions. Evaluators would punish schools and teachers who didn't teach this way because not teaching this way obviously meant that you were a bad teacher. Deep down, I knew that much of what I was doing was shallow, short term and trivial – surely it's wrong that I could train a barely literate child to pass their English language GCSE? – but this was what the system demanded and I got good at it.

....

* There's a veritable cottage industry of fake Einstein quotes out there and they're often flung heedlessly into education debates as some kind of proof or moral authority. I suspect old Albert might feel quite surprised. If you'd like to find out more, this website is a good starting place: http://skepticaesoterica.com/debunking-fake-albert-einstein-quotes.

As my views have evolved, I've become less and less comfortable with the status quo. It's led me to question many of the foundations on which my beliefs about teaching and education were founded: assessment, feedback, lesson grading and the entire concept of 'outstanding' teaching.

Much of what I was told had been shaped by assumptions made by such long dead thinkers as Jean-Jacques Rousseau and Herbert Spencer and that, since the 19th century, thinking on education has been broadly split between those identified as 'traditional' and those considered 'progressive'.* These terms are somewhat nebulous and resist attempts to precisely define them, but, broadly, the traditional school believes in the authority of the teacher and the centrality of knowledge, while a progressive approach can be described as child centered and believing that dispositions, skills and competencies are at least as important, if not more so, than 'mere facts'. If you're anything like me, you may find yourself repelled by one set of ideas and accepting the other as being self-evidently and obviously true. The problem is, we may not agree.

These ideologies fracture into myriad splinters and sub-groups. It's possible to hold aspects of each of these beliefs while simultaneously denigrating others. We can, for instance, claim that it is more important to enrich certain aspects of a child than others, or that wisdom is more important than intelligence. We can earnestly applaud efforts to make children easier to govern while raising an outcry against the pragmatic ideal of fitting children to jobs. This maelstrom of conflicting ideas and ideologies swirls beneath the level of consciousness in the minds of most teachers; we do what we do because it's right, goddam it! But everyone believes they're right. Can we really all hold such opposing beliefs and all be right? Hopefully, your reading so far has convinced you that this is unlikely.

For the record, here's what I believe: education should exist to make children cleverer; we can all become cleverer, no matter our starting point. In the name of social justice, I believe that professional ethics should not stand in the way of a working class child's chances of success. Socially disadvantaged students should have access to the same education as that

* It's not my intention to explore the history of education in this book, but if this is an area of interest I can recommend E. D. Hirsch Jr's *The Knowledge Deficit*, Daisy Christodoulou's *Seven Myths About Education*, Robert Peal's *Progressively Worse*, Martin Robinson's *Trivium 21c* and Kieran Egan's *Getting It Wrong from the Beginning*.

received in elite public schools. If these children are to have a chance at exercising free choice in how they live their lives, they must be explicitly taught the academic language needed to be academically successful. In the name of enrichment, I believe we should provide students with as broad and as deep a knowledge base as possible so they can think as broadly and as deeply as possible; after all, we cannot think about that which we do not know. I believe that creativity depends on knowing 'the rules' of the form in which we are working and that we should provide access to the most powerful conceptual knowledge that exists in the history of the subject disciplines we teach. I want children to have every advantage they can in order to allow them to choose to do whatever they want to do. But I don't give a damn about preparing them for work, as this is a small, narrow-minded endeavor. We might never be able to close the attainment gap between haves and have-nots but we should certainly strive mightily to shift the entire bell curve to the right.

Regardless of our beliefs, we are also endowed with a set of often tangled and contradictory values. It's important to comb out these values to see which are based on the unthinking adoption of others' assumptions, and which are essential for getting a good night's sleep. Our values inform us where to draw our lines in the ever shifting sands of policy and fashion. No amount of research or evidence can tell us what our values should be, and nor should it try. Values are about what we think the world *should* be like, not what it *is* like. Although what we value is open to debate, it cannot be shown to be 'wrong'. If you can look me in the eye and state with certainty that your values are better than mine, you're a fool. While everyone's values may be different, they all deserve a modicum of respect. Categorizing one person's values as having less worth than another's is unlikely to win over hearts and minds.*

If we genuinely want to improve education, we need to cut through all the nonsense about pedagogical preferences and start describing those

---

* We can, of course, argue about cultural relativism but it's rarely an argument that profits anyone. Arguing that the music of One Direction has the same worth as that of Mozart makes you look silly. Or worse, arguing that female genital mutilation is acceptable because all cultures have equal value would rightly be considered morally reprehensible. Ken Wilber's assertion that everything is "true but partial" is, I think, a blind alley – there are things that are always wrong, even if some people are happy to believe them.

values so precious to us that we would never compromise them. Then, and only then, might we find some common ground.

Former teacher and journalist Laura McInerney says:

> Improving education will only happen if we all have the humility to at least entertain the thought we might be wrong or over-exaggerating our concerns. We don't have to give in completely. I'm not about to become an evangelical advocate of any policy. But we also have to ensure that we're not just holding onto a dislike of a policy because it's comfortable or because we are too stubborn to admit we were wrong. Critical thinking means being critical of others, and of ourselves. If we lose that ability, we will have lost the most important learning faculty of all.[1]

Being critical of ourselves is one thing; maybe we can discipline ourselves to recognize our attempts to rationalize and justify our beliefs, but others rarely thank us for pointing out their flawed thinking. If it were as simple as showing others where they fall victim to cognitive dissonance and bias, all would be well. It's a rare thing to remain open to criticism; few of us have the mental toughness to submit our most treasured beliefs to a searingly honest examination. But it does happen, and it should be encouraged.

Should we do a 'bit of both'?

Whenever two or more competing ideas are in circulation there will always be those who call for compromise. To do a bit of both. To exercise a bit of give and take. The dictionary is instructive on this. The noun is defined innocuously enough: an agreement or settlement of a dispute that is reached by each side making concessions. But the verb's more damning definition is: the expedient acceptance of standards that are lower than is desirable. In his 1886 essay, *On Compromise*, John Morley asked, "How far, and in what way, ought respect either for immediate practical convenience, or for current prejudices, to weigh against respect for truth?"[2]

Compromise is the refuge of the unprincipled. As aphorisms go this is nicely pithy, but does it contain any truth? Well, that depends on our reasons for compromise. If it's to appease others then we have a problem.

As Margaret Thatcher said, "If you set out to be liked, you would be prepared to compromise on anything at any time, and you would achieve nothing." She was famous for refusing to compromise: "You turn if you want to. The lady's not for turning." I do realize I'm maybe on shaky ground with some readers by setting Old Maggie up as someone to emulate – inflexibility usually isn't a positive virtue. But she's got a point: if we're only interested in appeasing others, we will be buffeted by the winds of change and may well founder on the rock of opinion. Any attempt to grease the wheels by lowering standards is inexcusable.

Over the past few years,* many teachers have been asked to compromise what they consider common sense and told to talk for no longer than five minutes in a lesson and attempt to prove that children have made progress every 20 minutes. Education is an ideological battleground, and those in power have ever felt the need to impose their beliefs on teachers on how best to teach. Often the compromise has been for teachers to perform the Monkey Dance when observed and revert to 'what works' when the classroom door is closed. Teachers have felt under pressure to pretend they don't teach. On hearing that someone is planning to observe them they say, "Oh they won't want to see *that*, I'll have to change my plans. They won't want to see children working in silence; they'll expect some sort of show." This is an inherently dishonest position. It's not that the so-called progressive conspiracy has led to wide-scale changes in classrooms, it's that this kind of compromise has led to teachers feeling guilty. We reason, "Why would we be asked to do these things if they weren't the best things to do?" It's rare to be able to hold on to the belief that we're right when all the available evidence says we're wrong.

Consider again my list of educational practices about which I've changed my mind:

1. Good lessons involve children learning in groups with minimal intervention from the teacher.

---

* This refers particularly to the period beginning with Christine Gilbert's tenure as head of Ofsted in 2006 up to Sir Michael Wilshaw's appointment in 2012. Despite various structural changes and multiple revisions to Ofsted's guidance to evaluators, understandably many school leaders still fear the consequences of being criticized for not doing things the 'Ofsted way'.

2. Teachers should minimize the time they spend talking in class and particularly avoid whole-class teaching.

3. Children should be active; passivity is a sure sign they're not learning.

4. Children should make rapid and sustained progress every lesson.

5. Lessons should be fun, relevant to children's experiences and differentiated so that no one is forced to struggle with a difficult concept.

6. Children are naturally good and any misbehavior on their part must be my fault.

7. Teaching children facts is a fascistic attempt to impose middle class values and beliefs.

Can we simply do a bit of groupwork followed by a bit of teacher led instruction? Can we have a bit of 'passive' listening alongside a bit of 'active' learning? Yes, of course we can. But is this the same as suggesting they are equally as valuable? The question might become, *should* we do a bit of both? And if so, why? However, the choice between rapid and sustained progress is more complex – doing things quickly tends to preclude them lasting a long time. The choice between having fun and working hard is similarly complex. Great if you enjoy hard work, tough if you don't.

Now, I'm not saying we should never compromise. Clearly this would lead to a pointlessly uncomfortable existence. Compromise is often a practical and realistic approach to many of life's niggling little irritants. But would we compromise on our principles? On what we hold most dear? Speaking for myself, I'm prepared to compromise on anything except that which matters. This doesn't have to be antagonistic. Gandhi, known for passive resistance, was nothing if not a man of principle, and he had pretty clear views on this: "All compromise is based on give and take, but there can be no give and take on fundamentals. Any compromise on mere fundamentals is a surrender. For it is all give and no take."

But compromising feels so right. Or rather, it can feel like the noble choice despite the unsatisfactory outcome. No one wants to be labeled as uncompromising. But, then again, we're even less keen on being seen as unprincipled. Compromise is all very well as long as we can retain those pesky principles. My principles are my fundamentals. If I were prepared to compromise on what I believe most passionately to be true, what would I be other than a coward?

By these lights, compromise *is* a refuge, a hiding place for those without strongly held guiding principles. And that's fine. I don't say that if you lack these principles you are somehow lesser; there are many areas of my life where I have no strongly held opinion. I am therefore happy to compromise. But who among us compromises on what really matters?

Here are three principles on which we should not compromise:

- Children's behavior in lessons should never get in the way of the teacher teaching or other students learning; our expectation should be that children are respectful, hard-working and cooperative.

- Teachers should be supported by their school to enable them to teach to the best of their ability; extraneous demands should be stripped away to allow an expectation of professional excellence through reflection and development.

- Powerful knowledge is the right of every student.* We should never assume children from particular social classes should be taught differently to others.

One thing I'm more than happy to compromise on is how to teach. I have some views about what I think might work best and some evidence that supports these views. But I'd never attempt to compel anyone else into following my advice – I may well be wrong. And the likelihood that I'm wrong increases when applied to other personalities and contexts.

....

* Briefly, the more generalizable and theoretical knowledge is, the more powerful it is. Where it is tied to particular contexts it tends to be practical, procedural and of little use in other contexts. An example of this is to teach students to begin persuasive writing with a rhetorical question. This is far less powerful than teaching them the underlying concept that rhetoric is an ancient art dedicated to the manipulation of an audience.

The dichotomous box

Whenever we find a point on which we are unwilling to compromise, someone is usually delighted to dismiss our position as a 'false dichotomy' (and hence a waste of time). The answer, they claim, lies not at the margins but somewhere in the center. In this way we can dispense with the futile bickering between traditionalists and progressives, and those who champion the teaching of either knowledge or skills, because they are both right. We just characterize our adversaries as occupying an extreme position because it's easier to think in terms of black or white, but could this be yet another cognitive bias?

Human nature tends to create dichotomies – right or wrong, traditional or progressive, child centered or teacher led – and this way of thinking gets in the way of finding out how students learn best and ends with the belief that one size fits all.

Let's first explore the idea of a false dichotomy. This is a logical fallacy committed when we present only two options when in fact there are others. Typically, we would then go on to construct a straw man argument, which demonstrates that anyone holding the 'only other option' is clearly delusional.

Here are some patently false dichotomies:

- You're either for wearing school uniform or you're not.

- If you didn't see the gorilla you're either stupid or a liar.

- Either you have a fixed mindset or you have a growth mindset.

Each of these propositions presents what appears to be a rational choice but excludes other possible alternatives. Sometimes these are easy to spot but this is not always the case. In the last example, we may be dazzled by the simplicity and utility of this finding and not stop to consider whether there are other possibilities worthy of examination.

But lazily brushing aside someone's considered opinion as being a false dichotomy allows us to ignore potentially important issues. The fact that there's a dichotomy, false or not, alerts us to something which requires further examination in order that we make the most informed choices possible. In one sense all dichotomies are 'false' in that they are just ways of viewing the world. Sometimes a dichotomy can be a useful construct which helps us to think about choices and serves as a useful way of thinking.

For example, the positions taken by progressive or traditionalist educators lead to all sorts of seemingly unrelated disputes and confusions. If I genuinely believe that the best way to educate is to be guided by the inclination of the child and to respond to their impulses as a supportive guide then it makes complete sense that I will recoil in horror from a word as loaded with authoritarian meaning as 'obedience'. But, equally, if I think the best way for children to learn is to be instructed by an expert then it's obviously desirable for them to be obedient to that expert's instructions. The trick, if there is one, is to find a way to think outside the dichotomous box. What other alternatives are there? Are we perhaps falling victim to the anchoring effect?

The problem comes when we try to compromise. In the spirit of taking the best of both, many people are committing what I've come to think of as the 'and fallacy': you can't always eat your cake and have it. Some positions might really be mutually exclusive: Christianity and atheism, say. You could attempt to argue that there's a possible compromise between these positions but you'd probably be wasting your breath. Or what about science and astrology? Science depends on testing theories with well-designed tests while astrology requires no such 'proof' to be considered efficacious – we just have to believe in it. It's no good just to dismiss this dichotomy by saying that there's a time and place for both. There might well be a time and place for both but these times and places exclude each other. They do not overlap.

The decision of how to teach is complex. We choose a course of action based on our beliefs about what education is for, the demands of the subject we're teaching, our knowledge of the students we're teaching and the availability of pedagogical techniques in our teaching arsenal. If we believe first and foremost that education must be relevant to students' lives and experiences, we will select curriculum content and design lessons accordingly. History, mathematics and physical education are very different disciplines. One size is unlikely to fit all. The best way to teach fractions is very different to the best way to teach students to understand historical context. It may have more in common with the best way to learn how to serve in tennis, but the practicalities of practicing these skills requires completely different organizational skills.

We know no two children are the same: some appear to be much more able than others and seem to grasp tricky concepts more quickly. But does that mean we need to teach them differently, or just at a different pace? If a student is struggling to kick a ball, do they need more practice or a radical new approach to learning how to kick? For most children practice will be the answer. Those who require a different approach are so few as to be impossible to generalize from.

At some level, at least, we're aware of making these decisions, but one of the biggest factors that determines how we teach is informed by the availability bias. I remember receiving whole-school training on a technique called 'marketplace' some years ago. The trainer explained that we should teach new concepts by getting students to research different aspects of the topic and then turn the classroom into a bazaar where students hawk their wares. Quite apart from the fact that this is a time consuming and inefficient way to relay information, it's also pretty tedious when every teacher in the school uses the same technique over the days following the training. If someone tells us something is good, often we'll uncritically accept their advice and give it a go. If students seem to enjoy it we'll do it again. If they don't we'll shrug our shoulders and return to 'what works for me'.

Believing that you can cherry-pick the best approaches to teaching seems like good old fashioned common sense, but it might be flawed. If the evidence tells us that teacher led instruction is an effective way to teach and discovery learning is an ineffective way of teaching (and it does), why would you do a bit of both? You can only really hold this view if you think that one way of teaching is as good as another or that variety is more important than efficiency. Let's return for a moment to the dichotomy between science and astrology. I could claim that we might benefit from using astrology every now and then for the sake of variety or because we find it more motivating. But this is nonsense. When it matters we make choices based on the best available evidence rather than relying on hocus-pocus and guesswork. If we believe astrology is the best way to make decisions, then why wouldn't we always choose it when the stakes are high? Is it acceptable to simply claim it 'works for me'?

The crux of the matter is the belief that children will benefit by being taught by a variety of methods or that they will be more motivated to learn if given a choice about how to learn. Teaching cannot be child centered and teacher led at the same time. You have to make a choice. I'm not arguing that one position is better than the other, just that they are mutually exclusive. If you are choosing to do a 'bit of both' you fail to acknowledge that these positions are antithetical. When push comes to shove, if our lives were on the line, most of us would choose science and damn our principles! With the exception of religious crackpots, few of us would have a deep enough conviction in astrology to risk our lives on it. The difference is, our lives aren't on the line. It's not us who'll suffer if we do a bit of both.

The point, perhaps, is this: arguments polarize because the most interesting thinking often happens at the extremes. The middle ground is exactly that: the meeting of two competing principles. You can always choose to do a bit of both A *and* Z, but they will be diluted.

A   Z

The answer is rarely in the middle, but it can come from integration. The philosopher Hegel's theory of historical dialectic suggests a way that we could hold competing ideas in tension. He saw the development of new ideas in three stages:

1. Thesis – an accepted way of seeing the world.

2. Antithesis – a challenge to the accepted paradigm.

3. Synthesis – a resolution of the competing world views which holds each in creative tension.

If we applied this process to the ongoing debate on the purposes of education it might look a little like this:

1. Thesis – children should be taught what to think by an authoritative adult.

2. Antithesis – children will learn best if they are motivated and should therefore decide what they want to learn and how to learn it. The role of the teacher should be confined to providing suggestions and advice.

3. Synthesis – children should be taught what to think by an authoritative adult, encouraged to challenge and critique what they've learned and then express their new understanding of the world.

The synthesis I've arrived at above might be wrong, but it isn't a compromise. It takes contradictory ideas and attempts to force them together. But one word of warning: synthesizing something new from the clash of competing ideologies might lead us into believing in the inevitability of progress, that what's new is better than what has come before. This may be a mistake (see Chapter 6).

Instead of believing that there is an answer out there if only we search long and hard enough, developing *negative capability* – an ability to think about the mysteries of the world without needing to reconcile their contradictions – might be a way out of the dichotomous box.

The poet John Keats said this:

> Negative Capability ... is when man is capable of being in uncertainties, Mysteries, doubts, without any irritable reaching after fact & reason ... the sense of Beauty overcomes every other consideration, or rather obliterates all consideration ... the willingness to embrace uncertainty, live with mystery, and make peace with ambiguity. Thus, the conflicting nature of things must be understood to reach the imagination, where one can create ...[3]

As we've seen, often we just don't know. The truth is inconveniently messy. The way to square competing theories and ideas is not to find the middle ground but to force binary oppositions into creative tension. As the journalist and professional naysayer Christopher Hitchens put it, "The truth cannot lie, but if it could it would lie somewhere in between."[4]

We might want to resist the truth of this, but anything else is either boring or ridiculous. The Irish poet W. B. Yeats captured the nonsensical nature of much compromise when he said, "You know what the Englishman's idea of compromise is? He says, Some people say there is a God.

Some people say there is no God. The truth probably lies somewhere between these two statements."

The second part of this book is an attempt to bend the dichotomies back on themselves to find a satisfactory balancing point. Rather than reaching after certainties, maybe we could embrace the apparent chaos of liminality and seek to do both A and Z wholeheartedly and in full knowledge of the essential contradictions at work.

A   Z

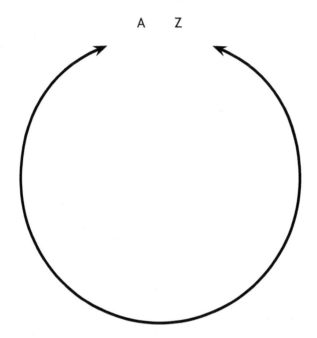

The act of learning is an attempt to live with negative capability. We need a stable, reliable world view in order to attempt a course of action. As soon as we act we destabilize reality. We then fix the instability once more to maintain our world view. A model of the world is only ever a way of holding reality and is always temporary. It will at some point fail. We justify our beliefs and actions in order to create meaning, which then becomes the basis of further intervention. We crave stability and certainty but we also seek to change the world.

Perhaps the fact that we're having this debate is a sign that the teaching profession is maturing. We are only just beginning to challenge our preconceptions and refine both custom and practice in light of research and evidence. As we'll see in the next chapter, the findings of science might overthrow some of our most cherished beliefs. Now that we've entered this liminal state, we need to stay with our uncertainty, hold off our need for closure and forge bravely, but skeptically, into the chaos.

Notes

1   Laura McInerney, What If Everything You Thought About Education, Was Wrong?, *LKMco* (8 August 2013). Available at: http://www.lkmco.org/article/what-if-everything-you-thought-about-education-was-wrong-08082013.
2   John Morley, *On Compromise* (London: Macmillan and Co., 1908). Available at: http://www.gutenberg.org/files/11557/11557-h/11557-h.htm.
3   John Keats, On Negative Capability: Letter to George and Tom Keats, 21 December 1817.
4   Christopher Hitchens, *Letters to a Young Contrarian* (New York: Basic Books, 2002), p. 21.

Chapter 5

You can prove anything with evidence!

Absence of evidence is not evidence of absence.

Martin Rees

A habit of basing convictions upon evidence, and of giving to them only that degree of certainty which the evidence warrants, would, if it became general, cure most of the ills from which the world suffers.

Bertrand Russell

The problem I face when weighing up the claims of education research is that I'm not a scientist, a researcher or even an academic. I'm just a teacher.* And, like most teachers, my exposure to research has until very recently been limited to what others have told me. And some of what I was told seemed frankly preposterous.

What happens when the evidence tells us something contrary to our lived experiences? We do what we do in the belief that it's for the best. As we've seen, when we're challenged we face cognitive dissonance. Either our beliefs and experience are wrong or the evidence is. When perceptions are in conflict it's entirely reasonable to ask for stronger evidence, especially when findings conflict with common sense and our direct observations. The burden of proof should always be with those making claims rather than with those expressing quite proper skepticism. As astronomer and science writer Carl Sagan said, "Extraordinary claims

---

* And even that's a fairly dubious credential as I no longer practice as a teacher. Maybe I should say, I'm not *even* a teacher.

require extraordinary evidence." But evidence can be twisted to say things that perhaps aren't so.

For instance, there's some very troubling evidence that suggests teaching assistants (TAs) are an expensive waste of time. This has generated newspaper headlines like this: "Studies have found that those students who receive help from teaching assistants make less progress than classmates of similar ability."[1] The source for this claim seems to be an Institute of Education project on the Deployment and Impact of Support Staff and was the largest ever study on the impact of support staff in schools.

Researchers compared the impact of varying degrees of support from TAs on students' progress in English, math and science by examining test results of over 8,000 students in 153 elementary and secondary schools in England and Wales, and from interviewing teaching staff and students. Much to everyone's surprise, the study found that students who received help from TAs made *less* progress than classmates of similar ability, social class and gender. In fact, the more support students received, *the fewer gains they made.*

On this evidence, schools should immediately fire teaching assistants. Or should they? The study failed to take into account the reasons why students received this support in the first place: lower achievement, learning and behavior difficulties, and social class. But it's not so much that teaching assistants cause lower attainment, it's that they usually work with groups of children who most need extra support. Often these children will require emotional and behavioral support too. Children with low prior attainment statistically make the least progress.

Before we make any rash decisions it's worth remembering that research only shows what has been, not what will be. What would the attainment of these students have been like had they not been supported? This could be a classic case of correlation being mistaken for causation.

We could interpret this evidence as proof that the more time students spend with teaching assistants, the less time they spend being taught by qualified teachers. But as hard-working teachers know, a good assistant can boost productivity, reduce stress levels and improve classroom practice. And if it really is the case that children receiving support from assistants do less well, then maybe it behoves schools to consider how to use them differently. It may not be that teaching assistants are a waste of money but that they're being utilized wastefully.

While it seems obvious that basing our practice on evidence is a very good thing, deciding what constitutes evidence is trickier to pin down than we might think. When you're caught up in the maelstrom of the classroom you see what you expect to see. That blinds us to other factors our attention has never been drawn to. So the question is: what are *you* not seeing – in the classroom, in your teaching? What is it that you're taking for granted? Where are the gorillas in your midst?

Apparently, pretty much everything teachers and students believe about learning is untrue and based on unsubstantiated theories, folklore and intuition.[2] We do what we've always done. We do what everyone else does. We do what feels right. (Or what someone else tells us is right.) And we do it based on very little in the way of empirical evidence. It's puzzling then that education seems to have uncritically accepted that imparting knowledge is bad. Or have we? My own suspicion is that most teachers put on a child-centered show when observed and then revert to teaching from the front when the classroom door is closed. The only real effect that being told teaching should be relevant, active and collaborative has had is to make us feel guilty for teaching.

Whenever someone tries to change our behavior, something is lost. If a teacher is great at lecturing and we force them to focus on planning group activities, the cost is twofold. Firstly, we take away what they're good at and, secondly, we make them do something they're bad at. This phenomena, "learning as loss",[3] might explain why we can be so resistant to new ideas that challenge accepted practice. As a species we tend to be loss averse, focusing far more on what we stand to lose than what we might gain. It makes something of a refreshing change for many teachers to be told that what they always believed was sensible – explaining, modeling, scaffolding and practicing – actually turns out to coincide with the findings of psychological research to be the most effective ways to teach.

But what if we had a gun to our heads? What if we were staking our lives and the lives of our students on the efficacy of the choices we make? Would that change our approach or shake our faith? Would we be willing to bet our lives that the strategies and techniques we advocate and practice are the best ones? There's very little I'd want to bet my life on, but if I did, I'd want to make sure it was based on the most impeccable of evidence.

Responding to evidence

We're constantly being confronted by evidence that challenges our existing beliefs. So how do we respond to this kind of breaking news? Do we bury our heads in the sand or take it on the chin? Do we have a fixed mindset or a growth mindset? Are we as open to change as we'd like to believe?

Acknowledging that 'we got it wrong' can lead to anxiety. It can force us to question our own being: if we got that wrong, then what else might we be mistaken about? Like most people, I've experienced being blind-sided by the shock of having the certainty that I'm right confronted by irrefutable evidence that I'm wrong. Take this example: I was due to fly home from Japan at 2 p.m. I get anxious about being late and wanted to make sure I'd arrive at the airport in good time, so I got up at 8.30 a.m., showered and ate a leisurely breakfast before packing up and wondering about what to do in the intervening hours. Knowing how pensive I get while waiting, I decided it would be best to get underway and catch the train to the airport. I dragged my bags to the station and dawdled, kicking myself for being such a poor traveller. Instead of spending my last hours doing something fun, I'd be hanging around in Osaka airport terminal for a few extra hours. When on the train, I dug out my ticket to double check which terminal I was leaving from and was shocked to discover that my flight was due to depart not at 2 p.m. but at 11 a.m. It was now 10:30 a.m. I can't tell you how sick I felt; I broke out in a cold sweat and sat there staring in blank incomprehension. How could I have been so wrong? I had known, been so certain, that I hadn't even felt the need to check. I might not have bet my life on the fact that I knew the time of my flight, but I'd certainly have bet several hundred dollars on it! And I'd have lost. In fact, that's exactly what I had to pay to book a new flight the next day.

The point of that sad story is that we often place unwarranted faith in what we believe. We can be so certain that we feel no need to check; we just know we're right. But we're all wrong, all the time, about things both trivial and vital.

Consider this little gem (Figure 5.1) that periodically does the rounds in education circles:

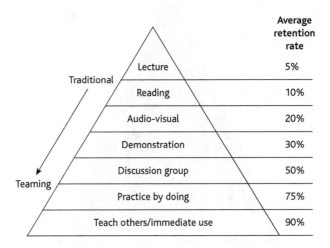

Figure 5.1. The learning pyramid*

Seductive, isn't it? The false sense of security comes from the fact that it bears out and validates our experience as teachers: we get to know our subjects so much better because we teach them, so it follows that the best way to retain new information is to teach it to someone else. And look: there are some statistics so it must be true! Well, unfortunately not. These claims can be dismissed in short order:

> If most educators stopped to consider the percentages, they would ask serious questions about the citation. They would inquire about the suspicious rounding of the percentages to multiples of ten, and the unlikelihood that learners would remember 90 percent of anything, regardless of the learning approach.[4]

---

* This is just one of the very many bogus cones of learning doing the rounds on the internet. For more examples visit: www.coneofexperience.com.

But it's not just the statistics that are unreliable; it's the fact that the whole thing has simply been made up. Figure 5.2 is Dale's actual cone of experience from his book *Audio-Visual Methods in Teaching*.[5] *

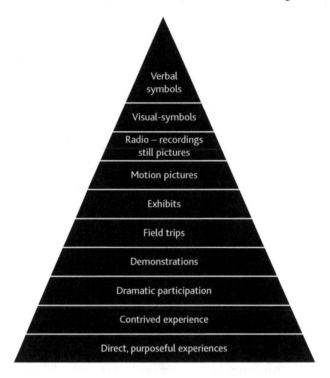

Figure 5.2. Dale's cone of experience

Spot the difference: no numbers! Dale also warned that the cone should not be taken literally – it portrays more concrete learning experiences at the bottom of the cone and more abstract experiences at the top of the cone. According to Subramony and colleagues, "The cone shape was meant to convey the gradual loss of sensory information" as students moved from lower to higher levels. "The root of all the perversions of the Cone is the assumption that the Cone is meant to be a prescriptive guide. Dale definitely intended the Cone to be descriptive – a classification system, not a road map for lesson planning."[6]

....

*   The text is available as a pdf at: http://ocw.metu.edu.tr/file.php/118/dale_audio-visual_20methods_20in_20teaching_1_.pdf. The cone is on p. 39.

The problem with any representation of the learning process is the dubious idea that a one size fits all, magic bullet approach to learning will work in every context for every student. Unsurprisingly, reality is a little more complex and such percentages are an attempt at simplification. Making lessons multimodal may well result in an increase in learning, but not always and certainly not as a de facto cause and effect. Sometimes it could be much more useful for students to get on with practicing something on their own than to have a discussion with their peers. It *might* be true that teaching others could be an effective way to learn, but what's the evidence beyond our intuition? This kind of belief is an emotional one and is pretty much like everything else that gets believed: a classic case of confirmation bias. But that doesn't excuse people making stuff up to support what they believe.

So if we can't rely on theory, lore and intuition, what can we rely on? There are some compelling voices in education that are happy to tell us that research in education is a chimera. Education professor Gert Biesta claims that 'what works' won't work.[7] Biesta is against using research to inform education policy because we don't know everything, because what we know might not be quite right every time and because it can be misapplied. Instead, he wants us to embrace a 'values-based' model based on what we, as educators, believe to be in the best interests of our children. Fortunately for Biesta, no one is holding a gun to his head and no one is likely to die if he's mistaken. I agree that evidence can only ever provide a very incomplete picture of what works and should not be solely used to determine policy.

Robert Marzano and colleagues, reflecting on the misinterpretation of his research, acknowledge that we can never really be sure *why* certain instructional strategies might be more or less effective. We should, they suggest, always base our decisions about *how* to teach on our knowledge of the students we teach, the subject matter we teach, and the contexts we find ourselves in.[8]

Caution is certainly required. While research might indicate that some approaches have a positive effect on student achievement in some situations, they could have a negligible or even negative effect in other situations. But Biesta goes further: he isn't even keen on 'evidence informed' practice and says that evidence should *always* be trumped by teachers' judgement.

While I have some sympathy with the idea of prioritizing teachers' judgement over mandated policy based on research evidence, there are two main problems Biesta doesn't really consider. Firstly, I think this kind of attitude is much more likely to be misunderstood and misapplied than giving due consideration to the admittedly incomplete picture that research might give us. It's likely to result in people treating nonsense like the 'pyramid of learning' as if it's fact and, metaphorically, lots of people missing flights. Whatever the problems with evidence, there are many more problems with guessing. As physicist Richard Feynman said, "It doesn't matter how beautiful the guess is, or how smart the guesser is, or how famous the guesser is; if the experiment disagrees with the guess, then the guess is wrong." The problem with many beautiful guesses in education is that there isn't even an experiment, let alone any evidence.*

The second problem is that I can't see any way to prevent education policy being based on research. E. D. Hirsch Jr. observed:

> Almost every educational practice that has ever been pursued has been supported with data by somebody. I don't know a single failed policy, ranging from the naturalistic teaching of reading, to the open classroom, to the teaching of abstract set-theory in third-grade math class that hasn't been research-based. Experts have advocated almost every conceivable practice short of inflicting permanent bodily harm.[9]

Removing research from education is probably impossible; the trick is to sift 'good' evidence from 'bad'.

A lot of what cognitive psychology tells us about what works is counter-intuitive, and therefore easy for us to ignore. Inconveniently, for anyone wanting to argue against using evidence to inform practice, the research findings I present in Part 3 are based on well-designed, consistent and repeatable trials. In other words, they 'work'. Here are a few of these findings:

- We're poor judges of how we learn best.

---

* Possibly, there cannot be any experiment of the same kind as there is in, say, physics because of the difficulty of carrying it out. Some things that it would be useful to do would be unethical – for example, having a 'control group' which received no teaching at all. There's also the almost impossible task of exactly matching groups of children and duplicating experimental conditions. Inevitably, teachers adapt to the nature of the class, regardless of how well they stay on script.

- Rereading and massed practice are the most popular but among the least effective ways to learn.

- Spacing and interleaving feel unproductive but are much more effective ways to learn.

- Allowing yourself to forget before attempting to retrieve will boost your ability to 'store' information.

- Making it harder to learn is more effective than making it easy.

- Every time we learn something new, we change the architecture of our brains.

Biesta may well be right in that we certainly don't know everything, and what we *do* know will inevitably be messed up by enthusiastic, well-intentioned folk like me. We have a history of ideas which are subject to testing and adaptation but we often hang on to reassuring lies instead of recognizing uncomfortable truths. But to suggest that teachers are somehow incapable of using evidence to guide their guesses as to what will work best for them is not just patronizing, it's silly. The irrefutable evidence that we are so often wrong about so very many things should at least give us cause to question our intuition, values and judgement.*

As part of that questioning, we also need to change the way we think about evidence. Just because we *know* something, doesn't mean we should *act* on it. We shouldn't see the findings of cognitive psychology as deterministic or restrictive; we should see it merely as a tool to help support our practice. Basic scientific knowledge of how students learn, how they interact and how they respond to incentives helps us to predict when things probably won't work. So, for instance, the finding discussed in Chapter 14 on the startling efficacy of the testing effect doesn't mean children should be made to do more tests. It just tells us that asking them

---

*   Reassuringly, perhaps, this is what makes science work: a scientist has a hypothesis, designs a test and observes the results. This then lays the groundwork for a theory which attempts to explain the results. If another scientist sees a flaw in the theory, they will design their own test and collect their own data. This gives them the opportunity to construct a new theory which better explains the available data. That we're wrong at any given time is inevitable – as more data is collected, as more becomes known about the world, so better theories will build on those that have gone before. It's clearly impossible to know everything, so we will only ever have a partial picture of 'what works'.

to recall what they've already learned is likely to help them remember it better. How you go about using this information is up to you. It could be used to justify boring kids with endless dreary pen and paper exercises or put to more innovative use, as in the example on pages 235–236.

Where research goes wrong

There are some other problems with education research we should consider. Let's imagine we want to conduct some research on the effectiveness of a new teaching strategy (strategy X). How would we go about it? Well, we'd probably want to test its effectiveness across a range of different groups of students and we'd probably consider getting several different teachers to try it out. We'd also want to have a control group which didn't get the intervention so that we could try to establish what sorts of things happen without the intervention of strategy X (and some would argue that it's unethical to deny children something that might benefit their education). Any particularly reputable research might also want to be a double-blind experiment* to try to avoid such confounds as the Hawthorne effect, but it's pretty tricky to keep teachers in the dark about how they're teaching their students, so in practice this is something that very rarely happens. We'd then need to decide on our success criteria – how will we know if strategy X works? For that we need something to measure, but what? Test results maybe?

OK, so we've set up our study and we've done the statistics and, guess what? It turns out strategy X is effective! It works! The overwhelming majority of studies show the successful implementation of ideas, frameworks, teaching materials, methods, technological innovations and so on. It doesn't seem to matter whether studies are well-funded, small scale or synthesizing analyses of other studies: almost everything studied by education researchers seems effective. Of course, there are some studies that report failures, but because of the perennial problem of under-reporting negative results they're rare. We have acres of information on how to

---

* A double-blind is an experimental procedure in which neither the subjects nor the people administering the test know why the experiment is being conducted. A double-blind experiment should help ward against some of those psychological effects we've discussed: observer bias, the placebo effect and the Hawthorne effect.

improve students' learning such that it seems inconceivable that learning would not improve. But almost every one of these successful studies has absolutely no impact on system-wide improvement. Why is this?

One of the problems we have in believing what's effective in education is that so many of the most valuable findings are counter-intuitive and deeply troubling. Teachers often exhibit mimicry – copying what they see others doing – but without trying to develop the understanding of the expert teacher. Education is so saturated with values, and so contested in its aims, that it cannot really be dealt with in the same way as physical sciences. We may pay lip service to this fact, but we still assume that all learning is part of the natural world and therefore conforms to the same rules that govern the rest of nature. I'm not sure that's true. Rather, learning is shaped by a combination of evolution, culture, history, technology and development, and as such it's a slippery devil.

Scientific method has to be appropriate to whatever field it is being applied. Methods may not be transferable between fields of study. Methodology is not always properly aligned with the problems we want to solve, resulting in what Wittgenstein described as a clash of "experimental methods and conceptual confusion".[10] If the most reliable of empirical evidence suggested beating children was the most effective way to get them to learn, we would reject this finding as being unacceptable, unethical and at odds with our values. Likewise, if a progressively aligned academic found rote drilling to be more effective than discovery methods they would find it straightforward to dismiss the finding as being too narrowly defined or harmful in some other, less empirical way. This is something we all do. Any evidence, no matter how robust, has to align with our ideologies and values otherwise it is ignored.

And then there's the issue that empirical evidence in education isn't empirical in the right way. As Wittgenstein observed, "The existence of the experimental method makes us think we have the means of solving the problems which trouble us; though problem and method pass one another by."[11] Education research is founded on the proposition that it's possible to establish causal links between discrete things, such as the link between strategy X and students' test results. But can it? Remember the problem of confusing correlation with causation – just because two events appear linked does not mean they are.

Even when events are clearly linked, there may still be problems. The diagnosis and treatment of ADHD is an interesting case in point. The Centers for Disease Control and Prevention in the United States (where they track the likes of Ebola and SARS) has monitored a 60 percent increase in the diagnosis of ADHD over the last decade. This is startling. Either the human genome is failing, leading to a bizarre increase in the number of prefrontal lobe related problems, or some other factor is at play. My money is on the 'other factor'.

Sir Ken Robinson observed that diagnoses of ADHD fall as you travel across the United States from east to west. He calls it the "plague of ADHD" and claims it is "fictitious". While various psychologists and pediatricians are convinced it does exist, it is not, Ken assures us, an epidemic. "These kids are being medicated as routinely as we had our tonsils taken out. And on the same whimsical basis and for the same reason – medical fashion."[12]

There are certainly some children who seem to choose when and where their ADHD will kick in (see page 84), but I'd be the first to accept that there are children for whom medication seems to make a real difference. Early in my teaching career, I taught a delightful, hard-working boy called Ricky. One day Ricky turned into a chair flinging monster. He screamed and raged and stormed out. I was flabbergasted; what on earth had happened? What had I done to this normally mild mannered boy? "Don't worry, sir," one of Ricky's friends told me. "It's just his ADHD. He forgot to take his pills today." I didn't know about the seemingly magical properties of Ritalin before that. Clearly Ken is right to say that denying the existence of ADHD – or indeed the dramatic effects of medication – is foolish.

Dr. Marilyn Wedge has pointed out that French children don't seem to suffer with ADHD:

> In the United States, at least 9% of school-aged children have been diagnosed with ADHD, and are taking pharmaceutical medications. In France, the percentage of kids diagnosed and medicated for ADHD is less than .5%. How come the epidemic of ADHD – which has become firmly established in the United States – has almost completely passed over children in France?[13]

How indeed. Ken blames computer games, boring schools and standardized testing. I don't know about you, but this sounds suspiciously simplistic and convenient. Wedge says that US physicians see ADHD as a biological condition best treated with biological interventions. This could be an example of the fundamental attribution error. French physicians tend to view ADHD as having contextual causes:

> Instead of treating children's focusing and behavioral problems with drugs, French doctors prefer to look for the underlying issue that is causing the child distress – not in the child's brain but in the child's social context. They then choose to treat the underlying social context problem with psychotherapy or family counseling.[14]

I'm not arguing that French doctors are right to do this – they may very well be laboring under their own misapprehensions – but if ADHD *is* caused by social context then prescribing medication would be a mistake.

In his book, *ADHD Does Not Exist*, Dr. Richard Saul makes a compelling case for doubting the diagnosis and treatment of very many who have been labeled as having ADHD.[15] Saul makes clear that the symptoms are all too real, but the medicalization of the condition has had severely negative consequences. He presents cases of children and adults who suffer with disorders which contain elements of attention deficit or hyperactivity and are then misdiagnosed. Sometimes the symptoms are normal. Sometimes they're not. Sometimes they respond well to medical intervention, but overwhelmingly it seems medication might be unnecessary.

We should always be aware of those who have a vested interest in the status quo – in this case, pharmaceutical companies that make a lot of money out of 'medicating' kids with drugs such as Ritalin. While Ritalin will have been subjected to a randomized controlled trial (RCT),* the issue is not whether Ritalin 'works', but with the cultural practice of diagnosis and prescription that encourage its use. Clearly Ritalin works, but maybe it's the practices of diagnosis and prescription that need to be subjected to an RCT. An RCT may demonstrate that certain drugs are effective but such proof doesn't provide any guidance as to their prescriptive application. Diagnostic practices are based on quite different sorts of assumptions and conditions.

....

* An RCT is a type of scientific experiment where subjects being studied are randomly allocated one or other of the different treatments under study. The RCT has become the gold standard for clinical trials, and there is an argument that the same standards and processes should be applied to education interventions.

There's also the issue of conceptual confusion. Sometimes researchers set out to prove something that would be impossible *not* to prove. Let's say I wanted to conduct a survey to determine how many students in Birmingham schools are under the age of 20. I could do all kinds of data analysis and design as many questionnaires as I pleased, but whatever I found would be trite as the causal connection I'm seeking to establish already exists as a conceptual connection. All I need to know is that school education in Birmingham ends at age 19 to work out that the existence of 20-year-old students is a logical impossibility. Although this is an obviously absurd example, it would appear that this kind of conceptual confusion is exactly the mistake made in much education research. Although the conceptual connections are usually a bit more subtle, the findings are equally meaningless.

Consider the example of a study on how 4-year-olds learn. Researchers from MIT set out to prove whether discovery learning was more effective than direct instruction. They claim their study shows that "children restrict their exploration both after direct instruction to themselves and after overhearing direct instruction given to another child; they do not show this constraint after observing direct instruction given to an adult or after observing a non-pedagogical intentional action".[16]

In order to reach this conclusion, the researchers gave children a toy with four tubes, each of which had an interesting feature: one squeaked, another contained a mirror and so on. In the first test the experimenter said, "I just found this toy!" As she brought out the toy she pulled the first tube, as if by accident, and it squeaked. She acted surprised ("Huh! Did you see that? Let me try to do that!") and pulled the tube again to make it squeak a second time. A second group of children were exposed to more formal instruction. This time the experimenter said, "I'm going to show you how my toy works. Watch this!" And then deliberately made the tube squeak but didn't show the children any of the other features of the toy.

Both groups were then left alone to play with the toy. Although children in both groups pulled the first tube to make it squeak, the children in the first group appeared more curious and spent more time experimenting: "In other words, direct instruction made the children less curious and less likely to discover new information."[17]

On the face of it that sounds pretty compelling, but let's interrogate that description for a moment. Firstly, both groups were shown how the toy worked by a teacher. The first teacher pretended she didn't understand the toy and the second teacher pretended she had given a complete description of how the toy worked. Children in the second group could be forgiven for thinking there was nothing further to find out – presumably they've learned to trust that teachers tell them all they need to know; to suddenly and deliberately lie to them would not have been expected.

Secondly, although we're not given any information other than the words the experimenters used, we might reasonably infer that the delivery of the second 'teacher' was a lot less enthusiastic. Of course, children will pick up on the way something is presented. One of the reasons Hattie claims that 'everything works' is that the enthusiasm of the teacher makes a huge difference.[18]

The MIT team seem to have decided that 'curiosity' is synonymous with 'to engage in discovery learning'. Curiosity has been equated with the teaching strategy the experimenters are promoting. Under these conditions there is no possibility that discovery learning could *ever* perform worse than explicit teaching in inducing curiosity because discovery learning *is* curiosity.

It is my suspicion that this is a failing found in a great many research studies. For instance, if you wanted to prove the following, "To develop competence in an area of inquiry, students must (a) have a deep foundational knowledge of factual knowledge, (b) understand facts and ideas in the context of a conceptual framework, and (c) organize knowledge in ways that facilitate retrieval and application",[19] it should become quickly obvious that (a), (b) and (c) are definitions of "competence in an area of inquiry". No amount of empirical research could ever demonstrate that these things are not connected!

Added to all this we have the research finding (oh, the irony!) that fewer than 1 percent of the education research findings that get published are replication studies.[20] (A replication study is one where researchers attempt to reproduce results with different test subjects.) Now, apparently the majority of replication studies in education (68 percent) manage to replicate the original findings, but when completely different teams of researchers conduct replication studies only 54 percent are found to be replicable. A cynic might wonder if there's a degree of vested interest at work here. Whether it's fear through lack of understanding, an unwillingness to value the work of others or plain old prejudice, this way of thinking manifests as an unwillingness to adopt an idea or product because it originates from another culture – a form of tribalism, often stemming from the illusion of asymmetric insight.

This might also suggest that instead of relying so enthusiastically on evidence we could put a little more faith in reasoning and analysis. If I present a reasoned analysis of why I think strategy X is likely to be effective with no supporting data, it'll be dismissed as 'mere speculation'. But my contention is this: I could conduct research on something that is analytically sound and ensure it cannot but fail to produce favorable evidence. Yes, there will be all sorts of variation between different groups of students and their teachers, but where a teacher is enthusiastic, research will likely provide a favorable finding. This seems obvious. If I can convince a teacher of the merits of strategy X, they'll work hard to get me the positive data I'm after with no connivance needed. Similarly, if they were sure I was a charlatan, there's no way they'd use strategy X unless they were forced to, and in that case the likelihood of the research finding being positive is remote in the extreme. So, either our personal beliefs are valued above all else or we have further examples of cognitive bias at work.

Does all of this effort to discover what works best trump the intuition of an experienced and thoughtful practitioner? Yes, sometimes it might. We don't know what we don't know, and without research to make these predictions we will inevitably rely on what we've always done. We're very good at jumping to conclusions that what we feel, intuitively, must be effective. But, as we've seen, we cannot trust our intuition because it leads us astray.

It's worth briefly exploring how some of our beliefs about education have been shaped. In the early 1800s, the ideals of the Enlightenment – scientific method, logic and reason – were in full swing. Everything could be counted, weighed and measured, and the truth about the world discovered, quantified and neatly labeled. As always, when the pendulum swings too far in one direction, it's about to swing back, and Romanticism – a belief that man should live in a more natural, prelapsarian state – was a reaction to the extremes of science. The Romantics espoused spontaneity, hidden potential and the benevolence of nature. These two ways of seeing the world have become super memes (see page 146), or what Daniel Willingham has termed "meta-beliefs" in education.[21]

A meta-belief is one which has taken on a life beyond the facts we believe about the world to become the prism through which we view the world. They make up the very fabric of thought and they lie at the center of an interconnected web of other, connected beliefs. We fail to think *about* these beliefs and instead think *with* them.

Willingham argues that we rely on a whole set of largely unexamined Enlightenment and Romantic meta-beliefs. An example of an Enlightenment meta-belief is that everything can be understood through science, or that reason and logic can be brought to bear to explain any problem. In fact, the human brain is such a powerful fetish that just showing a picture of it can make an audience 50 percent more likely to accept a statement as scientific fact.

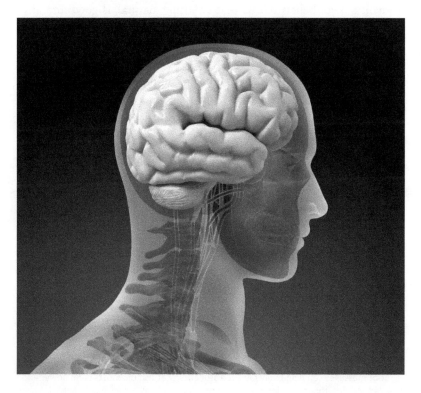

Figure 5.3. The brain

Whenever we cite research, we are drawing on the meta-belief that evidence is sufficient justification for action. When we accept the word of academics or authority figures over our own experience, we acquiesce to a meta-belief that those who are best qualified are most qualified to offer an opinion. We see Enlightenment meta-beliefs in action in the pseudo-scientific jargon used to advertise shampoo, and maybe some of the worst examples of mumbo-jumbo in education come dressed in neuroscientific jargon.* This might perhaps explain why we were so completely taken in by Brain Gym.** As professor of developmental neuropsychology Dorothy Bishop says:

> Neuroscientists can tell you which brain regions are most involved in particular cognitive activities and how this changes with age or training. But these indicators of learning do not tell you how to achieve learning. Suppose I find out that the left angular gyrus becomes more active as children learn to read. What is a teacher supposed to do with that information?[22]

Romantic meta-beliefs tell us that anything 'natural' is good and anything processed is bad. This suspicion of 'unnatural' intervention leads us to accept that education should be as natural as possible; any form of coercion is deemed appalling but even teachers passing on their hard won expertise can be seen as somehow interfering with the natural order. Children should find their own way and be guided by their innate curiosity. Some education experts express an almost mystical reverence for the goodness and wisdom of the prelapsarian child, whereas anyone who has to actually teach real kids knows only too well that they hunt in packs and can be savage in their interactions, both with each other and with any authority figure.

Anyone who talks about unleashing or unlocking children's hidden potential is acting on Romantic meta-beliefs about the world. This goes some way to explaining the totemic power of personalization, differentiation and independent learning – all these movements have at their heart a belief that children are special, unique and subject to mysterious hidden forces which can be harnessed, if only we're willing to strive to

---

* There have been theories suggesting that listening to Mozart can boost intelligence, foot massages can help badly behaved students, that fish oil boosts brain power and, I kid you not, that breathing through your left nostril will enhance creativity.

** For a comprehensive rebuttal of Brain Gym, see Ben Goldacre's *Bad Science*.

understand, love and accept each and every child and their special way of comprehending the world.

The point with both these sets of meta-beliefs is that there's a kernel of truth at their heart. Children *are* unique and some types of learning *are* innate; science *can* help us understand and reason and logic *can* improve aspects of our lives.

What type of research?

Understanding how our meta-beliefs operate can help us to understand how we view and approach education research. If we want to enquire into some aspect of education (or any other social science), whether we're aware of it or not, we'll make decisions about the following:

- Methods (What research tools will we use?)

- Methodology (How do we plan to conduct our research?)

- Theoretical perspectives (What assumptions about reality underlie the question we are asking and the kinds of answers we are looking for?)

- Beliefs about epistemology and ontology (What do we believe reality is, and how can we find out about it?)

The scientific (positivist) approach is to use the physical sciences as a model for investigation and experimentation. Adherents will likely believe that there is some objective truth which is discoverable through a deductive, theory testing approach. This is the 'scientific method'. They formulate hypotheses about the world which can offer explanations about how and why things happen. As a result they will choose research tools like surveys, random sampling, blind tests and the manipulation of variables. The advantage of such an approach is that it provides easily comparable data, which is verifiable and replicable.

The detective (interpretive) approach starts by critiquing the natural sciences as a model for investigating the social sciences. Interpretivists believe reality is subject to the context in which it is perceived and may even take the relativist view that there's no such thing as objective truth at all; instead of seeking to establish facts, they conclude that people are complex and that we should attempt to understand why they behave as they do. Society is, obviously, socially constructed. Their methods will be ethnographic studies, interviews, observation and analysis. Although this approach accounts for complex contextual issues, the evidence collected is often so complex as to be resistant to clear meaning and can be shaped to mean whatever the researcher says it means. Possibly you can detect my biases creeping in here.

So, are we left with dismissing interpretivism as less credible and positivism as inflexible? As Biesta points out, if hard data and emphatic conclusions fly in the face of our values, it isn't worth a damn. No matter how much empirical evidence we could come up with proving the effectiveness of rote learning, corporal punishment, circle time or group hugs, if it comes into conflict with our moral and ethical beliefs about the world we will ignore it. If you believe rote learning is vicious and boring, who cares how effective it is as a tool for learning? Interpretivism attempts to square this circle by thinking about meaning instead of facts. If you can never reliably control for all the variables in a classroom (e.g. time of day, time of year, weather, motivation, dispositions of teachers and students) then context overrides any 'objective' truth, and we can argue, "Well, it works for me."

Nobel prize winning physicist Carl Wieman, after many years of working closely with physics undergraduates, observed, "their success in physics courses was such a poor predictor of a student's ultimate success as a physicist".[23] He argues that rigorous education research is not so very different from 'hard' science as some might want to suggest. Good science has the power to make useful predictions; if research can be used to inform our actions then it is useful. It's unnecessary to accurately control and predict how every student in every context will behave or learn, just as a physicist has no need to control or predict how every single atom will behave in a physics experiment. All that is necessary is that we can predict an outcome that is both meaningful and measurable.

This tells us that the insights of cognitive science, gleaned over more than a century and predicated on well-designed, repeatable tests that build on prior research and which produce broadly consensual, meaningful and measurable outcomes, should not be dismissed as unlikely to work in the classroom. If the scientists are right, we could make a profound difference to how well our students learn. If all our empirical evidence turns out to be wrong, no one's died. It may not be worth betting your life on, but it outweighs the risk of going with a hunch.

To summarize, we cannot and will not find objective truth by investigating classrooms with the tools of the physical sciences. Context and values will make even the most robustly controlled trial meaningless. But the alternative is that 'evidence' means whatever anyone says it means and the person who shouts the loudest and the most authoritatively wins; it becomes a matter of persuasion and rhetoric.

Despite thousands of education research papers being published every year, teachers continue to do pretty much what they've always done. Instead of endlessly seeking to find out new things, we should think more carefully about the things we've already found out. Of course, first we need to be aware of what has been found out, and be willing to take it on board and use it. So we are up against cognitive dissonance and the need to assimilate these threshold concepts. (Threshold concepts will be addressed more fully in Chapter 7.)

I want to make a case that we could focus on the more controllable science of psychology and use the empirical evidence produced in laboratories to help us make educated guesses, predictions if you will, in order to guide our values and beliefs with data that exploits what we've discovered about the way children learn. Never mind that social sciences are different from natural sciences and that education research is so saturated with values; laboratory research that offers meaningful and measurable outcomes is far more worthy of our consideration than a classroom study, no matter how randomized or controlled.

That said, teachers conducting research into their own schools can only be a good thing, as long as no one seeks to generalize from such findings. While it may be very useful to experiment and test 'what works' in your own classroom, we can never discover what will work in anyone else's classroom beyond certain testable hypotheses.

Of course, specific intervention may not be effective with a particular student, but that doesn't mean that it will not be effective in a majority of cases. As teachers we're more concerned with trying out ideas than testing them. Daniel Willingham points out, "In basic research, the goal is the discovery of laws that describe natural phenomena. You take the world as it comes to you, and try to summarize it with general principles. Applied research, in contrast, is goal driven. You don't want to describe the world as it is; you want to change the world to make it better."[24]

As an example, I conducted a mini investigation into the effects of praise on feedback. I'll confess that I didn't put any effort into designing a fair test; I just wanted to see what would happen if I stopped praising my students and just concentrated on giving them instructional and corrective feedback. I explained to them what I was doing and why I was doing it, and after a six week period I asked them to evaluate how they thought the experiment had gone: 29 out of 30 students said they had found it easier to act on feedback and felt that they had improved as a result. One student said that she had struggled with not being praised for 'what went well' and had failed to make progress as a result. My conclusions? I would continue with not giving praise for the majority of the class but the student who felt she needed praise would get it.

Now, I'm not claiming my experiment has any value as science: it doesn't. But I decided to make this change after reading some research which predicted that my students might find praise counter-productive. What I had read was useful because it allowed me to test a theory that was underpinned by empirical evidence. I'll allow that I'm as susceptible to observer effects as anyone else and possibly students were experiencing the Hawthorne effect (see page 29). Maybe so, but even if my trial hadn't 'worked', I had still formulated a hypothesis which could be tested. Obviously, if I'd found my intervention to be ineffective for my particular students that would have been a useful finding too. Applied sciences may be different to natural sciences, but any research that offers meaningful and measurable outcomes is at least worth considering.

What is the unit of education?

It's a widely accepted axiom that "If you cannot measure it, you cannot improve it." Most education research is an attempt to measure the effects of teaching (or teachers) on learning (or students). But is this actually possible?

Let's first think about measurement in a very practical sense. Schools limit admission based on a sometimes very strict catchment area – if you want to make sure that your children attend a particular school you need to live within the catchment. For some very oversubscribed schools this can be a radius of less than a mile. If I measure the distance between my front door and the school I would like my daughter to attend, I need some agreed unit of measurement for my reckoning to mean anything; the local authority won't be interested in 'It's quite close'.

In order to work out how close, we agree on a measurement system and measuring devices which enable us to define the criterion of being inside or outside the catchment area. However, when it comes to measuring concepts such as progress, learning or teacher effectiveness things become much more complicated. We still feel the urge to convert things into numbers but often there is little agreement. We think we're being precise when bandying about such numbers but really they're entirely arbitrary.

Remember the scene from the film *Spinal Tap* where guitarist Nigel Tufnel proudly demonstrates a custom-made amplifier whose volume control is marked from 0 to 11, instead of the usual 0 to 10? Nigel is convinced the numbering increases the volume of the amp, "It's one louder." When asked why the 10 setting is not simply set to be louder, Nigel is clearly confused. Patiently he explains, "These go to 11." And how often have you heard an overenthusiastic school leader exhort teachers to give 110 percent?

Now, I say all this because it strikes me that we have no agreed measure of impact or progress in education. Kieran Egan argues, "failure to identify units of education is one key to understanding why so much educational research seems to have had no discernible beneficial effects on education".[25] Because we've fallen so heavily for the myth of progress, the need to measure it has become ever more pressing. One such measure, which has been widely gobbled up, has been the *effect size*.

The effect size (ES) allows us to quantify the magnitude of the difference between two groups. Armed with this measurement, we have decided we can move beyond simply stating that an intervention works to the more sophisticated consideration of how well it works compared to other interventions. Australian educationalist John Hattie has done much to popularize the effect size, and has analyzed a large amount of studies by imposing effect size on them. This begs the question, does the effect size give an accurate and valid measure of difference?

In order to answer this question we need to know what an ES actually corresponds to – that is, what is the unit of education? An ES of 0 means that the *average* treatment participant outperformed 50 percent of the control participants. An ES of 0.7 means that the *average* participant will have outperformed the *average* control group member by 0.7 standard deviations.* The baseline is that a year's teaching should translate into a year's progress and that any intervention that produces an ES of 0.4 is worthy of consideration.[26]

In his book, *Visible Learning*, Hattie went about aggregating the effects of thousands of research studies to tell us how great an impact we could attribute to the various interventions and factors at play in classrooms. He found that 'feedback', with a whopping ES of 1.13, topped the list of influences on student achievement. Direct instruction came in at 0.82, questioning at 0.41 and adjusting class size at -0.05.

So now we know. Giving feedback is ace, questioning is barely worth it and adjusting class size is pointless.** You might well have a problem with some of these findings but let's accept them for the time being.

An ES of $d = 1.0$ indicates an increase of one standard deviation. Hattie tells us: "A one standard deviation increase is typically associated with advancing children's achievement by two to three years, improving the rate of learning by 50%, or a correlation between some variable (e.g. amount of homework) and achievement of approximately $r = 0.50$. When implementing a new program, an ES of 1.0 would mean that, on average, students receiving that treatment would exceed 84% of students not receiving that treatment."[27]

. . . .

*   This means that an average person in the experimental group would be at the 76th percentile of the control group, or, to put it another way, if you divided 100 students into four 'ability sets', the average student in the experimental group would just about get into set 1.

** Note that 'testing' comes in at 0.3. In Chapter 14 we'll look at the overwhelming weight of evidence which suggests that testing is, in fact, one of the most effective ways to help students retain and transfer information. The problem is that what I refer to as testing is different to what Hattie means – we're divided by the same language.

Really? So if feedback has an ES of 1.13, are we really supposed to believe that students given feedback would learn over 50 percent more than those who are not? Is that controlled against groups of students who were given no feedback at all? Seems unlikely, doesn't it? And what does the finding that direct instruction* has an ES of 0.82 mean? I doubt forcing passionate advocates of discovery learning to use direct instruction would have any such effect.

At this point it might be worth unpicking what we mean by meta-analysis. The term refers to statistical methods for contrasting and combining results from different studies in the hope of identifying patterns, sources of disagreement or other interesting relationships that may come to light from poring over the entrails of qualitative research.

The way meta-analyses are conducted in education has been nicked from clinicians. But in medicine it's a lot easier to agree on what's being measured: are you still alive a year after being discharged from hospital? Lumping the results from different education studies together tricks us into assuming different outcome measures are equally sensitive to what teachers do. Or, to put it another way, that there is a standard unit of education. Now, if we don't even agree what education is *for* being unable to measure the success of different interventions in a meaningful way is a bit of a stumbling block.

And then to make matters worse, it turns out that the concept of the effect size itself may be wrong. There are at least three problems with effect sizes. They are the range of achievement, sensitivity to instruction and the varying duration of trials.

Firstly, the range of achievement of students studied influences effect sizes:

> An increase of 5 points on a test where the population standard deviation is 10 points would result in an effect size of 0.5 standard deviations. However, the same intervention when administered only to the upper half of the same population, provided that it was equally effective for all students, would result in an effect size of over 0.8 standard deviations, due to the reduced variance of the subsample.[28]

---

* It's not clear whether 'direct instruction' refers to generic teacher-led whole-class teaching or Siegfried Engelmann's Direct Instruction, in which lessons are scripted and which outperformed all other teaching methods in the largest and most expensive education study ever undertaken, Project Follow Through.

Older children will show less improvement than younger children because they've already done a lot of learning and improvements are now much more incremental. If studies are comparing the effects of inventions with 6-year-olds and 16-year-olds, and are claiming to measure a common impact, their findings will be garbage.

The second problem is how do we know there's any impact at all? To see any kind of effect we usually rely on measuring students' performance in some kind of test. But assessments vary greatly in the extent to which they measure the things that educational processes change. Those who design standardized tests put a lot of effort into ensuring that their sensitivity to instruction is minimized. A test can be made more reliable by getting rid of questions which don't differentiate between students, so if all students tend to get particular questions right or wrong then they're of limited use. But this process changes the nature of tests: it may be that questions which teachers are good at teaching are replaced with those they're not so good at teaching. This might be fair enough, except how then can we possibly hope to measure the extent to which students' performance is influenced by particular teacher interventions?

The effects of sensitivity to instruction are a big deal. For instance, Bloom claimed that one-to-one tutorial instruction is more effective than average group-based instruction by 2 standard deviations.[29] This is hardly credible. In standardized tests, one year's progress for an average student is equivalent to one-fourth of a standard deviation, so one year's individual tuition would have to equal nine years of average group-based instruction! Hmm. The point is, the time lag between teaching and testing appears to be the biggest factor in determining sensitivity to instruction. Outcome measures used in different studies are unlikely to have the same view of sensitivity to instruction.

The third problem is the time it takes to teach. Let's say we decide to compare two teachers using identical teaching methods, teaching two classes of children of exactly the same age. We test both classes at the start of a unit of work and at the end to see what impact the teaching has had. If children in both classes made identical gains, what would such a comparison tell us? Superficially it appears we're comparing like with like, but if it takes the first class one week to learn the material and the second class two weeks to learn the material then any such comparison is meaningless. The effect size would calculate both teachers as equally effective, but if the results are the same, one class learned twice as fast as the other. Any proper unit of education would need to account for the time it takes for students to learn something.

In meta-analyses there's little attempt to control for the first two problems. As long as studies make the duration of the trial, clear careful researchers can, and do, include the duration of the intervention as a moderating variable. This doesn't mean we shouldn't trust that those things Hattie puts at the top of his list don't have greater impact than those at the bottom, but it does mean we should think twice before bandying about effect sizes as evidence of potential impact.

When numerical values are assigned to teaching we're very easily taken in. The effects of teaching and learning are far too complex to be easily understood, but numbers are dead easy to understand: this one's bigger than that. This leads to pseudo-accuracy and makes us believe there are easy solutions to difficult problems. Few teachers (and I certainly include myself here) are statistically literate enough to properly interrogate this approach. The table of effect sizes with its beguilingly accurate seeming numbers has been a comfort: someone has relieved us of having to think. But can we rely on these figures? Do they *really* tell us anything useful about how we should adjust our classroom practice?

On their own, no. But if we're sufficiently cautious and see effect sizes as a very imprecise way to make a rough comparison, if we triangulate with the findings of cognitive science and the evidence of experienced teachers, then we might allow that an intervention is probably worth trying. After all, evidence is meant to be helpful. Arguably, if it's not helpful, it's not real evidence. If methodologies are being imposed then they're not based on evidence. Education researcher and author Geoff Petty says, "This strategy of top-down dictat does not work, it has been carefully evaluated and it fails. So if you are forced to do 'evidence-based teaching', you are not doing Evidence-Based Teaching! You are being bullied with an ineffective management strategy!"[30]

As ever, a mix of healthy skepticism and a willingness to think is always needed when looking at research evidence, but assigning numerical values and establishing hierarchies of effective interventions is only misleading.

Questions we should ask about research

If teachers are asked to change their practice in the name of research, whether it's a diktat from school leadership to teachers or from government to school leaders, they must be convinced. Imposing change does not work. So where new interventions are planned, Daniel Willingham suggests teachers should be encouraged to ask the following questions:[31]

1. **What problem is being solved and what is supposed to improve?**

    For instance, if a school is planning to buy its students tablet devices, what is meant to happen? If the answer is as vague as, "We don't want our kids left behind," then we should be entitled to ask what evidence is there that having tablet devices leads to an increase in performance.

2. **How will we know if the invention is successful?**

    It's important to know in advance how improvement will be measured and what kind of improvement will constitute a success. If you're introducing a new intervention to improve students' reading, how confident can we be that there's a meaningful way to measure whether the new intervention is better than what was done previously? We are notoriously biased in favor of novelty so we need to be sure that the answer is a lot better than 'this feels right'.

3. **When is the improvement expected to be apparent?**

    If a commitment to trying something new is open ended, we could end up waiting forever. It seems reasonable to know in advance when its progress will be evaluated.

4. **What will happen if the goal is (or isn't) met?**

    If the intervention doesn't seem to be going as planned, at what point will we admit defeat? Will we adjust what we're doing? Is there any kind of contingency?

5. **What evidence is there to support investing in the intervention?**

Where does the research come from? How secure are the findings? Is it classroom-based research, laboratory findings or just theorizing?

6. **Is the experience and expertise of teachers being acknowledged?**

If teachers are asked to try something that sounds fishy, it's not good enough to dismiss concerns with, "All the research supports it." The fact that it sounds implausible doesn't mean an intervention works, but teachers need to be given compelling reasons for ignoring the evidence of their experience.

This list shouldn't be taken as the definitive criteria that must be met before an intervention can be tried, rather it should be seen as a list of suggestions about what ought to be discussed. The information provided need not unequivocally support the intervention for it to be legitimate. It's not unreasonable to admit that the research support for an intervention is inconclusive yet mounting a case for why it should be tried anyway.

That's pretty much my position. The ideas in this book are based, at least in part, on a foundation of research, but some of it may be questionable. I've done my best to be duly critical and skeptical but I'm no academic. I've cherry-picked from the papers I've found most interesting and my interpretation will be as subject to bias as anyone's. I'm sure others can and will pick holes in some of the studies I cite. That is as it should be: pick away. We all benefit by improving on the errors of others.

Notes

1   John Stevens, Army of Teaching Assistants Faces the Axe as Education Department Attempts to Save Some of the £4billion They Cost Each Year, *Daily Mail* (3 June 2013). Available at: http://www.dailymail.co.uk/news/article-2334853/ Army-teaching-assistants-faces-axe-Education-department-attempts-save-4billion-cost-year.html.

2   This theme is discussed in Chapter 1 of Peter C. Brown, Henry L. Roediger and Mark A. McDaniel, *Make It Stick: The Science of Successful Learning* (Cambridge, MA: Harvard University Press, 2014).

3   James S. Atherton, Learning as Loss 1, *Doceo* (2013). Available at: http://www.doceo.co.uk/original/learnloss_1.htm.

4   Cisco, *Multimodal Learning Through Media: What the Research Says* (2008). Available at: http://www.cisco.com/web/strategy/docs/education/Multimodal-Learning-Through-Media.pdf, p. 3.

5   Edgar Dale, *Audio-Visual Methods in Teaching* (New York: Dryden Press, 1946).

6   Deepak Subramony, Michael Molenda, Anthony Betrus and Will Thalheimer, The Mythical Retention Chart and the Corruption of Dale's Cone of Experience, *Educational Technology* 54(6) (2014): 6–16 at 9, 10.

7   Gert J. J. Biesta, Why 'What Works' Still Won't Work: From Evidence-Based Education to Value-Based Education, *Studies in Philosophy and Education* 29(5) (2010): 491–503.

8   Robert Marzano, Debra Pickering and Jane Pollock, *Classroom Instruction That Works: Research Based Strategies for Increasing Student Achievement* (Alexandria, VA: Association for Supervision and Curriculum Development, 2003), p. 9.

9   E. D. Hirsch Jr, Address to the California State Board of Education, 10 April 1997. Available at: http://www.coreknowledge.org/mimik/mimik_uploads/documents/5/AddCASTB.pdf.

10 Ludwig Wittgenstein, *Philosophical Investigations*, tr. G. E. M. Anscombe (Oxford: Basil Blackwell, 1953), p. 120.

11 Ibid.

12 Sir Ken Robinson, Changing Paradigms. Speech given at the RSA (2008). Available at: https://www.thersa.org/discover/videos/event-videos/2008/06/changing-paradigms/.

13 Marilyn Wedge, Why French Kids Don't Have ADHD, *Psychology Today* (8 March 2012). Available at: http://www.psychologytoday.com/blog/suffer-the-children/201203/why-french-kids-dont-have-adhd.

14 Ibid.

15 Richard Saul, *ADHD Does Not Exist: The Truth About Attention Deficit and Hyperactivity Disorder* (New York: HarperCollins, 2014).

16 Elizabeth Bonawitz, Patrick Shafto, Hyowon Gweon, Noah D. Goodman, Elizabeth Spelke and Laura Schulz, The Double-Edged Sword of Pedagogy: Instruction Limits Spontaneous Exploration and Discovery, *Cognition* 120(3) (2011): 322–330. Available at: http://cocosci.berkeley.edu/Liz/BonawitzShaftoetalRevised.pdf.

17 Alison Gopnik, Why Preschool Shouldn't Be Like School, *slate.com* (16 March 2011). Available at: http://www.slate.com/articles/double_x/doublex/2011/03/why_preschool_shouldnt_be_like_school.html?wpsrc=sh_all_tab_tw_bot.

18 John Hattie, *Visible Learning: A Synthesis of Over 800 Meta-Analyses Relating to Achievement* (Abingdon: Routledge, 2008), p.15.

19 Suzanne Donovan, John D. Bransford and James W. Pellegrino (eds), *How People Learn: Bridging Research and Practice* (Washington, DC: National Academy Press), quoted in Kieran Egan, *Getting It Wrong from the Beginning: Our Progressive Inheritance from Herbert Spencer, John Dewey, and Jean Piaget* (New Haven, CT: Yale University Press, 2002), p. 166.

20 Matthew C. Makel and Jonathan A. Plucker, Facts Are More Important Than Novelty: Replication in the Education Sciences, *Educational Researcher* 43(6) (2014): 304–316.

21 Daniel Willingham, *When Can You Trust the Experts? How to Tell Good Science from Bad in Education* (San Francisco, CA: Jossey-Bass), pp. 49–79.

22 Dorothy Bishop, What is Educational Neuroscience? *BishopBlog* (25 January 2014). Available at: http://deevybee.blogspot.co.uk/2014_01_01_archive.html.

23 Carl Wieman, The Similarities Between Research in Education and Research in the Hard Sciences, *Educational Researcher* 43(1) (2014): 12.

24 Willingham, *When Can You Trust The Experts?*, p. 112.

25 Egan, *Getting It Wrong from the Beginning*, p. 158.

26 Robert Coe, It's the Effect Size, Stupid: What Effect Size is and Why it is Important. Paper presented at the British Educational Research Association annual conference, Exeter, 12–14 September 2002. Available at: http://www.cem.org/attachments/ebe/ESguide.pdf.

27 Hattie, *Visible Learning*, p. 7.

28 Dylan Wiliam, An Integrative Summary of the Research Literature and Implications for a New Theory of Formative Assessment, in H. L. Andrade and G. J. Cizek (eds), *Handbook of Formative Assessment* (New York: Taylor & Francis, 2010), pp. 18–40.

29 Benjamin S. Bloom, The Search for Methods of Group Instruction as Effective as One-to-One Tutoring, *Educational Leadership* (May 1984): 4–17. Available at: http://www.ascd.org/ASCD/pdf/journals/ed_lead/el_198405_bloom.pdf.

30 See http://geoffpetty.com/geoffs-books/evidence-based-teaching-ebt/.

31 Adapted from Daniel Willingham, Draft Bill of Research Rights for Educators, *Real Clear Education* (10 July 2014). Available at: http://www.realcleareducation.com/articles/2014/07/10/a_draft_bill_of_rights_for_educators.html.

Part 2
Through the threshold

Part 2
Through the threshold

This is your last chance. After this, there is no turning back. You take the blue pill – the story ends, you wake up in your bed and believe whatever you want to believe. You take the red pill – you stay in Wonderland and I show you how deep the rabbit-hole goes. Remember, all I'm offering is the truth, nothing more.

Morpheus, *The Matrix*

By now you should be feeling thoroughly tenderized. I hope that by first showing you some of the ways in which we so often go wrong, and then examining why we misunderstand each other when debating education, you will be more receptive to the main ideas of the book.

In Chapter 1, we examined why we should be wary of trusting our instincts and thought about how we deal with cognitive dissonance.

Chapter 2 dealt with a few of the cognitive biases we all fall prey to as we try to make sense of and simplify a terrifyingly complex world. The biases I introduced were the fundamental attribution error, confirmation bias, the backfire effect, the sunk cost fallacy, the illusion of asymmetric insight, group biases, the various observer biases (the anchoring effect, availability bias and the halo effect), the Dunning–Kruger effect and the ways we create perverse incentives.

In Chapter 3, I shared some of the assumptions with which I entered the teaching profession and outlined some of the ways I've come to change my beliefs over time. These included beliefs about behavior, the role of the teacher, how lessons should be taught and touched briefly on some thoughts about social class.

Then, in Chapter 4, I suggested that the reason there's so much disagreement about how to teach might be because we don't agree about what education is actually for. It is, however, vital to remember that even those who we most violently disagree with about *how* to teach still want the best for children. We forget this at our peril. We explored whether it's possible to compromise. I outlined my position that while it's probably fine to compromise on how to teach, we should not be prepared to compromise on our values. Looking at the middle ground is, perhaps, the worst way in which to compromise. I suggested we might do better to avoid certainty but also to hold the extremes together.

Chapter 5 looked at the role and limits of education research. We discussed ways in which we might think usefully about evidence and highlighted some problems with believing we could ever prove that some values are better than others.

With all that in mind, here are a few questions for you to consider before reading on:

- Have you perhaps experienced any of the cognitive biases as you've been reading?

- Have you changed your mind on anything so far?

- Is there anything about which you feel especially resistant?

- What are your values?

- What do you believe education is for?

- What should be the role of research and evidence in education?

You are now at a threshold. Passing through is hard and it will change you. The change is necessary. As you read, you might catch yourself feeling annoyed or frustrated and that, I think, is part of the process. Passing through the threshold doesn't mean you need to accept my explanations or understanding – in fact, I hope it means you'll be better able to express your reservations and disagreements – but pass through you must if the rest of the book is to make sense.

I say this as a challenge: I dare you to understand.

Firstly, I'm going to critique the idea of progress as it is commonly applied to education before teasing out some thoughts on what learning might be. We will then think about the vital role of memory in all of this.

Chapter 6
The myth of progress

We all want progress, but if you're on the wrong road, progress means doing an about-turn and walking back to the right road; in that case, the man who turns back soonest is the most progressive.

C. S. Lewis

Schools are driven by the need for students to make progress. And rightly so. No one sensible would ever argue against students making progress. But what does this mean in practice? We tend to believe that things get better, that mankind is on a journey to some perfect state in which irrationality will be banished. This is, I think, another meta-belief which shapes, and possibly distorts, our thinking. Darwin's evolutionary theory of natural selection is often interpreted as meaning that random biological mutations, which are then inherited and selected as being most fit for the context in which a species finds itself, are working towards some ultimate goal. They aren't. If we accept Darwin's theory, we also have to accept that our existence is a matter of chance. We are something of a fluke.

The philosopher of science, Karl Popper, thought something similar was happening in the realm of ideas. He saw the growth of knowledge as being the result of a process closely resembling natural selection. He thought that "our knowledge consists, at every moment, of those hypotheses which have shown their (comparative) fitness by surviving so far in their struggle for existence; a competitive struggle which eliminates those hypotheses which are unfit".[1]

But even a cursory glance at the history of ideas demonstrates that if this is true, it's a maddeningly slow process. In education alone many hypotheses which are unfit continue to lurch about our landscape. Maybe we can better understand the spread of ideas by considering the zoologist Richard Dawkins' theory of *memes* and *mimetic evolution*. In *The Selfish Gene*, he explains that just as genes are driven to replicate themselves through the process of natural selection, memes – ideas, tunes, images – also replicate themselves in a similarly self-interested way.[2] Through a process of cultural transmission, ideas spread themselves from person to person and from consciousness to consciousness regardless of whether they are good or bad ideas.

Obviously some memes are incredibly useful or beautiful – the ideas of central limit theorem, King Lear, growth mindsets, the electric light bulb, the idea of education itself – but others are not. There are still schools that practice Brain Gym, and, as we've seen, VAK continues to proliferate despite the lack of any supporting evidence of its efficacy. The learning pyramid (page 111) is one such meme that has spread exponentially with the advent of the internet despite it being baseless and wrong. It seems to me that all an idea needs in order to be accepted is to be shouted loudly enough and often enough for it to become something we no longer question. When this happens memes enter the realm of conventional wisdom and become self-evidently true in the minds of many; their survival is assured. Or as the economist John Maynard Keynes put it, "the power of vested interests is vastly exaggerated compared with the gradual encroachment of ideas".[3]

This is actually a useful reminder of why we're so poor at thinking rationally: our intelligence evolved through random mutation. The fact that we can think at all is blind chance. It's tempting to anthropomorphize natural selection and believe it behaves in the way *we* would behave. The startling realization about natural selection is not how well it works, but that it works at all. If we start to think that progress is not inevitable, then maybe we would find it easier to rid ourselves of the belief that learning is linear.

Our implicit belief in progress hoodwinks us into accepting that results should always be improving and things can only get better. We only have to remember the second law of thermodynamics: everything moves inexorably towards entropy and chaos.* Any temporary sense of progress is but a beguiling illusion, just another self-interested meme that replicates as it passes from mind to mind.

As I hinted at in Chapter 3, teachers have been exhorted to ensure their students make progress that is both rapid and sustained.[4] Let's just consider that for a moment. Progress should be both rapid *and* sustained. It should happen really quickly and should last for a really long time. Is it just me, or does this seem somewhat oxymoronic? Whenever I do something really quickly, it doesn't tend to last very long at all. Pulling an all-nighter before an important exam works in the short term but little of that information is likely to last for long. When I had to pass my GCSE math exam in order to qualify as a teacher, I took a past paper every day in the weeks leading up to the exam. By the big day I was something of an expert at math papers. Even though I aced the exam, I forgot almost everything within days. It felt like training a monkey – I could perform on the day but I had little or no understanding of what I was doing.

Take a look at these definitions:[5]

Progress	Sustained	Rapid
noun	*adjective*	*adjective*
1. Forward or onward movement towards a destination: "the darkness did not stop my progress". 2. Development towards an improved or more advanced condition: "we are *making progress* towards equal rights".	Continuing for an extended period or without interruption: "several years of sustained economic growth".	Happening in a short time or at a great rate: "the country's rapid economic decline".

You can certainly have 'movement towards a destination or an improved condition' (progress) that 'happens in a short time or at a great rate' (rapid) or which 'continues for an extended period' (sustained), but can

---

* The second law of thermodynamics states that the entropy of an isolated system not in equilibrium increases, because isolated systems always evolve towards thermodynamic equilibrium, a state with maximum entropy.

you have both at the same time? Is it actually possible for students' learning to improve in a short time or at a great rate and continue for an extended period?

I don't think it is. Of course we can have breakthroughs but these are rare. Sudden breakthroughs are usually the result of the steady accretion of understanding over time – the fact that they seem to happen quickly is misleading. We'll discuss the importance of these breakthroughs when we look at threshold concepts in Chapter 7. But for the most part, you have to make a choice between rapid and sustained and, this being the case, I'm going to vote for sustained. After all, progress that doesn't last isn't really progress, is it? This idea that progress can be rapid has led us into believing that meaningful progress can take place in individual lessons, and that learning follows a neat, linear trajectory. Children move from knowing nothing, to knowing a little, to knowing a lot in a smooth and easily navigable and safely predictable manner. This is self-evidently wrong as even a cursory examination of children's work over time makes clear. Progress is, if anything, halting, frustrating and surprising. Learning is better seen as integrative, transformative and reconstitutive – the linear metaphor in terms of movement from A to B is unhelpful. The learner doesn't *go* anywhere, but develops a different relationship with what they know.

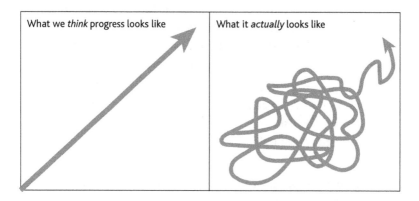

Figure 6.1. What progress looks like

Progress is just a metaphor. It doesn't really describe objective reality; it provides a comforting fiction to conceal the absurdity of our lives. We can't help using metaphors to describe learning because we have no idea what it actually looks like. Even though our metaphors are imprecise approximations, the metaphors we use matter. They permeate our thinking. Learning is often conceived as a staircase which students steadily ascend. The long shadow cast by developmental psychologist Jean Piaget has meant linear 'stage theories' have dominated the way we see the mysterious process of learning. As we know from our own messy journey through life, we often seem to step back or sideways as often as we step up. An alternative metaphor is offered by cognitive psychologist Robert Siegler, who has developed the theory that learning is like 'overlapping waves'. Piaget saw learning progressing in neat stages like a staircase: children would master level 1 before ascending to level 2, level 3 and so on. Instead, Siegler envisaged learning as "a gradual ebbing and flowing of the frequencies of alternative ways of thinking, with new approaches being added and old ones being eliminated as well".[6] He suggests that as we encounter new rules, strategies, theories and ways of thinking these wash through our minds like waves, sometimes obliterating what was there before, sometimes pushing suddenly forward in great surges.

This might be a more useful way to frame our thinking about progress. Siegler's image of surging and receding waves helps to explain the seemingly random retreats and swells we experience as we grapple with new skills and tricky concepts. Rather than feeling ashamed about 'slipping back' into the old ways of thinking and acting we thought we had outgrown, such episodes are better viewed as part of the natural ebb and flow of learning. Slipping back is part of the process of integrating new and troublesome concepts into our mental webs.

Various thinkers have tried to design ordered taxonomies that impose recognizable stages on to the way we learn and make progress. But a taxonomy is just another metaphor which fools us into believing that learning is hierarchical. The obvious result is grades, levels and other simplifications of something we don't really understand. The most famous among these is Bloom's Taxonomy, but the relative new kid on the block, the SOLO (Structure of Observed Learning Outcomes) taxonomy, makes similar assumptions.

Bloom's Taxonomy was first conceived back in 1954 and its levels (knowledge, comprehension, application, analysis, synthesis, evaluation and, later, creativity) are essentially plucked from the air and are certainly not supported by any research on learning. To say this is an oversimplification of how we learn is something of an understatement.

And maybe those 'higher-order thinking skills' at the top of the hierarchy aren't actually any more challenging than those at the bottom. Sometimes it's harder to remember than it is to create: recalling how an engine is constructed is far more challenging than designing an experiment to test the temperature at which water boils. Equally, it may be more difficult to understand than to evaluate. In fact, fully understanding a concept makes evaluation of it fairly straightforward. Just watch how quickly and precisely an expert baker like Mary Berry evaluates the shortcomings of a poorly baked cake, or an expert choreographer like Craig Revel-Horwood picks apart a badly executed tango; they do this because they have complete understanding – that is, epistemic knowledge of the 'underlying game'.[7] One could even suggest that their understanding came *after* attempting creativity and as a result of the arduous, effortful journey from novice to expert. The concepts of abstraction and specification (chunking up and chunking down) are problematic threshold concepts, and there's no model I know of that sufficiently accounts for how we actually learn and think.

The slippery nature of these higher-order skills means that they can appear somehow more advanced than the more readily definable and familiar skills. By teaching students content, by building their knowledge base, by making sure they can remember things and by ensuring they understand concepts, the higher-order stuff becomes much easier to wrap your head around.

Applying Bloom's Taxonomy consistently across domains is impossible. How could these generic levels apply to say, math, music, geography and athletics? Sure, we could classify any learning objective into either of the two lowest levels (knowledge or comprehension) or into any of the four highest levels (application, analysis, synthesis or evaluation) but what would it actually mean? The distinctions make no practical difference in diagnosing and treating gaps in students' learning and performance. Everything above 'knowledge' is usually considered higher-order thinking anyway, effectively reducing the taxonomy to just two levels.

When I first encountered SOLO it seemed different; here was a theory of learning instead of a theory of knowledge. Its vocabulary felt like a revelation. The idea that students would progress from pre-structural (knowing nothing) to uni-structural (knowing a little) to multi-structural (knowing a lot) to relational (able to make links between items of knowledge) to extended abstract (able to generalize and generate new hypotheses) makes a certain kind of sense. When we attempt to examine how students learn, it does seem as if they might be undertaking this kind of smooth, linear journey. Exciting possibilities about how I might design lessons to encourage students to respond in new and surprising ways were opening up before me. And there is no one more zealous than a convert; I wanted to spread the word.

Of the many benefits of using SOLO, the two I was most excited about were that it could help to develop a common understanding and shared language of learning, and it could make students' progress from just knowing facts to seeing connections very visible.

There was always the annoying niggle that there isn't really any evidence that using SOLO levels in lessons achieves any of the claims made for it, but what the hell, it seemed to be working for me and my students. But as time went by, I started noticing problems.

Consider this question: what makes you clever?

• Is it being able to generate revolutionary new thinking?

• Is it seeing links and connections between different concepts and ideas?

• Is it the quality and quantity of what you know?

The first two are beguiling. These applications of 'cleverness' seem self-evidently and obviously true: of course we want these things. But aren't they utterly dependent on the depth and breadth of what you know? What happens if you make a relational construct that is wrong? The answer, of course, is to go back to our store of knowledge and correct the misapprehension.

This observation led to the realization that the usefulness of SOLO was entirely dependent on the quality of knowledge the students possessed. I noticed that students were asked to make relational connections and abstract constructions at every key stage and beyond. The difference between students at ages 5, 11 or 18 is the quality and quantity of what they know. Finally, the penny dropped: teaching students how to analyze in isolation is pretty pointless. They need to have something to analyze. And if this sounds blindingly obvious to you, I can only hang my head in shame.

From there I started to consider whether I might have made other erroneous assumptions. Much of the time I had sunk into teaching the taxonomy was based on the flawed belief that it would help students to demonstrate progress. And make no mistake, it is great for getting students to demonstrate progress, but of what? If I accept that learning takes time and needs to build on a firm foundation of knowledge, then there really isn't any value in prompting students to show they're able to move from multi-structural to extended abstract in a single lesson. All this might demonstrate is the progress they've made in their ability to perform a particular task at a particular time. True extended abstract thinking can only develop over time.

But what about the importance of the shared understanding and common language of learning? If teaching children to use SOLO to identify their leaps from one stage on the ladder to another was artificial and superficial, did this at least provide a saving grace? Much to my chagrin, I decided it did not.

Teaching children a new cross-curricular language of learning assumes that the terms we use mean the same things at different times and in different places. But what if this common language was actually creating an illusion of shared understanding? What if we were using the same words to describe fundamentally different things? What if the time spent teaching students to understand what 'extended abstract' might mean in English, history, math, PE and art could be spent developing domain specific language that might be tailored to separate subject disciplines? I started to feel that SOLO was swamping the disciplinary 'what' with the pedagogic 'how' and that this resulted at best in wasting time and at worst in confusion.

Now, I am often reminded of the danger of throwing out the baby with the bathwater, but what if SOLO is the bathwater? SOLO might very well be useful for teachers to effectively plan learning outcomes – indeed, for some time after I stopped referring to it in lessons I continued to find it useful to refer to SOLO levels to help me think about progression.

But I have concluded that the tricks and gimmicks involved in explicitly teaching students about the taxonomy should be bypassed so we can concentrate on expanding domain specific knowledge. I'm not saying it's garbage, just that it's unnecessary. It may be useful for teachers to know about these structures, but in terms of teaching, students need to work out these things for themselves. Maybe it's enough just to teach them about our subjects without this potentially misleading meta-cognitive layer.

Suffice it to say that I quietly took down my SOLO displays, put away the hexagons and went back to teaching students how to get better at reading and writing without the need to ever mention terms like multi-structural. And no student ever said they missed it.

That would be that, except in the intervening years quite a cult has grown up. People are claiming that SOLO can make students independent, improve their exam results, make them better at the complex business of life, and is a wholly wonderful panacea. Let me make myself perfectly clear: if you've thought about this and have concluded that this is the best way to teach your students, far be it from me, or anyone else, to tell you you're wrong. After all, what do I know? But if you want to suggest that other teachers should also be using SOLO, the burden of proof lies with you.

The problem with all these taxonomies (we've had Biggs, Wills, Bateson, Belbin and dozens more) is their attempt to pin down the complexity of cognition in a list of simple categories. In practice, learning is a much more complex and messier set of cognitive processes and stubbornly resists any attempt to be sliced up so neatly. Thankfully, brain science has moved on and we have solid theory, especially about memory, which has put everything on a more empirical and scientific basis. Using Bloom's to design sequences of lessons is barely more useful than palm reading.

Learning and performance

One of the most useful things for teachers to be aware of is the distinction between learning and performance; every effort should be made to separate the two in our minds. The evidence is compelling: there are decades' worth of research and hundreds of studies which support the idea that learning is separate from performance and, more troublingly, that performance might not lead to learning.[8]

Performance is measurable, but learning can only be inferred from performance: it cannot be observed directly. That is to say, performance is easy to observe whereas learning is not. You can check a box to show that a student's performance has moved from x to y, but you can't necessarily tell whether learning has taken place.

There are instances where learning occurs but performance in the short term doesn't improve, and conversely there are instances where performance improves but little learning seems to happen in the long term. So, in a situation where the same skill is practiced over and over again in predictable conditions with immediate feedback, people appear to make dramatic progress. But after a delay, or if there are any environmental changes or minor differences in the task, it can appear as if no progress had been made; the apparently rapid progress made has not been sustained.[9]

Such performances are often fleeting and tell us little about what is actually going on inside students' heads. It seems to be so clear that if you can do something now then that must be evidence of learning, but this is very far from the case. One key thing that might improve how teachers teach and students learn is to recognize that short-term performance is a remarkably poor guide to long-term learning. Performance can be propped up by predictability and current cues that are present during the lesson but they won't be present when the information is needed later. This can make it seem that a student is making rapid progress but there may not actually be any learning happening. Here's an example:

The capital city of Poland is W_rs_w.

Any idea what the capital city of Poland is?

Warsaw? Oh, well done. Marvellous progress!

This is the Monkey Dance, and is a blunt but fairly accurate caricature of what goes on in far too many lessons. Teachers are primed to demonstrate their students' performance so that their observer can nod, smile and check away to their embittered heart's content. But there is no evidence of any learning taking place.

Professor Robert Coe of the Center for Evaluation and Monitoring at Durham University has dubbed these performance activities as "poor proxies for learning". Some of the poor proxies he describes are:

- Students are busy: lots of work is done (especially written work).
- Students are engaged, interested, motivated.
- Students are getting attention: feedback, explanations.
- Classroom is ordered, calm, under control.
- Curriculum has been 'covered' (i.e. presented to students in some form).
- (At least some) students have supplied correct answers (whether or not they really understood them or could reproduce them independently).[10]

When we see these things in a lesson we assume that learning is happening, but is it? Maybe at this point we should pause to consider what learning actually is (or might be). In order to move beyond these proxies, Coe has suggested this axiom: "Learning happens when people have to think hard."[11]

Or as Marcel Proust wrote, "We soon forget what we have not deeply thought about." It sounds probable that a process which requires attention, effort and the conscious mulling that fits new knowledge into existing knowledge to transform it is more likely to be memorable. Arguably, teaching is the attempt to induce cognitive change: to make students think differently. But thinking is similar to learning in that we can't see it. We can ask students questions and get them to write stuff down, but this will not necessarily reveal any but their shallowest thoughts. If we could agree on classroom activities that constitute thinking then we might have a useful tool to check out whether what's going on in our classrooms is likely to lead to learning.

But all this still doesn't tell us much about what learning actually *is*. As you might expect, this isn't going to be an easy question to answer. In fact, I'd go as far as saying there's probably no definition that would be accepted by everyone. Nevertheless, if we're going to talk about learning, I'm going to need to give you a definition so that you can at least follow my thinking, even if you then disagree.

Here then is my definition of learning: *the ability to retain skills and knowledge over the long term and to be able to transfer them to new contexts.*

I think these two areas, retention and transfer, are the hallmarks of learning. If learning happens over time, and we can only ever infer it from current performance, it makes sense that the best performances from which to make this inference are ones that occur in different times and places from where they were first introduced. So, if I taught you to play 'When the Saints Go Marching In' on the trombone, can you still play it six months later while parading up and down Kensington High Street? And if not, can you really be said to have learned it?

There is also, perhaps, a third, more mysterious aspect to learning: *it must result in a change of self.* We are what we know. When we learn something new it changes us. It allows us to think both *with* and *about* what has been learned. Once you've learned to play 'When the Saints Go Marching In', you feel a little bit more like a musician. If this change does not occur then all we're able to do is mimic without any real understanding.

These definitions are the subject of the next chapter.

Notes

1   Anthony O'Hear (ed.), *Karl Popper, Philosophy and Problems* (Cambridge: Cambridge University Press, 1996), p. 208.
2   Richard Dawkins, *The Selfish Gene*, new edn (Oxford: Oxford University Press, 2006).
3   John Maynard Keynes, Concluding Notes on the Social Philosophy Towards Which the General Theory Might Lead, in *The General Theory of Employment, Interest and Money* (Basingstoke: Palgrave Macmillan, 1936). Available at: https://www.marxists.org/reference/subject/economics/keynes/general-theory/ch24.htm.
4   Ofsted, *School Inspection Handbook* (January 2015). Ref: 120101. Available at: https://www.gov.uk/government/publications/school-inspection-handbook, p. 35.
5   See http://www.dictionary.com.
6   Robert Siegler, *Emerging Minds: The Process of Change in Children's Thinking* (Oxford and New York: Oxford University Press, 1998), p. 86.
7   David Perkins, *Making Learning Whole: How Seven Principles of Teaching Can Transform Education* (San Francisco, CA: Jossey-Bass, 2010).
8   Nicholas C. Soderstrom and Robert A. Bjork, Learning Versus Performance, in Dana Dunn (ed.), *Oxford Bibliographies Online: Psychology* (New York: Oxford University

Press, 2013). Available at: http://bjorklab.psych.ucla.edu/pubs/Soderstrom_Bjork_Learning_versus_Performance.pdf.

9   Robert A. Bjork, Disassociating Learning from Performance [video] (n.d.). Available at: http://gocognitive.net/interviews/dissociating-learning-performance.

10 Robert Coe, Improving Education: A Triumph of Hope Over Experience. Inaugural lecture, Durham University, 18 June 2013 (Durham: Center for Evaluation & Monitoring). Available at: http://www.cem.org/attachments/publications/ImprovingEducation2013.pdf, p. xii.

11 Ibid. p. xiii.

Chapter 7
Liminality and
threshold concepts

I am a part of all that I have met;

Yet all experience is an arch wherethro'

Gleams that untravell'd world whose margin fades.

For ever and for ever when I move.

Alfred, Lord Tennyson, *Ulysses*

We've already seen that learning is distinct from performance, but what is it? How can we ever hope to define the swirling, nebulous mass of thoughts that crowd our minds? Learning is a messy, complicated business, "a liminal process, at the boundary between control and chaos".[1] No matter how hard we try to exert control through teaching, there's no way we can ever really control what goes on inside someone else's head, and we're unlikely to ever accurately predict what a child will or won't learn as a result of our teaching.

It's obvious that if you can't remember what you've learned, you can't really claim to have learned it. But is there more to learning than that? Being able to transfer what you've learned in, say, a math lesson to a physics lesson, or from cognitive psychology to education, or even from the classroom to the exam hall, would appear equally important as remembering.

So, if we're going to make claims about what or whether students are learning, we need to be able to consider both how long they have retained information and whether they are able to use it in new contexts. Or, to put it another way, learning needs to be both durable and flexible. If our definition of learning doesn't include both of these qualities then it's probably flawed.

Liminality is a transitional, transformational state when we are in the initial stages of a process or occupying a position at or on both sides of a boundary; what the anthropologist Victor Turner described as "betwixt and between". This allows us to think about 'learning' as an essentially fluid process, existing at the threshold between knowing and not knowing. This state of restless flux is something all of us struggle to pin down even in our own minds. There is little hope of being able to pinpoint a moment in time and claim it to be the precise moment at which a student crosses a particular threshold.

Entering a liminal space engages us in the exciting process of mastery but can feel dangerous – grasping difficult new concepts changes us, and change is always uncertain. Although pre-liminal understanding of the world is vague, it's safe; some students prefer the safety of mimicry rather than the risk of mastery.[2]

Imagine yourself standing before a dark, ominous doorway. Through it you can glimpse something previously unimagined, but entering and crossing through entails a risk – anything might happen. But not passing through, while safe, means you will never fully see what's on the other side. Crossing a threshold also risks losing something; we have to let go of old ideas, which isn't always comfortable.

As well as passing through, the process of learning is also a voyage of discovery in which we boldly seek out brave new worlds. If our journey through life is full of adventure and adversity then we will learn from these experiences. If we never leave the safety of familiar environs and stay within the bounds of what is known then we're unlikely to develop or be much changed.

Although no metaphor can adequately describe it, learning can sometimes be a little like this. This led to a fascinating attempt by education professors Jan Meyer and Ray Land to map the unmappable and plot students' journeys within subject domains: the 'threshold concept'. They see threshold concepts as portals, "opening up a new and previously inaccessible way of thinking about something". If a student fails to pass through a threshold, they may not be able to progress further in a subject.

But once students do pass through they will experience "a transformed internal view of subject matter, subject landscape, or even world view".[3]

So, what makes a threshold concept different from, say, a key concept? Well, it appears that the areas of a subject at which students get stuck seem to be the most important bits. Further, more advanced ideas depend on the understanding of certain important fundamentals. In all subject domains and disciplines there are points which lead us into 'previously inaccessible ways of thinking'. If a concept is a way of organizing and making sense of what is known in a particular field, a threshold concept organizes the knowledge and experience which makes an epiphany or eureka moment possible.

Meyer and Land suggest a threshold concept will most likely possess certain important qualities.[4] Some of the adjectives we could apply to these concepts are:

- **Integrative:** Once learned, they are likely to bring together different parts of the subject which you hadn't previously seen as connected.

- **Transformative:** Once understood, they change the way you see the subject and yourself.

- **Irreversible:** They are difficult to unlearn – once you've passed through it's difficult to see how it was possible not to have understood before.

- **Reconstitutive:** They may shift your sense of self over time. This is initially more likely to be noticed by others, usually teachers.

- **Troublesome:** They are likely to present you with a degree of difficulty and may sometimes seem incoherent or counter-intuitive.[5]

- **Discursive:** The student's ability to use the language associated with that subject changes as they change. It's the change from using scientific key words to talking like a scientist.

Think about learning to read. At some point you started to grasp the fact that the funny squiggles on the page represent the sounds we make when we speak. Over time this liminal state solidified into an ability to decode writing and turn it back into sounds. For most of us, this dramatic shift goes unnoticed and unremarked; it just happens. But it transforms us. From then on we are incapable of experiencing writing or texts without this knowledge. We may struggle with new words and unfamiliar structures but we know that the meaning is there, waiting to be unlocked. This change is irreversible; there is no going back to how we were. This change of state offers us an insight into the adult world, it reveals what was previously mysterious and it sets us off on a journey that gives us access to all recorded human thought. But once we've passed through this particularly elusive, troublesome threshold, it all seems so obvious and changes us so utterly that we find it hard to recognize a time before we knew how to read.

Remaining on the other side of the threshold has serious consequences. Failing to learn how to read is endemic – there's a handful of such students in most schools who are never fully able to get to grips with the curriculum content. Failure to grasp other, less fundamental, threshold concepts results in mimicking what others are able to do without ever really understanding what or why.

We should pause to ask whether we can teach without exposing students to threshold concepts. We probably could, but why would we want to? One of the common criticisms of a transmission model of teaching is that students can just find out the information they need on the internet. If teaching was simply about getting kids to learn stuff then this would be valid. But we don't just want them to retain knowledge; we want them to be changed by it. And that's why we need teachers to help us cope with the troublesome nature of the passage through thresholds.

The problem we have as teachers is that because we've already passed through these thresholds, we routinely underestimate how difficult it is to master a tricky concept. This is the curse of knowledge, sometimes called hindsight bias. This can lead us to believe either that we're more skilled than we actually are or, more usually, that learning a new task is easier than it actually is. Thinking in terms of threshold concepts helps us to remember how hard it can be to master this troublesome knowledge.

I get very excited about the idea of 'troublesome knowledge'. Far from being something we should be alarmed about, Land suggests that knowledge *should* be troublesome and that teachers *should* be troublemakers.[6] If our teaching doesn't confront and confound students' beliefs and expectations then it will be a superficial and impoverished affair. But what does troublesome knowledge mean?[7]

Some knowledge is troublesome because it's associated with risk, discomfort and unease; it's akin to eating the fruit of the tree of knowledge of good and evil. Once you've lost your innocence, there's no regaining it. Some knowledge can be troublesome because it's where we get stuck.

To help us think about how best to deal with this kind of knowledge, it's worth considering why students get stuck. It's easy to see why students might get stuck with something that's conceptually difficult. We know abstractions can be hard to grasp and work hard to explain these tricky aspects of our subjects. Sometimes we just need to continue showing examples and accept that students need to occupy a liminal space for some time until the penny drops.

More difficult though is knowledge which seems alien. Just as we saw in Chapter 1, new information that conflicts with old information produces cognitive dissonance. If we are to help students through this kind of difficulty, we need to help them to see the world through others' eyes and accept the possibility that there may be room for different interpretations.

There's also the problem of the assimilation paradox: it can be much more difficult to unlearn erroneous prior knowledge than it is to learn something entirely new. Because what we know is bound up with so many existing schemas, it can be very hard to root out errors and mistakes. For instance, if we were to use what we know about human growth and respiration to understand plant growth, we might well end up with false beliefs, such as "Plants use soil for food" and "Plants breathe CO_2". If we're unaware of these misconceptions then students may just end up adding new information into a faulty knowledge base and creating an increasingly inaccurate understanding of the world.[8]

Very often, though, students get stuck because a lot of what we know is tacit, unspoken and assumed. It may be that we don't know something well enough to articulate it, or it may be that we simply assume everyone already knows it. This tacit knowledge can be very basic – such as the assumption that all students know how to skim read a text – or quite complex. We might, for instance, assume that students understand the meaning of a word like 'analysis' ("I want you to analyze this passage." "What do you mean, sir?" "Look, just analyze it, OK?"). An expert takes their ability to analyze for granted – they don't have to explain it to be able to do it. This is what education professor David Perkins calls the 'underlying game': the unacknowledged repertoire of skills and knowledge an expert has available to them – the stuff we use to think with. Students also need access to this knowledge; if we don't tell them what we know they'll struggle to intuit it. So, if we want to avoid students getting lost in liminal space, we need to be explicit about exactly what we mean and strive to articulate everything we know about a subject.

Once we've done the hard work of wrapping our heads around the concepts of liminality, thresholds and troublesome knowledge, we then need to know what to do with it. How might knowing all this change our practice? Anarchic though it may sound, a hunt for the threshold concepts of our subjects is not (just) about lobbing grenades into the placid ponds of our students' minds; it could also be a way to overcome the bloated edifice of the curriculum. Because we fear that students won't grasp the basics, we tend to overstuff the curriculum with content and overburden ourselves and our students. While there's no substitute for knowledge (you can't think about something you don't know), less could well be more, certainly in the initial stages. Understanding and recognizing the most important conceptual areas of our subjects upon which all else rests might help us to make better decisions about both what and how to teach.

Some useful work has been done, particularly in the domains of mathematics and the sciences, to unpick and describe what these threshold concepts may be. A threshold concept in physics is gravity, in biology there's evolution, the concept of opportunity cost in economics,* deconstruction in literature and so on. Tracing students' mastery of these concepts may allow us a somewhat more accurate insight into what they might be learning. It's hard for someone who's grasped a concept – for instance, that a writer selects language and structure to manipulate the reader – to believe that anyone else might not understand something so obvious and fundamental. That's the problem: it's only obvious once you know. And once you know, once you're on the other side of the threshold, it's not at all obvious what's changed. Suddenly we 'get it', but we may not

---

* Opportunity cost – the concept that we always make choices, and that these choices then preclude other courses of action, not only opens up the subject of economics but also, as we saw in Chapter 2, helps us to understand the consequences of decisions we make in education.

be at all clear how we got it or even be able to articulate what it was we got.

So how can we identify the threshold concepts of our subjects? Most obviously, they're the places students commonly get stuck. What are the knots of your subject? The bits that give you the most trouble in communicating to classes? Often these areas are the points at which many seemingly unrelated pieces of knowledge coalesce into meaning. With this as our starting point, we can start to map out what these concepts might be for a particular subject area.

For my subject, English, the threshold concepts might be:

- Understanding the relationship between grammar and meaning.

- Understanding the effect of context, both on writers and readers.

- Understanding the need to use supporting evidence for ideas.

- An awareness of the ways in which language can affect readers.

- Understanding how different ways of structuring text can produce different effects.

- Understanding that language can be analyzed to reveal a variety of meanings.

You could certainly argue for others to be included, but each of these concepts is, I think, fundamental to being able to perform at the highest level in English language and literature. Until they are grasped, the ability to find and make meaning is limited.

Piecing together these concepts and mapping them on to the curriculum is the very opposite of misguided attempts of generic taxonomies to describe linear and universal stages of learning. It might not feel comfortable, but it's essential that we acknowledge that there's no straightforward linear route from 'easy' to 'difficult'. Mastery of a threshold concept is a messy business and will often require retracing our steps back, forth and across unfamiliar conceptual terrain. The idea of a threshold concept is in itself a threshold concept. We find it hard to grasp not just because of its transformative implications but also because it's tough to wrap your head around: what's the difference between a threshold concept and a more traditional way of looking at the basic principles of a subject? Is it just a fancy name for something we're already familiar with? This is a briar patch through which it can seem too onerous to pass and it's all too easy to get stuck. This might help us to appreciate the frustration our students often feel for what, to us, seem the most straightforward and natural ways of thinking.

Passing through this particular threshold is a gateway to understanding some of the other threshold concepts explored in this book. I mentioned these in the introduction but by now they should make a little more sense:

- Seeing shouldn't always result in believing (Chapter 1).
- We are all victims of cognitive bias (Chapter 2).
- Compromise doesn't always result in effective solutions (Chapter 4).
- Evidence is not the same as proof (Chapter 5).
- Progress is a gradual, non-linear process (Chapters 6 and 7).
- Learning is invisible (Chapter 8).
- Current performance is not only a poor indication of learning, it actually seems to prevent it (Chapters 8 and 9).
- Forgetting aids learning (Chapter 9).
- Experts and novices learn differently (Chapter 10).
- Making learning more difficult can make it more durable (Chapter 11).

Each of these has changed the way I think about teaching and education and each has had a destructive effect on my previous beliefs. Now that I've wrestled with and absorbed these ideas, there's no going back. It's troublesome stuff, but once you get it, it changes the way you think about education. In response, I've had to integrate everything I do and think to fit with my new understanding – some of what I thought was right has had to be revised, other things have been rejected utterly. My views are still shifting and as they shift so do I – this has pleased some people and upset others. And what could be more discursive as an attempt to express my new thinking than the act of writing a book?

Notes

1   Dylan Wiliam, Assessment, Learning and Technology: Prospects at the Periphery of Control. Keynote address to ALT-C, Nottingham, 5 September 2007. Available at: https://www.alt.ac.uk/sites/default/files/assets_editor_uploads/documents/altc2007_dylan_wiliam_keynote_transcript.pdf, p. 5.
2   Glynis Cousin, An Introduction to Threshold Concepts, *Planet* 17 (December 2006): 4–5. Available at: http://www.et.kent.edu/fpdc-db/files/DD%2002-threshold.pdf.
3   Jan Meyer and Ray Land, Threshold Concepts and Troublesome Knowledge: Linkages to Ways of Thinking and Practising Within the Disciplines, ETL Project Occasional Report 4 (May 2003). Available at: http://www.etl.tla.ed.ac.uk//docs/ETLreport4.pdf, p. 1.
4   Adapted from http://www.ee.ucl.ac.uk/~mflanaga/thresholds.html.
5   David Perkins, The Many Faces of Constructivism, *Educational Leadership* 57(3) (1999): 6–11.
6   Ray Land, Threshold Concepts and Troublesome Knowledge [video] (2011). Available at: https://www.youtube.com/watch?v=WR1cXIdWnNU.
7   David Perkins, Constructivism and Troublesome Knowledge, in Jan Meyer and Ray Land (eds), *Overcoming Barriers to Student Understanding: Threshold Concepts and Troublesome Knowledge* (London and New York: Routledge, 2006), pp. 33–47.
8   Stellan Ohlsson, Resubsumption: A Possible Mechanism for Conceptual Change and Belief Revision, *Educational Psychologist* 44(1) (2009): 20–40.

Chapter 8
Learning: from lab to classroom

As we acquire more knowledge, things do not become more comprehensible but more mysterious.

Albert Schweitzer

No discussion of learning would be complete without considering the remarkable work of the late Professor Graham Nuthall of Canterbury University in New Zealand. Between 1997 and 2004, Nuthall conducted one of the most robust and interesting pieces of education research I've come across. The Project on Learning was an ambitious, long-term study looking at how students aged from 9 to 11 learn from their classroom experiences. The project focused on how students' knowledge and thinking are progressively shaped by classroom activities, and how teachers influence this development. He wired up 12 different classrooms with microphones and miniaturized video cameras and, over several months, recorded what went on. A team of researchers then transcribed the classroom recordings and started to crunch through the data. Teachers and students were interviewed both at the time and six months after the recordings to try to pinpoint what and how students were actually learning.

Remarkably, Nuthall's data analysis on individual students' experience allowed him to predict, with 80–85 percent accuracy, exactly which concepts, principles, generalizations and procedures each student would learn and remember. Some of what he discovered seems plain, old-fashioned common sense, but much was quite surprising and seems to confirm the laboratory results of cognitive scientists. This triangulation of testing under controlled conditions and classroom observation demands our attention. Anything that can be predicted and then demonstrated to take place in real classrooms allows us to be reasonably certain that these findings are likely to be relevant in every classroom.

We'll return to Nuthall's findings at various points, but for now let's focus on the observation that teachers believe that "engaging in learning activities ... transfers the content of the activity to the mind of the student". Although we might not really believe this, we certainly tend to act as if it's true. But, "as learning occurs, so does forgetting ... learning takes time and is not encapsulated in the visible here-and-now of classroom activities".[1] This is what I've come to call the input/output myth and is the subject of the next chapter. As we've already established, there's not much use in being able to do something at the end of one lesson but not remembering how to do it next lesson. That's hardly progress, is it?

Nuthall tells us that even though we all go through essentially the same learning process, background knowledge, experiences, interests and motivations can be wildly different. He saw learning as making connections between all this stuff that kids bring *to* the classroom with what they encounter *in* the classroom. Because of this diversity of experience, roughly a third of what students learn will be unique to them. Let me put that another way: one in three things a student will have learned by the end of a teaching sequence will not be known by *any other student*. In a class of 30 students that's a hell of a lot of unique knowledge. I may have a clear learning objective which I intend all students to learn, but my feeble attempts will be dwarfed by what's going on in students' heads.

He also observed that students tend to know about 40–50 percent of whatever we're trying to teach them.[2] This sounds straightforward enough: why don't we just teach them the 50–60 percent they don't already know? Well, there are two reasons. Firstly, they don't all know the same 40–50 percent of stuff and, secondly, if you attempt to teach kids something about which they know absolutely nothing, they'll have nothing to connect it to. The likelihood is that it won't make the perilous journey from working memory to long-term memory. That is to say, it'll be forgotten fairly quickly.

Now, obviously we've all managed to successfully learn about things of which we previously knew nothing, so it can't be that this knowledge vanishes completely. Although newly learned concepts don't seem to stick very well, they must be in there somewhere. Nuthall's observations about forgetting are fascinating because they equate so closely with research into memory, learning and forgetting. In the next chapter, we'll look at what might be going on when we appear to forget stuff, but for now it's worth noting Nuthall's observation that another prerequisite for learning seems to be the number of times we encounter information. Single, isolated experiences rarely seem to turn into learning; students need opportunities to come at things from different angles in order to make sense of new information and slot it usefully into the network of stuff they already know. He suggested that if students had encountered a concept on at least three different occasions, or in different contexts, there was about an 80 percent chance they would still know it six months later.

When we're given new information we hold it in working memory and connect it to other new information and experiences, as well as relating it to and evaluating it against known concepts. If the new information becomes sufficiently integrated then it will be 'learned' – that is, retained in long-term memory.

Nuthall's research also indicates that learning doesn't happen as a direct result of classroom activities. Instead, it arises from the way students *experience* these activities. This difference may seem trivial, but it's the essential difference between 'teaching' and 'learning'; just because we've taught something doesn't mean they'll have learned it. What's important is how students go about trying to make sense of what we tell them. And students are *always* attempting to do this, whether they're aware of it or not. Sometimes this attempt to integrate new knowledge results in learning and sometimes it doesn't.

According to Nuthall, we can understand this process much better if we acknowledge that a good deal of what students end up learning they learn from each other. As they go through the process of trying to fit new ideas into the webs of prior knowledge, students will usually talk to each other. They'll share ideas and help each other as they stumble through the liminal spaces between old ways of holding the world and new insights. But a lot of what they learn from each other is full of misconceptions and confusion. Terrifyingly, Nuthall estimates that 80 percent of the feedback students get on their work is from each other, and 80 percent of that is wrong.[3]

Nuthall argued that students learn better when they can self-select or self-generate activities. If we put them in groups we'll give them opportunities to interact with each other; if we don't they'll still interact but in a way that teachers won't be able to monitor and thus prevent misinformation spreading. He suggested that during whole-class instruction we attempt to literally direct students' learning by forcing them to pay attention only to the content we intend them to learn. But students will be reacting to new concepts and information whether the teacher is aware of it or not; they talk to themselves and each other all the time. When the class is set up for students to direct their own learning, the teacher can listen to this because it will be explicit. When the teacher is at the front, directing, they cannot, either because they're unaware of it or because they perceive it as bad behavior.

Much of what students know is bound up in their peer culture. In Chapter 24 we will consider the psychology of motivation and how we might go about motivating students in order not only to make them more willing to learn but also to affect students' social standing. If we only ever provide traditional academic routes to learning, the 'most able' will have all the power and the 'least able' will quickly, and unsurprisingly, become disaffected. The notion of ability is as much about how we see ourselves and how others see us as it is about intelligence. I challenge some of the received wisdom about ability in Chapter 22.

Finally, learning should be memorable. Students don't just learn the curriculum; they remember the context in which they learned it. If something dramatic and exciting happens then they'll remember it – just as I remember my biology teacher accidentally dropping a human skeleton on the floor. Sadly, though, these moments of drama tend to dominate and now I have no idea what that biology lesson was about. How students experience an activity is as much a part of what they learn as the intended curriculum content. This suggests that we should find ways to harness our built-in predisposition for stories and find ways to contextualize content without losing the detail.*

....

*   Martin Robinson, author of *Trivium 21c*, told me a lovely story about his daughter learning about climate change. She rushed home and, in a voice of portentous doom, explained how sea levels were rising and that everyone was going to die. "That's very interesting," Martin said, "so what's climate?" She didn't know. In the enthusiasm to teach the content, the most important concept had been lost.

....

'Thinking' doesn't happen in a vacuum – it has to be tied to stuff that students already know. Therefore we have to design lessons that get them to think about the connections they already know and how it relates to the new stuff we want them to learn. In this way, new learning becomes integrated into the webs of information they are building up in long-term memory.

This suggests we should plan opportunities for students to revisit new ideas. This is borne out not just by the research on spacing and inter-leaving but also from the observations of Nuthall's Project on Learning. Nuthall noticed that about 80 percent of information would be retained after three separate re-presentations.[4] That's not to say we should simply repeat lessons – ideally, the information should be presented in different ways to allow students to see connections with what has gone before. This observation fits snugly with some of the research on memory we'll look at in the next chapter.

Have you ever noticed that when you reread a book or watch again a favorite film you spot things you don't remember from last time round? Maybe we missed them or maybe we've just forgotten them, and it's not until we view the information again that we fix it in our minds. Possibly we're not just seeing new content; we're also cross-referencing it with everything else we know. Just as the ancient Greek historian Heraclitus observed, we can't step into the same river twice. Every time we encounter a piece of information we're different; we have the capacity to add to schemas in new and interesting ways.

All this begs a couple of important questions. Firstly, what should we do differently as a consequence of Nuthall's research? And, secondly, what might be the threshold concepts of the subject you teach, and how would knowing this help you to teach differently?

The first question is perhaps easier to answer. We need to acknowledge that we just don't know what's happening in classrooms. I realize this sounds like a council of despair but actually it could be liberating. If we accept that 'learning' is far too mysterious to see and confidently check off as having happened, we can at least be reasonably sure that multiple presentations of material are far more likely to result in learning than simply covering content. This prepares the ground nicely for Part 3, in which I will introduce the concept of 'desirable difficulties' and explain what we could do to find order in the chaos.

We also need to be aware of how little we know about the way students learn in groups. In order to monitor what students are learning, we need to assess what they know at the beginning of a teaching sequence and compare this to what they know when they are tested. We've already seen that everyone will start off knowing different things and this will, of course, result in them learning different things. If we're not sure what the starting points were then we'll have no idea how effective our teaching might be. If it's true that much of what students learn comes from their peers, we need to be aware of the culture in our classroom. We will benefit from knowing what they're interested in, what they're good at and who is popular. If we allow opportunities for different students to shine at different times then we will validate all the children we teach. Setting up tasks that require different combinations of skills and knowledge might ensure that there are opportunities for everyone to learn because everyone will get to connect new information to different sets of prior knowledge.

As to the second question, identifying threshold concepts is possibly the easy part. You just need to look at those curriculum areas which cause the most confusion and on which other, more advanced areas depend. More difficult is knowing what to do with this information. My suggestion is that once we've identified this troublesome knowledge we need to make sure that it's these areas of content to which we apply the concept of desirable difficulties, and in particular, the ideas of spacing (Chapter 12) and interleaving (Chapter 13) to the curriculum.

But before we go on to a discussion of the solutions, we need to look more closely at what might happen when we learn. For this we will explore the frankly bizarre workings of human memory.

Notes

1   Graham Nuthall, The Cultural Myths and Realities of Classroom Teaching and Learning: A Personal Journey, *Teachers College Record* 107(5) (2005): 895–934 at 928.
2   Graham Nuthall, *The Hidden Lives of Learners* (Wellington: New Zealand Council for Educational Research Press, 2007), p. 35.

3   Cited in John Hattie, *Visible Learning for Teachers: Maximizing Impact on Learning* (London: Routledge, 2011), p. 131.
4   Nuthall, *The Hidden Lives of Learners*, pp. 80–81.

Chapter 9
The input/output myth

Memory is the cabinet of the imagination, the treasury of reason, the registry of conscience, and the council chamber of thought.

St. Basil

Before we go any further, have a go at remembering the following list: *class, learn, chalk, student, teacher, whiteboard, bell, assembly, corridor, lesson, detention, book, hall*.

We'll see how you did in a page or so.

Why should teachers need to know *anything* about memory? Shouldn't they just get on with teaching and leave remembering to the kids? Well, as the old truism goes, "If they're not learning, you're just talking." If you're minded to accept the definitions and arguments offered in the previous chapters, then you should be ready to agree that memory plays a pretty substantial role because, "If nothing has changed in long-term memory, nothing has been learned."[1]

So, if an important part of teaching is trying to induce changes in students' long-term memories, it strikes me that a working knowledge of some of the theories about how our memories work might be essential if we are to design teaching sequences that actually stick in students' minds. It's certainly true that we tend to remember what's most useful and interesting to us; so at least part of our task should be to deal in information which fulfils these criteria.

There's certainly little point in teaching stuff if our students don't then remember it. Memory is the most important process we must harness if they are to make any progress at all: "Everything in life is memory, save for the thin edge of the present."[2] This is an idea that's been around for thousands of years. If Aristotle was right that we are what we repeatedly do – we are, in a very real sense, our habits – then what else is habit but memory, learned ideas and behaviors?

One of the problems we face is how we think about memory; what happens and what we *think* happens are two dramatically different things. Memory is not a single static edifice; it's both a *selective* and an *interpretive* process. Making a division between 'memory' and, say, 'reasoning' suggests there is some sort of central system which governs all our mental processes. Daniel Dennett says this belief in a mythical 'center' which houses our consciousness causes us to underestimate how much processing must be accomplished by the relatively peripheral systems of the brain.[3]

But maybe you disagree. Maybe you think it's more important for students to understand rather than merely remember. My contention is that these two are inseparable. Our reasoning *is* our memory, and vice versa. Certainly it's impossible to understand something that you cannot remember – you may once have understood it, but what use is that? Can we remember something we don't understand? The obvious answer is, yes, of course we can, don't be so stupid. But think about it for a moment. Plenty of people remember Einstein's formula $E = mc^2$ without having any kind of understanding of relativity.* And I can remember the mnemonic, Richard Of York Gave Battle In Vain, without comprehending how light is diffused through a prism. Isn't this evidence of remembering without understanding? Well, no. If I remember an item of knowledge like a formula or mnemonic then I *understand* what this item is. I *know* it's different from understanding a complex scientific theory. My problem is that I *neither understand nor remember* the theories – I merely know what I don't know. But, if I labored mightily to understand these concepts then I would also remember them, at least for as long as I was able to use my understanding to act appropriately. When the memory fades, so does the understanding.

---

* This is hardly surprising as, I was surprised to find, $E = mc^2$ has nothing whatsoever to do with relativity. It actually describes mass energy equivalence: energy = mass x the speed of light^2 which means that for a little bit of mass you get an awful lot of energy. Hence nuclear power.

Returning to antiquity for a moment, Plato expressed these ideas much more eloquently:

> Now see if it is possible in the same manner to possess knowledge without having it. Suppose a person had caught wild birds, doves or any other sort, and built a dove-cage in his dwelling and fed them. In a certain way we should say he always had them, because he possesses them. ...
>
> In another sense we should say he has none of them, but he has got a power over them, since he has made them subject to him in a domestic enclosure of his own. He can take and hold them when he likes, catching any one he wishes, and he can let it go again. And it is up to him to do this as often as he thinks proper.[4]

Simply having the birds isn't enough, you have to catch them when you need them. Through reasoning and understanding we can learn when and how to catch the birds we need. As Dennett puts it, "Learning to reason is, in effect, learning knowledge retrieval strategies."[5]

Why do memories fade? It turns out that for all practical purposes our brains have a seemingly limitless capacity for storing memories. So why is it that students never remember to use capital letters, and why can't I remember my car registration?

Human beings have been speculating about the vagaries of memory for thousands of years, and as far back as Plato it's been clear that there are at least three separate processes involved in remembering: encoding (acquiring memories), storage (putting them somewhere) and retrieval (finding them when we want them). Each of these processes might have implications for how we teach.

We intuitively feel that remembering Pythagoras' theorem is different from remembering where we left our whiteboard pen, so it seems clear that memory is not a single monolithic edifice but a set of connected processes. Cognitive psychologists tend to agree there are fundamental differences between sensory memory, short-term or working memory and long-term memory. As we've already seen, if nothing changes in long-term memory then nothing has been learned; it is on this area that we will focus.

Firstly, let's look in detail at the three processes of memory, encoding, storage and retrieval. Encoding is getting information in, storage is finding a place to keep it and retrieval is finding it again when we want it. But be wary, although this metaphor might seem to suggest that remembering is a conscious process, it isn't.

One of the most common misconceptions about memory is that we record events in the same way a video camera does and then replay faithful copies of these events whenever we desire. This is appealing but just plain wrong. Our blind spots mean that we fail to see gorillas and motorcycles when they're present; it's not too great a stretch to suggest that we sometimes see things that aren't there. Memories are constructed based on our feelings about what we are experiencing. We then filter these experiences through our own unique set of values, knowledge and previous experience. We remember the peak of these experiences, good or bad, and tend to forget how long they lasted. It's because memories are reconstructed from the most intense of our experiences that two people can witness the same event but end up remembering something quite different.

Let's quickly revisit the list of words I asked you to memorize at the beginning of this chapter. How many can you recall? Did you remember the word 'school'? When these kinds of experiments are conducted, about 40 percent of people remember words that weren't on the list they memorized. 'School' was suggested because all the other words are semantically linked to it. This tells us that much of what we believe to be memories of real experiences and factual data is in fact an illusion. We substitute what we actually heard or saw with what seems likely or what we'd prefer to be true. And, for the most part, we do it entirely unknowingly.[6]

As teachers, this gives us yet another headache. How can we be sure that what we taught is what will be remembered? The short answer is, we cannot. But through bitter experience we will become intimately acquainted with common misconceptions and mistakes. Although there will always be children who throw us surprising new curve balls, the majority of mistakes made become tediously familiar over time. These common encoding errors should be specifically and explicitly addressed rather than tackled ad hoc. The best teachers are expert enough to be able to seemingly predict with uncanny accuracy the likely mistakes their students will make, and this body of pedagogical content knowledge is something all teachers and schools should seek to build.

Let's for a moment assume that what students remember is the same as what we teach. How best do we absorb information? We've already seen that we can't rely on theories such as learning styles, so what should we do? There's little doubt that what we remember has more to do with our emotional investment in what we encounter. It shouldn't be too controversial to suggest that manipulating students' mental state might have a profound effect on what they subsequently remember. So how might we go about this?

One suggestion is to train our memories, just as the ancient Greeks and Romans used to. Science journalist turned memory champion Joshua Foer says that anyone can improve their ability to remember. We often talk about people with great memories as though it were some sort of innate gift, but that's not the case. Anyone can improve their memory. He says, "We remember when we are able to take a piece of information and experience it. We remember when we pay attention. We remember when we are deeply engaged."[7] Most importantly, we remember when we transform new information so that it fits into our interconnected webs of information and makes sense.

He suggests a process called elaborative encoding, which is really just a fancy way of saying that information should be made more meaningful. Consider the Baker/baker paradox. We are much more likely to be able to remember that someone has the job of a baker than we are to remember that their name is Baker. That's because we have all sorts of rich associations with bakers: the smell of fresh bread, flour-dusted aprons and white paper hats. Whereas as the name Baker is essentially meaningless, it doesn't connect to anything else we know. In neurobiological terms, when we learn someone's profession a larger number of synapses are strengthened as we make connections to both 'bread' and 'bakeries'.[8] The ancient technique of memory palace* is a great way to take advantage of our brain's fantastic visual/spatial memories.

Nowadays it is rare indeed for children to be taught anything by rote. Or, to use a less pejorative term, by heart. Essentially, rote learning remains a

---

* Sometimes referred to as the method of the loci, this memory technique is employed by those who enter memory competitions to remember vast amounts of information. Items to be remembered are mentally associated with specific physical locations. The method relies on remembering these spatial relationships to establish, order and recollect unrelated, context-less information.

much maligned and neglected method of teaching. As we saw in Chapter 5, certain ways of thinking about education are so ingrained that they become meta-beliefs; a term like rote learning "becomes understood increasingly literally and separately from the complex of education ideas that originally gave it meaning".[9] We don't even consider whether rote learning might sometimes be an effective tool; we just know, deep in our hearts, that it's an instrument of evil, born in some bleak Gradgrindian hellhole and perpetrated on children in order to crush their eager little spirits. It is clearly anathema to the ideals of progressive education as it is unnatural, unpleasant and laborious.

And, of course, learning things by rote can lead to some humorous mistakes: "Three kinds of blood vessels are arteries, vanes, and caterpillars."[10] Clearly, this student has been made to parrot the different blood vessels but has confused the sounds. In the case of 'vanes' this just results in a spelling error, but 'caterpillars' shows they have little or no understanding of the information they've learned. If they had they would know that blood is unlikely to flow through our bodies inside caterpillars. Obviously, no one sees this as desirable, which has led to the unthinking rejection of learning by heart. In its turn, this has deprived children of "developing those resources that come along with a wide and immediate access to some of the world's greatest poetry and prose".[11]

And just in case you still believe that 'you can just Google it', knowing where to go to find whatever it is you need to know "perpetuates the absurdity that this is the same as knowing something. Knowledge does not exist in books or in computer files. They contain only codes that require a living mind to bring them back to life as knowledge. Knowledge only exists as a function of living tissue."[12]

This well-intentioned but disastrous move away from memorizing the richness of what the world has to offer has impoverished everyone who has fallen under its sway. Learning things by heart is something we do automatically, especially as very young children. It comes naturally whether we're recalling the words to nursery rhymes or reeling off stories word for word before we can read. The key is engagement: "If you're really engaged, memory comes pretty automatically."[13]

Here are some reasons to learn something by heart:

- The challenge of memorizing stuff, whether it's a Shakespeare sonnet or the 7 times table, can be enjoyable.

- We become better at retaining information through the practice of trying to retain it. And what does practice make? Permanent!

- We notice details we would otherwise miss.

- Multiple readings or viewings might help us to better understand the material we're learning.

- Committing something to memory means we'll always have it with us without the need to look it up.

Another much more counter-intuitive way to improve encoding is to explore the Bjorks' theory of 'desirable difficulties'. In brief, the idea is that by making information more difficult to encode we can improve our ability to retrieve it later. This is discussed at length in Chapter 11.

Storage

At one time we believed memory decayed over time; now it would seem our brains have the capacity to store everything we will ever learn. No one really knows precisely how, or even where, memory is stored, but there are a number of interesting theories. The video camera misconception suggests that memories are stored, accurately and intact, as on a DVD. But effectively storing memories is about linking and connecting what we experience in a vast web of interrelated concepts or schemas. This is the aviary within which the captured birds of our knowledge fly. Although we don't like to admit it, unlike an electronic storage device, our memory is not static. Every time we access a memory we reconstruct it differently and color it with the context in which it's recalled. This leads to misremembering the details of experiences and, sometimes, creating memories of events which never actually happened. The term 'storage strength' "is a measure of how interconnected or entrenched information is, how related it is to everything else that's in our memories".[14]

As we've seen, to store memories we must first transfer them from working memory to our long-term store. There's a whole host of experiments conducted on normal, healthy individuals as well as brain-injured patients with memory deficits which make the division between short-term and long-term memory clear. This is also supported by convergent evidence from biological research.

Working memory

Working memory is synonymous with awareness. The act of paying attention, of reading these words or listening to a colleague complain about their class' lack of homework, fills up our working memory. But our working memories are always full, even when we're not focusing on something in particular. We are constantly absorbing and processing sensory data from the world around us. This is like a computer program running in the background – it doesn't require effort on our part and we can't turn it off.

We can store some immediate experiences and a little bit of knowledge, but working memory also allows us to reach back into our long-term memory and pull bits of it into the foreground as needed. We can then process this mix of what we're experiencing and what we previously knew to make decisions and achieve our goals. People with high working memory capacity tend to be good storytellers, they tend to solve and do well in exams, they have good verbal reasoning and they are likely to write well. Clearly a high working memory capacity is a distinct advantage.

In the 1950s, George Miller defined the limits of short-term memory as 7 ± 2 items. This means that most us can retain a seven-digit telephone number without too much effort but anything longer is problematic. But if we're trying to hold on to anything more complex this capacity is severely reduced, and in the hullabaloo of the classroom students will be lucky if they can remember four or five things. If I asked you to remember a sequence of numbers or words, and then gave you a series of tasks that demanded your attention, the likelihood is that you would forget two or three items in the sequence.

Let's give it a go. Memorize this list: *butterfly, suitcase, four, Swindon, triangle, raining, box.*

Now perform the following tasks:

1. Turn the page.

2. Calculate 14 × 9 in your head.

3. Spell out your mother's maiden name backwards.

4. Draw a picture of what you imagine is behind you.

5. Look at the footnote.*

In a classic experiment, grandmasters, expert chess players and novice players were asked to examine chess games in progress and attempt to memorize the positions of the pieces on the board. Unsurprisingly, the grandmasters were a lot better at this than anyone else. Some bright sparks immediately assumed that playing chess must improve your memory! But before anyone got too overexcited, there was another way of considering the grandmasters' apparently superior memories. To test this out, the researchers repeated the experiment but this time they placed the chess pieces completely randomly. This time the grandmasters were no better at remembering the pieces' positions than anyone else. In fact, they were often slightly worse as the randomly distributed positions made no sense and probably made them a little bit cross.

Why might this be? Well, consider the chessboard in Figure 9.1. If you were to look at it for five seconds you ought to be able to memorize the positions of at least seven pieces.

Figure 9.1. The Italian Game

---

* If you've managed to avoid cheating, you will have used a significant portion of your working memory capacity. How many of the items can you remember? If the answer is three or four you can feel pleasantly smug. If it's one or two, don't be too alarmed. This is well within normal parameters. Some people can hang on to as many as ten, but this is rare.

Unless you know quite a lot about chess you're likely to find this task incredibly taxing. But the more you have studied the game, the easier the task becomes. If you know the starting positions for each of the pieces, you will only need to keep track of those that have moved. If you have played chess to competition level, the task is easy. Then you may have recognized this position as the opening of the Italian Game. If so, you only have to remember a single item – the task becomes very simple indeed.

Our problem is that life comes at us thick and fast. In an average school day, children will be bombarded with new information, instructions and distractions. If they are to have any hope of extracting meaning from it, they need to be able to process it. This processing might be in the form of a discussion, a series of questions, a written exercise or some other kind of activity. This onslaught of information and processing leads to cognitive overload which we will discuss further shortly.

But back to working memory. We have to realize that our limited capacity to hold on to information has lots of different impacts on us. We need strategies to successfully negotiate our deficiencies. Some of these are pretty obvious, but here are a few things we could do in the classroom.

We need to think about and process new information immediately and repeatedly. We need to process what's going on the moment it happens, not 10 minutes later, not a week later, at the moment. So we need ask meta-cognitive questions like:

- Do I agree?

- What might I be missing?

- What else do I need to know?

- What assumptions are being made?

- How can I apply this in my life?

Although we do this naturally, the more explicitly we are able to get students to 'think hard' about subject content, the more likely they are to remember it. We also need to repeat this process. We need to practice. So, not only do we need students to think in our lessons, we also need them to go home and continue thinking about what they've learned.

Maybe the most useful kind of homework might in some way force students to continue the conversations we have in lessons.

We also need to think elaboratively. We need to make teaching relevant to students, but we often make the mistake of thinking we have to find out what they like. This leads us to plan lessons themed around *The X Factor* or the World Cup, in the belief that we are in some way making the content more relevant. Instead, we should consider what we have already taught and try to link new information to the webs they're building up in lessons. Where these schemas are insufficiently embedded we can create 'knowledge gaps' by making students curious about what we want them to learn.

I recently read *The Wonders of the Solar System* by Brian Cox. When discussing Saturn's rings he begins by asking, "Have you ever wondered what the rings of Saturn are made of?" I had wondered! And I wanted to know. By the end of the chapter it turned out that they're made of dust. Ice covered dust. My knowledge of Saturn's rings had been woefully inadequate and simply being told the fact that its rings are made of dust might not have been absorbed, but by activating my curiosity it ensured that I wanted to fill the gap in my knowledge. This kind of teaching is akin to digging a pit, filling it with the stuff we want children to learn, covering it with leaves and then beckoning them to follow us.

As well as thinking elaboratively, we should also use the power of imagery and think illustratively. We need to take advantage of our wonderful capacity to think in images. Maybe we should get students to write notes in this way to focus on what their ideas *look like*. As we saw in our discussion on the memory palace, it's much easier to bring to mind a picture and then the associated links will follow.

We can also overcome the limits of our working memories through organization and support. The more structure we provide, the easier it is to transfer across to long-term memory. If we can show how new knowledge links to existing knowledge, we can assist the growth and formation of new schemas. Life provides continual scattergun blasts of new information, but if our teaching is carefully sequenced then students are much more likely to retain it.

Finally, we need to provide appropriate support. We need to acknowledge that everyone starts life as a novice and that novices think in qualitatively different ways to experts. A novice will know very little about a subject and will have correspondingly little to draw from long-term memory to help them think and make new connections. In Chapter 10, we will discuss some potential solutions to this problem.

Cognitive load

Cognitive load is the amount of information we're trying to process in working memory at any one time – it's how hard we're thinking. But as we've seen, working memory is extremely limited – we all have a cognitive limit, the maximum number of pieces of information we can process at one time. If this is the first time you've encountered any of the information in this chapter, your head will probably be starting to hurt. This is due to the cognitive load of trying to pay attention to so many new pieces of information at once. To bypass our cognitive limit we arrange information as interrelated webs of knowledge or schemas. Rather than being a useless store of inert facts, items stored in long-term memory are "sophisticated structures that permit us to perceive, think, and solve problems".[15] These schemas allow us to treat multiple elements (chess pieces) as a single element (the Italian Game). They are the cognitive structures that make up our knowledge base. Schemas are built up and acquired over a lifetime, and, quite literally, the more we know the better able we are to think.

Whenever we give students something to think about in the classroom, they need to process it with working memory. The less we tax working memory, the easier we find it is to store new schemas and add to existing schemas. Once our working memory is full, new information displaces what was previously being stored and we become overloaded.

The power of forgetting

Behavior psychologist B. F. Skinner famously quipped, "Education is what survives when what has been learnt has been forgotten." It's a great line but may conceal an important fact about the way we learn. Most of us believe that as we learn we build up memories and as we forget these

189

memory stashes decay. This is wrong. The godfather of memory research, Hermann Ebbinghaus noted that when we 'lose' information, such as French vocabulary or the process for working out the circumference of a circle, we can relearn this information much faster than if we had not previously learned it. This would seem to suggest that information isn't really forgotten but lurks somewhere beneath conscious awareness as memory engrams.*

The rate at which we forget depends on all sorts of factors including students' prior knowledge and motivation to learn, the contextual cues present at the time of instruction, how long information needs to be retained and, most crucially, the type of material we want students to learn. Some things are 'stickier' than others; we're excellent, for instance, at remembering stories.

Ebbinghaus first conducted his experiments into remembering and forgetting in 1885. He wanted to test the outer limits of memory and so practiced trying to retain lists of nonsense syllables. He found that, on average, we predictably forget about 70 percent of what we study within a few days. As Figure 9.2 shows, the curve of forgetting is initially very steep and then flattens off.**

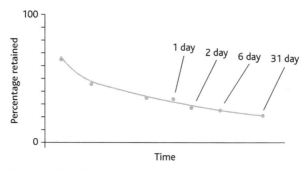

Figure 9.2. Ebbinghaus' forgetting curve

Although it would be foolish to say exactly how much each individual student will remember and forget, what we need to accept is that

....

* An engram is an impression made physically in the neural tissue of the brain by any mental stimulus which helps explain the persistence of memory.

** It's important to remember that the forgetting curve is based on the average score of a group of students (or one student learning and forgetting lots of things). In reality, you might remember each piece of information today and forget it tomorrow. The forgetting curve just shows the average tendency.

forgetting is endemic and predictable – everyone forgets at broadly similar rates over time.

Unlike 19th century psychologists, we're probably not interested in remembering nonsense. Most of what we want students to learn is much more memorable, but even so, the likelihood of getting the correct answer in a test decays steeply at first and then levels off. We do all in our power to prevent students from forgetting what we have taught them. This seems entirely correct and not open to debate: forgetting is clearly the enemy of learning.

Well, according to Robert and Elizabeth Bjork, the way our memories work is a good deal more complex than that. For all practical purposes, our capacity to store new information appears limitless – our brains have sufficient space to comfortably store every experience we're likely to have over our lives. But what's incontrovertible is that sometimes we cannot access or retrieve these memories. In an attempt to explain this, the Bjorks came up with the new theory of disuse.[16] They say that everything we've ever encountered has a retrieval strength (how easily we can recall that thing right now) and a storage strength (how well we know something – the quantity of schema to which an individual item is linked). Retrieval strength correlates with our ability to recall information when we want it, and storage strength is simply how deeply embedded individual items are in schemas. Although retrieval strength completely determines our ability to recall memories, fascinatingly it's storage strength that governs how *quickly* we forget and regain information. There's stuff rattling around in my brain that I *know* I know, I just can't always remember what it is.

Some things, like the phone number we've had for the last 10 years, have extremely high storage and retrieval strengths; we can recall the number whenever we need it because we've had to recall it so many times over such a long period. Other items are well stored but we're not always able to bring them to mind when we want them. To return to Plato's aviary, these are birds that don't come when we whistle.

What about the phone number you had before the one you have now? At one time you were able to bring it to mind with ease, but now you struggle to recall it. Sometimes we *know* we know something – it's on the tip of our tongue – but we can't bring it to mind. You know that feeling you get when watching a film and you're racking your brain to remember that actor's name? It's in there somewhere, but for the life of you it won't come. Then, hours later, you sit bolt upright in bed at 4 a.m.: it was Stewart Granger! No? Just me? If you can't find a thing when you need it, you might just as well not know it. We've all suffered from the frustrating phenomenon of knowing we know something but being unable to dredge it up from the murky recesses of our minds. Just because a memory is stored does not mean we will always be able to access it.

Then there are items with poor storage strength but high retrieval strength. These items might be analogous to birds we've only recently added to our collection. We're very pleased when we first acquire them but then lose them among the flock of more familiar birds. Imagine you've just been given a new phone number – what do you do? If you're like me, you'll repeat it over and over until you've stored it in your phone. We panic at the thought of forgetting the number, but once it's in the phone's memory we can relax. But as we'll see, by focusing our attention on something and attempting to increase its retrieval strength, we might prevent it being stored.

This has important implications for the classroom. Pretty much everything about the way lessons are taught explicitly emphasizes students' current performance. We give them cues and prompts to prevent them in the forgetting answers, but then we're surprised when they've forgotten them next lesson. If we really wanted to remember a new phone number, the best approach might be to allow ourselves to forget it. This sounds pretty stupid, but maybe it's the act of trying to recall that helps store memories.

Weirdly, the higher the retrieval strength of an item of memory – that is, how easy it is for us to recall a piece of information *right now* – the smaller the gains in storage strength from additional study or practice. So, if something is highly accessible, virtually no learning can happen! No matter what you do, there will be no additional increases in storage. But, and this is the exciting part, as we forget and retrieval strength dips, then when we study or practice there's a noticeably larger increase in storage strength. As Bob Bjork puts it, "Forgetting, rather than undoing learning, creates the opportunity to reach additional levels of learning."[17] So, as time passes and we forget some of what we were able to retrieve, any re-presentations of information will result in a boost to learning in the long term. Contrary to our expectations, harnessing the power of forgetting might be the best way to increase the amount we learn.

Teacher and musician Gerald Haigh offers this example:

> Some years ago, after I'd played some ragtime at a piano workshop, the concert pianist running the course encouraged me to learn Scott Joplin's Maple Leaf Rag, which I had always thought out of my reach. Thus encouraged, I learned it as I always do, a bar, or even less, at a time, never going on until the studied section is secure. As a result, at the end, I really did know it. I played it a few times for friends and at a music festival.
>
> Then I left it and moved on to other pieces. Earlier this year, though, I decided to revive Maple Leaf Rag. I got it out and tried it and, perhaps unsurprisingly, it was a struggle. I played it, but with hesitations and wrong notes. Immediately, I stopped. I knew it was no use trying just to correct the details, which would have been a bit like painting and patching the rust on an old car – cover one bit up and you soon discover another so you end up with an unsatisfying ramshackle old car.
>
> So I simply set to and learned the piece over again from the beginning. And do you know, four things happened. None, when you think about it, are particularly surprising:
>
> * The learning was much quicker the second time.
> * I uncovered errors I had consistently missed the first time.
> * I discovered musical subtleties, touches of Joplin genius, which I had also missed the first time.
> * The end result was better than before – more mature, more confident, more musical.[18]

Gerald notes that he's far from the only one to have discovered this:

> The piano forum pianostreet.com has a thread dedicated to this phenomenon. Experiences related there vary, but there's a consistent feeling that a piece comes out better the second time. For example:
>
> "Things not only come back much faster, but to a much higher level. Technical problems you once faced often just melt away, and you can often gain a much better understanding of the 'big picture' of the piece the second time."[19]

So, if all this stuff about progress, learning and memory is true, what effect should it have on the way we teach? First and foremost, we need to be aware of how information is encoded and held in short-term memory before being stored in long-term memory. If students are expected to pay attention to too much at once they will become overloaded and fail to memorize what they need to learn.

Then we need to remember that learning can be consolidated by being given meaning. Narratives are intrinsically memorable in a way that other means of presenting information are not. We should tell students stories in such a way that they can see links and connections with what they already know so that the information sticks.

And, finally, we should keep in mind how memory works and the powerful role played by forgetting. Learning and forgetting occur at about the same rate, and one of the few things we can depend on is that students will forget much of what they appear to learn. But whether they seem to know it or not, most of this 'forgotten' knowledge will still be rattling around in there somewhere. And once something has been forgotten it is much easier to relearn.

Notes

1   Paul Kirschner, John Sweller and Richard Clark, Why Minimal Guidance During Instruction Does Not Work: An Analysis of the Failure of Constructivist, Discovery, Problem-Based, Experiential, and Inquiry-Based Teaching, *Educational Psychologist* 41(2) (2006): 75–86 at 77.
2   Michel Gazzaniga, quoted in Endel Tulving and Fergus Craik (eds), *The Oxford Handbook of Memory* (New York: Oxford University Press, 2005), p. 703.
3   Daniel Dennett, *Consciousness Explained* (London: Penguin, 1993), p. 39.
4   *The Theaetetus of Plato*, tr. Benjamin Hall Kennedy (Cambridge: Cambridge University Press, 1881).
5   Dennett, *Consciousness Explained*, p. 223.
6   Adapted from Henry Roediger III and Kathleen McDermott, Creating False Memories: Remembering Words Not Present in Lists, *Journal of Experimental Psychology: Learning, Memory & Cognition* 21(4) (1995): 803–814.
7   Joshua Foer, Feats of Memory Anyone Can Do, *ted.com* [video] (February 2012). Available at: http://www.ted.com/talks/joshua_foer_feats_of_memory_anyone_can_do?awesm=on.ted.com_Foer&utm_campaign=&utm_medium=on.ted.com-static&utm_source=t.co&utm_content=awesm-publisher.
8   Kathryn McWeeny, Andrew Young, Dennis Hay and Andrew Ellis, Putting Names to Faces, *British Journal of Psychology* 78 (1987): 143–146; Gillian Cohen, Why is it Difficult to Put Names to Faces? *British Journal of Psychology* 81 (1990): 287–297.
9   Kieran Egan, *Getting It Wrong from the Beginning: Our Progressive Inheritance from Herbert Spencer, John Dewey, and Jean Piaget* (New Haven, CT: Yale University Press, 2002), p. 67.
10 Richard Lederer, Student Writing Bloopers, in *Anguished English: An Anthology of Accidental Assaults Upon Our Language* (Charleston, SC: Wyrick, 1987). Available at:

http://blogs.sha613.org/msebersolegrade8/files/2014/10/Student_Writing_Bloopers-119vgxg.pdf.

11 Egan, *Getting It Wrong from the Beginning*, p. 67.

12 Ibid. p. 68.

13 Justin Snider, Rote Memorization: Overrated, or Underrated? *HechingerEd* (11 February 2011). Available at: http://hechingered.org/content/rote-memorization-overrated-or-underrated_3351/.

14 Robert A. Bjork, The Theory of Disuse and the Role of Forgetting in Human Memory [video] (n.d.). Available at: http://gocognitive.net/interviews/theory-disuse-and-role-forgetting-human-memory.

15 John Sweller, Cognitive Load During Problem Solving: Effects on Learning, *Cognitive Science* 12(2) (1988): 257–285 at 260.

16 Elizabeth Bjork and Robert A. Bjork, Intentional Forgetting Can Increase, Not Decrease, Residual Influences of To-Be-Forgotten Information, *Journal of Experimental Psychology: Learning, Memory, and Cognition* 29(4) (2003): 524–531.

17 Bjork, The Theory of Disuse and the Role of Forgetting in Human Memory.

18 Gerald Haigh, Revisiting Lost Learning, *The Learning Spy* (30 November 2014). Available at: http://www.learningspy.co.uk/learning/revisiting-lost-learning-gerald-haigh/.

19 See http://www.pianostreet.com/smf/index.php?topic=47079.0.

Chapter 10

The difference between experts and novices

Thinking is the hardest work there is, which is probably the reason why so few engage in it.

Henry Ford

The ability to think about thinking – or meta-cognition as it's become known – makes a huge difference to our ability to perform well. The problem is that we're shockingly bad at transferring knowledge learned in one context to another without explicit instruction and advice. Daniel Willingham explains that this is because, "The processes of thinking are intertwined with the content of thought."[1] In other words, our ability to think about a thing depends on how much we know about it. The more we know, the better able we are to think.

It seems we are predisposed to examine the 'surface structure' of a problem rather than recognizing that its underlying 'deep structure' is the same as something we already know. I've often lamented that for a 'skills-based' subject like English, students are appallingly bad at transferring the skills learned, say, when analyzing poetry to those needed when analyzing non-fiction texts. In the minds of their teachers it's straightforward, but for some reason students just don't seem to intuit this. One answer, as we all know, is to remind them. Again. And again. But we won't always be there to remind them, so where does this leave us?

Well, we can usefully think in terms of novices and experts. While novices and experts will obviously have different amounts of subject knowledge, they also approach problems completely differently. Novices set about solving a particular problem as soon as it's set. This, inevitably, means concentrating on detail and ignoring structure.

Ignoring the wood for the trees

The novice immediately plunges into the wood and begins looking carefully and intently at the trees. Not many trees can be seen at any one time and it's impossible to see anything in the distance. There's a bewildering amount of detail but few clues as to the relevance of any of it. The light is poor in the novice's wood and none of the potential paths offer any indication of the way out or through. Some turn out not even to be real paths and sense of direction is soon lost. Under such circumstances novices can only plan small stratagems, which will take them a short way, and hope for the best. It's seldom absolutely clear whether any path is really relevant to the ultimate goal. It is often necessary to retrace steps and abandon particular paths. Sometimes it is difficult to tell whether a path has been tried before or not. Inevitably, it's largely a trial and error approach. Novices quickly forget most of the relevant details of a problem and lose the sense of the route taken to reach a solution. As Sweller puts it, "Novices, not possessing appropriate schemas, are not able to recognize and memorize problem configurations and are forced to use general problem-solving strategies such as means-ends analysis when faced with a problem."[2]

While the novice is blundering speculatively about in this dark wood, the expert has remained outside, thinking about problem structure, perhaps even walking away from the wood to some higher ground for a better overview. As experts, we deliberately consider other woods and the general and specific structures of problems they have posed. We review knowledge of woods in general and specifically and think about structure, but also about solution – what do we really want from addressing this particular wood, and is it worth addressing? We may take time for a cup of tea and some peace of mind. We may look up information on the internet which we foresee we might need. We will, in fact, deliberately employ meta-cognition. The expert enters the wood later, but is then able to recognize which trees, or patterns of trees, are meaningful. They might also consider other topographical features, the alignment to the sun, wind direction or the tracks of particular animals. The expert will have understood whether it is worth working in this wood at all and, if so, what to look for, why and where. Experts only look for, and at, particular features and know what they all mean. There will be few surprises in there.[3]

An expert understands the particular problem but also the generalities of this kind of problem. An expert will recognize the probability that this wood is similar to other woods in important respects and the need to consider this deliberately before proceeding swiftly and directly to their goal. Experts are much more likely to learn something that will be of value for next time a similar problem is encountered, particularly if any part of it has been tricky.

Working in that wood as a novice can be oppressive and scary. Novices will have only rather general impressions and will notice and recall very few important details. Worse, little of what they recall will make much sense and almost none of it will be memorable or remembered. At some point when students are 'lost in the woods', teachers will be forced to intervene to minimize the sunk cost of wandering about and not getting anywhere. Ideally, this guidance will come before students begin to practice a new skill, rather than as a result of misconceptions being embedded.

One major difference, therefore, between the novice and the expert is that the former will soon run out of steam and become frustrated, and even perhaps actually averse, while the expert will remain interested, especially if he feels he has been challenged. Novices risk demotivation the more difficulty they encounter; experts become ever more motivated by it. This suggests a positive way of harnessing the sunk cost fallacy: experience of failure makes it easy to give up, but perseverance and the experience of success makes us invest in a course of action.

Explicitly teaching students how to become consciously familiar with the methods they use to learn, how and why they work, and when and how to apply them *could* help them think more like experts, but we need to remember that children are not experts and that the only way they're likely to become experts is by learning facts about the subjects we teach. Remember the discussion of rote learning in the previous chapter? We need to draw a distinction between rote learning and *inflexible knowledge*.

What we ultimately want is for students to have a flexible understanding that can be applied to a wide variety of new situations, but this is unlikely to happen by magic. Inflexibility is a necessary stepping-stone to expertise.

So what's the difference? Think about Meyer and Land's definition of threshold concepts on page 160. I doubt that many of you will have learned this by heart, but if you have you may well be able to recite it without it meaning very much. If this was the first time you've encountered the threshold concept then you may only have grasped what they are at a superficial level. For instance, you may be able to apply your understanding to the following question: which of these descriptions best fits the definition of a threshold concept?

a.   Knowing that poems often contain metaphors.

b.   Knowing how to write a paragraph analyzing the use of metaphors in a poem.

c.   Knowing that metaphors substitute meaning to enable new insights into what is being compared.

Although I'm confident you will have been able to apply what you have learned to this question without difficulty, you may yet feel unable to seek out and define the threshold concepts of the subjects you teach. This is an example of mimicry and inflexible knowledge. Once you have sufficiently mastered this new piece of knowledge it will be firmly embedded within your web of schemas. At this point, you will be equally able to pick holes in my arguments or use the information to better teach your students.

Daniel Willingham suggests that "inflexible knowledge is meaningful, but narrow; it's narrow in that it is tied to the concept's surface structure, and the deep structure of the concept is not easily accessed. 'Deep structure' refers to a principle that transcends specific examples; 'surface structure' refers to the particulars of an example meant to illustrate deep structure."[4]

The obvious solution would be to encourage students to think about content in deeper, more abstract terms, so that they are better able to generalize what they learn to new contexts. Regrettably this doesn't work. Because students have yet to pass through the thresholds that lead to expertise, any attempt to shortcut the process is only likely to lead to mimicry and inflexibility. We can't expect them to see deep structure until they've amassed sufficient expertise in the shallows. They need to learn the concrete before they can generalize to the abstract. We need to get used to recognizing metaphors and exploring what they mean before we can make use of the abstract generalizable contained in the third definition above.

We want our students to have an understanding of the deep structure of a domain of knowledge, but we have to be patient. If we want someone to have an insight, simply telling them what the insight is 'meant to be' robs them of seeing it for themselves. Instead, we can tell them as much about the surface features of a problem as we can and wait for them to join our dots. Mimicry is a necessary waiting room in the chaos of liminal space. Feeling frustrated that children know, say, their times tables, but are unable to do long division, is silly. As they learn more facts, see more examples and get more practice, they will slowly but surely move towards an expert's understanding of the subject.

When it comes to meta-cognition, just being made aware of meta-cognitive techniques might actually be unhelpful. What would help is careful explanation of the troublesome knowledge they need to experience the 'Aha!' moment of emerging from liminality.

This is another of the threshold concepts so essential to an understanding of how children learn. It's counter-intuitive, but once it's grasped, it changes the way in which we think about how to teach.

Independence vs. independent learning

Understanding both what meta-cognition is and why it's useful might be a step towards autonomous and confident competence, rather than the nebulous nonsense that masquerades as 'independent learning'. Up until relatively recently most teachers have accepted that students will only become independent if we make them learn independently. In essence, this usually means independently of the teacher. This is something of a tall tale. We all want children to become independent – to go out into the wide world and without having to rely on us.* If we really want them to flourish, we need to give them free and unfettered access to our expertise.

Every year a well-worn narrative unfolds: university admissions tutors claim undergraduates are unable to learn independently and accuse schools of 'spoon feeding'. Quite rightly, schools point out that they do loads of independent learning and so it must be the fault of universities themselves because of all those tedious unidirectional lectures. And never the two shall meet. I reckon we've made a mistake: doing independent learning can, all too often, result in dependency. If we really want our students to be self-sufficient then we need to teach them in such a way that will result in them actually becoming independent.

For the record, Figure 10.1 shows the teaching sequence I recommend following in order to ensure students become increasingly independent:

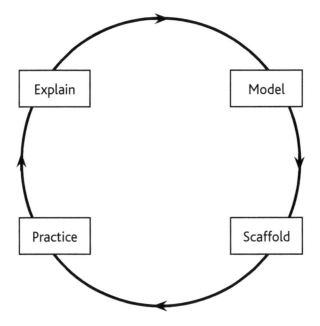

Figure 10.1. The teaching sequence for independence

---

* And even if we don't much care about that, then we at least want them to perform well in their examinations without us having to cheat!

Briefly, we start by explaining the context about which we want students to learn and then building their vocabulary field about the subject. The more they know, the better able they will be to think. Then we deconstruct worked examples and model our thought processes so that students will be able to break down and understand how an expert approaches a task. When students know how to approach a task like an expert, we then need to provide scaffolding that supports them to work at a level beyond their current capability. And then we must give students opportunities to practice what they have learned so that it becomes embedded in long-term memory.*

Learning is more like a marathon than a sprint.** As we've seen, learning depends on changes being made in long-term memory. This tells us we should be less concerned about what's going on in individual lessons and more focused on longer term learning goals: what will students know or be able to do next lesson, next month, next year? To ensure that students make these long-term changes to memory we need to keep in mind Robert Coe's contention that learning is most likely to occur when we have to think hard. Unless we think deeply about a topic we are unlikely to learn much about it. This connects neatly with Willingham's proposition that, "Memory is the residue of thought."[5] What we think about is what we will remember; thinking hard is more likely to result in long-term retention.

So far so good. However, as Daniel Kahneman points out, "Anything that occupies your working memory reduces your ability to think."[6] Even maintaining a walking speed above about four miles per hour will occupy working memory and therefore reduce our ability to think. If someone asks us to think about a complex problem when we are walking we will, most probably, stop in order to give the matter our full attention. Think about what you do when called upon to make a complex maneuver when driving: if we reverse park we often turn down the radio so that we can concentrate better.

This presents us with something of a vicious circle: until we have 'thought hard' about a subject we will be unlikely to have transferred essential

----

* This teaching sequence is discussed at length in *The Secret of Literacy*, pp. 19–60.

** In fact, it's probably more like orienteering.

knowledge from our working memory to long-term memory; but unless we think hard, such transfer is unlikely.

The problem was neatly expressed by Ralph Waldo Emerson when he said, "Every artist was first an amateur." Willingham elaborates: "Whenever you see an expert doing something differently from the way a non-expert does it, it may well be that the expert used to do it the way the novice does it, and that doing so was a necessary step on the way to expertise."[7]

Experts and novices think in qualitatively different ways. The difference between an expert and a novice is that a novice hasn't had time or opportunity to build up the schemas of an expert. Neither have they taken on board the *episteme*,* the underlying game of the expert. Learning requires a change in the schematic structures of long-term memory and is demonstrated by progress from clumsy, error prone, slow and difficult performance to smoother, effortless performance. As we become increasingly familiar with the material we're learning, the cognitive characteristics associated with the material are altered so that it can be handled more efficiently by our working memory. In order to be an expert, first we have to be a novice. The problem with independent learning is that it attempts to shortcut this process by assuming that if we get novices to work on the kinds of problems experts work on then they will think like experts. Sadly this is not the case.

This is why I think teacher instruction and worked examples may be vital. And I'm not alone. Education professor and cognitive scientist Barak Rosenshine includes the following strategies as being both borne out by the evidence from experiments in cognitive science and also confirmed by classroom-based research: provide models, guide student practice, provide scaffolds for difficult tasks, require and monitor independent practice.[8] Further, in their literature review, *What Makes Great Teaching?*, Coe et al. cite pedagogical content knowledge and quality of instruction (which includes modeling, scaffolding and practice) as the two highest-yield teaching strategies.[9]

....

* Plato used *episteme* to mean knowledge, as in 'justified true belief', in contrast to *doxa*, common beliefs or opinion. Epistemology, the study of knowledge, is derived from the same root.

Explaining new concepts clearly provides students with the knowledge they need in order to think. You cannot think about something you know nothing about. You doubt me? Give it a go. If you know nothing about quantum physics, all you can do is repeat the words over and over, or wonder what it might be. You can't actually think about it. On the other hand, the more you know, the more sophisticated your thinking is likely to be. I am able to think deeply about education, but regrettably I am incapable of thinking at more than an insultingly superficial level about the mysteries of the quantum universe.

The more we know on any given subject, the more we'll be able to think about. And the more we're able to think about, the greater our ability to think *with*. For instance, I know enough about grammar to be able to parse a sentence – to break it into its component parts and identify the function of each. I can also use the meta-language of grammar to label these components. I can think about the effects of grammatical structures to consider a writer's intentions and nuances of meaning. This is more than pedantry. Because of the quantity of what I know, I can diagnose, often quite precisely, what it is others might not know. All this has become a very conscious part of the way I use language. When I read, and even more so when I write, I think *with* grammatical knowledge.

Understanding, then, depends on having sufficient knowledge of a subject; the more you know, the greater your capacity for understanding. If I want students to produce anything of worth, I need to give them access to my expert thought processes. I need to 'show' them how I think by talking through an example. If I don't do this and instead rely on, say, three bullet pointed success criteria,* then students will only have a very vague idea of how to go about producing what I want.

It also turns out that we don't learn well from watching experts perform. I used to believe that I could become better at tennis by watching Wimbledon. This wasn't something I arrived at as a fully articulated conclusion, but it seemed somehow reasonable to think that by watching the best tennis players in the world I might get better at tennis. I didn't.

----

*   Success criteria are a checklist of what students need to include in a piece of work for it to be considered successful. If they have had these criteria exemplified, modeled and have had the opportunity to practice using them, then they are useful. If they are merely presented as a means for students to self-assess their work, then they are usually a waste of time.

Frustratingly, it wasn't until I took some lessons and had a coach explain how to stand, how to hold the racket, how to move and, crucially, how to think, that I started to see how to improve. And at that point I also had a vastly improved understanding of what Federer et al. were up to.

The explain and model stages of the teaching sequence can either be *deductive* or *inductive*. With a deductive approach to teaching, the teacher provides the material students need to think about and reduces the quantity of information they are required to hold in working memory. We provide guidance to make up for the knowledge they haven't yet got around to storing in long-term memory, and this allows them to concentrate on thinking rather than on remembering.

If you use an inductive approach, you will show examples of how a concept is used in the hope that students will 'notice' how the concept works. Students come to understand rules and generalizations by noticing what examples have in common. It's worth acknowledging that both deductive and inductive approaches are valuable for teaching concepts, generalizations, processes and skills, depending on the subject matter and the students you're teaching. An inductive approach is less predictable – will students notice the principle you want them to learn? If not, it's much more efficient to just tell them and then focus on understanding the connections.

There's no doubt that a deductive approach is a more efficient way to cover basic content, but there's some compelling research suggesting that students tend to understand and remember more when learning occurs inductively, but only if this is combined with an interleaved approach to studying content.[10] This suggests that students best learn a rule by seeing examples containing the rule mixed up with examples that don't.

Once the basics are understood, the scaffold stage is where students can be asked to think in increasingly challenging circumstances. The scaffolding we provide should allow students to consider things which seem impossible; it should seek to make the impossible possible. And then students are ready to practice by tackling problems of increasing complexity in an effort to move them from competence to mastery. If we're content with mere competence, we're unlikely to get to the point where our understanding of complex concepts can be drawn into working memory as complete chunks whenever needed. The changes that will have taken place in long-term memory must be practiced in order for students to be truly independent.

The first two stages are about freeing up working memory to allow students to think and therefore remember, and the final two stages are to provide support and opportunity to ensure that thinking becomes increasing less dependent on the teacher. As students become more expert, as they start to emerge from the liminal spaces between threshold concepts, they become increasingly able to think hard about a subject and will become increasingly likely to learn more about that subject.

Applying the label of expert only to adults is perhaps problematic. More knowledgeable and experienced students might also be considered experts in particular fields. This being the case, we need to be aware of the *expertise reversal effect*: instructional techniques that reduce working memory load may become counter-productive when applied to students who have developed a degree of expertise. It's sensible to think that the more you know, the less guidance you need. In fact, too much direction is likely to prove a distraction. Students may be prevented from taking advantage of their memorized schemas and working memory might even become overloaded by the additional, and pointless, input: "From this perspective, the expertise reversal effect can be understood as a form of the redundancy effect. It occurs by co-referencing the learners' internal available knowledge structures with redundant, external forms of support."[11]

It may be that as students become knowledgeable with sufficient practice, they begin to think like experts. Clearly, at that stage it would not be desirable for them to continue receiving explanations or working on examples of what they had already mastered.

Can we teach meta-cognition?

We not only need meta-cognition as such, but we also need to *know* that we need it – and we need to be told this. Again and again. We need to be told that there are broad principles and general approaches that structure and color detail, and we need to be told that we must deliberately seek and consider these before we get bogged down in this detail. But no one spontaneously learns that what isn't learned, isn't learned. As Nassim Taleb says, "The problem lies in the structure of our minds: we don't learn rules, just facts, and only facts. Metarules (such as the rule that we have a tendency to not learn rules) we don't seem to be good at getting. We scorn the abstract; we scorn it with passion."[12]

Experts have extensive specialist knowledge but, every bit as importantly, they have also been trained to step back and meta-think rather than plunge straight in. As teachers, we become accomplished at finding the structures of our subjects and isolating the relevant; we learn to tell the difference between general understanding and the deliberate application of general understanding. But we've had to be trained to do this; it is no more 'natural', no more an innate skill for us than it is our students. It doesn't seem so very long ago that I was flailing in the classroom, clueless about what I was supposed to be doing. All is, in other words, not lost.

Teaching meta-cognition, or any other meta-skill, demands the deliberate deployment of two venerable and unfashionable teaching methods: scaffolding and modeling. To model critical awareness when reading texts, students need to see this way of thinking in action. It must be made obvious that the teacher actually uses such meta-cognition in real life, that their set of techniques is genuinely useful. When addressing issues or solving problems, teachers must think aloud to show how they use meta-cognitive techniques. Critical reading would be a perfect opportunity for such modeling. Before and during reading we can actively model the meta-linguistic questions and ideas we keep actively running in our minds. We can provide a commentary of our thinking. We can overtly show that we routinely interrogate texts at the meta-linguistic level and are alert to agenda, immediate purpose and wider ambition.

Scaffolding requires that we make explicit, and go on making explicit, the frameworks of meta-cognition and the deliberate need to build and then invoke them: the need to step backwards; to reach peace of mind; to engender confidence in one's own abilities, experience and common sense and to deploy these; to take a deliberately wide, overall view; to invoke general theory; to consider related issues; to recall similar instances and compare them with present issues; to think generally about situational structure; to critique the present and particular presentation of issues; to consider an author's putative purpose and read in the light of it; and so on. As these are not innate mental habits, and do not transfer well into new situations, the deliberate need to engage in such general, proactive, critical and enquiring thinking about thinking must be made explicit repeatedly.

We seek to produce students able to choose appropriately from among a selection of self-correcting and self-management strategies, and who can take a strategic overview of their performance and attitudes towards their performance. The path to mastery isn't smooth, but it becomes a lot less bumpy when we accept that it's hard and that we're supposed to struggle.

Here are some examples of the students I have taught explicitly using the meta-cognitive techniques they've learned:

- Mnemonics: The student who taught me how to spell rhythm (Rhythm Helps Your Two Hips Move).

- Word roots: The student who has looked up 'revolution' and found, to his interest, 'revolve' and 'revolutionary'.

- Evidence of improvement: The student who turns up with three drafts of a piece of writing which get more focused and better written as they go. There are words written several different ways on the drafts with the wrong spellings crossed out. He has also retained the drafts without embarrassment.

- Seeing from another's point of view – subtext: The student who muses, "What we really need to think about is what the author is up to – where are they coming from?"

- Self-reflection: The student who says, "I wrote it this way because …"

- Curiosity: The student who, until recently, always crouched protectively over his work now pushes his writing over and asks, "Is that how you spell it?"

- Self-monitoring: The student who says, "Slow down sir! I can't take it all in. Can you tell me bit by bit?"

These students are engaged in their own learning, and they see it from outside as well as from inside. They have the tools for tackling new situations and they have the understanding to look for the appropriate tools in their toolbox. They are drivers rather than passengers.

So, can we teach meta-cognition? Yes. *But it is not a subject!* Making students meta-aware should be part and parcel of the process of teaching the content of the curriculum. We need to find effective ways of scaffolding what we want students to learn and modeling the way we want them to apply this learning. If we get this right, we might minimize students' inability to transfer knowledge between domains. Arguably, this is what expert teachers do already; we just need to be more explicit about what we're doing and, crucially, why we're doing it.

Strategies for embedding these ideas about progress, liminality, troublesome knowledge, memory and meta-cognition in teaching will be considered in Part 3.

Notes

1 Daniel Willingham, Critical Thinking: Why Is It So Hard to Teach?, *American Educator* (Summer 2007): 8–18 at 8. Available at: http://www.aft.org/sites/default/files/periodicals/Crit_Thinking.pdf.

2 John Sweller, Cognitive Load During Problem Solving: Effects on Learning, *Cognitive Science* 12(2) (1988): 257–285 at 259.

3 Hugo Kerr, *The Cognitive Psychology of Literacy Teaching: Reading, Writing, Spelling, Dyslexia (& A Bit Besides)* (n.d.). Available at: http://www.hugokerr.info/book.pdf.

4 Daniel Willingham, Inflexible Knowledge: The First Step to Expertise, *American Educator* 26(4) (2002): 31–33 at 32. Available at: http://www.aft.org/periodical/american-educator/winter-2002/ask-cognitive-scientist.

5 Daniel Willingham, *Why Don't Students Like School? A Cognitive Scientist Answers Questions About How the Mind Works and What It Means for the Classroom* (San Francisco, CA: Jossey-Bass, 2009), p. 54.

6 Daniel Kahneman, *Thinking, Fast and Slow* (London: Penguin, 2012), p. 30.

7 Willingham, *Why Don't Students Like School?*, p. 110.

8 Barak Rosenshine, Principles of Instruction: Research-Based Strategies That All Teachers Should Know, *American Educator* 36(1) (Spring 2012): 12–19.

9 Robert Coe, Cesare Aloisi, Steve Higgins and Lee Elliot Major, *What Makes Great Teaching? Review of the Underpinning Research* (London: Sutton Trust, 2014). Available at: http://www.suttontrust.com/wp-content/uploads/2014/10/What-makes-great-teaching-FINAL-4.11.14.pdf, p. 2.

10 Monica S. Birnbaum, Nate Kornell, Elizabeth L. Bjork and Robert A. Bjork, Why Interleaving Enhances Inductive Learning: The Roles of Discrimination and Retrieval, *Memory & Cognition* 41 (2012): 392–402. Available at: http://bjorklab.psych.ucla.edu/pubs/Birnbaum_Kornell_EBjork_RBjork_inpress.pdf.

11 Chee Ha Lee and Slava Kalyuga, Expertise Reversal Effect and its Instructional Implications, in Victor A. Benassi, Catherine E. Overson and Christopher M. Hakala (eds), *Applying Science of Learning in Education: Infusing Psychological Science into*

Part 3
What could we do differently?

Part 3

What could we do differently?

If you have always done it that way, it is probably wrong.

Charles F. Kettering

If you accept that linear progress is an unhelpful myth, and that attempts to make something essentially mysterious and hidden conform to a predictable narrative are foolish at best, then you might be feeling a little concerned about what to do next. In every educational institution some, if not most, of what is done routinely will be wrong. But there's no going back. You've taken the pill and you can't just shut your eyes and pretend everything is the same.

The good news is that this can and should be a liberating experience. It's not that everything you do is wrong, it's often just our reasons for doing it that are questionable.

So, while learning is forever invisible, we can plan for it by designing a curriculum which anticipates the threshold concepts of the subjects we teach and by paying close attention to what science has revealed about how we learn. Despite our clear and obvious differences, this is broadly similar for the vast majority of people: we tend to get stuck in the same places and are subject to the same limitations of memory.

Part 3 details a suite of solutions that have been rigorously tested in laboratory conditions and successfully trialed in real classrooms. Much of the evidence about how best to learn is surprising. Part of the surprise is that our old friend intuition has led us so badly astray. All too often, what we *think* works best is just what *feels* best; as we will see, the reverse is often the case.

Chapter 11
Deliberately difficult

A grindstone that had not grit in it, how long would it take to sharpen an ax? And affairs that had not grit in them, how long would they take to make a man?

Henry Ward Beecher

Everyone wants an easy life. Students want learning to be quick and easy, just as teachers want to find ways to speed up the learning process. Intuitively, we believe the best way to get children to learn is to present information as simply as possible and provide support to help them perform to the best of their ability. But in light of what we know about memory, forgetting and how we learn, this might be an inherently short-term approach to teaching:

> The most fundamental goals of education are long-term goals. As teachers and educators, we want targeted knowledge and skills to be acquired in a way that makes them durable and flexible. More specifically, we want a student's educational experience to produce a mental representation of the knowledge or skill in question that fosters long-term access to that knowledge and the ability to generalize – that is, to draw on that knowledge in situations that may differ on some dimensions from the exact educational context in which that knowledge was acquired.[1]

Who could argue with this? After all, isn't this what teaching is fundamentally about? We might have other aims and consider education to have additional purposes, but if we're not promoting learning and raising achievement, what on earth are we doing? The reason for the confusion is the input/output myth. We labor under the misapprehension that what we teach, students will learn. Regrettably, the truth is a whole lot more complicated than that.

As we've seen, learning and forgetting are inextricably linked. This is bad enough, but on top of that is Nuthall's bewildering discovery that students' learning is mostly unique. In the highly structured world of the classroom, the 'items' learned by no more than one other student range from about 45 percent to just under 90 percent.[2] That is to say, on most occasions the vast majority of our students fail to learn well over half of what we teach. Terrifying! How can we possibly keep track of their progress?

Nuthall suggests that there are three different 'worlds' in operation in a classroom. There is the visible world of the teacher, the murky, mysterious world of students' peers and the rarely glimpsed, private world of the individual students. We get to see our teaching, we get to see the students answering questions and performing tasks designed to demonstrate their progress, but we seldom, if ever, get to see inside students' heads. We literally have *no idea* what's going on in there. And any attempt to claim otherwise is foolishness.

So what do we do? We fall back on the comforting sureties on the input/output myth and convince ourselves that students' performance correlates with their learning. Because we associate fluency and familiarity with learning, we fail to accurately judge what we do and don't know. Although it would be lovely if all the various quick fix, magic bullet solutions out there actually worked, regrettably methods that help us to make progress tend to make learning seem harder rather than easier.

What can be done?

One of the most troubling counter-intuitive discoveries in the field of cognitive psychology is that current performance is a poor indicator of future learning. It seems that the better our performance is at the point we encounter new information, the less likely we are to retain and be able to transfer this information to different fields. Bafflingly, if we want to improve learning we might have to reduce performance by introducing what Professor Robert Bjork calls "desirable difficulties".[3] It turns out that making it more difficult for students to learn means that they actually learn more! Maybe increasing difficulty during the process of encoding might have a positive impact on our ability to retrieve information.

Intuitively, you might believe the best way to master the information in this book would be to reread it, but rereading is one of the least effective ways of learning. What makes it seem effective is that it produces the illusion of knowing; as you reread you become more familiar with the material and believe you know it. But you don't, you just think you do. Psychologists refer to this phenomenon as 'fluency'. We routinely misjudge the depth of what we know. Possibly these misjudgements occur because rereading isn't sufficiently cognitively demanding. If you really want to master material you need to make your life a little more difficult: give yourself tests on each chapter, try to recall the content a week from now and then a month later. Working harder will result in better learning, whereas the easier it is to recall something, the smaller the increase in learning.

If you want to see rapid improvement then by all means give students clear cues about the answers you're looking for, and do a whole load of massed practice. If you watch *that* lesson it looks great! The teacher is happy, students are happy and observers can check away delightedly on their clipboard. But come back and test what the students still know next week, next month, next year and the situation might be a little more bleak.

On the other hand, if you're after sustained improvement then you want to introduce as much variability into your teaching as possible: change rooms, change seating, change displays; remove the comforting and familiar background to lessons; mix up topics. These desirable difficulties will slow down performance but will lead to increased long-term retention and transfer of knowledge between contexts.

And therein lies the problem: everyone prefers the feeling of 'rapid progress'. Even if we're aware of the distinction between learning and performance, the hard fact is that the route to sustained progress feels uncomfortable. We have to delay gratification. We have to take the risk that an observer won't check the 'progress' box on their observation pro forma. We might look bad so we don't do it. However, when we are after long-term learning, current performance is not a reliable index of how effective a lesson has been.

Let's assume that you're willing to take the risk. What should you do? Bjork's research suggests that there are certain difficulties we can introduce that appear to have a desirable effect on our ability to retain and transfer information between contexts. These desirable difficulties include:

- Spacing out material to be learned over planned intervals.

- Interleaving or mixing topics together instead of presenting them in neat termly blocks.

- Testing students' ability to retrieve information instead of simply showing it to them again.

- Giving clues rather than complete solutions so that students have to generate rather than simply repeat answers.

- Introducing variety and unpredictability into classroom environments.

- Reducing and delaying the feedback teachers give to students.*

What all these difficulties have in common is that they encourage a deeper, more complex processing of material than people would normally engage in, which makes information more likely to transfer from working to long-term memory (see Chapter 10).

Making learning easier boosts retrieval strength in the short term and this leads to better performance. This feels good and produces a sense of *cognitive ease*. When something feels comfortable and familiar, it makes us feel good. And when we feel good, we're relaxed, not thinking. Because the deeper processing that encourages the long-term retention is missing, that retrieval strength quickly evaporates. The very weird fact of the matter is that forgetting creates the capacity for learning. If we don't forget, we limit our ability to learn. Therefore, we actually want students to forget some stuff!

Remember, though, learning happens when we think hard, so we need to create conditions which induce *cognitive strain*. Strain is unpleasant

---

* Coe et al., in their 2014 literature review *What Makes Great Teaching?* (p. 17), give special mention to spacing, testing and generation as being of 'high utility' in the classroom, and Dunlosky et al. (2013) single out 'practice testing' and 'distributed practice' (spacing) as being of high utility based on laboratory testing as well as classroom-based research. I should point out that interleaving is only classified as having 'moderate utility', mainly down to a lack of classroom study.

and stressful. We're wary of the unfamiliar and so we concentrate. When we're forced into situations where we have to pay attention and make an effort, we have to think. When learning is difficult, we make more mistakes and, naturally, that leads us to infer that what we're doing must be wrong. In the short-term, difficulties inhibit performance – more mistakes to be made and more apparent forgetting – but it is this forgetting that actually benefits students in the long term. Relearning forgotten material takes less time and effort with each attempt. All of the strategies outlined in Part 3 are predicated on this simple but counter-intuitive premise.

There are two important points that I need to make clear at the outset. The first is that a difficulty is only desirable if it's not *too* difficult. Making classroom instruction so difficult that no one is able to work out what's going on would be an unmitigated disaster. A desirable difficulty is one that makes it harder for us to retrieve what we've stored in memory. Difficulties are only desirable when they induce effortful but *successful* recall of learned material. We're after struggle, not failure.

The second point is a reminder that we should mistrust our intuition. If we seem to be rapidly improving, there's good reason to believe that we're falling victim to the illusion of knowledge. The comforting sense of developing fluency and familiarity will blow us off course because anything of worth is hard to achieve. If we want to be sure we're *really* learning, we need to accept the necessity of stumbling and effortful steps towards a distant but achievable goal. Struggle is a sign not of failure but of progress.

Notes

1   Robert A. Bjork and Marcia C. Linn, Introducing Desirable Difficulties for Educational Applications in Science (2002). Available at: http://iddeas.psych.ucla.edu/IDDEASproposal.pdf, p. 5.
2   Graham Nuthall, *The Hidden Lives of Learners* (Wellington: New Zealand Council for Educational Research Press, 2007), p. 68.
3   Bjork and Linn, Introducing Desirable Difficulties for Educational Applications in Science.

Chapter 12

The spacing effect

Cramming seeks to stamp things in by intense application before the ordeal. But a thing thus learned can form few associations. On the other hand, the same thing recurring on *different days* in different contexts, read, recited, referred to again and again, related to other things and reviewed, gets well-wrought into mental structure.

William James, *Talks to Teachers on Psychology*

Of all the 'desirable difficulties', the spacing effect is perhaps the most straightforward and easiest to accept. The benefits on long-term retention have been demonstrated for all manner of materials and tasks, types of learners and time scales. In fact, Hermann Ebbinghaus was going on about his 'forgetting curve' well over a century ago, and the spacing effect he discovered is one of the most widely accepted effects unearthed by experimental research on learning and memory.* Ebbinghaus discovered that he could learn a list of 12 nonsense syllables by restudying it 68 times but, by spacing repetitions over three days, he could get that down to 38 repetitions – almost half the amount of study time for the same result. The conclusions seem clear: our memories are strengthened if we wait for a while before restudying rather than repeating the exercise straightaway.

In our efforts to cover the curriculum, we jump from topic to topic, ensuring students are familiar with each topic and then moving on. Typically,

....

* Of all the difficulties Bjork suggests, this is the only one analyzed by Hattie in *Visible Learning*. He gives spaced vs. massed learning an effect size of $d = 0.71$, which is high. Of more interest, perhaps, is the finding that spacing increases the students' rate of acquisition by $d = 0.45$ and retention by $d = 0.51$. This is on top of any other effects for strategies like feedback and direct instruction.

though, we will forget a good deal of the information we encounter within a few days of learning it. As we saw in Chapter 9, forgetting is the route to better learning. It might, with sufficient planning, be possible to expect students to remember far more of what we want them to learn.

Ebbinghaus also conducted experiments into how information could be retained for as long as possible. He found that if we allow some forgetting to take place before reviewing the material to be learned, the curve of forgetting starts to flatten off (see Figure 12.1).

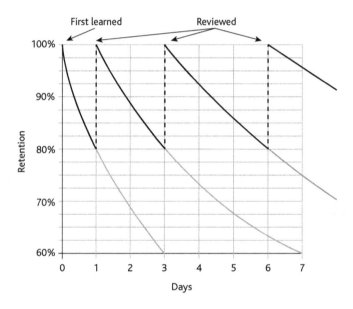

Figure 12.1. The spacing effect

It makes complete sense that if we revisit information at regular intervals we are much more likely to remember it, but the real reason this is so effective is that, as we forget, we are more receptive to learning new information. And, what's more, because new learning (or relearning) depends on what has gone before, the optimal spacing of curriculum content also enhances the transfer of knowledge between contexts and can provide a foundation for subsequent new learning.

So what exactly is the most optimal interval to space out teaching? Is there an ideal moment to practice what you've learned? We know that if we practice too soon, retrieval strength is too high and we waste our time. But if we practice too late we will have forgotten too thoroughly to relearn it. The research on forgetting we looked at in Chapter 9 suggests the best time to practice is just at the moment we're about to forget. Unfortunately, although forgetting follows a predictable pattern, it appears that this moment is different for every person and each bit of information.

In a study designed to establish the optimal spacing required to learn foreign vocabulary, Harry Bahrick spent nine years experimenting with different spacing intervals to see which was the most effective. Struggling to find suitable test subjects willing to commit almost a decade to the project, Bahrick eventually convinced his wife and children (all fellow psychologists) to participate. Together they began the laborious process of learning lists of German vocabulary over differently spaced intervals. They found it wasn't only the number of days between each session that had a major impact on what was retained, but also the number of sessions (this is known as the *repetition effect*). Testing themselves after 14 day, 28 day and 56 day intervals they found, much to their surprise, that the effect was strongest for the 56 day interval.[1]

So, what stops us taking advantage of this powerful effect in schools? One problem is students' perpetual moan that they've 'done this before'. Another more serious obstacle is the effort we would need to put into planning a curriculum to ensure content was spaced in the best way possible. Bahrick found that 13 sessions spaced 56 days apart yielded comparable retention to 26 sessions with a 14 day interval. Neither of these lends itself well to the complexity of the subjects we have to teach.

To accommodate 26 sessions spaced 14 days apart requires 364 days, and you need 728 days for 13 sessions spaced 56 days apart. Neither of these is particularly feasible in a school year of about 160 days. Does this mean we shouldn't bother? No, of course not. What Bahrick's work tells us is that stretching out the space between study sessions is not only possible but desirable. What we need to establish is just how great an interval and how many repetitions we can reasonably squeeze in.

Guess what? There's an app for that! Polish computer scientist Piotr Wozniak invented an algorithm to calculate when forgetting is 'just right'. Wozniak was frustrated in his attempts to become fluent in English by just how long it took to memorize and then practice the newly acquired vocabulary. He identified an inherent contradiction in trying to determine the optimum interval to restudy information. On the one hand, "Intervals should be as long as possible to obtain the minimum frequency of repetitions, and to make the best use of the so-called spacing effect." But on the other hand, "Intervals should be as short as possible that the knowledge is still remembered."[2] His program, SuperMemo (www.supermemo.com), is designed to provide the perfect interval and number of repetitions for users to learn new information at the point of optimum forgetting. Ideally, material to be learned should be reviewed one or two days after initially studying it, then again after a week, a month and so on.

It seems that by allowing ourselves to forget before further study, not only do we filter out competing information but we also get more practice in trying to actively recall what we want to learn. Bahrick suggests this might be because, "With longer spaces, you're forgetting more, but you find out what your weaknesses are and you correct for them. You find out which mediators – which cues, which associations, or hints you used for each word – are working and which aren't. And if they're not working, you come up with new ones."[3]

One question you might have is, what if I want to learn something for a test I'll be taking in six months' or ten days' time? Happily, we now know the optimum spacing intervals to retain information for different time periods (see Table 12.1 based on research by Cepeda et al.[4]).

Table 12.1. Optimal intervals for retaining information

Time to test	Optimum interval between study sessions
1 week	1–2 days
1 month	1 week
2 months	2 weeks
6 months	3 weeks
1 year	4 weeks

If you've got a test next week, wait a day or so before restudying the material you've covered. If the test is in a month, give yourself a week to forget. And if your test is a year hence, you're best off waiting at least a month. The further away the test date, the longer the interval between study sessions.

None of this is especially novel – it's well-known that learning is a recursive process – and teachers know that some looping back is required for students to grasp the trickier bits of the curriculum. Meyer et al. see learning as an excursion or journey which, although it has an intended destination, will not be fixed to a particular route – almost like a road trip where there's a plan to make deviations and explore places of interest as they come along. Particularly interesting or confusing scenes will be revisited. "The eventual destination may be reached, or it may be revised. It may be a surprise. It will certainly be the point of embarkation for further excursion."[5]

This deviation, digression and revisiting can perhaps be anticipated if we take especial care to distribute carefully spaced revisions of the threshold concepts we most need our students to grasp.

Another concern with spacing curriculum content is deciding what you're going to teach while you're waiting for students to forget what they've learned. This is where the concept of interleaving comes in.

Notes

1   Harry P. Bahrick, Lorraine E. Bahrick, Audrey S. Bahrick and Phyllis E. Bahrick, Maintenance of Foreign Language Vocabulary and the Spacing Effect, *Psychological Science* 4(5) (1993): 316–321.

2   Piotr Wozniak, General Principles of SuperMemo (n.d.). Available at: http://www. supermemo.com/english/princip.htm.

3   Interview with Harry Bahrick, quoted in Benedict Carey, *How We Learn: Surprising Truth about When, Where, and Why It Happens* (London: Random House, 2014), p. 75.

4   Nicholas Cepeda, Edward Vul, Doug Rohrer, John Wixted and Harold Pashler, Spacing Effects in Learning: A Temporal Ridgeline of Optimal Retention, *Psychological Science* 19 (2008): 1095–1102.

5   Jan Meyer, Ray Land and Peter Davies, Implications of Threshold Concepts for Course Design and Evaluation, in Jan Meyer and Ray Land (eds), *Overcoming Barriers to Student Understanding: Threshold Concepts and Troublesome Knowledge* (London and New York: Routledge, 2006), pp. 195–206 at p. 202.

Chapter 13
Interleaving

Making mistakes simply means you are learning faster.

Weston H. Agor

How would you go about learning a new skill, memorizing a series of dates or solving an equation? Most of us tend to review the basics, complete a few related practice exercises, reach an acceptable level of proficiency and then move along to the next topic. This approach is known as blocking, or massed practice. Massed practice allows us to focus on learning one topic or skill area at a time. The topic or skill is repeatedly practiced for a period of time and then you move on to another skill and repeat the process. Interleaving practice, on the other hand, involves working on multiple skills in parallel.

If you want to learn 1, 2 and 3 then a blocked practice session would look like this: 111–222–333. An interleaved practice session could be either randomized (132–123–213) or studied in series (123–123–123). How you interleave doesn't seem to be too important; the only constraint is that we should avoid teaching the same topic consecutively. This means that instead of delivering topics in the traditional semester blocks, we instead work out in advance the information we need students to learn over the duration of a course and mix it up so that in any given semester they might study six or seven different topics.

This may appear more straightforward in a 'skills-based' subject like English but may look very daunting for teachers of math or science. If you deliver your course in blocks, students' performance will be much higher at the end of a semester. But if you interleave your curriculum, their learning will probably be much deeper at the end of the course.

Blocking leads to deceptively compelling short-term gains. It 'feels right' to teach this way. But as we've seen, our instincts can be misleading. If our intuition tells us we should block content, we should probably interleave.

Before radically overhauling a curriculum, you probably want some idea of how effective it is to interleave content. There have been numerous studies comparing the effects of interleaving vs. massed practice over the past few decades. One of the most recent studies involved teaching students how to calculate the volumes of four geometric solids: wedge, spheroid, spherical cone and half cone.[1]

Students were split into two groups: an interleaved group and a massed group. The interleaved group were given all four tutorials and then completed 16 practice problems that were mixed so that each set of four problems included one of each type of problem from each tutorial. The massed group were given one tutorial and then four related practice problems (e.g. spheroid tutorial followed by spheroid practice problems) before moving on to the next three solids. Both groups completed two practice sessions and a test, each spaced one week apart. The results confirmed the findings of previous studies. Although the massed group performed 29 percent better than the interleaved group on the practice sessions, when it came to the final test the interleaved group performed 43 percent better than the massed group.

But why is this? What happens in our brains when we mass, or block, as opposed to when we interleave our learning? Maybe it's that studying in blocks provides the 'illusion of knowing' and gives us a false sense of security; we think we're getting better. In contrast, interleaving creates anxiety, the feeling that things are unpredictable and therefore we need to take more care. The exact cognitive mechanism by which interleaving works is a matter of debate, but there are two competing theories: retrieval practice and discriminative contrast.

Retrieval practice hypothesis

In order to practice a skill, the brain needs to access the knowledge it has and bring it into working memory. With block practice this occurs when the first practice problem is started and does not happen again while the remaining problems are worked on. With interleaving practice, the brain needs to bring the appropriate knowledge into working memory for every practice problem. This may cause the pathways for those memories to strengthen and allow for better retention.

Imagine trekking through dense jungle – because there's no path, the going is difficult. But once you've hacked through the undergrowth once, each subsequent journey is easier. Massed practice is like making a single trip, whereas interleaved practice involves travelling back and forth repeatedly. The more times you walk the path, the better the chance you'll be able to find it again later.

Discriminative contrast hypothesis

Another theory is that working on similar skills simultaneously forces the brain to differentiate between the two skills. When you only practice one skill over and over, the brain knows what is coming next and doesn't have to work as hard. With interleaving, the brain is forced to figure out what skill each practice problem calls for. This forces us to focus more intensely and leads to better retention.

Picture your commute to work. If the traffic is clear you can set your cruise control and zone out, but if there's a jam you have to concentrate to avoid bumping the car in front. Massed practice is like using cruise control or satellite navigation; it's possible to disassociate from the act of driving and end up at a destination with no memory of the drive. But in heavy traffic we dare not let our thoughts wander because of the need to continually adjust our speed and direction.

These mechanisms are not mutually exclusive and there may be others at play that haven't yet been discovered.

Tips for interleaving teaching

There's ample evidence for the positive effects of interleaved practice in a variety of domains including learning simple motor skills, recognizing different painters' styles, learning badminton serves, interpreting electrocardiograms and identifying birds. The diversity of knowledge and skills that have been studied, and the strength of the effect that has been seen, makes me optimistic that this technique can be used to learn almost anything if applied correctly.

There's little point asking students to interleave a topic they haven't yet learned about. Clear explanations and modeling are a vital first phase. Depending on the subject you teach, interleaving curriculum content can just be annoying. No one would benefit from interleaving lessons on *Macbeth* with lessons on *Great Expectations* – that would just ruin the narrative. But if we concentrate on ensuring that the threshold concepts which underlie curriculum content are interleaved, then students might 'feel the benefit' as my old granny used to say.

If students are really going to learn tricky new concepts, we need to gradually increase their difficulty to make sure they are having to work hard. It's the working hard that helps us to encode new information in a way which makes it easier to retrieve. Massed practice allows students to get in a groove, which leads to the illusion of knowing. Ideally, revisiting material should feel jarringly unfamiliar – remember, the point is not to improve current performance. Most of the research on interleaving has been on inductive learning. As we saw in Chapter 10, inductive learning is where students are expected to work out rules and principles from seeing different examples of a concept.

Interleaving can be introduced alongside other desirable difficulties. It's essential to make sure you revisit previously learned topics. This also has the happy advantage of leveraging the spacing effect. Also, don't just restudy material – design tests to practice recall of what has been taught. The testing effect is so powerful and important that it's discussed separately in the next chapter.

Let's say we want to maximize our students' performance in their GCSEs and it's now January. Let's assume that breaks down to 15 weeks of teaching with one one-hour lesson per week. What should we do? According to Table 13.1, if we have, say, five topics to study, we should space study intervals about three weeks apart, like so:

Table 13.1. Example of a spaced and interleaved revision timetable

	Topic 1	Topic 2	Topic 3	Topic 4	Topic 5
Week 1	1st interval				
Week 2		1st interval			
Week 3			1st interval		
Week 4	2nd interval			1st interval	
Week 5		2nd interval			1st interval
Week 6			2nd interval		
Week 7	3rd interval			2nd interval	
Week 8		3rd interval			2nd interval
Week 9			3rd interval		
Week 10	4th interval			3rd interval	
Week 11		4th interval			3rd interval
Week 12			4th interval		
Week 13	5th interval			4th interval	
Week 14		5th interval			4th interval
Week 15			5th interval	5th interval	

In the example above, topics 1–3 benefit from having dedicated lessons for the first interval and also get one extra spaced repetition. If one area of the curriculum is given greater weight in the exam or is trickier to retain, then this should further help us decide how to prioritize our time.

Although acing exams is great, I'm really not that interested in students merely passing tests. As I stated in Chapter 4, I'm much more interested in making students cleverer. Spacing and interleaving the presentation of curriculum content results in knowledge being stored better and lasting longer. And the more you remember, the more you know, and the better able you are to think.

This all sounds fabulous, so why don't we do it? Apart from the fact that it takes thinking and planning to implement effectively, the only real argument against interleaving is that students don't like it. Even though laboratory tests and classroom trials have demonstrated that it's clearly a more effective way to learn than massing practice, the fact that performance is lower during instruction fools us into believing that it must be ineffective. Even showing the evidence of improved test results can just lead to a backfire effect, with over 65 percent of students simply discounting the evidence and continuing to do what they've always done.[2] Part of the problem is that by increasing performance during instruction and then massing practice, we encounter the 'illusion of knowing' and that warm, fuzzy feeling of cognitive ease. In order to counter this, any attempt to interleave the curriculum requires us to patiently explain both what we're doing and why.

Notes

1   Doug Rohrer and Kelli Taylor, The Shuffling of Mathematics Problems Improves Learning, *Instructional Science* 35 (2007): 481–498.
2   Monica S. Birnbaum, Nate Kornell, Elizabeth L. Bjork and Robert A. Bjork, Why Interleaving Enhances Inductive Learning: The Roles of Discrimination and Retrieval, *Memory & Cognition* 41 (2012): 392–402. Available at: http://bjorklab.psych.ucla.edu/pubs/Birnbaum_Kornell_EBjork_RBjork_inpress.pdf.

Chapter 14
The testing effect

A curious peculiarity of our memory is that things are impressed better by active than by passive repetition. I mean that in learning (by heart, for example), when we almost know the piece, it pays better to wait and recollect by an effort from within, than to look at the book again. If we recover the words in the former way, we shall probably know them the next time; if in the latter way, we shall very likely need the book once more.

William James, *The Principles of Psychology*

Tests are garbage, right? Like me, you may find yourself baring your teeth at the thought of being drilled to death or inflicting endless rounds of mind numbing tests on your students. That's no way to learn, is it? All that is going to do is produce 'inert knowledge' that will just sit there and be of no use whatsoever, right? Wrong. Apparently, the 'retrieval practice' of testing actually helps us induce "readily accessible information that can be flexibly used to solve new problems".[1]

This doesn't mean that we need more summative assessment. As you know, most tests are conducted in order to produce summative information on how much students have learned, and as such have (possibly rightly) attracted lots of ire. But maybe this is a very narrow way to view the humble test.

As we've already seen, 'the illusion of knowing' fools us into thinking we've learned when we haven't; we think we know more than in fact we do. For instance, you may well have some pretty fixed ideas about testing.

Which of these study patterns is more likely to result in long-term learning?

1. Study study study study – test

2. Study study study test – test

3. Study study test test – test

4. Study test test test – test*

Most of us will pick (1). It just feels right, doesn't it? Spaced repetitions of study are bound to result in better results, right? Wrong. The most successful pattern is in fact (4). Having just one study session, followed by three short testing sessions and then a final assessment will outperform any other pattern. Who knew?

The research suggests that we should be using testing as part of our teaching and learning repertoire. This is something that, quite literally, never occurred to me until reading about the benefits of the testing effect. In order to qualify, testing experiences need to be low risk (i.e. there must be no consequences for failure), frequent and designed to include variation and distracting difficulties, such as providing competing alternative answers to trigger retrieval of information that might be tested at another opportunity. Surprisingly, there doesn't need to be any feedback provided on what you got wrong.

The implications are fascinating. One of the first things we might need to reconsider is what might constitute a test. That is to say, we should move away from the limited definition of testing being merely a pen and paper based exercise conducted under exam conditions. Testing can (and should) include some of the tricks and techniques we've been misusing and misunderstanding as Formative Assessment. In fact, it doesn't really matter how we test students as long as our emphasis changes. Testing should not be used primarily to assess the efficacy of your teaching and students' learning; it should be used as a powerful tool in your pedagogical armory to *help* them learn.

Maybe this is really obvious and everyone else has always understood the fundamental point of classroom assessment, but I don't think so. The point of formative assessment is to find out what students have learned

....

* When I've used this example to demonstrate the counter-intuitive nature of the testing effect, various people have expressed a surprising dislike for the word 'study'. By study I mean the revision of previously studied material.

and to adjust teaching to fill in any gaps. This deficit model means that teachers (and students) might be laboring under some quite fundamental misunderstandings.

The benefits of testing include direct effects on retention and indirect benefits on meta-cognition, teaching and learning.[2] While all are interesting and worth pursuing, here I'm going to discuss how I've tried to use the direct benefits of testing.

Retrieval aids later retention

It appears that studying material once and testing three times leads to about 80 percent improved retention over studying three times and testing once. The research evidence suggests that it doesn't matter whether people are asked to recall individual items or passages of text – testing beats restudying every time. Now, we all know that cramming for a test works. However, these studies show that testing leads to a much increased likelihood that information will be retained over the long term. This implies that if we want our students to learn whatever it is we're trying to teach them then we should test them on it regularly. And by regularly I mean every lesson. What if every lesson began with a test of what students had studied the previous lesson? Far from finding it dull, most students actually seem to enjoy this kind of exercise. If you explain to them what you're up to, and why, they get pretty excited at seeing whether the theory holds water.

Testing appears to be the way forward if we want to make sure students remember (i.e. learn) the stuff we're teaching them. Getting students to summarize what they've learned in a paragraph at the end of each lesson and setting homework designed to test students' recall of lesson content is a start. In an effort to improve students' learning, I've experimented with beginning lessons with multiple choice questions – three related to the previous lesson, one related to the previous semester's study and one on material covered the previous year.

History teacher Harry Fletcher-Wood suggests another interesting way to exploit the testing effect is to get students to master important concepts and memorize essential information. Considering the historical periods they would be studying, he gathered information on famous people, wars, inventions, works of art and literature and organized them into a table with the relevant dates. The table was then turned into a card sort activity – a kind of jigsaw containing pretty much everything students would need to know about their history curriculum.

Then he began each lesson by asking students to complete the card sort. As you'd expect, they struggled and made lots of basic errors. He persisted, and after a few lessons the students became irritated: "We've already done this," they'd cry. "Yes, but you can't do it," came the reply. Before long they actually came to enjoy the challenge of completing the familiar activity in the quickest possible time.

Eventually, after repeated exposures to this low stakes test, students' recall improved significantly, and they began to be able to make links between times and events. While it might be true that facts are useless and dull in isolation, it's essential to realize that no fact ever exists in isolation. Knowing the dates of Queen Victoria's reign isn't just a fact to be 'regurgitated'; it allows us to place anything labeled as 'Victorian' – inventions, works of literature, scientific discoveries – within a precise period of time and to see how events might relate to each other.

Increasing knowledge leads directly to more questions and greater curiosity. As students' knowledge of the historical period they were studying increased, they became better able to think about each of the isolated pieces of knowledge. Students' most interesting questions can come from the seemingly dullest corners of history:

Q. Why did population collapse from Roman times to the Anglo-Saxons?

A. This seems to be due to the decline in trade and changes in social organization.

Q. Why was there another huge fall during the Middle Ages?

A. There you have the catastrophic effect of the Black Death; suddenly, the effect of losing 40 percent of the population hits home.

Q. Why doesn't life expectancy change significantly until the Victorian period?

A. Now the problems with medical technology become apparent.[3]

Testing causes students to learn more from the next study episode

This is also pleasingly referred to as 'test-potentiated learning'. Basically it means that having followed a study test test test (STTT) pattern of lessons, the next STTT pattern will result in *even better* retention: the more tests you do, the better you will be at learning!

This particular field of study belongs to Japanese psychologist Chizuko Izawa, who between 1966 and 1970 investigated the extent to which learning takes place during testing. She examined three hypotheses:

1.   During a test students will neither learn nor forget.

2.   Learning and forgetting *could* occur during a test.

3.   Taking a test might influence the amount of learning during a future study session.

Guess what? Propositions (1) and (3) turn out to be correct. But doesn't this contradict the testing effect? Well, apparently not; the testing effect can be interpreted as a slowing of forgetting *after* the test. And the real kicker is that this potential improvement occurs *whether or not students get any feedback on their tests!*[4]

Testing improves transfer of knowledge to new contexts

This one is the grail! Many educators have whole-heartedly embraced the notion that we shouldn't teach students *what* to think, but instead we should teach them *how* to think. If we can teach students to solve problems, think critically and be creative, what need of old-fashioned school subjects? Unfortunately it turns out that these skills are tied to domain knowledge. If you can analyze a poem, it doesn't mean you can analyze a quadratic equation, even though we apply the word 'analysis' to each activity. Likewise with evaluation, synthesis, explanation and all the other words to be found at the top of Bloom's Taxonomy. The ability to transfer skills across domains might be something of a myth. Often, people who seem able to transfer skills have often memorized schemas across a wide range of subject domains.

But what if testing could improve the transferability of skills and knowledge? What then? Could retrieval practice really help the transferability of knowledge?

Let's start by defining 'transfer'. How about, "applying knowledge learned in one situation to a new situation"? And let's be a little more cautious than the examples given above. Can we teach students how to analyze non-fiction texts and then expect them to be able to analyze poetry? This is a real cause of anxiety of mine because, frustratingly, it's hard. Within a 'skills-based' subject like English we ought to be able to do this. But, year after year, I've found myself stymied by students' damnable inability to see that analyzing in one context is exactly the same as analyzing in another. Rebranding the skill as 'zooming in'* has helped but it's still an uphill struggle; they need constant prodding and reminding.

Ebbinghaus was experimenting the transferability of skills way back in the 1880s; more recently Susan Barnett and Stephen Ceci have proposed a taxonomy for transfer studies which attempts to describe the dimensions against which transfer of a learned skill might be assessed. So could testing make the difference? There have been a number of different studies on the effects of testing on the ability to transfer skills and there is lots of evidence for 'near transfer' (the ability to transfer learning between closely related domains).

It's also been demonstrated that 'far transfer' may be possible.** In this experiment, subjects studied prose passages on various topics (e.g. bats, the respiratory system). Subjects then restudied some of the passages three times and took three tests on other passages. After each question during the repeated tests, subjects were presented with the question and the correct answer for feedback. One week later subjects completed the final transfer test. On the final test, subjects were required to transfer what they had learned during the initial learning session to new

---

*   This idea is fully explained in *The Secret of Literacy*, pp. 100–102.

**   Near transfer is relatively straightforward: most people can transfer the ability to, say, operate one toaster to another without difficulty. Far transfer is the ability to transfer a skill learned in one discipline to another. So, a student who can analyze a poem may not be able to analyze an equation.

inferential questions in different knowledge domains (e.g. from echolocation in bats to similar processes used in sonar on submarines). The results showed that subjects were more likely to correctly answer a transfer question when they had answered the corresponding question during initial testing.[5]

Is this conclusive? Maybe not, but it's compelling. That's not to say that teaching students to analyze poetry will result in better analysis of quadratic equations, but if it helps them transfer between non-fiction and poetry we should be quite pleased.

Testing helps with retrieval of material not tested

Even more surprisingly, testing can facilitate retrieval of material that was *not* tested – yes, you read that correctly. Taking a test will help you to remember even the stuff that wasn't actually tested. This concept of retrieval-induced facilitation sounds almost magical and seems at odds with the concept of retrieval-induced forgetting. But the contradiction only exists in the short term; the more incidences of retesting, and the longer you leave the final test (at least 24 hours), results in clear improvements of material that has not been tested in the STTT pattern of learning.

....

The depth of the questions students are able to ask relies on their knowledge and understanding, as does their ability to make sense of the answers. Testing is an effective way to build students' capacity to recall the facts we most need them to know.

Because testing helps us to identify whether we have learned and understood the information we've been studying, it provides a useful meta-cognitive insight. Simply rereading notes leads to a growing sense of familiarity which we assume means we have learned the material, but when we test ourselves we can clearly see what we don't know. More time testing and less time re-presenting material will lead to improved recall and can make future study even more beneficial. But how much time?

According to a study conducted by Arthur Gates way back in 1917, we should devote between 30–40 percent of our time (less time is needed with older students) to the initial study of a topic and the remaining 60–70 percent to testing.[6] In 1939, Herbert Spitzer went even further, and after conducting a massive study on the effect of testing on over 3,000 children, concluded that the most dramatic results occurred when children were first tested once or twice in the week following their initial study. After studying a text passage just once, these students scored about 50 percent on a test taken two months later. In contrast, waiting two or more weeks before the first test meant that students scored only about 30 percent in the final test.[7] To be most effective, testing needs to be utilized sooner rather than later. Much more recently, Jeffrey Karpicke and Henry Roediger showed not only that the benefits of testing become more apparent over time, but also that these benefits can be applied in real classrooms to the study of meaningful material.[8]

It seems obvious that testing is a desirable difficulty that requires more effort to retrieve items from memory, but there's also speculation that testing takes advantage of our memory's elaborative processes and actually stores tested information anew. Instead of simply strengthening existing storage strength, testing could result in multiple copies being pressed into different mental schema. Each time we attempt to retrieve something, we're actually re-storing it. And the harder the test, the greater the benefit to memory.

If the testing effect is then combined with the potential of spacing and interleaving, the effects might be extraordinary.

Notes

1 Henry L. Roediger III, Adam L. Putnam and Megan A. Smith, Ten Benefits of Testing and their Application to Educational Practice, in Jose P. Mestre and Brian H. Ross (eds), *Psychology of Learning and Motivation*, Vol. 55: *Cognition in Education* (San Diego, CA: Academic Press, 2011), pp. 1–36 at p. 3.

2 Ibid.

3 Adapted from Harry Fletcher-Wood, What I Learned from Learning the Periodic Table and Other Thoughts on Memory and Retention of Historical Knowledge and Understanding, *Improving Teaching* (20 November 2013). Available at: http://improvingteaching.co.uk/2013/11/20/what-i-learned-from-learning-the-periodic-table-and-other-thoughts-on-memory-and-retention-of-historical-knowledge-and-understanding/.

4   Chizuko Izawa, Reinforcement-Test Sequences in Paired-Associate Learning, *Psychological Reports* 18 (1966): 879–919; Chizuko Izawa, Function of Test Trials in Paired-Associate Learning, *Journal of Experimental Psychology* 75 (1968): 194–209; Chizuko Izawa, Optimal Potentiating Effects and Forgetting-Prevention Effects of Tests in Paired-Associate Learning, *Journal of Experimental Psychology* 83 (1970): 340–344.

5   Susan Barnett and Stephen Ceci, When and Where Do We Apply What We Learn? A Taxonomy for Far Transfer, *Psychological Bulletin* 128 (4): 612–637.

6   Arthur I. Gates, *Recitation as a Factor in Memorizing* (New York: The Science Press, 1917).

7   Herbert F. Spitzer, Studies in Retention, *Journal of Educational Psychology* 30(9) (1939): 641–656.

8   Henry L. Roediger III and Jeffrey D. Karpicke, The Power of Testing Memory: Basic Research and Implications for Educational Practice, *Perspectives on Psychological Science* 1(3) (2006): 181–210.

Chapter 15
The generation effect

Nothing comes from nothing (*Ex nihilo nihil fit*).

René Descartes

Another desirable difficulty we can introduce is to get students to 'generate' information instead of just reading it. The act of grappling with an answer or struggling to solve a problem, rather than just noting down the answer or solution, requires more from us and therefore means we are more likely to better store information in long-term memory. We are also more likely to remember information when we have to produce (or generate) some or all of the material ourselves rather than simply seeing the correct answer.

We can make testing even more effective by requiring students to generate short answers to questions rather than merely selecting from multiple choice questions. Writing an essay results in even stronger learning benefits. This sounds a lot less counter-intuitive than some of the other desirable difficulties we've looked at and, in some ways, is far more aligned with a more progressive understanding of effective teaching.

If I wanted you to learn the names of different kinds of fruit, I could ask you to simply read and recall their names or I could give you a prompt, such as "Apple or o_____", and 'orange' would immediately come to mind. This results in retrieval-induced forgetting; when retrieving information from memory, the retrieved memory will be strengthened. However, competing memories will be less accessible afterwards. This implies that remembering doesn't only produce positive effects for the remembered facts or events; it might also lead to forgetting of other, related things in memory. Unsurprisingly, over the short term you would remember those items you had generated much better than those you hadn't.

So why does it work? Psychologists aren't really sure, but one explanation is that the act of trying to retrieve what you know from the murky depths of memory *before* you know what the answer will be strengthens the connections between schemas. The information to be generated is a gap. The effort of trying to fill the gap with freshly learned knowledge provides even more links and connections between what you already knew and what you've just learned. The greater the number and strength of these connections, the more likely you are to remember new stuff.

This is similar to opening knowledge gaps as described on page 188. If you have a tooth extracted, your tongue is incapable of leaving the gap alone. If we're confronted with a gap in what we know, we may either become curious or frustrated, but we're likely to keep worrying at it until we've filled it. There's also evidence to suggest that not only solving a problem but attempting to solve a problem and providing an incorrect solution might be more beneficial than simply being told an answer you already know.[1] But hang on, does this mean we should just let kids work everything out for themselves rather then ever telling them stuff? Intuitively, I'd want to say that you must already *know* the solution; anything else is just guessing. But research into the *pretest effect* suggests guessing might be more beneficial than you might think.

Pretesting

One extraordinary admixture of the generation and testing effects is the pretest. You'd think that being given a test on a topic you'd never previously studied would be a spectacular waste of time. But you'd be wrong. Numerous studies have demonstrated that getting wrong answers alters how we think about the questions we're asked. Even if we answer a multiple choice question wrongly and are then shown the correct answer, we are far more likely to remember that information. Unlikely as it sounds, generating a wrong answer increases our chances of learning the right answer.

This seems surprising. It's been speculated that this benefit must come from students gaining greater fluency due to their exposure to the questions they will be tested on, but apparently not. In one study, researchers sought to assess the effect of pretesting above and beyond just letting students know what will be tested. Before taking a test, students were divided into four groups. One group was given the text on which they would be tested – passages with key facts marked, a second group was given the opportunity to memorize the questions they would be asked, a third group was given an extended study period and a fourth group was given a pretest. Even though they got almost every pretest question wrong, students in the pretesting group outperformed all other groups on a final test, including those students who had been allowed to memorize the test questions. It would seem that the act of unsuccessfully attempting to answer questions has a greater effect on learning than studying the questions on which you are to be tested.[2]

But how does testing work when we've never learned a thing in the first place? Should we encourage students to just guess? Well, yes – it would seem 'just guessing' at the correct answer increases the chances of learning the correct answer at a later date. One study found that as long as you're given appropriate feedback, you'll still see a testing benefit even if you get the answer wrong on a pretest.[3]

A study by psychologists Rosalind Potts and David Shanks found that generating an answer produces better results than just being tested. They divided their subjects into three groups. One group was given the meaning of a new word, the second group was asked to guess at a definition and the third group was given a short list of suggestions from which they had to pick an answer. Each group was tested and given feedback on whether their answers were correct before being given a final test. In all three groups, those students who generated their own answers were consistently the best performers. Surprisingly, picking from among meanings provided by the experimenters provided no advantage over simply reading the definition.[4]

Potts and Shanks suggest that the act of generating our own guess involves us more and thus leads to increased attention. Both reading and choosing from a list require little thought and so fail to strengthen storage in long-term memory. Another explanation is that making mistakes alerts us to our ignorance, whereas reading information fools us into confidently believing we know the answers. Could it be that when we *know* we don't know we're more likely to learn?

....

It's no surprise that many students prefer to be told the answers to questions they should be able to work out on their own. While it's easier for everyone concerned to give in to this preference, we generally accept that it's better for students to do a bit of thinking and attempt to find their own answers.

Some people have decided that research into the generation effect suggests that we should avoid teacher led instruction because children need to generate answers for themselves. I'd argue that careful explanation and modeling is far from the passive process that it is sometimes portrayed as being. If students were merely expected to read and listen, and never to articulate their thoughts through speech or writing, then this might be a reasonable criticism. But when instruction challenges students to generate responses, make guesses and make the process of learning more effortful, then all will be well.

Notes

1   See the sources cited in Peter C. Brown, Henry L. Roediger and Mark A. McDaniel, *Make It Stick: The Science of Successful Learning* (Cambridge, MA: Harvard University Press, 2014), p. 267.
2   Lindsey E. Richland, Nate Kornell and Liche Sean Kao, The Pretesting Effect: Do Unsuccessful Retrieval Attempts Enhance Learning?, *Journal of Experimental Psychology: Applied* 15(3) (2009): 243–257.
3   Nate Kornell, Matthew Jensen Hays and Robert A. Bjork, Unsuccessful Retrieval Attempts Enhance Subsequent Learning, *Journal of Experimental Psychology: Learning, Memory, and Cognition* 35 (2009): 989–998.
4   Rosalind Potts and David R. Shanks, The Benefit of Generating Errors During Learning, *Journal of Experimental Psychology: General* 143(2) (2014): 644–667.

Chapter 16
Variety

All cases are unique, and very similar to others.

T. S. Eliot, *The Cocktail Party*

Schools tend to be organized so as to reduce variety as much as possible. Timetables dictate the same pattern of lessons week in, week out; we teach the same lessons in the same classrooms, which are, in turn, organized in set patterns; and children are assigned seats according to inflexible plans.

This makes complete sense in terms of the most efficient way to run a school. However, when teaching takes place in the same narrow, predictable manner, students' experiences become tied to the context in which they first encountered whatever it is we want them to learn. Fine if you only ever want them to recall that information in your lesson, but if you want them to still know later what they knew at the time you taught them – and if you want them to be able to use whatever you've taught them somewhere other than in your classroom – then this might be a problem.

Variation is perhaps the physical manifestation of interleaving. Not only should we interleave different topics, we should also vary the conditions in which students learn. Even just changing the room in which teaching takes place can enhance recall on a later test. Most advice given to students on how to revise usually suggests that they find a secluded, convenient space to study, but some research suggests that studying the same material in two different rooms, rather than twice in the same room, leads to increased recall of that material.[1]

Instinctively, we believe that preparing students for exams might work best if we made them practice in conditions as similar to the conditions in which they'll end up taking the exam. We give them the same timed conditions, make them familiar with the exam papers they'll get in the real thing and sometimes we even try to get them practicing in the same room they'll eventually take the exam. This might not be the most effective preparation.

In one experiment, children aged from 8 to 12 were tested on their accuracy at throwing beanbags at a target. One group practiced trying to hit the target at the same distance they were to be tested at, while the second group practiced throwing their beanbags at targets at a variety of different ranges. You might expect the group that had practiced throwing at the distance at which they were to be tested to perform better, but you'd be wrong. Initially there was no difference between the two groups, but after a delay the children who had varied their practice by trying to hit targets at different distances were significantly better. The reason for this startling finding isn't clear, but the benefits of trying out different practice routines seems to be clearly preferable to simply doing more of the same.[2]

That would be reasonable if all we wanted was for kids to toss beanbags about, but does this finding tell us anything useful about teaching children to write essays or perform calculations? Well, yes. This has been replicated over many other studies, all of which have demonstrated that when a test after training takes place under novel conditions the benefits of variation during learning are even larger.

Notes

1   Steven M. Smith, Arthur Glenberg and Robert A. Bjork, Environmental Context and Human Memory, *Memory & Cognition* 6(4) (1978): 342–353.
2   Robert Kerr and Bernard Booth, Varied Motor Skill Practice is Beneficial for Beginners, *Perceptual and Motor Skills* 46 (1978): 395–401.

Chapter 17
Reducing feedback

Less is more.

Robert Browning, *Andrea del Sarto*

The idea that giving less feedback is beneficial might come as a bit of a shock. Giving feedback is commonly and widely accepted as the best, brightest and shiniest thing we can be doing as teachers, and the more of it the better. Ever since Professor Hattie published *Visible Learning* in 2008, we have had conclusive proof: according to Hattie's meta-analyses, feedback has the highest effect size of any teacher intervention.[1] QED. And this has led, unsurprisingly, to an avalanche of advice on how to give feedback more efficiently, frequently and effectively. Teachers the world over have rejoiced.*

It seems so obvious that giving students feedback on how they can improve their performance is the right thing to do that for the most part we've grudgingly accepted increasing workloads as the unavoidable price we have to pay to do the best for our students. But is feedback worth the time we devote to it?

One consideration is the finding that teachers confidently state that they give a great deal of feedback to students in lessons, but "when students were asked what feedback they experienced in classrooms, many reported the level as being low to virtually nil".[2] How can we account for this except to assume that one or other group must be lying or mistaken? Well, there might be another interpretation. Teachers may well spend a fair amount of time giving feedback to students in their class, but an

....

* Not.

249

individual student may equally well spend relatively little time receiving feedback. If there's one teacher and, say, 30 students to a class, the teacher might spend 15 minutes giving feedback to students, but each student would only get 30 seconds of individual attention.

Giving lots of feedback may not be having much in the way of impact. But there's a more serious issue to take into account. What if the act of giving feedback simply improves students' performance at the cost of long-term learning? I'm not an especially good driver, but I'm a truly terrible navigator. This used to mean that I would get lost. A lot. When I first moved to Bristol in 2001, I bought an atlas of the city and when driving somewhere new I would have to stop the car periodically to try to align the map to the streets around me. Needless to say, I found this pretty stressful. Luckily, I'm a lot better at recognizing landmarks than I am at reading maps. Slowly, through a process of trial and error, I started to learn how to find my way around. I've got to the point where I know the city pretty well.

Then, a few years ago, I bought a GPS. It was a blessing. For the first time in my life I could set out on a journey confident I would be able to make it to a new destination without getting horribly lost. Following my arrow shaped avatar along the purple path unfolding before me was a joyous and liberating experience. But as you know, GPSes are not perfect. Sometimes they suggest bizarre routes and sometimes they seem to freeze just when you need them most. I hate those moments of uncertainty; that helplessness as I flounder without the feedback I have become so accustomed to. The relief when the arrow pops back is palpable. Even when I make a mistake I'm able to remain calm; the GPS simply reroutes or points me back the way I came. I can safely say that my experience of driving has been revolutionized. GPSes are just about perfect at giving feedback.

But I don't learn any new routes. Why is that?

John Hattie and Helen Timperley say that for feedback to be considered effective it must answer three questions:

- Where am I going? (What are the goals?)

- How am I going? (What progress is being made toward the goal?)

- Where to next? (What activities need to be undertaken to make better progress?)[3]

My GPS answers these questions very effectively; the gap has been reduced, but I still don't learn. The problem is I get *too much* feedback. I know where I am, where I'm going and what I need to do next *all the time*. I never have to struggle. And because I never struggle, I never learn.

Interestingly, Hattie and Yates also see GPSes as a metaphor for feedback. They do, however, point out that a GPS is programmed only to look forward. It forgets past routes and wrong turns, and its suggested routes will be the same for all users heading to the same destination. Different drivers will have different starting points, but routes will converge on a common goal. "Despite the obvious gulf in technologies, we can see the GPS as providing a heuristic analogy as to how students can use teacher-sourced feedback in the classroom context."[4]

My contention is that this is a situation enacted all too often in schools. Our well-intentioned efforts to let students know exactly what they should be doing next might short-circuit learning. The 'gap' between where we are and what we should do next might be important. If someone fills the gap, we don't have to think. And if we don't have to think, we won't learn. Could filling this gap too quickly be counter-productive?

Perhaps we've been a little uncritical on just how best we should be thinking about feedback. Take a look at this sentence from the abstract to Hattie and Timperley's 2007 paper, 'The Power of Feedback': "Feedback is one of the most powerful influences on learning and achievement, but this impact can be either positive or negative."[5]

That's rather startling, isn't it? Although feedback is hugely powerful, its "impact can be either positive or negative". Maybe just giving feedback willy-nilly is something to be avoided; perhaps we need to be a bit more mindful about what we're doing. Dylan Wiliam also reminds us (in Table 17.1) that giving feedback can often backfire and have startlingly unintended consequences.

Table 17.1. Possible responses to feedback

Response type	Feedback indicates performance ...	
	Exceeds goal	**Falls short of goal**
Change behavior	Exert less effort	**Increase effort**
Change goal	**Increase aspiration**	Reduce aspiration
Abandon goal	Decide goal is too easy	Decide goal is too hard
Reject feedback	Feedback is ignored	Feedback is ignored

This table illustrates just how easy it is to get it wrong. How often might our feedback result in students making less effort, aiming lower and abandoning goals? Too often. Clearly, there are cases where no feedback at all might be preferable.

Baldly stating that giving feedback is always desirable misses much of the nuance in Hattie's research. Seven of the studies on feedback analyzed by him actually report effect sizes below his 'hinge point' of 0.4, although the average effect size is 0.79.*

But as Hattie acknowledges, some forms of feedback are more effective than others. Hattie offers us a list of 'feedback effects'. Right at the top is 'cues'. Now, it comes as absolutely no surprise to me that using cues will boost students' performance. How could it not? But as we've already explored at length, increasing performance is not the best route to improve learning. At number 2 is the unhelpfully labeled 'feedback'. How is feedback a feedback effect? All we are told is, "Those studies showing the highest effect sizes involved students receiving information feedback about a task and how to do it more effectively." Hattie and Timperley say

---

* In Chapter 5 we saw that almost every intervention can be said to 'work' at some level, so Hattie came up with the idea of the hinge point to suggest when an intervention was worth exploring and when it should be ignored.

students are most likely to respond positively when feedback is given on correct rather than incorrect responses, and when "goals are specific and challenging but task complexity is low".[6] They also suggest that feedback is best when it doesn't threaten students' self-esteem.

Let's just sum that up. In order to be considered effective, feedback should only provide information on correct responses, only be given on simple tasks and make you feel good. So as long as kids do simple tasks and get all the answers right, feedback will be effective. What's the point of that? Fortunately, Hattie and Timperley propose a somewhat more sophisticated model for effective feedback which takes into account four different levels at which feedback may be received: task level, process level, self-regulation level and self-level. This model has gained some traction in schools and has been widely, if uncritically, adopted. But what does it mean, and does it actually enhance learning (and not just performance)?

Well, here's some of the interesting stuff. While Hattie and Timperley acknowledge that there have been lots of studies that have found problems with the timing of feedback, they say that they're flawed because they don't take the four levels of feedback into account. They point out that immediate feedback "can result in faster rates of acquisition", but this fails to recognize that speeding up rates of acquisition is likely to have a negative impact on long-term retention and transfer. Weirdly, one study found that delaying feedback had a negative effect for 'easy items' but had a whopping effect size of 1.17 for 'difficult items'.[7]

As Hattie sees the job of a teacher as making work as difficult as possible,* this would strongly suggest that delaying feedback might be a concept worth exploring further: "Simply providing more feedback is not the answer, because it is necessary to consider the nature of the feedback, the timing, and how the student 'receives' this feedback (or, better, actively seeks the feedback)."[8] We need to be a lot more critical of being told that anything is 'the answer'. Moreover: "With inefficient learners, it is better for a teacher to provide elaborations through instruction than to provide feedback on poorly understood concepts ... Feedback can only

....

*   In a 2008 interview with Warwick Mansell in the *TES*, Hattie said, "A teacher's job is not to make work easy. It is to make it difficult. If you are not challenged, you do not make mistakes. If you do not make mistakes, feedback is useless."

build on something; it is of little use when there is no initial learning or surface information."[9]

So that's clear. Whatever we do, we need to make our instruction and our teaching as effective as possible before we attempt anything else. This is undoubtedly true, and so we should give thought to how we might best design sequences of effective teaching. Guess what? There's no one answer.

Now, at the risk of disappearing down the rabbit hole of research, it's also worth reading Soderstrom and Bjork's ideas about all this:

> One common assumption has been that providing feedback from an external source (i.e., augmented feedback) during an acquisition phase fosters long-term learning to the extent that feedback is given immediately, accurately, and frequently. However, a number of studies in the motor and verbal domains have challenged this assumption. *Empirical evidence suggests that delaying, reducing, and summarizing feedback can be better for long-term learning than providing immediate, trial-by-trial feedback.* However, the very feedback schedules that facilitate learning can have negligible (or even detrimental) performance effects during the acquisition phase ... *Numerous studies – some of them dating back decades – have shown that frequent and immediate feedback can, contrary to intuition, degrade learning.*[10]

Why is this? Well, apparently, "feedback that is given too immediately and too frequently can lead learners to overly depend on it as an aid during practice, a reliance that is no longer afforded during later assessments of long-term learning when feedback is removed".[11] Or, to put it another way, giving students feedback turns them into crazed feedback junkies, causing them to fall to pieces when they're in a situation (i.e. an exam) where they can't get their fix. If this is true, and feedback is merely a crutch to prop up performance during the 'acquisition phase' of learning, then we could be in real trouble. This doesn't sound quite so counter-intuitive when we think about the GPS problem.

I want to make absolutely clear that this does *not* mean that we should avoid giving students feedback on how they're doing. But it does suggest that judiciously withholding, delaying and reducing feedback can boost long-term retention and lead to sustained learning. The next time you're considering giving a student feedback, maybe it's worth letting them struggle for just a little bit longer. It could be that immediate feedback negates the need for memorization. Just as we outsource our memory of phone numbers and appointments to diaries and gadgets, we might be allowing students to outsource their knowledge of 'what to do next' to their teachers.

How might we build this thinking into grading and feedback policies? If teachers are expected to spend ever increasing hours on grading and giving feedback, what effect will this have on their ability to teach effectively? If feedback can have a negative impact on students who have not acquired sufficient knowledge, or lack confidence in their ability to achieve goals, time would be better spent ensuring they have the requisite knowledge and/or trying to establish viable goals to which they can commit. Who, in my classes, does this apply to?

Feedback is dismissed by students who are not interested in achieving the goal their teacher has set for them. In these cases there may be either no 'gap' to close or students select an alternative goal that may not involve learning anything constructive. Too many students assigned 'aspirational' targets simply dismiss them as unachievable. But school accountability systems designed to show the rigor of progress data rarely acknowledge a capacity to change targets to something more credible in students' eyes and re-engage their sense of a purpose.

Feedback has become the magic bullet *du jour* for determining teacher quality – previously it has been sharing learning objectives, group discussion and multi-part lesson plans. But the burden of grading that is expected of teachers may be unsustainable, and may, in a few years, be replaced by a newer, more fashionable totem. What will have been the opportunity cost?

Getting feedback right

There are perhaps only three reasons that make giving feedback worthwhile:

1. **To provide clarity**: Most mistakes are made because students are unclear on precisely what they should be doing. Providing feedback that points out misconceptions and provides clarification is an essential first step. If we don't get this right all else is for naught.

2. **To get students to increase effort:** This is the hoary old chestnut at the heart of every success. Trying harder makes a big difference. Getting students to understand what they should be doing is hard enough, but motivating them to actually do it is the master skill.

3. **To get students to increase aspiration:** There's certainly some merit in overlearning concepts and practicing to the point that errors are eliminated, but feedback may not be necessary to achieve this. Once a goal has been met or exceeded students need to aim for something more challenging. No challenge means no mistakes, and no mistakes means that feedback is unlikely to be useful.

If we understood which of these purposes we were engaged in, our feedback might be a lot more useful and a lot more likely to produce the results we desire. As always, if we've dealt satisfactorily with the *why*, we are much better placed to think about *how*.

Providing clarity

It ought to go without saying that if students aren't clear about how to improve, they're unlikely to get any better. The chances are that they will embed mistakes through repeated practice and end up getting good at doing it wrong. This is not to be encouraged. It should be reasonably obvious to us when a student has misunderstood something and when they have made a mistake due to carelessness or lack or effort. We face a dilemma: we know if we just point out some of the mistakes students have made that we allow them to embed bad practice, but if we point out every mistake we overload students' ability to learn.

So here's my tentative solution. If we insist that students annotate every piece of work with the mistakes they are able to spot, our clarification can then be applied with pinpoint accuracy to the exact spot they have identified as where they are ready to learn. They will receive feedback only on those areas they've identified as containing errors or misunderstandings.

We all know that students' self-assessment is often garbage, so let's prevent them from writing meaningless descriptive comments about how they *feel* about their work and instead let's make them proofread, error check and highlight the areas where they are uncertain or where they might have taken a risk. This approach makes students meta-cognitively engage with their work and think in a more meaningful way about what they've produced.

I realize there is a weakness here: what about those errors which students make unknowingly or in the belief that they are right? These are errors which they may be unable to spot and therefore are errors that they will continue to make. What do we do about this? Again, we're faced with a choice: we can either tell them what to do or we can probe their misunderstanding by asking questions. I don't believe there's a right answer on this one; I think it's up to you as a teacher to use your professional judgement to decide whether it will have more impact to tell or question. But it's worth knowing that there are consequences for every choice.

If we choose to tell students the answer then they may not value it. It may be that they fail to remember the answer as they haven't had to think about it. But, equally, it could be that they will both remember and value the answer; the outcome is uncertain. If we choose to ask a question to probe a student's understanding, we run the risk that they won't arrive at a correct answer and their misconceptions will be embedded. There's also the problem that it takes time to think about something new and students may decide to ignore the question. However, if they do decide to answer the question, and they have the necessary knowledge to think meaningfully about it, then they are perhaps more likely to both remember and understand the correct information.

The preceding ideas have been condensed into Figure 17.1:

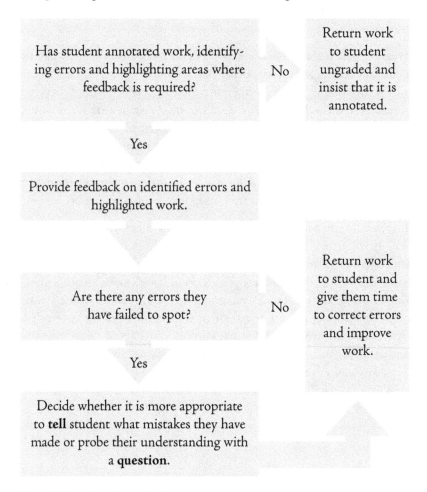

Figure 17.1. Feedback for clarification

Increasing effort

Once we are reasonably sure that students understand how to improve, our next step is to check that they can actually be bothered. It's become something of a cliché to say that success depends on hard work, but essentially that's the message we need to convey. Tragically, far too many students would rather be seen as lazy than stupid. It's much more preferable not to try because then you have an excuse for failure: "Of course I could've done it, but I couldn't be bothered." Why is this considered so much more socially acceptable? Well, that's actually fairly straightforward. Most people see effort as something that is transient but intelligence as something that is fixed. It seems obvious that if we believe we can't get clever then it might not make much sense to try.

But we know that's not true, don't we? We readily accept that training improves sporting performance and that music and drama improve with rehearsal. Why is it that so many of us are so convinced that practice won't make us smarter?

Firstly, we need to consider why students expend effort and how they perceive success.[12] The main reason students decide to invest effort are:

1. To do better than others.

2. To avoid doing worse than others.

3. Their intrinsic interest in the task.

4. To improve their performance.

If your main motivation is to look good (reasons 1 and 2) then it follows that you will only invest effort if your chances of success are high. If it looks like you might fail, not trying is a rational response. If your motivation is based on how absorbed you are in a particular task (reason 3) then it's likely you'll carry on trying for as long as your interest continues. This is far better than a desire to look good but it is still fragile. What if you found the task boring? Would you continue to try? The difficulty here for teachers is that feedback is only likely to be effective when students are interested in the task. What we want is for students to improve even when the task doesn't immediately interest them. In fact, any feedback will probably be irrelevant as students will be sufficiently engaged to make their own trial and error improvements, just as they do in activities like skateboarding or mastering computer games. The fourth reason is the one we should seek to develop. How can we give feedback which harnesses students' desire to improve their performance?

Students tend to attribute their performance to:

1. Their ability.

2. The performance of others.

3. Their intrinsic interest in the task.

4. How hard they tried.

5. Their experience from previous learning.

When students believe their success (or failure) is due to their ability (or lack of it) then it's hard to offer constructive feedback. All they want to hear is 'well done'. Any criticism is perceived as a lack of appreciation of their ability. If feedback undermines their belief in their ability, this may have a catastrophic impact on any impact they will make. Likewise, if they see their success as being due to the underperformance of others, there's little positive likely to come from asking them to try harder. Why should they? If students see their performance as a consequence of the interest they have in a task then feedback is not going to make much difference – they're either interested enough to try harder or they're not. What we want is for students to see their success as being directly caused by their effort. The trick then is to design feedback that is focused on convincing students that they need to improve their performance, and that this can be achieved through hard work.

What would seem clear from this is that if our feedback is to have any impact on learning it must be directed at the task rather than at the students themselves. Kluger and DeNisi suggest that future research should focus less on the impact feedback has on performance and more on the sorts of responses triggered in students when they're given feedback.[13] And, as luck would have it, Carol Dweck has spent her career doing exactly that.

When we think about success and failure we find it almost impossible to avoid the fundamental attribution error. The way we perceive success or failure is dependent on three factors:

1. **Personalization:** The extent to which we believe success is influenced by internal or external factors. An *internalized* factor might be that we believe we produced a good piece of work whereas an *externalized* factor might be our belief that the teacher likes us.

2. **Stability:** Whether success is perceived to be transient or long lasting. A *stable* attribution would be the belief that we're good or bad at a particular subject. An *unstable* attribution would be our

understanding that we were lucky or that we prepared well for a test.

3. **Specificity:** Whether success in one area is interpreted as being likely to lead to success in other areas. A *specific* attribution is that success or failure in one area has nothing to do with how we will perform in other areas. *Global* attributions would lead us to conclude that being bad at one thing would mean we were bad at everything.

Clearly, students will be more likely to act positively on feedback if they attribute success or failure to internal, unstable and specific factors. If they believe their performance is due to external, stable or global factors, then it would be logical to conclude that nothing can be done. If our purpose for giving feedback is to prompt students into making greater effort then we need to do the following:

*   Target feedback to increase task commitment.

*   Design feedback that will be attributed to internal factors that students can control.

*   Design feedback that makes students consider unstable factors that are dependent on effort.

*   Make feedback as specific as possible (bit obvious this one!).

The point of all this, as Wiliam concludes, is for students to believe that "It's up to me" (internal) and "I can do something about it" (stable).[14]

All this advice is summarized in Figure 17.2:

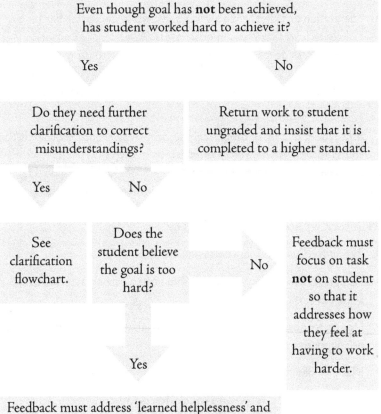

Figure 17.2. Feedback to increase effort

Increasing aspiration

Many high achieving students will be naturally hungry and will want to take every opportunity to improve even further, but some won't. What do we do about those students who meet our expectations but are satisfied with doing just enough to get by?

There are two issues to deal with here:

1. How can we formulate feedback that has the effect of raising aspiration?

2. What do we do about those students who, when they meet or exceed expectations, decide they don't need to exert as much effort, or that the goal they've met is too easy?

On the first question, the Education Endowment Foundation reports that "On average, interventions which aim to raise aspirations appear to have little to no positive impact on educational attainment."[15] This is bad news. They suggest there is evidence that most students do actually have pretty high aspirations, which implies that a lot of underachievement stems from a gap between aspirations and the knowledge and skills needed to achieve them.

More worryingly, there's little evidence that targeted interventions have met with any consistent success in raising students' aspirations. Even where low aspirations might have been successfully raised, it is not clear that any improvement in learning necessarily follows.

The message seems to be that we are better off spending our time on increasing attainment rather than worrying ourselves about imponderables such as aspiration. So, is trying to design feedback aimed at raising aspirations doomed to fail? And if it is, what do we do with those students who are making the grade? Do we just leave them to it? As Table 17.1 indicates, the effects of feedback are far from certain. If students believe they have met or exceeded a goal, ideally they will decide to aim higher and adopt a more demanding goal. Unfortunately, feedback is just as likely to have a negative impact. It may be taken as a signal to ease off and exert less effort, or, if success seems to come too easily, students may decide the goal itself is beneath them and abandon it.

If we're not careful, *any* feedback we give may well have a detrimental effect. There's no point in giving feedback that fails to raise students' aspirations. To do that we need to make sure students are making mistakes. If they're not, how can they improve? Lessons should be sufficiently challenging that making mistakes is inevitable; if it isn't then it's unlikely that students will be learning much. If lessons are too easy, it's the teacher's fault. And if it's our fault, the solution is to consider how to design tasks that don't place a ceiling on achievement.

An uncontrolled study

I was fortunate to be involved in an extremely unscientific project which looked at how we add value to high attaining students. A group of 10th grade students who were achieving A* grades across a range of subjects were put forward and, following a conversation, we realized that almost all of them felt that their success was *despite* not *because of* their teachers' efforts. One said, "I've never had any feedback which helped me improve." Maybe this is understandable: busy teachers who are being held account-able for the progress of their students are not going to prioritize those who are already achieving at the top of the scale. But surely someone has to?

We explained to the students that we were going to give them a series of challenges designed to get them to make mistakes so that we could give them meaningful feedback on how to improve their performance.

Firstly, we tried getting them to complete tasks in a limited time: if we deemed that a task should take 30 minutes to complete, we gave them 20 minutes to finish it. The thinking was that one condition for mastery is that tasks can be completed more automatically. Also, by rushing they would be more likely to make mistakes. This had some success.

Next, we gave the students tasks in which they had to meet certain demanding conditions and criteria for success. These were difficult to set up and always felt somewhat arbitrary in nature. For instance, in a writing task, we made it a condition that students could not use any word that contained the letter e. This kind of constraint led to some very interesting responses but, ultimately, the feedback we were able to give felt superficial and was deemed unlikely to result in improvement once the conditions were removed.

Finally, we decided that we would try grading work using A level rubrics. This had a galvanizing effect. Suddenly, students who were used to receiving A* grades as a matter of routine were getting Bs and Cs. The feedback we were able to give was of immediate benefit and had a lasting impact. When interviewed subsequently, one student said, "For the first time I can remember, [the teacher's] grading was useful – I had a clear idea of how I could get better."

Now, this is of course highly anecdotal and not worth a hill of beans in terms of academic research: there were no controls and our findings cannot claim to be in any way reliable or valid. But they're interesting. Perhaps the most powerful aspect for the students who took part was the novelty of teachers being interested in exploring how to add value to them.

Designing assessments that allow students to aspire beyond the limits is no mean feat. It should go without saying that it's unhelpful to place artificial glass ceilings on what students might achieve. The notion of 'performances of understanding' suggests a potentially useful model.

Israeli academic Yoram Harpaz suggests that students are asked to demonstrate understanding in ways which inevitably limit how they are able to perform. His three levels of performance are:

1. To present knowledge.

2. To operate on and with knowledge.

3. To criticize and create knowledge.

The first level requires students to explain and express ideas in their own words; the second moves into analysis, synthesis and generalizations; and the third asks students to look for contradictions, ask difficult questions and expose assumptions.[16]

Although these performances are not intended to be seen as hierarchical, it's possible to trace potential progression both within each category of performance and across the categories. Interestingly, most assessments tend to be capped at some point with the 'operate on and with' category. Very few assessments are interested in exploring students' ability to 'criticize and create knowledge'. As ever, we teach what we assess, and if it's not assessed, it's not valued. How much scope would the dialectic process of questioning, exposing assumptions and formulating counter-knowledge give to students stuck at the top of the assessment tree? How much more productive might our feedback be if it were to encourage student to criticize what they have been taught?

Figure 17.3. captures this advice:

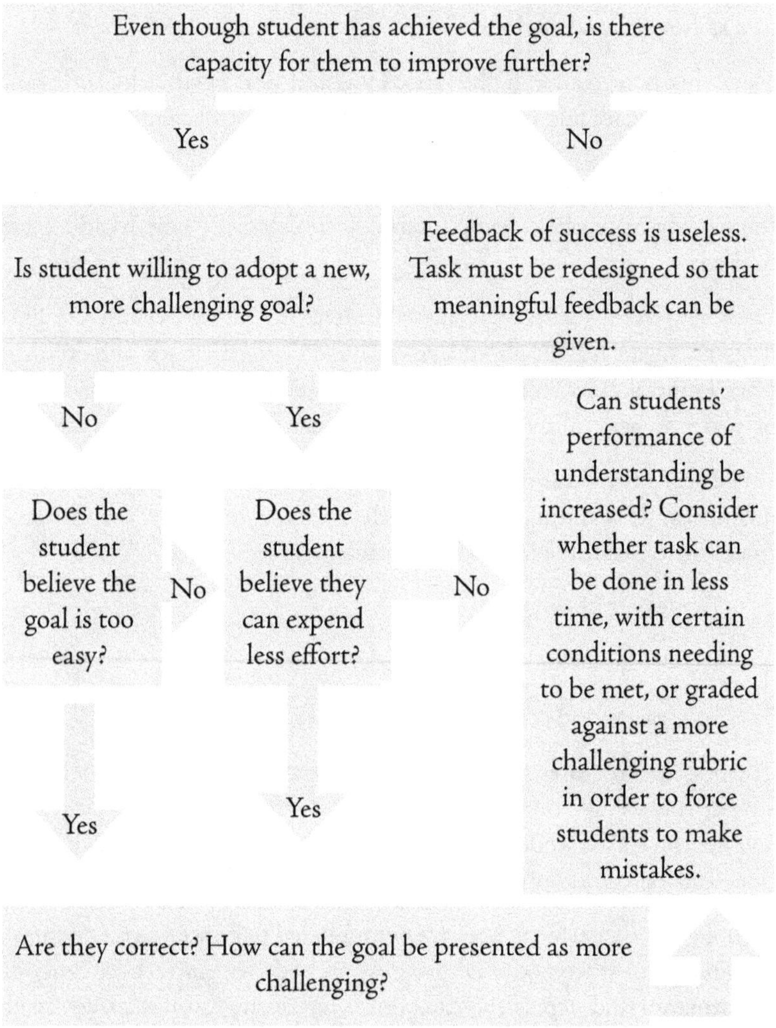

Even though student has achieved the goal, is there capacity for them to improve further?

Yes   No

Is student willing to adopt a new, more challenging goal?

Feedback of success is useless. Task must be redesigned so that meaningful feedback can be given.

No   Yes

Does the student believe the goal is too easy?   No   Does the student believe they can expend less effort?   No

Can students' performance of understanding be increased? Consider whether task can be done in less time, with certain conditions needing to be met, or graded against a more challenging rubric in order to force students to make mistakes.

Yes   Yes

Are they correct? How can the goal be presented as more challenging?

Figure 17.3. Feedback to increase aspiration

....

In response to my thoughts on why and how we might give feedback, Dylan Wiliam added the following advice:

> Sometimes, what a student needs is a (metaphorical) kick up the back-side: "You haven't put any effort into doing this work, so I'm not going

to put any effort into grading it." Sometimes the support we give to students may be emotional rather than technical – getting them to believe they can do something they themselves don't believe they can.

That's why I don't think that feedback should be descriptive. I think it should be productive – the only interesting thing that feedback does is what it does to the learner, and specifically whether it prompts them to do what we want them to do (raise aspiration, or increase effort, according to the situation), which is why I suggest that feedback should, in general, be more work for the recipient than the donor. Another thing to remember is that much feedback is one-to-one tuition (I don't know of a single teacher that can grade two books at the same time) and much of the time the student isn't even listening. So if it's worth our while as teachers giving students written feedback, it is worth taking lesson time to get them to respond to it. So, as a general rule, I advise teachers not to give feedback unless the first 10 to 15 minutes of the next lesson is allocated to students responding to the feedback.

Moreover, a great deal of grading feedback seems to me to be done more for proving that the student's work is being graded than improving learning. Teachers tell me that they have to be able to convince administrators they are doing their grading, but there are other ways to do this. I have seen many elementary school teachers give feedback to their students orally, but then require their students to go back to their seats and make notes about the discussion which (a) develops literacy skills; (b) creates a mnemonic for the student about the substance of the exchange; and (c) proves the teacher has been doing their job. I have seen one pre-kindergarten teacher give oral feedback to students and then get the students to go to the video pod to record their immediate reactions to the feedback which the student or the parent can access at a later date. *There are much more effective ways of structuring feedback interventions than just grading students' work.*[17]

....

So, that's it. Getting feedback right is a difficult business, but I hope that some of the questions I've raised and the issues I've discussed are useful in helping you to think more about both 'why' and 'how' you're providing feedback. I'm afraid, though, that the 'what' is up to you.

Notes

1 John Hattie, *Visible Learning: A Synthesis of Over 800 Meta-Analyses Relating to Achievement* (Abingdon: Routledge, 2008).

2 John Hattie and Gregory Yates, Using Feedback to Promote Learning, in Victor A. Benassi, Catherine E. Overson and Christopher M. Hakala (eds), *Applying Science of Learning in Education: Infusing Psychological Science into the Curriculum* (Washington, DC: American Psychological Association, 2014), pp. 45–58 at p. 46.

3 John Hattie and Helen Timperley, The Power of Feedback, *Review of Educational Research* 77(1) (2007): 81–112 at 86.

4 Hattie and Yates, Using Feedback to Promote Learning, p. 49.

5 Hattie and Timperley, The Power of Feedback, 81.

6 Ibid. 85–86.

7 Ibid. 98.

8 Ibid. 101.

9 Ibid. 104.

10 Nicholas C. Soderstrom and Robert A. Bjork, Learning versus Performance, in Dana Dunn (ed.), *Oxford Bibliographies Online: Psychology* (New York: Oxford University Press, 2013). Available at: http://bjorklab.psych.ucla.edu/pubs/Soderstrom_Bjork_Learning_versus_Performance.pdf, p. 23 (my emphasis).

11 Ibid.

12 Ruth Butler, Task-Involving and Ego-Involving Properties of Evaluation: Effects of Different Feedback Conditions on Motivational Perceptions, Interest, and Performance, *Journal of Educational Psychology* 79(4) (1987): 474–482.

13 Avraham Kluger and Angelo DeNisi, The Effects of Feedback Interventions on Performance: A Historical Review, a Meta-Analysis, and a Preliminary Feedback Intervention Theory, *Psychological Bulletin* 119(2) (1996): 254–284. Available at: http://mario.gsia.cmu.edu/micro_2007/readings/feedback_effects_meta_analysis.pdf.

14 Dylan Wiliam, *Embedded Formative Assessment* (Bloomington, IN: Solution Tree Press, 2011), p. 119.

15 See http://educationendowmentfoundation.org.uk/toolkit/toolkit-a-z/aspiration/.

16 Yoram Harpaz, Teaching and Learning in a Community of Thinking: Theory and Practice (n.d.). Available at: http://yoramharpaz.com/presentations/teaching-andlearning-in-cot-en.pdf.

17 Dylan Wiliam, comment on my blog post, Getting Feedback Right, *The Learning Spy* (10 April 2014). Available at: http://www.learningspy.co.uk/featured/gettingfeedback-right/#comment-5452 (my emphasis).

Chapter 18
Easy vs. hard

We do these things not because they are easy, but because they are hard.

John F. Kennedy

If you've been paying attention so far you may have noticed a potential problem with making learning harder. If we accept the need to minimize cognitive load then introducing desirable difficulties at the point of acquisition appears incongruous.

This returns us to some of the concepts we explored in Part 2:

- Working memory is severely limited.

- Experts and novices think differently.

- We rely on memorized schemas to solve complex problems.

According to Daniel Willingham, one of the reasons students struggle with school is that we make them think too much, and thinking is hard. Experts get around the restrictions of limited working memories by retrieving whole schemas (connected webs of information) from long-term memory. Because novices don't have these memorized schemas to rely on, they're forced to pay attention to too many separate pieces of information at the same time, and this often leads to cognitive overload.*

....

* This is the point of memorizing basic foundational knowledge such as number bonds: unless students have memorized 3 + 7 = 10, they'll have to calculate it anew each time they encounter a problem containing these numbers.

As we discussed in Chapter 10, not only do experts know more but they also think differently. Novices concentrate on the detail of a problem and ignore its structure. The neural architecture of an expert appears different from that of a novice. So, when we ask novices to approach problems like experts, their lack of deep knowledge prevents them from thinking meta-cognitively.

This would appear to be a clear-cut case for making learning easier. Annie Murphy Paul attempts to force these colliding perspectives together with the recommendation that we do both.[1] But is this a helpful dichotomy? As we've seen, polarity can be a useful thinking tool. Instinctively, I want to see this as a situation where you can't just do a bit of both. Paul suggests we reduce cognitive load at the point of instruction and only introduce difficulties once new concepts have been mastered; first we make learning easy, and then we make it hard. But is that actually possible? If it's the struggle that is the path to mastery, is it really sensible to wait for the learning to happen *before* introducing desirable difficulties?

In terms of memory, most teaching is about improving retrieval strength. We provide cues and contexts that make it easier for students to retrieve information during instruction. But if instead we're interested in improving storage strength we need to think differently. If we create the conditions that best allow learning to occur and recognize that 'struggle' is an essential part of coping with liminality, then we might be better placed to guide students through the troublesome thresholds of the curriculum.

We acquire information through explicit explanation and modeling. I don't see much benefit to giving students garbled information. (Although, according to one study, charisma and quality of exposition may have very little bearing on how well information is retained, so I could be wrong.[2]) The trouble is that, left to our own devices, we're likely to forget about 70 percent of everything we've learned (see Chapter 9).

Once new information has been encountered we need to make it stick. The least useful thing to do is to teach or review what's just been taught: if we want it to be retained we're better off using testing, generation, spaced retrieval practice and interleaving different topics. This is deeply counter-intuitive because it feels hard. If study is easy it produces the illusion of knowing; we think we're learning. Reducing performance makes us feel like we're not getting any better, but the evidence is, time and time again, that making learning deliberately difficult makes learning better. And, weirdly, forgetting makes space for us to better store information. Items we've *not* practiced retrieving are more likely to be forgotten in the short term, but forgetting increases the chances of retaining information that is recalled in spaced retrieval practice.

In struggling to integrate information into schemas we have to struggle with what we're learning. If we've forgotten part of the schema we have to work hard to dredge it up from long-term memory. It's an effort – we make mistakes and get it wrong. It might feel like we're not improving, but we are. As we saw in Chapter 12, we *might* be able to remember up to 90 percent of what we learn by taking advantage of the forgetting curve and spaced retrieval practice.

In *Thinking, Fast and Slow*, Daniel Kahneman tells us that our minds are composed of two agents: fast, intuitive, effortless and automatic (System 1) and slow, deliberate, effortful and reflective (System 2).[3] We need the process of slow, deliberate System 2 thinking to allow us to build up the necessary schemas which, in the long term, will lead to better, lightning fast, automatic System 1 thinking.

Now, obviously, this isn't the complete picture. I'd be the first to point out that there's more to education than getting stuff in and making it stick. But hopefully no one will dispute that this is an essential consideration and one it behoves us to get right. Yes context matters. Of course motivation matters. Naturally no single way of approaching a problem will work in every situation with every student. There is no magic formula for success. Expert teachers will always be required to make expert judgements about what might constitute the right level of difficulty for each student. But this is about our ability to make meaningful predictions about what might be effective for most students in most situations.

In summary, we can't wait until students have mastered a subject before introducing difficulty; it's the difficulty that leads to mastery. Cognitive load theory reminds us that students will struggle to solve complex problems with minimal guidance. The best way to build long-term memory to overcome the limitations of working memory might be to reduce classroom performance and 'think hard about subject content', in order to improve storage strength of the concepts needed to think like experts. If we want learning to be easy, we need to make it hard.

Notes

1   Annie Murphy Paul, Making Learning Easier and Making It Harder: Both Are Necessary, *Annie Murphy Paul* (20 March 2014). Available at: http://anniemurphypaul.com/2014/03/making-learning-easier-and-making-it-harder-both-are-necessary/.
2   Shana K. Carpenter, Miko M. Wilford, Nate Kornell and Kellie M. Mullaney, Appearances Can Be Deceiving: Instructor Fluency Increases Perceptions of Learning Without Increasing Actual Learning, *Psychonomic Bulletin & Review* 20(6) (2013): 1350–1356.
3   Daniel Kahneman, *Thinking, Fast and Slow* (London: Penguin, 2012).

Part 4
What else might we be getting wrong?

Part 4

What else might we be getting wrong?

In Part 1 I sought to explain why we might be wrong about many of the things we've come to believe about education. We've discussed the power of c_____ _____, explored some of the problems we have in agreeing what education is for and thought about some of the limitations and concerns that come from uncritically accepting education research.

Test your recall:

1.   Name three cognitive biases and explain them to a colleague.

2.   Suggest four different purposes of education.

3.   What is 'negative capability'?

4.   What does Biesta say is wrong with evidence-based education?

5.   What is Hattie's 'hinge point' for effective interventions?

With this in mind, in Part 2 I introduced my thoughts on p_____, l_____ and m_____. These are the t_____ _____ of the book.

Test your recall:

1.   What's the problem with rapid progress?

2.   Explain the difference between learning and performance.

3.   What does 'liminality' mean?

4.   Name three qualities of threshold concepts.

5.   What does 'cognitive overload' mean?

In Part 3 I presented R_____ B_____'s concept of d_____ d_____ and explained how they might be applied in the classroom.

Test yourself:

1. When does a difficulty become undesirable?

2. What is the optimum spacing of foreign vocabulary?

3. How did Harry Fletcher-Wood make use of the testing effect?

4. Suggest two reasons why it might be beneficial to reduce or delay feedback.

5. What are the stages of the teaching sequence for independence?

Now, in Part 4, we will start to think through the consequences of grasping the threshold concepts we discussed in Part 2 and consider some of the other things we might be wrong about.

Chapter 19

Why formative assessment might be wrong

I owe my success to having listened respectfully to the very best advice, and then going away and doing the exact opposite.

G. K. Chesterton

Formative assessment, or Assessment for Learning as it's commonly branded, is so prevalent in schools that it's almost impossible to escape our biases and view it with sufficient clarity to assess how useful a concept it might be. Once again, though, we need to stand back from our practice and consider whether what we believe about it could be wrong.

Of course it's important for teachers to know where their students currently are, where they need to get to improve and what they need to do to get there. But Dylan Wiliam's 'big idea' of formative assessment – that we should "Use evidence about learning to adapt teaching and learning to meet student needs"[1] – might be holed beneath the waterline. The assumption that you can assess what students have learned in an individual lesson, and then adjust future teaching based on this assumption, is flawed: there's no meaningful way to assess what students have learned during the lesson in which they are supposed to be learning it. You cannot see learning; you can only see performance.

If we measure performance then we can infer what *might* have been learned, but such inferences are highly problematic for two reasons: (1) performance in the classroom is extremely dependent on the cues and stimuli provided by the teacher, and (2) performance is a very poor indicator of how well students might retain or transfer new concepts.

Let's consider the five 'key strategies' Wiliam presents as the bedrock of 'embedded' formative assessment.

1. Clarifying, sharing and understanding learning intentions and success criteria

The basic premise of letting kids know what they're supposed to be learning is fine. But I do have a bone to pick with success criteria. Wiliam recommends sharing grade schemes with students so that they will know whether they have successfully achieved the learning intention. 'Student friendly' grade schemes are, he contends, "useful as students are introduced to a discipline".[2] But many rubrics are inherently meaningless and rarely provide anything meaningful to students. In subjects such as English this is especially pronounced: grade schemes draw a distinction between 'confident' and 'sophisticated'. One is apparently better than the other, but any difference is arbitrary. Exam boards are forced to provide exemplar work for teachers to understand the process by which they arrive at their decisions. Instead of wasting their time with vague, unhelpful success criteria, why not spend time deconstructing exemplars and modeling the expert processes we would use to complete a task?*

As 'success criteria' has joined the lexicon of educational buzz words, it has become increasingly reduced to a list of bullet points of what students ought to include in their work. This might be reasonable as long as they have been derived from deconstructing an exemplar, patiently scaffolded and then practiced. Giving students detailed information about how to be successful can be enormously powerful, but just giving them a checklist encourages a very superficial understanding of what they should do to be successful.

Broadly, I'm in favor of sharing with students the intention behind what they are being asked to do. Anything that adds clarity to the murky business of learning has to be a good thing. However, an intention (outcome, objective or whatever you want to call it) along the lines of: 'To be able to ... (insert skill to be acquired or practiced)' or 'To understand ...

---

* For a detailed explanation of how to go about this, see *The Secret of Literacy*, pp. 36–38.

(whatever the teacher wants students to learn)' is unlikely to be much help. All too often our learning intentions are lesson menus: here is what you should know or be able to do by the end of today's lesson. Unless we have very low aspirations for our students, they are unlikely to do more than merely mimic the understanding or expertise we want them to master. If, instead, we were to share our intention for students to learn threshold concepts, then we could tell them that it might take them weeks to wrap their heads around such troublesome knowledge. We could remind them that in this lesson they are making progress towards a goal and that there is no expectation for them to 'get it' in the next hour or even the next week. As discussed in Chapter 6, learning is not a neat, linear trajectory, it's liminal. Students not only need to spend time in that confusing, frustrating in-between space, they also need to know how important it is to be there as long as need be. If learning intentions rush or limit this experience then they might be doing more harm than good.

To a teacher, laboring under the curse of knowledge, the meaning behind our intentions is clear. But to students, standing at the threshold, not knowing the things we take so much for granted, they are often impossibly vague:

Learning objective: To understand the influences that affect personal economic choices

Success criteria:

I can:

- Explain how limited resources create the need for choices.

- Identify the costs and benefits of a choice.

- Identify and evaluate incentives.

- Analyze choices and predict consequences.

This may seem clear to an expert, but to a novice it's a checklist of barely understood ideas that will lead only to shallow mimicry (see Chapter 7). Even worse are the misguided attempts to differentiate learning intentions and success criteria. There's a requirement in many schools to break these down into levels or grades, with students expected to access work at their target grade. As we saw in Chapter 2, this leads to both students and teachers anchoring themselves on data never intended for this purpose and which gives tacit permission for low expectations.

Here is an example of the sort of thing we should avoid:

Learning objective: To be able to work out meaning using clues

Success criteria:

- C – I can explain what words mean.

- B – I can explore alternative meanings.

- A–A* – I can analyze and evaluate words and phrases to work out the writer's intentions and impact on the reader.

The assumptions made in this example are breath-taking. If you've already understood the concepts of language analysis and that writers use linguistic techniques to shape readers' responses then this is, perhaps, a useful checklist. But if you're a novice still struggling to integrate these ideas then it's a recipe for superficiality and low expectations.*

In summary:

- **Learning intentions**: Yes, over the long term, but never as neat, self-contained lesson objectives. And, please God, let's stop wasting everyone's time by forcing students to write and underline them every lesson!

- **Success criteria**: Yes, if they're the product of teaching and clearly modeled, scaffolded and practiced. No, if they're a vague checklist of surface features.

---

* I'm allowed to be rude about this example as it's one I used myself some years ago.

2. Eliciting evidence of learners' achievement

Basically, this is about how we use questions. We make decisions about how and what to teach based on what we know about students' understanding. It's widely considered unprofessional for teachers to move on without questioning students to find out what they have learned. But apparently less than 10 percent of the questions asked by teachers actually cause any new learning.[3] How on earth would we know that? All we can infer is that we don't *think* any learning was caused, and that's not the same thing at all.

Wiliam argues that there are only two valid reasons for questioning: "to cause thinking and to provide information for the teacher about what to do next". I'm happy with the first of these reasons but I'm not quite so sold on the second. If we ask questions, no matter how well-designed, and then use the responses we elicit to decide whether we should 'move on', we are in serious danger of overlooking that "as learning occurs, so does forgetting" because "learning takes time and is not encapsulated in the visible here-and-now of classroom activities".[4]

If students don't know the answer to our questions, we can remediate. If misconceptions are revealed then we have an opportunity to explore them. But if they answer our questions correctly it means very little. Just because they know it *now* doesn't mean they'll know it next lesson or in an exam. A correct answer is, perhaps, the least useful response we can hope for and might just be an example of mimicry. Far from hoping for neat answers to exit tickets,* the ideal circumstances in which to finish a lesson may be for students to be actively struggling with difficult concepts.

Let's quickly recap the three distinct states on a student's journey from not knowing to knowing:

- **Not knowing**: At this point nothing relevant has been stored and so nothing can be retrieved.

---

* An exit ticket is the name given to a question, often written on a piece of paper (hence ticket), that students must answer before being allowed to leave the lesson.

- **Liminality**: Students have begun to lay down relevant knowledge in long-term memory but it is weakly integrated with prior knowledge and so poorly stored. In order to cope with the confusion of 'kind of' knowing something, students often mimic what they think their teachers want them to do. This leads to a sort of 'cargo cult understanding' where you get the superficial aspects but have no idea what's happening beneath the surface.

- **Knowing**: At this point, new knowledge has been securely integrated within existing webs of prior knowledge and students have made it part of their 'working vocabulary'. They understand the deeper aspects of the new knowledge and can therefore apply it to a range of situations which leads to even better storage.

Of course, an exit ticket can spot complete misunderstandings but that could still be potentially misleading and counter-productive. If we use AfL techniques to assess understanding in the lesson we're only likely to find evidence of mimicry. Some students will be able to mimic well, others won't, but no one will have understood a difficult new concept at a deep level. We should assume that everyone, regardless of what the exit ticket says, is in a liminal state, and so design our schemes of work to make use of what we know about building students' capacity for retention and transfer, rather than getting sidetracked by techniques which merely reveal current performance.

Asking questions might be important for stimulating discussion. Wiliam tells us that "Engaging in classroom discussion really does make you smarter."[5] If he's right then it's certainly incumbent on us to ensure all students participate in these discussions. But creating the conditions for effective classroom discussions has very little to do with finding out what students know and everything to do with provoking thought.

As we've seen, students are unlikely to transfer concepts from working to long-term memory until they have encountered them on *at least* three occasions.[6] So, who cares what they know at the end of a lesson. Better to assume that they are highly likely to forget it.

3. Providing feedback that moves learning forward

Who could argue against providing feedback that moves learning forward? Nobody disputes that feedback is powerful, but as we saw in Chapter 17, too often feedback leads to lower performance. The key to moving learning forward is that feedback must provoke thinking, and that's a lot harder to accomplish and predict than we might imagine.

4. Activating students as instructional resources for one another

What does it mean for students to 'own' their learning? Wiliam argues that cooperative learning is "one of the greatest success stories of educational research".[7] He advocates a range of techniques for encouraging cooperative learning that puts the child at the center of the classroom and moves the teacher to the side. But there is always an opportunity cost: if we ask students to spend a lesson working things out in groups, that is a lesson we cannot spend teaching them. Cooperative learning certainly has a place, but it should only come after careful explanation and modeling.

Often peer assessment is presented as a useful strategy for improving students' attainment. But in light of Nuthall's discovery that most of the feedback students get on their work is from each other, and most of that is wrong, it's clear that this is hugely unreliable.[8]

5. Activating students as owners of their own learning

It's a truism that no one can teach you anything; they can only help you to learn. And yet we insist on holding teachers and schools to account, but not students. It's no surprise that teachers often seem to work a good bit harder than the students they're meant to be teaching.

Students can certainly develop sufficient insight into their own learning to improve it, but simply expecting them to assess their work using student-friendly grade schemes is unlikely to result in much success. Much better to develop their error checking skills; proofreading is hugely useful in making students engage meta-cognitively with their work, as well as ensuring that the feedback teachers give is targeted at the point at which students are ready to learn.

Many of the strategies discussed by Wiliam and enshrined in formative assessment have worth, and if considered carefully enough will have a positive impact on students' progress. However, the 'big idea' that you can assess learning and respond usefully is wrong.

Why I might be wrong

In response to my critique, Dylan Wiliam argues the following:

> It is impossible to assess what students have learned in an individual lesson. As John Mason once said, "teaching takes place in time, but learning takes place over time".[9] The ultimate test of any teaching is long-term changes in what students can do (or avoid doing, such as getting pregnant or taking drugs). The problem with such an approach to teaching is that if we wait until we see the long-term evidence, it will be too late. An analogy with automobile manufacturing may be helpful here.

> In the 1970s and 1980s, the major American and European car-makers had smart people designing production processes through which vehicles progressed, and then, at the end of the process, the finished product would be inspected to see if it worked properly. The Japanese, building on the work of W. Edwards Deming (an American) realized that it would be far better to build quality into the manufacturing process. If something was wrong with a car, any worker on the production line had the authority to stop the production line to make sure that the problem was fixed before the vehicle moved along the production process. This approach is often described as 'building quality in' to the production process, rather than 'inspecting quality in' at the final stage. Another way of describing the difference is a move from quality control to quality assurance.

> Similarly, in teaching, while we are always interested in the long-term outcomes, the question is whether attending to some of the shorter-term outcomes can help us improve the learning for young people.

This is an extraordinarily complex task, because we are trying to construct models of what is happening in a student's mind when this is not directly observable. Ernst von Glasersfeld saw that the models teachers construct come not from learners but from their own conceptual elements. A teacher "can never compare the model he or she has constructed of a child's conceptualizations with what actually goes on in the child's head ... the best that can be achieved is a model that remains viable within the range of available experience".[10]

So I agree that we can never be sure that the conclusions we draw about what our students have learned are the right conclusions. This is why my definition of formative assessment does not require that the inferences we make from the evidence of student achievement actually improve student learning – learning is too complex and messy for this ever to be certain. What we can do is increase the odds that we are making the right decision on the basis of evidence rather than hunch.

In terms of the five strategies, much of chapter 3 of my book *Embedded Formative Assessment* (where I discuss learning intentions) is spent railing against success criteria, and arguing that a shared construct of quality (what Guy Claxton calls a "nose for quality"[11]) is what we should be aiming for, although on those rare occasions when we can spell out the rules for success, we should, of course do so. Michael Polanyi's work on 'personal knowledge' now over 50 years old, is still the definitive work on this, in my opinion.[12]

In terms of eliciting evidence (which is definitely not just questioning by the way, as I go to considerable lengths to show), then of course we never really know what is happening in the student's head but I am confident that teaching will be better if the teacher bases their decisions about what to do next on a reasonably accurate model of the students' thinking. There will also, I suspect, be strong differences across disciplines here. Asking a well-framed question in science may reveal that a student has what Jim Minstrell calls a "facet of thinking"[13] that is different from the intended learning – for example, a student may think that a piece of metal left outside on a winter's night is colder than the wooden table on which it rests, when in fact the temperature of the two are the same (the metal feels colder because it conducts heat away from the hand faster). You may not get rid of the facet of thinking quickly, but knowing that the student thinks this has to be better than not knowing it.

As for feedback, there really is a lot of nonsense talked about how feedback should and should not be given. People say that feedback should be descriptive, and maybe a lot of the time it should be, but people forget that the only good feedback is that which is acted upon, which is why the only thing that matters is the relationship between the teacher and the student. Every teacher knows that the same feedback given to one student will improve that student's learning but to another student, of similar achievement, will make that student give up. Teachers need to know their students, so that they know when to push, and they know when to back off. There will be times when it is perfectly appropriate to say to a student that this work really isn't worth grading because they have 'phoned it in' and other times when this would be completely inappropriate. Just as importantly, students need to trust their teachers. If they don't think the teacher knows what he or she is talking about, or doesn't have the student's best interests at heart, the student is unlikely to invest the effort required to take the feedback on board. That is why almost all of the research on feedback is a waste of time – hardly any studies look at the responses cued in the individual recipient by the feedback.

The quote about collaborative/co-operative learning being one of the success stories of educational research comes from Robert Slavin, who has probably done more high-quality work in this area than anyone.[14] The problem is that few teachers ensure that the two criteria for collaborative learning are in place: group goals (so that students are working as a group rather than just in a group) and individual accountability (so that any student falling down on the job harms the entire group's work). And if a teacher chooses to use such techniques, the teacher is still responsible for the quality of teaching provided by peers. As David notes, too often, peer tutoring is just confident students providing poor quality advice to their less confident peers.

Finally, in terms of self-assessment, it is, of course, tragic that in many schools, self-assessment consists entirely of students making judgments on their own confidence that they have learned the intended material. We have over 50 years of research on self-reports that show they cannot be trusted. But there is a huge amount of well-grounded research that shows that helping students improve their self-assessment skills increases achievement. David specifically mentions error-checking, which is obviously important, and my thinking here has been greatly advanced by working (in Scotland) with instrumental music teachers. Most teachers of academic subjects seem to believe that most of the progress made by their students is made when the teacher is present. Instrumental music teachers know this can't work. The amount of progress a child can make on the violin during a 20 or 30 minute lesson is very small. The real progress comes through practice, and what I have been impressed to see is how much time and care instrumental music teachers take to ensure that their students can practice effectively.

So in conclusion, David has certainly provided an effective critique of 'assessment for learning' as enacted in government policy, and in many schools, but I don't see anything here that forces me to reconsider how I think about what I call formative assessment. I remain convinced that

> as long as teachers reflect on the activities in which they have engaged their students, and what their students have learned as a result, then good things will happen.[15]

This defense rests on the idea that although we can never be sure what's going on in a child's mind, "teaching will be better if the teacher bases their decisions about what to do next on a reasonably accurate model of the students' thinking". Wiliam makes a rather interesting and surprising point: it doesn't matter that we can't know what's going on in our students' minds because his "definition of formative assessment does not require that the inferences we make from the evidence of student achievement actually improve student learning".

Hang on, what then *is* formative assessment? Wiliam's definition proposes that an assessment functions formatively, "to the extent that evidence about student achievement is elicited, interpreted, and used by teachers, learners, or their peers, to make decisions about the next steps in instruction that are likely to be better, or better founded, than the decisions they would have taken in the absence of the evidence that was elicited".[16]

He offers some important features of this definition:

> The definition of formative assessment does not entail any view of what students should be learning – it can be used to improve the learning of anything. Most of the psychological work on memory has been done in laboratory settings on learning that is easy to test. Sometimes, we want to develop dispositions or attitudes that are very different from the kinds of knowledge that feature in most psychological studies.

> The definition of formative assessment does not entail any view of what happens when learning takes place – in other words, it is independent of any psychology of learning.

> The distinction between summative and formative is grounded in the function that the evidence elicited by the assessment actually serves, and not on the kind of assessment that generates the evidence.

> Anyone – teacher, learner or peer – can be the agent of formative assessment. The focus of the definition is on decisions, not evidence.

> The decisions are about 'instruction', which may sound to UK readers as espousing a transmission approach to teaching, is used here in the US sense of the planned engagement of students with activities that will result in learning.

> The definition does not require that the inferences about next steps in instruction are correct. Given the complexity of human learning, it is impossible to guarantee that any specified sequence of instructional activities will have the intended effect. All that is required is that the evidence collected improves the likelihood that the intended learning takes place.
>
> The definition does not require that instruction is in fact modified as a result of the interpretation of the evidence. The evidence elicited by the assessment may indicate that what the teacher had originally planned to do was, in fact, the best course of action. This would not be a better decision (since it was the same decision that the teacher was planning to make without the evidence) but it would be a better-founded decision.[17]

No one is seriously arguing that we should avoid making teaching decisions based on evidence, or that it's a bad idea to reflect on the process of teaching and learning. But, and it's a big but, what evidence? And what learning?

If we are to accept that it is best to "use evidence about learning to adapt teaching and learning to meet student needs", we need to be pretty clear about what we're doing. How far should we consider the limits of working memory? Or possibly the role of retrieval-induced forgetting? If we were to accept, for instance, the concept of desirable difficulties and the finding that current performance is a very poor indicator of future learning, then maybe the very worst thing we could be doing is making decisions based on students' responses to cues and prompts in the classroom. If this is the route we follow, we're more likely to encourage mimicry than mastery.

If we were to accept the evidence on learning and memory then possibly the most sensible approach is to design a curriculum which spaces, interleaves and tests students on the threshold concepts of our disciplines. We should acknowledge that if we want students to retain, transfer and be changed by their lessons, then maybe we should ensure they do not leave lessons thinking that they understand. Even if they've experienced an epiphany during the lesson, we still want them to continue mulling it over and sorting it into long-term memory. Instead, we should encourage them to recognize that anything of worth takes time and cannot be quickly grasped without repeated encounters and plenty of practice.

Then, instead of doubting ourselves, we should reflect on how well we have stuck to these principles.

It is overwhelmingly more complex to see whether a student has learned something during a lesson than it is to check whether a car has been sufficiently well-constructed. Any attempts to elicit evidence from students during the teaching process is fraught with difficulty, and the only really helpful response is one along the lines that Wiliam refers to on the properties of wood and metal. As he observes, knowing that a student is laboring under a misapprehension is better than not knowing it. Definitely. But what about when students are able to answer your questions? If we take this as a measure of our teaching's effectiveness, then we could be sadly and spectacularly mistaken. Maybe they're only able to mimic what they think we want. Finding out that students know the right answer during a lesson is the most useless piece of feedback we can get. Who cares? It is only in ascertaining whether a change has taken place over the long term that we will get any useful feedback on the effectiveness of our teaching.

So, in conclusion, all that formative assessment within lessons can tell us is what students *haven't* learned, never what they *have* learned. That's not to say that it isn't extremely useful to check out misconceptions and reveal areas of ignorance, but it might be incredibly damaging to use formative assessment in lessons as a justification for believing we can 'move on' or to believe that we know with any certainty whether students are 'making progress'.

Notes

1   Dylan Wiliam, Assessment for Learning: Why, What and How. Talk delivered at the Cambridge Assessment Network Conference, University of Cambridge, 15 September 2006.
2   Dylan Wiliam, *Embedded Formative Assessment* (Bloomington, IN: Solution Tree Press, 2011), p. 65.
3   Ted Wragg quoted in ibid. p. 79.
4   Graham Nuthall, The Cultural Myths and Realities of Classroom Teaching and Learning: A Personal Journey, *Teachers College Record* 107(5) (2005): 895–934 at 922.
5   Wiliam, *Embedded Formative Assessment*, p. 81.
6   Graham Nuthall, *The Hidden Lives of Learners* (Wellington: New Zealand Council for Educational Research Press, 2007), p. 69.

7   Wiliam, *Embedded Formative Assessment*, p. 133.
8   Nuthall, *The Hidden Lives of Learners*, p. 35.
9   See Peter Griffin, Teaching Takes Place In Time, Learning Takes Place Over Time, *Mathematics Teaching* 126 (1989): 12–13.
10 Ernst von Glasersfeld, Learning as a Constructive Activity, in Claude Janvier (ed.), *Problems of Representation in the Teaching and Learning of Mathematics* (Hillsdale, NJ: Lawrence Erlbaum Associates, 1987), pp. 3–17 at p. 13.
11 Guy L. Claxton, What Kind of Learning Does Self-Assessment Drive? Developing a 'Nose' for Quality: Comments on Klenowski, *Assessment in Education: Principles, Policy and Practice* 2(3) (1995): 339–343.
12 Michael Polanyi, *Personal Knowledge: Towards a Post-Critical Philosophy* (London: Routledge & Kegan Paul, 1958).
13 Angela DeBarger, Carlos Ayala, Jim Minstrell, Pamela Kraus and Tina Stanford, Facet-Based Progressions of Student Understanding in Chemistry. Paper presented at the 2009 annual meeting of the American Educational Research Association. Available at: http://chemfacets.sri.com/downloads/ChemFacetsTR1.pdf.
14 Robert Slavin, Eric Hurley and Anne Chamberlain, Cooperative Learning and Achievement, in William M. Reynolds and Gloria J. Miller (eds), *Handbook of Psychology*, Vol. 7: *Educational Psychology* (Hoboken, NJ: Wiley, 2003), pp. 177–198.
15 Dylan Wiliam originally contributed this critique on my ideas about formative assessment as a comment on my blog post, Why AfL Might Be Wrong and What To Do About It, *The Learning Spy* (12 March 2014). Available at: http://www.learningspy.co.uk/myths/afl-might-wrong/.
16 Paul J. Black and Dylan Wiliam, Developing the Theory of Formative Assessment, *Educational Assessment, Evaluation and Accountability* 21(1) (2009): 5–31 at 9.
17 This response originally appeared as a comment on my blog post: The AfL Debate: Does It Matter Who's Right?, *The Learning Spy* (28 April 2014). Available at: http://www.learningspy.co.uk/assessment/afl-debate-whos-right/.

Chapter 20
Why lesson observation doesn't work

The power of accurate observation is commonly called cynicism by those who have not got it.

George Bernard Shaw

It's small wonder that we're obsessed with ascertaining the quality of teachers, what with the great and the good telling us that teacher quality is the most important ingredient in students' success.

It's become something of a truism that "the quality of an education system cannot exceed the quality of its teachers".* This is an interesting assumption that sounds plausible, and certainly, taken in the round, assessing teacher quality and then working to develop teachers is an entirely laudable aim. Possibly though this leads us into error. If we believe that bad teachers are dragging down our education system, this might make us keen to identify which teachers are good and which are bad. This mistaken belief goes some way to explaining our apparent inability to see beyond the lesson observation as a means of achieving this goal.**

If we were to shift our thinking slightly and say instead that it's not the quality of teachers, it's the quality of *teaching*, we might believe and

---

*   This is often attributed to the 2007 McKinsey report, *How the World's Best Performing Education Systems Come Out on Top*, but a footnote reveals the quotation actually comes from a South Korean government official.

**   It really is a mistaken belief based entirely on the unsupported assertions of Eric Hanushek in his 1992 paper, 'The Trade-off between Child Quality and Quantity' and adopted wholesale by the Sutton Trust in their 2013 report, *Testing Teachers*.

behave very differently. Any teacher can teach badly and most can teach well. If we were to believe that all teachers could improve then maybe we would think differently about how to hold them accountable.

It is almost universally accepted that the best way to hold teachers accountable and to drive improvement in the quality of teaching and learning in a school is to conduct graded lesson observations. But what if we're wrong? Lesson observation distorts teaching; it makes teachers focus on performance instead of learning and creates a system which is more interested in short-term fluff than real improvement.

Graham Nuthall identified the problem as stemming from the belief that a busy, active classroom where everyone is happily engaged in some kind of project which requires them to think about thorny issues and solve intractable problems looks great.[1] If you preside over a classroom like this, you're more than likely going to get a thumbs up. But this is based on the mistaken belief that you can recognize great teaching and learning just from looking.

Robert Coe has even gone as far as suggesting that lesson observation is the new Brain Gym, questioning both its validity and impact.[2] He points out that there isn't even one single, solitary study that provides real evidence that observations lead to improvement in teachers' practice.

In Chapter 1 we looked at the various problems with the belief that we can rely on our senses for accurate information about the world. This should at least give us pause for thought: what makes us so sure we can accurately and reliably judge teaching and learning? Robert Coe made the following points which neatly summarize much of what we discussed in Part 2.[3]

Observation produces a strong emotional response

We bring our cognitive biases to bear on the lessons we observe. If we like a thing it must be good; if we don't it's obviously bad. These emotional reactions happen so quickly and are so overpowering that they blind us to other interpretations. As social psychologist, Robert Zajonc subtitled his 1980 paper, "preferences need no inferences". Instead they "reduce the universe of alternatives",[4] and we are left only with the need to justify what we have been suckered into believing is objectively true.

Learning is invisible

We rely on poor proxies to make judgements about whether students are learning (see page 155). What we see enacted in lessons is students' current performance – what they can do *now*. Worryingly, good performance is not necessarily a sound indicator of learning. By praising lessons where teachers create the conditions for improved student performance we may well be undermining the likelihood that they can retain and transfer what has been studied. Instead, we should consider how students are drawing on what has been covered in previous lessons. Unless understanding is left open children will stop thinking in-between lessons. Students need to know that their understanding is necessarily incomplete. Obviously, we hope they will see superficial connections between the content covered in one lesson and the next, but we should acknowledge that they are unable to see the deep structure of a teaching sequence because their knowledge is, as yet, too inflexible.

Lessons are the wrong unit

Understanding liminality and the difference between performance and learning undermines the primacy of the lesson as a unit of planning. Because a curriculum is divided up into units – terms and lessons – our thinking about how to teach is constrained. The school year is sectioned into six more or less equal terms, and so it's become law that each year is split into six self-contained units. Similarly, the school day is divided into units of delivery – lessons – and the lesson is usually viewed as a self-contained unit of learning. If you're observing a single lesson, what can you hope to see?

Whatever students might *appear* to do in lessons, learning takes time. If we rely on learning taking place within neat hour long blocks then the complexity of what can be learned is necessarily limited. That might be fine if all we wanted to impart were superficial, atomized blocks of knowledge or mechanistic procedures for writing essays or performing calculations. If, however, we want students to grasp the complex and troubling nature of the underpinning concepts of the subjects we teach then an hour is not going to be enough.

Math teacher Bodil Isaksen says, "Thinking about an individual lesson leads us down the wrong path to the wrong solutions. Inspiration is not something cultivated by a one-off lesson. It is the product of day-in day-out ethos and teaching ... Our planning is weakened by lesson-based thinking. It makes it too easy to forget about cohesion and natural progression over time."[5]

Lessons always will be the unit of delivery in schools – there's probably no other practical way to carve up the curriculum – but they do not have to be the unit of planning. Dividing schemes of work into individual lessons distracts teachers from concentrating on what is to be learned over time. If we expect children to make progress over the course of a lesson then we will look for and value superficial features of delivery. When we accept that anything of worth takes time we can tell students that what we want them to learn is too difficult to pick up in a single lesson – it will take them weeks, months perhaps, to begin to understand what it's taken us years to become expert in.

Accepted 'good practice' may be more fashionable than effective

We are often victims of the 'cult of the new' (the availability bias in another, more fashionable guise). Just because a teacher is doing something pedagogically interesting, doesn't mean it's effective. Needless to say, observers are often unduly influenced by fashions and fads. If you're convinced that every lesson should be crammed with independent learning, groupwork or higher-order questioning then you will tend to prefer those lessons which confirm your particular bias. If you're one of the legions who believe that teachers shouldn't talk then you'll be impressed when you see this happening. This is human nature at its worst; teaching methods just don't matter. In fact, they could be considered dangerous. This led Dylan Wiliam to ask, "How can we stop teachers doing 'good' things?"[6] Asking teachers to change will, at least in the short term, make them worse at teaching. Time spent mastering new fads and fashions is time that can't be spent doing what you've already mastered.

We assume that if you can do it you can spot it

Classroom observation is a very different skill from teaching (although there are, of course, overlaps). Grading lessons based on students' progress is problematic because it takes an almost Herculean effort of will to concentrate on the students and not be distracted by the teacher. Because the vast majority of observations are undertaken by teachers, we are naturally fascinated by what our colleagues do. Being good at a thing might actually be a distraction, and there's some research to indicate that non-experts' judgements of teachers are no different to those of experts.[7]

We don't believe observation can miss so much

Focusing on one area leads to inattention blindness; it's almost guaranteed that we will miss the gorilla. And if we do see the gorilla, what else will we miss? The Dunning–Kruger effect (see page 62) tells us that the least skilled people are the most likely to believe they are right. We're tremendously poor at predicting what we will be able to do and are often victims of our intuition. Very often the facts are counter-intuitive. A useful rule of thumb, in all areas of life, might be to assume that what 'feels right' is often a comforting lie.

Context matters

Teaching that seems to produce good learning will vary from day to day and lesson to lesson. Sometimes certain approaches work and sometimes they don't. Friday period 5 will have a very different atmosphere to Tuesday period 2. The same kids approach learning differently depending on what they already know, where they are in the teaching sequence, meteorological conditions, how recently they've eaten, what they've eaten, the phase of the moon and a whole host of other imponderables. Any half-way decent teacher will adapt their teaching in an attempt to meet these ever changing needs. What you might do with one class on one day will be entirely different from what you might do at another time with a different group of kids.

If we're basing our observation on some checklist of what constitutes good teaching, we have two problems: (1) how will we know if we've seen it if we can't tell just from looking? and (2) how sure are we that our checklist is right?

Although maybe anyone can spot a car crash, and although most observers can appreciate seeing a master practitioner at the height of her powers, what we see in an observation is just the background of teaching. Judging a professional based solely on a snapshot is foolhardy and unfair. The belief that there are good and bad teachers is almost universal. Many people have the fixed mindset belief that good teachers are born not made; that they have the kind of personality that students love; that teaching comes naturally. At the other end of the scale are those who rapidly lose control of what is going on in their class; they seem as if they'd be happier doing something else and their students are unlikely to learn very much.

But what if the same teachers, working in different circumstances, could perform quite differently? If I was asked to teach a PE lesson to a bunch of truculent 16-year-olds I'd never met, I'm certain I'd be terrible. And I'd probably be equally out of my depth if I was expected to teach a phonics lesson to an pre-kindergarten class. Perhaps these are extreme examples, but we've all had classes that we've felt ashamed to be observed teaching. Does being seen strutting my stuff in front of a class I know well and have an excellent relationship with make me outstanding?

It might be helpful to further illustrate the problem by describing two different lessons I have observed.

Lesson 1

This was one of the most impressive lessons I've ever seen in terms of how slickly organized it was. In the space of 50 minutes, students took part in a bewildering array of activities. They had a starter in which they were asked to analyze a text and describe, using keywords, the techniques that had been used. They then had to get out the piece of work they had been working on for the past few lessons and set themselves a goal for the lesson. They then had to complete their chosen goal, take part in a discussion assessing their progress and giving advice to other students on their table for the next lesson. That all this was possible is a testament to the fact that the students had obviously been thoroughly drilled in the expectations of how to behave. There wasn't a second of wasted time, the students worked independently for the vast majority of the lesson and the teacher's input was minimal as they wandered the class giving brief suggestions here and there. If a student asked for help, they would be questioned on how they might work out the answer for themselves without recourse to the teacher – they were clearly well used to this and knew how to go about solving the problems they encountered. The students' engagement and behavior for learning were exemplary. It all looked amazing.

But was it? Well, on the face of it, the lesson was incredibly well-planned, it was clearly a typical example and the students were enthusiastic about their experience. Their performance in the lesson was tip-top. But were they learning? Well, frankly, I was disappointed by the quality of their writing. Oh well, I thought, that's just because they're in 7th grade. I stamped on these nagging doubts and both the other observer and I were more than happy to chalk the lesson up as outstanding. But were we wrong to do so?

Lesson 2

This lesson was a shambles. For a start, the objective was overly complicated and confusing, with most of the students unable to explain what they were supposed to be doing. There was no differentiation – everything was pitched right at the top with little support for those who might struggle. While some students were clearly enjoying the challenge, others were distracted and off-task for extended periods. In one activity, students read a very complex text and then had to answer a number of fiendishly difficult comprehension questions that required background knowledge which many of them didn't have. Chaos ensued. The teacher allowed the class to struggle and then intervened to didactically explain, at some length, what they should have been doing. This too was clearly a typical lesson and many of the students complained that they often 'didn't get it' and that Miss didn't explain things clearly enough for them to make distinct progress. These were kids who knew what to expect and were vocal about demanding it. As an observer, I couldn't help but agree – it was hard to see that any but a few very able students had made any progress. Again, we were unanimous: the lesson was clearly and wholly 'inadequate'.

There's no question that the students in lesson 1 were happier, performing better, more engaged and better behaved. The weird thing was that the teacher of lesson 2 got consistently higher exam results – over the previous five years she had outperformed every other member of the department by a fairly significant margin. She is quirky, fiercely intelligent, remarkably knowledgeable about her subject and constitutionally incapable of turning out a 'good' lesson. The exam results for the teacher of lesson 1 weren't bad, but neither were they what you would expect given the clockwork nature of her lessons. Could this be an example of short-term performance gains actually getting in the way of long-term retention and transfer?*

In the course of a single day, even the best teachers are capable of teaching a full range of lessons from inadequate to outstanding. Anyone can have a bad day, or a good one. The correlation between lesson grades and exam results is poor: teachers who deliver outstanding performances in lessons do not necessarily produce outstanding outcomes, and vice versa.

---

* Once in an exam analysis meeting, a school leader who taught in a particular department said that the reasons the exam results of that department were so poor was because of their outstanding teaching. They concentrated on independent learning and refused to 'spoon feed'. This obviously meant kids did less well in the test. I kid you not – that really happened.

What if I'm wrong?

Robert Coe says:

> [I]f it is true that despite the huge efforts we have made to improve education not much has changed, there are important lessons for us to learn. One would be that effort and good intentions are not enough; we have to work smarter, not just harder. Another would be that we must look carefully at the strategies we have been using to improve, and replace them with some different ones. A third lesson is that a more critical and realistic approach to evaluation may be required. An uncritical belief that things are improving may be comforting, but is ultimately self-deceiving and unproductive.[8]

Grading observation lessons provides particularly cold comfort.

As with everything we do, cognitive bias will be at work to prevent us from seeing that we might be mistaken. Many teachers and school leaders take the view that while grading lessons might not be perfect, there's no better alternative. But of all the imperfect methods we could use to evaluate teacher effectiveness, this is the least perfect. Gradings are completely unreliable. We'd get a more statistically valid and less biased assessment if we flipped a coin. Here are the killer stats from the multi-million dollar MET Project: if a lesson is given a top grade by one observer, there's a 78 percent chance that a second observer will give a different grade. And if a lesson is given a bottom grade, there's a *90 percent chance that a second observer will give a different grade!*[9] Another robust piece of research found that fewer than 1 percent of lessons judged inadequate are genuinely inadequate and only 4 percent of lessons judged outstanding actually produce outstanding learning gains. And overall, *63 percent of judgements will be wrong.*[10] All grades reveal are our bias and preferences. Believing in the accuracy and impartiality of lesson grades is inherently dishonest.

Another argument is that quality assurance procedures require that we evaluate teacher effectiveness. Yes, teachers must be held accountable, but is there another way? There are no easy answers to this, but schools should look at as many sources of data as possible to make these complex decisions. If a teacher is struggling, grading them as inadequate will only demoralize them further. Instead, we should give clear standards that teachers are expected to meet. These could include:

- A baseline quality of students' work.

- A minimum standard of grading.

- Students' performance in public exams.

- Attendance and punctuality.

- Professionalism in interactions with students, staff and parents.

If you're struggling or underperforming in any of these areas, then maybe you should expect and deserve to be put on performance review.

But what about the view that some teachers *like* having lessons graded? Doesn't this give us a good reason to carry on? Well, they might well enjoy someone validating their teaching (especially if they're good at putting on a show), but then they might also like to have fairy dust scattered over their classroom. A belief in the validity of lesson grading makes no more sense than a belief in witchcraft. And for all the difference it will make to improving teaching and learning, you might as well wave a magic wand about.

Can we make classroom observation more effective?

Does this mean that there is now no place for classroom observation? Should we abandon it altogether? Every instinct screams no, doesn't it? Anecdotally, I've learned a lot from observing teachers in action and I'm certain that I'm not alone. So how can we make lesson observations a little bit better?

Don't make assumptions

If you're in the privileged position of being able to watch a fellow professional do their thing, go in with the mindset that you are there to learn. Make a note of what you see and what questions you might ask. When you have the opportunity to discuss an observed lesson with the teacher who taught it, discussion should be framed using questions like these:

- Were there any surprises?

- How might you have done that differently?

- Can you explain what was happening when ...?

- Were you aware of ...?

- What do you think the impact of x might be?

Listen to the answers and learn from them. If the teacher asks for or is interested in your opinions, wait for them to ask you. Otherwise, try to keep your mouth shut. This is hard, but if you accept the reality that you are not the expert you think you are, and that the teacher you've observed will know their class and their subject better than you, all will be well. At some point you might be tempted to share what you would have done. Resist this temptation. It is a pointless piece of self-indulgence to try to download your 'expertise' on to another teacher. They won't thank you for it, it won't change their practice and it's probably wrong.

Make it reciprocal

It's my contention that we learn more from observing than we do from being observed. It's a truism that those who observe most teach least. Therefore, the most useful thing school leaders with lighter teaching loads can do is to use their time to cover colleagues so that they can observe each other. Why doesn't this happen? Because we're obsessed with the idea that 'we know best'. Even if this is true and we do actually know best, what benefit is that to the teachers we lead? A much more useful approach is to lay the groundwork for an inquiry model of classroom observation which allows teachers to investigate and reflect on aspects of their own teaching.

Focus on instructional support

One of my favorite models for classroom observation is the one taken by Doug Lemov and the Uncommon Schools network. The idea is ridiculously simple: you look at the data to find out which teachers have the best results and then you observe them to find out what they're doing. Lemov's teaching manual, *Teach Like A Champion*, is a compendium of some of the strategies common to these über-teachers which can be practiced and replicated by us mere mortals.[11]

According to the Classroom Assessment Scoring System (CLASS),[12] teachers' interactions can be divided into three broad categories: emotional support (classroom climate, teacher sensitivity, regard for student perspectives), classroom organization (behavior management, productivity, strategies for engaging students) and instructional support (strategies that foster content knowledge, strategies that foster analysis and reasoning skills, strategies that foster knowledge of procedures and skills, quality of feedback, instructional dialogue). Researchers have found that teachers are consistently much better at providing emotional support and organizing classrooms than they are at giving instructional support.[13]

What this suggests is that teachers only tend to improve at the 'easy' things. Providing effective emotional support and effective classroom organization are essential; if we neglect them we have chaos. The frightening truth is that we can get away with low quality instructional support if we know how to engage kids and make them behave. If it's true that many teachers stop improving after a few years in the job (see page 316) this might explain why. As soon as students stop throwing chairs about and more or less do what we want, we're content. It takes a rare individual to decide independently to leave this comfort zone. We will only improve through deliberate practice and that means doing things we can't currently do. And what teachers seem to find hardest is instructing students in their subjects. Telling teachers what to do to improve and then relying on them to make the unlikely decision to struggle is the continuing professional development (CPD) model espoused by most schools, and, as you can see, it's doomed to failure.

The training run by Doug Lemov and Uncommon Schools is all about isolating the elements of great teaching and practicing them over and over. The thinking is that what we practice we get good at. If we've practiced an instructional technique we're much more likely to use it. And here's where classroom observation can be used to focus on guided practice of these instructional techniques that are likely to have the most impact.

Watch the teacher and the kids

The current trend in education is for observations to focus on students' learning. John Hattie is very clear that we should only ever focus on students, insisting, "I never allow teachers or school leaders to visit classrooms to observe teachers; I allow them to observe only students."[14] Superficially this makes a certain kind of sense, but we need to ask whether we're interested in how teachers teach or how students learn? Or are both important?

If you walk into a classroom it's hard not to look at the teacher. But by observing teachers are we really only focusing on hot air? We routinely ask questions of teachers: are they differentiating? How are they asking questions? Are they using this or that strategy? This approach to observation runs the risk of merely inviting the observer to give their advice on how the teacher could teach 'more like me'. All this results in is cosmetic change for change's sake. At best it's well-meaning but ineffective, and at worst it's bullying and used as a club to force compliance. Why should we change the way we teach just because an observer has a preference we don't happen to share?

Isn't it more reasonable to ask what the effect of the teaching is? If we accept Hattie's suggestion that all observations should be either from the students' point of view or of the students, what might we lose? If observations were focused only on what the students were doing, instead of the teacher's interactions, would we have a sounder basis on which to make judgements and offer advice?

Well, the bad news is this might be a red herring. Watching only the students in lessons focuses teachers on performance rather than learning, and encourages them to concentrate on short-term approaches which result in 'rapid' progress, often at the cost of sustained progress. Maybe it might be more productive, especially if we want to improve instructional support, to observe what the teacher is doing. This might lead to a more nuanced discussion post observation because a teacher is much better placed to discuss their actions rather than speculate on the unknowable nature of the students' minds. And if the focus is guided practice, then it becomes essential to watch what teachers are doing in order to give the feedback and support to embed improvement.

Dylan Wiliam often talks about teachers needing to improve, not because they're not good enough but because they can be even better.[15] Clearly it's preferable for teachers to decide themselves how they might improve their practice and we should absolutely avoid simply telling them what to do. But if we accept the need for systemic improvement then we need to consider how we might help teachers actually improve instead of just blandly asking them what they prefer. Here are three suggestions.

1. Find out what teachers are good at and start from there

Feedback to teachers is usually focused on what could be improved rather than what was good. The problem here is that if we only ever focus on negatives then we end up making people feel negative. Even when observers try to balance their feedback in favor of 'what went well', we often only end up hearing what was wrong. To avoid this we could focus on expanding the good things or, as Chip and Dan Heath would have it, growing the "bright spots".[16]

Imagine you're a parent and your child comes home with the following school report:

English	A
History	A
Science	A
Geography	B
French	B
Math	E

What would you focus on? The E grade leaps out at us and we automatically want to find out what's going wrong in math. But the real story of this report is that things are going well in every other subject. If we shifted our perspective to find out what's working everywhere else, we might actually end up with a better plan of action for addressing the weak performance in math.

Of course, that's not to say we should ignore problems and simply lavish praise on areas where teachers are successful. Where there are serious and urgent issues it's probably silly to scratch around for pointless reasons to say well done. This is one of the problems with mandating that teachers' feedback should take the form of two stars and a wish or on 'what went well' and 'even better if …' Sometimes nothing went well! And there's research to suggest that feedback on success rarely results in improvement.

But when working to help good teachers improve performance, what if instead of just focusing on what teachers are getting wrong, we invested some time in improving what they're already good at? It's hard to hear that you're failing. It's hard to improve if you're focused on what you're bad at, but we all enjoy talking about our passions, and most people are prepared to spend time on what they enjoy. That would be my starting point: get to know the teacher, find out what they're good at and work out how to do more of it.

2. Focus on strengths
instead of weaknesses

We learn more from observing others than we do by being observed. Typically, schools 'support' teachers by scrutinizing their performance ever more closely. This strikes me as unlikely to result in anything much except making people ill. We need a certain amount of stress to keep us on our toes but too much stress is counter-productive. Instead, I'd rather observe with the teacher I'm supporting. We can then talk about what we've seen, how children appear to be making progress and discuss how our expectations have been confounded by the complexity of learning. It might also be worth focusing on the teacher's identified strengths. How can what they've seen help them to improve what they're already good at?

3. Do difficult things

And if all this sounds a bit too touchy-feely, my third step would be to give teachers really difficult things to do. If we make mistakes we can learn from them. Mistakes become normalized and we're more confident in taking risks. It's easy to succeed if the bar is set low. Success holds little satisfaction if everyone can achieve it at the first attempt. If we have high expectations then it must follow that students will fail to meet them. Our job is not to lower the bar but to help students deal with the frustration of not being able to get over it. Yet.

The same holds true for teachers. Anyone can improve over the short term with masses of one-to-one attention and support. For all the fear and confusion around accountability, I think the bar is often set pretty low. Hoping that children learn exclusively through the medium of big paper and sharpies is certainly setting the bar perilously low. Much better to, for instance, work on improving teacher talk than minimizing it. The harder it is to achieve success, the more valuable it is. This might seem counter-intuitive and it is certainly provocative, but I'm pretty sure that we are only likely to change when we encounter things that startle us out of received (and sometimes very sloppy) wisdom.

Notes

1 Graham Nuthall, *The Hidden Lives of Learners* (Wellington: New Zealand Council for Educational Research Press, 2007), pp. 25–26.
2 Robert Coe, Classroom Observation: It's Harder Than You Think, CEM Blog (9 January 2014). Available at: http://www.cem.org/blog/414/.
3 This section is adapted from Robert Coe, Improving Education: A Triumph of Hope Over Experience. Inaugural lecture at Durham University, 18 June 2013. Available at: http://www.cem.org/attachments/publications/ImprovingEducation2013.pdf.
4 Robert B. Zajonc, Feeling and Thinking: Preferences Need No Inferences, *American Psychologist* 35 (1980): 151–175, quoted in Jonathan Haidt, *The Righteous Mind* (London: Penguin, 2012), p. 65.
5 Bodil Isaksen, A Lesson is the Wrong Unit of Time, *Bodil's Blog* (25 January 2015). Available at: http://blog.bodil.co.uk/?p=80.
6 Dylan Wiliam, Stopping People Doing Good Things. Keynote speech at the SSAT conference, Birmingham, November 2010.
7 Bill and Melinda Gates Foundation, *Ensuring Fair and Reliable Measures of Effective Teaching: Culminating Findings from the MET Project's Three-Year Study* (2013). Available at: http://metproject.org/downloads/MET_Ensuring_Fair_and_Reliable_Measures_Practitioner_Brief.pdf.

8   Coe, *Improving Education*, p. ii.

9   Kata Mihaly, Daniel F. McCaffrey, Douglas O. Staiger and J. R. Lockwood, A Composite Estimator of Effective Teaching (8 January 2013). Available at: http://www. metproject.org/downloads/MET_Composite_Estimator_of_Effective_Teaching_ Research_Paper.pdf.

10   Michael Strong, John Gargani and Ozge Hacifazlioglu, Do We Know a Successful Teacher When We See One? Experiments in the Identification of Effective Teachers, *Journal of Teacher Education* 62(4) (2011): 367–382.

11   Doug Lemov, *Teach Like a Champion: 49 Techniques That Put Students on the Path to College* (San Francisco, CA: Jossey-Bass, 2010).

12   See http://curry.virginia.edu/research/centers/castl/project/ class-ongoing-development.

13   Megan W. Stuhlman, Bridget K. Hamre, Jason T. Downer and Robert C. Pianta, *What Should Classroom Observation Measure, Part 2: A Practitioner's Guide to Conducting Classroom Observations* (n.d.). Available at: http://curry.virginia.edu/uploads/ resourceLibrary/CASTL_practioner_Part2_single.pdf.

14   John Hattie, *Visible Learning for Teachers: Maximizing Impact on Learning* (London: Routledge, 2011), p. 138.

15   Dylan Wiliam, Every Teacher Can Improve [video] (December 2012). Available at: https://www.youtube.com/watch?t=19&v=eqRcpA5rYTE.

16   Chip Heath and Dan Heath, *Switch: How to Change Things When Change is Hard* (New York: Random House, 2011).

Chapter 21
Grit and growth

All good is hard. All evil is easy. Dying, losing, cheating, and mediocrity is easy. Stay away from easy.

Scott Alexander

So far we've talked a lot about learning as if just presenting the right material in the right way will have the desired effect. As we know, children are complex and classrooms more complex still. We're probably interested in more than students 'merely' acquiring new skills and knowledge within the domains of the subjects we teach. We may also have an interest in fostering a 'love of learning' and turning students into 'lifelong learners'. Whatever the current trend might be, we want our students to somehow be changed and improved by their experiences in school.

One of the most intractable barriers we have in the face of these worthy goals is our students' attitude to effort. It's embedded in our language: easy does it, hard luck, easy on the eye, don't take it so hard. Why is it that we have come to view things that are 'hard' as bad and effort as the preserve of fools? Rightly, this attitude is something we're pretty keen to address. And to our great good fortune there's lots of interest in the various desirable 'non-cognitive' skills, ranging from motivation to perseverance to resilience. While much thought has been put into how we might go about teaching these qualities, much less thinking has gone into whether we can or should.

One of the most popular theories to take hold in education in recent years is Carol Dweck's theory of mindsets. The finding that students with a growth mindset learn best has been around for a while and ought to need little in the way of introduction. Briefly, we should encourage students to focus more on the process of learning and less on performance; to see mistakes as opportunities; and to believe that anyone, no matter their starting point, can become significantly better at something if they're only prepared to try. People with growth mindsets will make effort for its own sake whereas the fixed mindset is all about success. Failure at a task is seen as evidence of personal failure. Struggle is seen as evidence of lack of ability. This is particularly toxic as hard work is the only real route to mastery, and if hard work is seen as something only losers have to dirty their hands with, well, why would you bother?

Less well-known, but increasingly influential, is the theory of grit. There's a school of thought which says, "Sometimes learning is not fun. Instead, it is just hard work; it is deliberate practice; it is simply doing some things many times over."[1] This idea has been around for centuries and forms the basis of the Protestant work ethic. Recently it's had something of a renaissance. As far back as the 1890s, psychologists have been telling us that it takes 10 years to become an expert in whatever field you choose to pursue.[2] K. Anders Ericsson confirmed that although mastery might be within the reach of ordinary mortals it required 10 years of deliberate, effortful practice. This was seized upon by Malcolm Gladwell in his book *Outliers*, and converted to the neat round figure of 10,000 hours. This has since become something of an industry with books like *Bounce* and *The Talent Code* dominating bestseller lists. Ericsson has publically distanced himself from Gladwell and the notion that 10,000 hours of any old practice will result in mastery. Instead, he has emphasized the concept of 'deliberate practice'. This is intentional, aimed at improving performance, set just beyond your current skill level, combined with immediate feedback and repetitious. When these conditions are met, practice improves accuracy and speed of performance on cognitive, perceptual and motor tasks.

Angela Duckworth and colleagues explored the concept of grit, and looked at deliberate practice in relation to success at spelling bees. They found that the best spellers engage in prolonged deliberate practice, despite this being the least enjoyable and most effortful of all the different preparation activities they might choose. "Grittier spellers engaged in deliberate practice more so than their less gritty counterparts, and hours of deliberate practice fully mediated the prospective association between grit and spelling performance."[3]

So what can we learn from all this? Mainly that there's no substitute for hard work. And, perhaps, without the feeling that what you're doing is actually a bit of an effort, you won't ever achieve real mastery; taking a shortcut is more likely to result in mimicry.

When I was first introduced to Carol Dweck's research the scales fell from my eyes. It was an epiphany, a veritable Damascene conversion. And like Saul before me, I quickly became an evangelist. All we have to do is convince students to work harder and embrace struggle. Any sign of frustration or lack of willingness is evidence of a fixed mindset, and fixed mindsets are bad. The growth mindset, in contrast, is a panacea. All we have to do is convince students to think better and accept that the path to success is far from smooth.

Dweck suggests that about 40 percent of people have what she terms a fixed mindset and another 40 percent have a growth mindset. The remaining 20 percent are a bit of both. But the exciting news was that we could shift these percentages. By adjusting the way we spoke about intelligence and used praise, we could cure children of the curse of the fixed mindset. Although this way of seeing the world has been a game changer in many schools, clearly there's a need for caution. We're in danger of this becoming yet another educational meme; a meta-belief that warps and distorts as it becomes increasingly and uncritically consumed.

Clearly there's a relationship between effort and outcomes, but to suggest there's no such thing as innate talent or natural aptitude is just silly, as even the most cursory review of the science of behavior genetics will tell us. Of course effort, hard work and perseverance matter; they're just not the only ingredients of success. Getting too excited about grit and the growth mindset is dangerously wishful thinking. The growth mindset theory is a useful theory for describing how we approach learning, but it's not a fact. It's important to remember that evidence, even the evidence of the saintly Dr. Dweck, is not the same thing as proof. Other studies have not been able to replicate Dweck's original results, finding instead that if students with a growth mindset were overly concerned with academic performance they tended to behave similarly to those students with a fixed mindset.[4] Attempts to alter beliefs about intelligence and attitude may very well backfire if students' 'ego investment' in school is not also addressed. Dweck herself admits that a growth mindset alone is insufficient to affect students' performance at school.[5]

But is it true that fixed mindsets are bad and growth mindsets are good? On reflection, I think the truth may be a little more complicated than that. We all have an enormous capacity for growth. This capacity (plasticity) is how we acquire new skills and incorporate new knowledge into pre-existing schemas; without it we wouldn't change at all. We also have a biological predisposition to fix new learning in place and make it part of us. If we didn't have a fixed view of multiplication or conjugating the French verb *avoir* then we'd never be able to make use of our capacity to grow and change.

Regardless of what theorists might claim about mindsets, we have evolved to grow and fix new learning in place. If nothing is settled – or fixed – growing is so much more troublesome. Daniel Dennett suggests that through a process of cultural transmission, "We somehow *install* an already invented and largely 'debugged' system of habits in the partly unstructured brain."[6] This sounds a bit mysterious but might perhaps explain our apparently innate capacity for learning language.

When we talk about fixed mindsets in education perhaps we are concerned that some students have an overdeveloped propensity to hold on to ideas and are afraid in some way to let go of their concepts of themselves. Or do students have a fixed view of things about which they feel content? Could it be that those possessing the much vaunted growth mindset let go of potentially valuable ideas too readily? Might they be more easily swayed or fooled than their fixed mindset peers? Could those with a fixed mindset be more likely to express dissatisfaction with the status quo (if *we're* not at fault then it must be the environment – *viva la revolución!*)? And might an individual with a growth mindset too eagerly accept adverse conditions as their lot? Either way, I think labeling students as either fixed or growth is too simplistic, especially if we think of one of the labels in essentially pejorative terms.

This would seem to be another example of how we get stuck in the dichotomous box. It may be that we need both a fixed and a growth mindset in order to master new learning; the process of growing our webs of knowledge and then fixing this new understanding of the world in place seems the very essence of learning. Rather than the comforting certainty of valuing one mindset and trashing the other, we should instead seek the negative capability of embracing two seemingly contradictory ideas and try to embrace both mindsets.

This very fixed view of the growth mindset has led to teachers blaming students' lack of progress on their mindset. This probably isn't something we want to encourage and has caused something of a backlash against Dweck and Duckworth. The complaint is that if we attribute an individual's failure to a fault or lack in their character then we are apportioning blame; a lack of success can be explained by a weak will and a poor attitude. Possibly this is an example of the fundamental attribution error.

The counter-argument is that society should be held to account for the failure of those at its margins; if we fail, it is down to our lack of opportunity and the prejudices we encounter. No one would argue that life is fair; it isn't. Being born into social advantage hugely increases our chances of being successful; being born into poverty is a crushing burden.

Various pundits have argued that grit and resiliency are only prescribed for low-achieving students and, sure as eggs are eggs, low achieving students will be those from the most deprived socio-economic backgrounds or those who suffer from mental health problems, special educational needs or for whom English is a second language. That these children are more difficult to teach is not their fault; instead of demanding that they demonstrate grit, maybe we should look at the gravel in our own eyes.

Is there something in this? Is it unfair to ask the dispossessed to suck it up and try harder? Does this mean the research on motivation theory is being used to hold children to account, while ignoring the impact of other contextual factors that might influence children's attainment? The prevailing view certainly seems to be that children raised in affluent families outperform their less privileged peers. So is it wrong to hold the disadvantaged accountable for their performance? Is the theory of self-actualization through effort the preserve of an advantaged elite?

There are fears that the theory of mindsets might be either misinterpreted or used simply as another way of blaming victims. If students are told or end up believing that the reason for their lack of success is their mindset, might this not imply that our success is completely within our sphere of control and that society has no role in or responsibility for our travails? These are worthwhile questions to ask, and if the answer to any of them is yes then we may have a serious problem. But is this how schools and teachers are interpreting Dweck's research?

Let's consider each of these concerns in turn. If it's true that only 'low scoring' children are expected to display resilience, then something is seriously amiss. Teachers recognize instinctively that it's really not OK to refer to innate ability when discussing the work of low ability students. We never say, "Oh well, what can you expect of children in a bottom level?" or "No wonder you couldn't do it, you're thick!" But we'll happily say to those in top levels, "You're so clever!" and "That's what I'd expect of someone in this class." As a result, there are very many privileged, able students who have a fixed understanding of their ability and who have not developed the resilience to cope with setbacks or take risks.

If anything, we're likely to have very low expectations of grit in children from less privileged backgrounds. We're much too quick to shrug and think, "Well, what can you expect of kids like these?" As a result, we demand less and accept poor attainment and low standards. But if we took the view that the destiny of these students *was* within their control, at least to a certain extent, wouldn't we be more likely to have higher expectations?

The argument that the research of Dweck and Duckworth has led to an ideological stance that 'blames' children for low attainment may be true in some schools, but all too often, far from schools and teachers holding students accountable for their success, teachers are more likely to be blamed for their students' failures. The focus on closing the attainment gap between children from socially disadvantaged backgrounds and those who are not ensures that schools are anxious to give less privileged students every opportunity and advantage they can. We fall over ourselves to offer any and every intervention available.

Whatever role society has to play in the likely outcomes and relative success of students, isn't it more rather than less empowering to let children know that they have some small measure of agency and control? One rather obvious message from Dweck's research is that a fixed mindset is not fixed. We can all change our intelligence, personality and character. Isn't this good news for those who might feel most trodden down by society's grimy heel? Surely, any other message is horribly fatalist and consigns children to remain at the bottom of the pile.

Yes, of course we are constrained by our backgrounds and the circumstances of our birth; there's no doubt that economic disadvantage, race, gender and many other factors have a huge impact on our life chances. But do we also need to be constrained by our beliefs of what is and isn't possible?

For me, the biggest change has been that I used to believe that it was my job to make work as easy as possible for my students so that they didn't have to deal with the frustration of getting stuck. Now it seems to me that a teacher's job should be to make work as challenging as possible. If students don't struggle they won't make mistakes, and if they don't make mistakes they're unlikely to learn very much. This fundamentally changes the way I've come to think about the expectations we have for students of differing abilities.

We should establish what students *think* they can do and then tell them they can do better. Perhaps the worst thing we can say is, "Do your best." Maybe our best isn't good enough. The job of teachers is to help students get there. Sometimes, however, it may not always be productive to persist in the face of challenge. For example, persevering to accomplish goals that are extrinsically motivated, unimportant to the student or in some way inappropriate could potentially "induce stress, anxiety, and distraction, and have detrimental impacts on a student's long-term retention, conceptual learning, or psychological well-being".[7]

One useful insight from all this is in maintaining a clear distinction between 'mastery' and 'performance'. In Chapter 7, we saw that improving students' performance leads at worst to mimicry without understanding and at best to mere competence. Many students feel the pressure to perform and focus on demonstrating their competence and outperforming others. A performance goal might be to get an A in an exam or for a teacher it might be to get a certain percentage of their class achieving a particular progress measure.

If mastery is our goal, we make a decision to be the best we can be at something. When students focus on mastery rather than performance they are more likely to find lessons interesting, persist in the face of difficulties, seek help when stuck and see the point of what they're studying. Motivation over the long term is easier to maintain because mastery goals are just beyond reach. People with a growth mindset tend to be more interested in competing with themselves than gaining external feedback and validation. Teaching for mastery will not only lead to the rounded and resilient students we all want, but it is also likely to lead to improved exam performance.[8]

If we really want students to develop a growth mindset that will equip them with grit, resourcefulness and resilience, we need to stop focusing on what they can *do* and accept that the central tenets of Assessment for Learning are fatally flawed. Any classroom practices that encourage teachers or students to believe that assessment *proves* learning must be rooted out and exposed as the harmful nonsense it often is.

So, what's stopping us?

There are two huge obstacles in our path. The first is the institutionalized nature of schools themselves. Everything about schools is set up to value performance over mastery and learning. It would be a brave school indeed that sought to unpick the fabric of classrooms and curriculums and introduce a structure that supported sustained instead of rapid progress. But why are schools like this?

Well, that's the second and perhaps more intractable problem. In Chapter 7, we explored the idea that we intuitively believe increasing students' performance is a good thing. It feels good to perform well and it's uncomfortable to struggle. Students are happier with lessons in which they perform well, teachers feel happier designing schemes of learning which allow students to jump from one feel-good performance to the next, and school leaders feel happier with a curriculum that checks boxes, covers content and – with a fair trailing wind, lots of last minute intervention and determined teaching to the test – will result in a predictably decent exam performance. Anything that confirms this bias is welcomed; anything that contradicts it is dismissed.

It's all very well to tell students that we want them to get cleverer through taking risks and making mistakes, but nothing in the way we behave supports this message. We are deeply suspicious, for instance, of teachers struggling and would much prefer to cultivate competence rather than run the risks required for real mastery. According to one controversial study, teachers stop improving after three years of teaching.[9] Our learning curve is steep to begin with – we improve or we quit – but after three years, generally speaking, we achieve competence. Children have stopped throwing chairs about and pretty much do what they're told, and we relax. Although we become increasingly familiar with course materials, we tend not to challenge ourselves to do things beyond our current level of expertise. It's as rare for teachers to step outside their comfort zones as it is for children. If we want to achieve mastery, we need to run the risk of failure, struggle and discomfort.

The message is: don't trust your gut. If it feels right, it's probably wrong. Easy isn't actually easier. Deliberately choosing the harder, more difficult option may be the best way to ensure our students are learning. In the next chapter we'll look at how difficulty and struggle might be a better way to think about teaching for students of different abilities.

We may *say* we value growth mindsets in our students but we have a systemically fixed mindset to teaching and education. If we want change, we need to stop making the same old mistakes and start making some new ones. Teaching has become increasingly high stakes. The consequences of having a poor lesson observation or a bad set of exam results can be pretty awful. Embracing challenges and mistakes is all very well, but if some scumbag is waiting to clobber you for them, your growth mindset won't last long. Teachers are incentivized to cover their backs and find excuses for any mistakes. And let's be clear: we *all* make mistakes. If we want to engender a growth mindset in education we need to remove the consequences of failure. We need to make it OK for teachers to admit their mistakes and, in so doing, learn from them.

Notes

1   John Hattie, *Visible Learning for Teachers: Maximizing Impact on Learning* (London: Routledge, 2011), p. 108.
2   William Bryan and Noble Harter, Studies on the Telegraphic Language: The Acquisition of a Hierarchy of Habits, *Psychological Review* 6(4) (1899): 345–375.
3   Angela Lee Duckworth, Teri A. Kirby, Eli Tsukayama, Heather Berstein and K. Anders Ericsson, Deliberate Practice Spells Success: Why Grittier Competitors Triumph at the National Spelling Bee, *Social Psychological and Personality Science* 2 (2010): 174–181 at 178.
4   Jennifer Crocker, Marc-Andre Olivier and Noah Nuer, Self-Image Goals and Compassionate Goals: Costs and Benefits, *Self and Identity* 8 (2009): 251–269.
5   David Glenn, Carol Dweck's Attitude, *Chronicle of Higher Education* (9 May 2010). Available at: http://chronicle.com/article/Carol-Dwecks-Attitude/65405/.
6   Daniel Dennett, *Consciousness Explained* (London: Penguin, 1993), p. 293.
7   Nicole Shechtman, Angela H. DeBarger, Carolyn Dornsife, Soren Rosier and Louise Yarnall, *Promoting Grit, Tenacity, and Perseverance: Critical Factors for Success in the 21st Century* (US Department of Education Office of Educational Technology, 2013).

Available at: http://tech.ed.gov/files/2013/10/OET-Draft-Grit-Report-2-17-13.pdf, p. viii.

8 Corwin Senko, Chris S. Hulleman and Judith M. Harackiewicz, Achievement Goal Theory at the Crossroads: Old Controversies, Current Challenges, and New Directions, *Educational Psychologist* 46(1) (2011): 26–47.

9 Steven G. Rivkin, Eric A. Hanushek and John F. Kain, Teachers, Schools, and Academic Achievement, *Econometrica* 73(2) (2005): 417–458.

Chapter 22
The dark art of differentiation

There are no differences but differences of degree between different degrees of difference and no difference.

William James

Differentiation is one of the darkest arts in teaching. Of all the impossible tasks expected of poor, overworked teachers, differentiation is one of the most troublesome. The generally accepted position is that differentiation is wholly good, and this is the cause of the wracking guilt felt by harrowed teachers: it may well be good, but it's hard work. In a large study of differentiated instruction in the United States, teachers were provided with extensive professional development and ongoing coaching.[1] Three years later, the researchers wanted to know if the program had had an impact on student learning. But they were stumped. In an interview, one of the team said, "We couldn't answer the question because no one was actually differentiating."

So what exactly *is* differentiation? Ideally, instruction is supposed to be customized for every student: everyone should receive a unique curriculum that meets their individual and unique needs. Teachers produce tailor-made assignments or provide the specific one-on-one help that enables every child to achieve their potential. If this sounds unrealistically onerous to you, then you're not alone. Perhaps it sounds more reasonable to say that differentiation is a process of acknowledging that every child is different and treating them accordingly. Even this leads to overworked, overstretched teachers feeling guilty about not being able to do the impossible. Author and teacher Francis Gilbert says on the subject, "The whole thing is a duplicitous gimmick ... In reality schools just do not have the resources, time or space in the curriculum to implement it."[2] American education writer James Delisle is even more uncompromising: "Differentiation is a failure, a farce, and the ultimate educational joke played on countless educators and students."[3]

But maybe, just maybe, our anger and guilt is misplaced. Maybe differences matter less than we suppose. Obviously we're all different. Just like snowflakes, human beings are all special, unique and entirely individual. But as the philosopher, C. S. Peirce is reputed to have said, "For a difference to be a difference, it must make a difference." Like snowflakes, maybe those differences aren't as important as we might sometimes like to think. When it snows the difference between individual flakes is irrelevant. For all that we each possess our very own unique permutations of DNA, the fact that our physiognomies are broadly the same means we learn and behave in broadly similar ways. Of course we have an infinite variety of differences in ability, but the way we learn is surprisingly similar. Freud called this "the narcissism of the small difference", and Richard Sennett observes that, "We share in common and in roughly equal measure the raw abilities that allow us to become good craftsmen: it is the motivation and aspiration for quality that takes people along different paths in their lives. Social conditions shape these motivations."[4] Teaching is complicated because students are so different, but possible because they're so similar.

If every class is, in a very real sense, a mixed ability class, then, regardless of our views on selection or setting, all teachers need to cater for students with a range of skills, aptitudes and dispositions. Does this mean we have to kill ourselves producing individual lesson plans for all the uniquely different little buggers we teach? Like many of the slippery terms used in education, differentiation can mean all sorts of things depending on who's talking and in what context. Does it mean coping with difference? Learning for all? Success for all? As the landscape has changed over the past few years, there's an increasing consensus that 'success' should be differentiated; our examinations demand winners and losers. Where does this shifting terrain leave us? Claiming that differentiation just means we're special and different, and should be treated as such, is bland to the point of meaninglessness.

So let me offer my definition of differentiation: getting all students to do something they find challenging. Every student should struggle, no matter their ability.

Nuthall points out that, "Ability appears to be the consequence, not the cause of differences in what students learn from their classroom experiences."[5] If we differentiate classroom experiences based on our perceptions of students' abilities then we guarantee our predictions will come to pass. But how should we make decisions about who needs to struggle less? As we saw in Chapter 19, formative assessment only allows us to make (often erroneous) inferences about what's happening inside students' heads. That's fine if we're making decisions about whether we need to explain a point in more detail or provide more opportunity to practice a tricky concept, but it's nowhere near precise enough to decide that certain students should not be taught certain content.

You'd think that for a practice as widespread and onerous as differentiated instruction there would be some compelling evidence in its favor, wouldn't you? Fascinatingly, teacher and *TES* columnist Greg Ashman seems to have uncovered disturbing evidence that differentiation might not be at all effective. Data from the 2013 Teaching and Learning International Survey (TALIS) conducted by the Organization for Economic Cooperation and Development (OECD) reveals that 63 percent of teachers in England say they frequently give different work to students in the same class, compared to only 25 percent of teachers in higher performing countries. Ashman plotted a graph (see Figure 22.1) comparing the TALIS survey with the most recent Program for International Student Assessment (PISA) math scores.

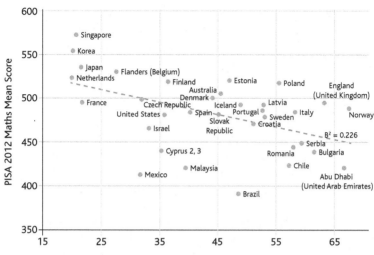

Figure 22.1. Possible effects of differentiation on PISA scores

Source: Greg Ashman, Your Own Personal PISA – What Does the TALIS Show Us?, *ResearchED* (2014).

Ashman says, "I expected some countries with high performance to have low levels of differentiation. However, I also expected the graph to have no overall shape with other high performing countries using this strategy a great deal. I didn't expect to see the rough negative trend that appears to be present."[6]

Admittedly this is just a correlation, and one that isn't even as precise as Figure 1.5. We certainly can't say with certainty that differentiation doesn't work, but neither can we say it does. And surely we should be able to have some confidence in a practice that adds such a significant burden to teachers' workloads. Opportunity cost might go some way to explaining this finding. If a teacher is busy producing differentiated resources for students what will they not have time to do instead?

Thankfully, there's another, perhaps better, way to differentiate. In considering the methods of some of the most successful education systems in the world, education professor and assessment expert Tim Oates reckons that the most successful education systems are built on the assumption that all students are capable of understanding. If this assumption seems ever to be in doubt then "ideas are elaborated in different ways in order to encourage individual understanding".[7]

The kind of teacher led instruction Oates is referring to has been tarred with a very grubby brush over the past few decades. Let me make clear that I am not advocating mono-directional lectures being perpetrated on children. It's just that at certain points in the unfolding of a curriculum, students – because they are novices – benefit most from being taught by experts. As soon as they acquire some expertise then, of course, they should be allowed, indeed encouraged, to forge ahead on their own. My view is that although teacher led instruction might have its flaws and failings, it's more effective than any other form of instruction. Just as democracy is the best worst form of government, teachers explaining difficult concepts to children is the best worst form of teaching.

If we accept that progress is messy – more akin to Siegler's 'overlapping waves' than Piaget's neat stages of smooth, linear progression – and if we further accept that students might need to occupy liminal spaces for slightly longer than a lesson or two, then we should be concerned that ill thought out ideas about differentiation might lead to teachers denying students access to ideas that might take time to click into place. If all we value is increasing short-term performance, then it follows that this is what many students will also value. They will avoid making mistakes and see setbacks and struggle as evidence of failure. When lessons are made as challenging as possible, students will make more mistakes. Mistakes are the very stuff of learning. If your students aren't struggling and making mistakes, perhaps you're not doing your job. The only way to prevent struggle is to lower expectations. And, as the cliché goes, nobody rises to low expectations.

Great expectations

Dylan Wiliam once said, "You show me a teacher who's satisfied with what they're doing, and I will show you a teacher with low expectations."[8] I take some comfort from this. If we make learning hard, sometimes we'll get it wrong and sometimes students will fail to get what we want them to get. But not to try – to make learning easy and guarantee success – that's the real failure.

A few years ago, I taught a transition lesson to a class of 6th grade students to prepare them for the 'step up' to big school. I didn't find out I would be doing this until that morning and I was handed an armful of resources to use with them. I forget now what the lesson was supposed to be on but I do remember thinking it was laughably patronizing. So, just for the hell of it, I decided to teach them a lesson I'd taught to my 11th grade class analyzing the language of Shakespeare's Sonnet 116. Certainly, some of the students struggled but all were able to complete the task I'd set. Afterwards, I asked them to tell me on a scale of 1–10 how hard they had found the work (1 being insultingly easy, 10 being ear-bleedingly difficult). And guess what? They gave me a 5! When I told them the lesson's provenance, I'm not sure if they were more impressed with themselves or disappointed by the lack of challenge presented by secondary school. The point was, I treated them all as if they could do it and, by God, they *could* do it! If I'd told them in advance that they were going to tackle poetry from the GCSE literature anthology it might have 'seemed impossible', but because I didn't they assumed it was possible.

No doubt we'd all want to argue that we have high expectations for our students, so it's helpful to remember that improving short-term performance is teaching that seeks to make learning easier for students. Teaching that explicitly seeks to improve long-term retention and transfer of skills and knowledge is teaching that will result in students making mistakes.

Because of the prevailing belief that students should visibly make progress within lessons, teachers are encouraged to minimize the mistakes students make. There's no real progress in knowing the answer to a question you've just been told. We might *say* we have high expectations, but if we fear to let students fail might our words be revealed as mealymouthed and meaningless?

Teachers' emotional responses can be interpreted as low expectations. It's very hard to maintain high expectations of students you perceive as 'low ability'. Supportive and sympathetic teachers might be communicating that they don't expect quite so much from their students.

> The teacher's reaction suggests that the outcome was in the control of the student, which implies that the student has high ability. Alternatively, students may interpret sympathy by the teacher as a reflection

of lower expectations of them, that is, that the outcome was uncontrollable and thus the student has low ability.[9]

Fascinatingly, when teachers are irritated or annoyed by poor outcomes, students tend to interpret this reaction as demonstrating that the outcome was within their control. After all, who would get angry with something that was simply beyond your ability? It could be that withholding sympathy and support will actually result in students deciding we have higher expectations of them.

If we seek to make classwork easier, students may decide we have low expectations. It's not too great a surprise to find that if students become aware that they are being treated differently, they decide they are less capable. In one study, researchers identified teachers as either 'high-differentiating' or 'low-differentiating'. High-differentiating teachers went to some trouble to provide additional, alternative or simplified materials for students they perceived as more or less able, whereas low-differentiating teachers tended to treat all students similarly. Contrary to most conceptions of what makes good teaching, the study reported significantly worse outcomes for students who had high-differentiating teachers.[10]

It's too easy to say that we should aspire for all students to get over the same high bar. We also need to acknowledge that we'll need to use different ladders *and* think carefully about concealing the ladders. If we treat students differently, they'll behave differently. All students will need to spend time in liminal space but some need to be there for longer. Effective differentiation aims to start with an end point and plan how to get all students there. Sometimes we just need to admit that this takes time and is, frustratingly, beyond our capacity to control.

The mindset of differentiation

This is where the growth mindset may be most useful. Liminality isn't comfortable, and if we're going to make students struggle then they'll get frustrated. Dweck calls the fear of failure the "tyranny of now", and talks about using the "power of yet" to help view struggle differently.[11] She describes a high school in Chicago where students had to pass a set number of courses in order to graduate – if they didn't manage to pass a course they were awarded the grade 'Not Yet'. As she says, "if you get a failing grade, you think, I'm nothing, I'm nowhere. But if you get the grade 'Not Yet' you understand that you're on a learning curve. It gives you a path into the future."[12]

This sounds great, but we need to be mindful of the pitfalls discussed in the previous chapter – the last thing we want is for students to feel tyrannized by the "power of yet". When students fear failure they stop thinking. If they stop thinking they short circuit the possibility of learning. To that end, Dweck tells us we should praise wisely. We will discuss some of the problems with praise in the next chapter.

So that is how I think we should best approach differentiation. Not as a back-breaking exercise in producing teetering piles of pointless paperwork, but by having consistently high expectations of every student we teach, regardless of their ability, and by encouraging them to make and learn from their mistakes. Meeting these expectations takes time. It's as meaningless to expect to see differentiation in a single lesson as it is to see progress. Effective differentiation will take place over months, not hours.

Scaffolding expectations

Of course, it's not enough *just* to expect children to meet challenging expectations without offering any support. Children need different ladders. So what do we do with students whose self-esteem is in tatters? Make them feel better by lowering our expectations? Or struggle to get them to believe that everyone who has experienced success has done so through hard work, perseverance, support, learning from mistakes and making damn sure they try and try again. Obviously, high expectations on their own are insufficient, but they are necessary.

If we assume all children are capable of understanding the threshold concepts of our subjects, we need to think about how we will support them through their liminal journey. There are two important principles here:

1. Scaffolding should be used to enable children to do something they would find too difficult to attempt without support. Just as engineers use scaffolding to help them erect skyscrapers, so should we view the support we give children of different abilities.

326

Similarly, builders tend not to use scaffolds to build a six-foot wall, so neither should we support children by making something simple easier.

2. We should never use scaffolding unless we have a plan for removing it. Writing templates and other interventions at the point of production are very difficult to take away and so children end up becoming dependent on them. Scaffolding at the point of speech and thought is much easier to embed and dismantle. My suggestion is to provide the barest minimum of support to enable children to produce the very best work of which they are capable and then take away that support as quickly as possible.

....

If differentiation means anything it's that we need to resist easy explanations and lazy assumptions. Yes, we're all different, but so what? Other people's minds are hidden to us – we will never know how anyone else learns and to assume that we can is dangerous. But we can perhaps make some assumptions about people in general. We know that forgetting and liminality are predictable side effects of trying to assimilate new information. Everyone will process differently depending on what they already know, but it seems we all go through broadly similar experiences.

Obviously enough, some children have particular needs that must be met. It's not differentiation to provide equal access for students with learning difficulties or physical impairments – it's a basic human right. But where is the line drawn? Many children arrive at school with hideously complex and sometimes harrowing backstories. Of course we must be mindful of their fragile sense of self, but there is little teachers can do to change these unique and tangled problems. Schools need to provide all kinds of support, *but teachers should teach*. And teach as if every child is capable of achieving extraordinary things. The alternative is all too predictable.

And if altering our expectations is problematic, so too are other forms of differentiation. Asking teachers to spend time producing additional resources and wasting time with differentiated lesson plans is at best a distraction. At worst it makes us feel guilty and leads to lowering expectations. When considering what is and isn't reasonable to expect of teachers, my bottom line is this: any policy predicated on the idea that teachers' workload can, or should, increase is doomed to failure. But any policy which makes it easy for teachers to take risks and maintain high expectations of students is likely to succeed.

Notes

1   Carol A. Tomlinson, Catherine M. Brighton, Holly L. Hertberg, Carolyn M. Callahan, Tonya R. Moon, Kay Brimijoin, Linda A. Conover and Timothy Reynolds, Differentiating Instruction in Response to Student Readiness, Interest, and Learning Profile in Academically Diverse Classrooms: A Review of Literature, *Journal for the Education of the Gifted* 27 (2/3) (2003): 119–145.
2   Francis Gilbert quoted in Phil Beadle, *How to Teach* (Carmarthen: Crown House Publishing, 2010), p. 190.
3   James Delisle, Differentiation Doesn't Work, *Education Week* (6 February 2015). http://www.edweek.org/ew/articles/2015/01/07/differentiation-doesnt-work.html?qs=differentiation+doesn%27t+work.
4   Richard Sennett, *The Craftsman* (London: Penguin, 2009), p. 241.
5   Graham Nuthall, *The Hidden Lives of Learners* (Wellington: New Zealand Council for Educational Research Press, 2007), p. 213.
6   Greg Ashman, Your Own Personal PISA – What Does the TALIS Show Us?, *ResearchED* (2014). Available at: http://www.workingoutwhatworks.com/en-GB/Magazine/2014/10/Your_own_personal_PISA.
7   Tim Oates, Why Textbooks Count: A Policy Paper (November 2014). Available at: http://www.cambridgeassessment.org.uk/Images/181744-why-textbooks-count-tim-oates.pdf, p. 12.
8   Dylan Wiliam, Assessment, Learning and Technology: Prospects at the Periphery of Control. Keynote address to ALT-C, Nottingham, 5 September 2007. Available at: https://www.alt.ac.uk/sites/default/files/assets_editor_uploads/documents/altc2007_dylan_wiliam_keynote_transcript.pdf, p. 3.
9   Wilhelmina J. Vialle and Stuart Woodcock, Are We Exacerbating Students' Learning Disabilities? An Investigation of Preservice Teachers' Attributions of the Educational Outcomes of Students with Learning Disabilities (2011). Available at: http://ro.uow.edu.au/cgi/viewcontent.cgi?article=2356&context=edupapers.
10 Christine M. Rubie-Davies, Teacher Expectations and Perceptions of Student Attributes: Is There a Relationship?, *British Journal of Educational Psychology* 80 (2010): 121–135.
11 Carol Dweck, The Power of Believing That You Can Improve, *TED* (December 2014). Available at: https://www.ted.com/talks/carol_dweck_the_power_of_believing_that_you_can_improve/transcript?language=en.
12 Jason S. Moser, Hans S. Schroder, Carrie Heeter, Tim P. Moran and Yu-Hao Lee, Mind Your Errors: Evidence for a Neural Mechanism Linking Growth Mind-Set to Adaptive Posterior Adjustments, *Psychological Science* 22 (2011): 1484–1489.

Chapter 23
The problem with praise

Praise is inextricably bound up with many of the issues discussed in this book. It's hard to separate praise from feedback; it often seems fundamental to motivation (which we'll discuss in the next chapter) and it's become synonymous with developing students' growth mindsets.

In a landmark study, Carol Dweck and her team divided 4-year-olds into two groups and asked them to complete a series of puzzles. When they completed a puzzle, one group was praised for their intelligence and talent. Researchers said things like, "You're so clever," and "I'm so impressed with your intelligence." The children were then asked to attempt another puzzle and were given the choice of a more difficult puzzle or one that was at the same level of difficulty. Most chose a puzzle of about the same difficulty. The second group were praised for their effort. Researchers said, "Well done for trying so hard," and "I'm impressed at how well you stuck at that." These children were much more likely to choose a more difficult second puzzle. The speculation is that praising children for their intelligence makes them see struggle as threatening. If they struggle, they can't be clever. But praising effort, improvement and perseverance helps us to feel that challenge is worthwhile. Dweck says, "When students were praised for effort, 90 percent of them wanted challenging new tasks they could learn from." This is pretty clear, isn't it? She goes on to say that, in contrast to ability praised students who gave up at tasks as they got more difficult, "The effort-praised students still loved the problems, and many of them said that the hard problems were the most fun."[1]

But this is inconsistent with some of Dweck's earlier findings. Hattie tells us, "Kamins and Dweck (1999) compared the effects of praising a person as a whole (for example, 'You're a clever girl') with the effect of praising a person's efforts ('You're excellent in putting in the effort'). Both led to zero or negative effects on achievement."[2] Another study found that praising effort has, at best, a neutral or no effect when students are successful. But praise is likely to be negative when they struggle because this leads to a more 'helpless or hopeless' reaction.[3]

So what should we believe? Does this mean we should stop praising children altogether? Maybe. The much debased currency of 'what went well' prevents teachers stating that sometimes work has no merit – sometimes nothing went well.* If it's not good enough we should say so. Teachers can feel compelled to praise for the barest minimum of effort: "Managed to hand your homework in on time this week? Well done." Hattie and Yates suggest, "If you praise a good deal, students learn you are a teacher that praises a good deal, and that is all. This is not a commodity you can increase and expect the effects of praise will increase."[4]

Praise can be particularly negative when students begin to fail or struggle to understand what's being taught. One study noted that almost half of teachers' feedback was praise, and that "premature and gratuitous praise confused students and discouraged revisions".[5] But surely all this suggests is that praise should be separated from feedback. It makes sense that making a value judgement (praise) could have a negative impact on students' likelihood to act on information on how to improve (feedback). Why should they improve their work if it has been praised? As Hattie says, "for feedback to be effective in the act of learning, praise dissipates the message".[6]

But perhaps the most toxic effect of praise is that it can lead to learned helplessness: students come to depend on the presence of praise to be involved in their work. One study found that when students were provided with feedback with and without praise, feedback *with* praise led to lower engagement and effort![7]

American educationalist Alfie Kohn considers praise patronizing, manipulative and an abuse of power. It could be that praise acts to lower students' interest in a task and it can result in a reduction of quality. "The

---

* It has become increasingly popular over recent years for teachers to respond to students' work by telling them 'What went well' (WWW) before pointing out what might be 'Even better if ...' (EBI). In many schools, these prompts are mandated for all written feedback.

effect of a 'Good job!' is to devalue the activity itself – reading, drawing, helping – which comes to be seen as a mere means to an end, the end being to receive that expression of approval. If approval isn't forthcoming next time, the desire to read, draw, or help is likely to diminish."[8] The problem is that praise is always judgemental – a positive judgement is no more likely to benefit students than a negative one.

So, that seems pretty clear, doesn't it? Praise might have the following deleterious effects:

- It leads to low engagement and effort.
- It has no positive effects on achievement.
- It leads to learned helplessness.
- It's confusing.
- It's patronizing.

The problem is that this seems to contradict our lived experience; we *know* how good praise can make us feel, don't we? Surely to goodness we should be suspicious of research that seems to fly in the face of the evidence of these experiences. When I've shared some of these findings with teachers, the cognitive dissonance has been unbearable. On the whole, I urge caution. I'd recommend distancing ourselves from buffoonery like the praise sandwich and two stars and a wish,* as these certainly decrease the likelihood of students acting on feedback. At best positivity for its own sake is a waste of time, at worst it's transparently manipulative.

But no one would disagree with the power of a sincere compliment – the difficulty is in knowing the difference. Maybe we should start thinking about how best to *encourage* students to learn. Is there a meaningful distinction between such concepts as praise, encouragement and appreciation?

....

* The praise sandwich is a piece of constructive criticism 'sandwiched' between two positive statements. 'Two stars and wish' does exactly what it says it does: two positive comments for every suggestion for improvement.

If praise is to be sincere and useful, Kohn makes the following four recommendations:

1. Make praise as specific as possible.

2. Avoid phony praise.

3. Avoid praise that sets up competition.

4. Don't praise people, only what people do.

How might these points be rebranded as 'encouragement'? My guiding thought is that when we're attempting something difficult, would we rather hear, "Well done!" or "You can do it"? Would we rather be praised or encouraged?

Let's deal with each of them in turn.

1. Make praise as specific as possible

No one, I think, would take issue with this. Most students easily see through such meaningless nonsense as 'Well done' and 'Good job'. These utterances are merely social, signifying precious little. But if you look over any set of students' books, these phrases crop up far more often than is comfortable. We do it out of habit and as a sort of placeholder – something to write while we consider what we really want to say. And, interestingly, the younger the student, the more likely we are to slap on a 'Well done'. It's abundantly obvious that being specific is always more useful than being vague.

Sometime ago I tried an experiment. I told a class of 8th grade students that I would avoid using praise when I graded their work over the course of a semester. I consciously avoided generic pats on the head and focused on just giving them specific instructions on how to improve. At the end of a six week period, I asked them to give me feedback on my feedback by answering these questions:

- How did it make you feel?

- How easy was it to act on?

- Is your work better as a result?

Hardly scientific, but the consensus was that they didn't feel much either way. They felt my comments were easy to act on and that their redrafted work was better. One student said she wanted me to tell her what she did well. So I did. No one said it made them feel bad and everyone felt that they had been able to improve their work. Although I didn't praise anyone, they all felt *encouraged* by knowing how to improve their work. Here's some confirmation bias:

> Praise for task performance appears to be ineffective, which is hardly surprising because it contains such little learning-related information.[9]

> Praise addressed to students is unlikely to be effective, because it carries little information ... and too often deflects attention from the task.[10]

Students *like* praise, but so what? They like eating popcorn, watching music videos and goofing off with each other, but I'm sure I'm not alone in wanting to minimize these activities in the classroom. Students are often very poor at knowing what is good for them and their preferences are usually a weak indicator of what will work best.

2. Avoid phony praise

As a rule, it's always best to avoid insincerity. But as I thought about it, what I realized is that it can be devilishly difficult to spot phony praise. The way teachers interact with students is embedded over time. Just as students can suffer with learned helplessness, so can teachers. Changing habits is hard. If students are badly behaved we can easily find ourselves applauding them for basics like showing up on time, sitting in their seats and doing the bare minimum of work. What do they learn from this? My suspicion is that when they get a 'Well done' for sitting down, it normalizes bad behavior. They start saying stuff like, "Look, I've written two sentences and not punched anyone. Surely I deserve some Vivo Miles."

3. Avoid praise that sets up competition

Much as we might wish otherwise, life ain't fair. Students' performance is relative and it's useful to know how well we're doing compared to others because then we can do something about it. Someone has to be at the bottom of the pile, but it doesn't have to be *us*.

As we've seen, making mistakes is an unavoidable part of life. We need to be honest about our mistakes but not to celebrate them as some sort of victory. Instead we should help students overcome setbacks and see mistakes in the context of longer-term goals. We should help them to be gracious in defeat and to acknowledge the success of others. "To do that, we need to refuse all the meaningless plastic and tin destined for landfills. We have to stop letting the Trophy-Industrial Complex run our children's lives."[11]

I'm not sure that avoiding competition is a worthy goal. Telling a student, "You're the best in the class," isn't bad because it creates competition but because it's divisive. It's the praise that's the problem, not the competition. Encouragement could well work by engendering competition. What about saying, "You haven't done as much as everyone else on your table" or "Kayleigh has come up with the best range of ideas so far"?

4. Don't praise people, only what people do

I've saved this one for last deliberately. This is the one that runs counter to so much recent training in schools. Dweck tells us that the way to a growth mindset is to praise students' effort rather than their ability, but Kohn disagrees suggesting that praising students' effort is as likely to backfire as praising their intelligence. Praising effort might suggest low expectations – *Well done for trying but someone of your ability is never going to actually succeed.* "To the extent that we want to teach the importance of making an effort – the point being that people have some control over their future accomplishments – praise really isn't required at all."[12]

Instead, Kohn recommends 'process praise', or praising what people *do*. So, instead of lavishing praise on students' effort, however heroic, we should instead focus on their *efforts*. This may seem an insignificant distinction but adding that 's' could make all the difference. Our effort may be too bound up in who we are, but our efforts are clearly separate from us. Effort is something we have to dredge up from within, but our efforts are what we have produced. The main difference is that instead of commenting on what students are doing (which is inextricably bound up with who we are at that moment), we're commenting on what they've done. And this takes us full circle. If I'm commenting on the work a student has produced, I'll do much better to give them kind, helpful and specific instructions on how to improve it further.

Now, maybe I'm overcomplicating all of this. Some studies conflate process praise and praising effort, using the terms interchangeably.[13] But the point isn't to second guess ourselves or try to catch people out; it's to really think about the likely effects of what we say. I'm not saying *not* to praise kids – all I'd urge is that you think about why you're doing it and what you want to achieve.

Whether or not process praise helps students to develop the ability to cope with struggle, it's a fact that the better you know your students, and the better they know what to expect, the better your ability to differentiate will be. Routines need embedding. It takes preparation and patience for students to trust that struggle; not being able to do things *yet* is positive.

Notes

1   Carol Dweck, *Mindset: The New Psychology of Success* (New York: Ballantine, 2007), p. 72.
2   John Hattie, *Visible Learning for Teachers: Maximizing Impact on Learning* (London: Routledge, 2011), p. 121. See also Melissa L. Kamins and Carol S. Dweck, Person vs. Process Praise and Criticism: Implications for Contingent Self-Worth and Coping, *Developmental Psychology* 35(3) (1999): 835–847.
3   Yvonne Skipper and Karen Douglas, Is No Praise Good Praise? Effects of Positive Feedback on Children's and University Students' Responses to Subsequent Failures, *British Journal of Educational Psychology* 82(2) (2011): 327–339.
4   John Hattie and Gregory Yates, Using Feedback to Promote Learning, in Victor A. Benassi, Catherine E. Overson and Christopher M. Hakala (eds), *Applying Science of Learning in Education: Infusing Psychological Science into the Curriculum* (Washington, DC: American Psychological Association, 2014), pp. 45–58 at p. 47.
5   Ken Hyland and Fiona Hyland, Feedback on Second Language Students' Writing, *Language Teaching* 39(2) (2006): 83–101 at 87.
6   Hattie, *Visible Learning for Teachers*, p. 121.
7   Ursula Kessels, Lisa M. Warner, Julia Holle and Bettina Hannover, Threat to Identity Through Positive Feedback About Academic Performance, *Zeitschrift für Entwicklungspsychologie und Pädagogische Psychologie* 40(1) (2008): 22–31.
8   Alfie Kohn, Criticizing (Common Criticisms of) Praise, *Alfie Kohn* (3 February 2012). Available at: http://www.alfiekohn.org/blogs/criticizing-common-criticisms-praise/.

9   John Hattie and Helen Timperley, The Power of Feedback, *Review of Educational Research* 77(1) (2007): 81–112 at 87.

10   Ibid. 97.

11   Ashley Merryman, Losing Is Good for You, *New York Times* (24 September 2014). Available at: http://www.nytimes.com/2013/09/25/opinion/losing-is-good-for-you.html?_r=2&.

12   Kohn, Criticizing (Common Criticisms of) Praise.

13   Kyla Haimovitz and Jennifer Henderlong Corpus, Effects of Person versus Process Praise on Student Motivation: Stability and Change in Emerging Adulthood, *Educational Psychology* 31(5) (2011): 595–609. Available at: http://www.reed.edu/motivation/docs/Haimovitz_Corpus_AERA.pdf.

Chapter 24

Motivation: when the going gets tough, the tough get going

Our greatest weakness lies in giving up. The most certain way to succeed is always to try just one more time.

Thomas A. Edison

Why is it that some kids arrive at school motivated to work hard, while others can't be bothered? What explains this difference? The crucial question for teachers is, how does motivation work?

The problem we face is that learning requires effort, attention, concentration, discipline and motivation. As we've discussed, what we teach is subject to rapid and substantial forgetting. Because of this, no one is likely to learn something unless they're sufficiently interested in it. But even when students are interested, concentration spans are short and attention is easily disrupted. What's more, the act of concentrating and the effort of maintaining self-control places great stress on mental resources, which are subject to overload. Self-control strategies are insecurely learned, relatively unpracticed and easily depleted.[1]

Motivation is driven not so much by the relevance of the content as the challenge of the task. If students are sufficiently curious about what they're learning, the effort involved seems worth it. If a task is too easy or too hard, we can't be bothered. Being asked to do a word search might be fun for a while but it soon becomes dull. Equally, being asked to perform complex calculations in your head is unlikely to have much appeal for most students. We are motivated by problems that are both challenging *and* attainable — otherwise we get frustrated, bored or complacent.

Teaching needs to stretch but not overwhelm students. Now, obviously challenge is relative; what's challenging to me might be straightforward to you. How then do we get the level of challenge 'just right'?

Much of what goes on in classrooms is predicated on the belief that if kids are sufficiently engaged in an activity, they will learn from it. But it doesn't take a genius to spot that we can really enjoy something without learning a whole lot from it. For instance, most children will enjoy spending lessons watching cartoons, but they're unlikely to learn much curriculum content this way. This leads us inexorably down the path of 'dumbing down' and fun for fun's sake. Nuthall's research "shows that students can be busiest and most involved with material they already know. In most of the classrooms we have studied, each student already knows about 40–50% of what the teacher is teaching."[2] We tend to be motivated to get stuck into tasks we're comfortable with, but that won't result in us learning much. Motivation to work is not enough. We have to be willing to grapple with uncertainty. As Nuthall says, "Learning requires motivation, but motivation does not necessarily lead to learning."[3]

Our misunderstanding of the relationship between motivation and learning filters through into how we conduct assessments. When given a test, some students will quietly get on with it, some will be looking busy but not writing very much, some will doodle and others will put their heads on the desk and dribble. Guess which ones will do best on the test? Those students who care about doing well will do the best. But what of those students who knew what to do to get the answer but didn't do it? Tests are an accurate measure of how keen we are on taking tests; they are not that great a measure of what we've learned.

So this offers us two choices. We could either forget about learning altogether and simply focus on motivation – a bit of a 'hit and hope' approach. Or we could attempt to strip out some of what passes for engagement and teach demanding content in as impassioned a way as we can manage. Instead of tempting kids with shiny baubles, teach them and they will come. But what if they're not interested in our subjects? What if they think math, poetry or the Treaty of Versailles is boring?

Daniel Willingham argues that content doesn't drive interest. What could be more interesting to a teenage boy than sex education? He recalls how the long anticipated lesson where human sexuality was first explained was crushingly tedious: "It's not that the teacher talked about flowers and pollination – he really did talk about human sexuality – but somehow it was still dull. I wish I could remember how he did it; boring a bunch of hormonal teenagers with a sex talk is quite a feat."[4] Quite so. In my case, all I remember of that lesson was the teacher using a rubber glove to demonstrate the purpose of an erection. She picked up the flaccid thing and showed how difficult it was to get one of the fingers through a hole, and then inflated it saying, "Look – it goes in easily now."

The content of a lesson may be sufficient to whet your appetite, but it won't sustain your interest if the lesson is dull. The very real difficulty with getting students to engage in something difficult is that it will require them to expend effort. Generally speaking, they're not keen to do this. To unpick this we need to consider what goes through students' minds and how they are incentivized to make effort.

Math teacher David Thomas has used game theory (see Table 24.1) to show the process students might go through in deciding whether or not to exert effort in lessons.

Table 24.1. The effort matrix

		Teacher	
		Good lesson	**Bad lesson**
Student	**Good lesson**	Academic success Social success	Academic failure Social failure
	Bad lesson	Academic failure Social success	Academic failure Social success

Source: David Thomas, Trying is Risky, *Mr Thomas' Blog* (9 February 2014). Available at: http://www.mrthomasmaths.com/2014/02/trying-is-risky/.

In every lesson students have a choice: will they make an effort or not? Teachers can, at least to some extent, control the quality of their lessons. Any teacher, no matter how skilled, will teach a mix of 'good' and 'bad' lessons. Clearly this is hugely reductionist and there will be many shades of grey in-between, but essentially a lesson is good when students learn having chosen to exert effort and bad when they have not. For each pair of inputs there are two results, one academic and one social. There are many ways for students to enjoy the approval of their peers but only one route to academic success, and this requires both teachers and students to make a positive input.

So what governs the choices students make? To some extent, this depends on a host of imponderables, such as time of day, the weather or the results of playground disagreements, but on the whole students assess whether a lesson is likely to be good and choose their level of participation accordingly. Game theory suggests that students are likely to be risk averse. If they perceive the probability of a lesson being only 50 percent good then most students will not consider this lesson worth investing effort in; if they did they would risk failing socially. The goal for teachers is to convince students that the probability of a lesson being good is as high as possible. Unfortunately, this isn't totally within the sphere of teachers' control. Students' decisions will be affected by their prior experience of the subject, their self-esteem and the school culture. To make the risk of exerting effort pay off teachers need to plan lessons to make sure any effort will result in some measurable success.

The greatest challenge to economic modeling is the rationalist delusion. People – especially students – don't always act rationally. There's little rationale for sabotaging their own learning in the way some seem to, and it doesn't always result in social success.

Behavioral economics offers another way of looking at motivation. Remember Kahneman's System 1 and 2 thinking: System 1 is always on, always processing, always making snap judgements and decisions – often we're not even aware of what we're doing. But when we're faced with difficulty, System 2 flips on and takes control of our thinking. The problem is that this requires concentration. If we're distracted we quickly revert to autopilot and run on instinct and impulse. Thus our lives are a tug of war between head and heart. As System 1 urges us to act on impulse, System 2 attempts to regulate our behavior through self-control.

Because of the effort involved in staying focused, Kahneman suggests System 2 thinking is essentially lazy. We have an in-built reluctance to invest any more effort than is strictly necessary. We conduct our mental lives by the law of least effort. The effortful thinking that we demand of stdudents requires discipline and self-control. But this kind of thinking and the effort involved in not giving in to the path of least resistance and slacking off is hard work. Our best intentions are worn down by any distraction. This could be cognitive load, but it could also be lack of sleep, hunger or the need to empty our bladder. And at the same time, we're more likely to be selfish and inconsiderate in other areas if we're maintaining focus on a particular task. I often find that when I'm immersed in writing, some instinct makes me snap impatiently at offers of a cup of coffee or requests that I empty the dishwasher.

Expending effort leads to *ego depletion*. We have a limited reserve of self-control. If we're exerting control in one area, we don't have it to spare in another. If you're tired, you're more likely to overeat; if you're concentrating on a complex cognitive process, you're less likely to be polite. And when it comes to school work, the more your ego is depleted, the more likely you are to give up.

This has led psychologists to wonder whether our reserves of self-control and motivation are strictly finite or whether they can be built up through training. Apparently they can. In several experiments, people were able to resist the effects of ego depletion when given a strong enough incentive. University of Oregon researchers explored attempts to raise intelligence by improving control of attention. They found that "Training attention not only improved self-control, scores on non-verbal tests of intelligence also improved and the improvement was sustained for several months."[5]

School demands extraordinary efforts of cognitive work and self-control from students every day. Some students seem to have less self-control than others. The paradox is that the students with the least self-control often need it most. Self-control depletes, habit rescues. The only way out of the paradox is for us to strengthen students' System 2 thinking by building the habit of self-control.

How? Probably the most straightforward answer lies in embedding consistent classroom routines. This makes it easier for students to do what is expected of them because they don't have to think about it; they do the same things lesson in, lesson out. Obviously this requires a lot of self-control and effort from poor, overworked teachers. We're as much in danger of ego depletion as anyone else.

Motivation is inextricably bound up with emotion. This is referred to by psychologists as the *affective domain*. Just knowing how students go about encoding, storing and retrieving curriculum content doesn't mean they'll actually do it. How they feel matters even more. Recall the Pygmalion effect discussed in Chapter 1: what happens is influenced by our expectations. How a teacher treats a student or a class affects their motivation. People live up to our expectations of them. And nobody rises to low expectations.

As a student, what makes you look forward to the lesson? Often it's not so much *what* you have next, as *who* you have next. Emotional interactions between teachers and students are some of "the most powerful hidden dynamics of teaching", according to Robert Marzano, as they are "typically unconscious".[6]

Three charioteers

As we saw in Chapter 1, rational, forceful persuasion is far from the most powerful form of influence. If we want to win over hearts and minds we need to understand how to make such an appeal. The art of rhetoric has been around for millennia and any attempt to motivate our students will benefit from an understanding of the 'three charioteers' of rhetoric: ethos (our credibility and authority), pathos (an appeal to emotions) and logos (an appeal to logic).

This helps us to see a teacher's influence on students' motivation through the eyes of the students. There are questions that all students implicitly and subconsciously ask of teachers when being taught by them.

Ethos: How much credibility does this teacher have?

Some of our credibility is bound up in our experience. As new teachers, we're perceived as having limited authority so it's hard to get students to take us seriously. When we've worked at a school for a while it becomes gradually easier. However, if we're perceived as being ineffectual this will increasingly work to our disadvantage.

We need to show students not only that we mean business and we'll do what we say we'll do, but also that we're worth taking seriously. If they don't trust that we know whereof we speak, they'll soon stop listening.

- How can you demonstrate that you want great things for your students?

- How can you encourage their efforts with genuine, sincere praise?

- How do you model hard work and self-control?

Pathos: How much does this teacher care?

Children quickly decide, "Why should I care if you don't?" Obviously, this isn't logical and results in cutting off your toes to spite your feet, but that doesn't make it any less prevalent or powerful.

Most people respond well to the sense that they're cared about, and children need to feel that we understand and will encourage them. If we give homework but don't grade it, they'll stop making an effort. If students see us as human, they'll treat us as human. So any advice along the lines of not smiling until Christmas is a guaranteed way to weaken our ability to influence our classes.

- How can you take the time to understand each student by asking them about *themselves?*

- How can you affirm each student by catching them making the effort?

- How can you show that you see their viewpoint: 'I know this isn't your only subject!'

Logos: How much does this teacher help me succeed?

Students need to believe both that we have something worth teaching and that the challenges we set make them feel successful. The more they experience success, the more effort they'll put into succeeding. But the success they experience needs to feel worthwhile – if it's too easy, it's not valuable.

- How can you trust them with rewarding challenges?

- How can you hold them to ever higher standards?

- How can you support them even more patiently?

The more students (implicitly) answer these questions positively, the more students will feel motivated to work hard. *The harder you work on your empathy for them, the harder they'll work for you.*

Trust is a better predictor of teacher success than expertise. A teacher may know their subject inside out, but if their students don't trust them they won't feel very motivated. It works both ways though: subject expertise builds trust; students love being taught by someone who loves their subject and knows best how to share it.

The challenge is this: while students with the most difficult emotions are the hardest to deal with, they're precisely the kids in most need of emotional affection, affirmation and encouragement. Whenever teachers say, "You're so bright, but your behavior isn't good enough and you're not working hard enough," the message students hear is: "I'm so bright, I don't need to behave or work very hard." Eventually interactions turn hostile, and both teachers' and students' emotional reactions become resentful.

If students grappling with the most tangled emotions are the ones most at risk of a downward spiral of complacency, negativity, resentment and hostility, what can we do? Simply attempting to level the un-level playing field for those who experience negativity at home by rewarding their intermittent efforts, while neglecting those students who quietly and consistently work hard, is counter-productive. If the worst behaved kids get rewarded most, the school perpetuates disruption and dis-incentivizes effort.

Ultimately, this is a dilemma as much for school leaders as for classroom teachers. We all need to find a way to internalize the habit of self-control that will last a lifetime, or at least until home time. A culture of trust is vital, and it starts with modeling: unless we as teachers, and the school at large, practice what we preach on being motivated and loving learning, how do we hope to inspire enduring motivation in kids? The happier teachers are in their work, the happier students are to work hard. The higher the standards of behavior that we hold kids to, the more they realize that we care about them in the long term. We shouldn't indulge them by placating and pleading, then lose patience and snap into anger and annoyance. Instead, we should embody purpose, not power, as guiding adults making tough choices, especially when it gets difficult.

Hearts matter as much as minds. Those of us excited by the potential of cognitive science to improve teaching should not blind ourselves to students' emotional connection with us. To neglect the affective domain is to miss an important piece of the puzzle of student motivation. And the more difficult the emotions the kid brings to the classroom, the greater the emotional impact we have a chance to make on their lives. Tender, loving care can make all the difference.

Motivation and mindset anchoring

The unofficial motto at Eton, one of the most prestigious schools in the world, is 'Effortlessly superior'; it's only acceptable to be better than everyone else as long as you're not trying. But this is a pernicious and inherently dishonest position to take. Maybe there are some people so blessed that they don't have to work hard to achieve success, but how much more might they achieve were they to break a sweat now and again? The reality is that while we might pretend not to try, almost all real success is based on hard work and effort. Why should we have come to value the appearance of laziness? This way of seeing the world leads us to look at the apparently effortless performance of an expert and assume that they're just talented, and it's all right for them. How many of us give up on a goal when we realize just how great the gulf is between where we're starting from and mastery?

Beliefs matter; mindset matters; work ethic matters. Our ideas about effort stem from our mindset. If you believe in effortless intelligence, it leads to avoidance of effort and fear of failure. If you believe in hard work and overcoming setbacks, this leads to success. As we've seen, growth mindsets change the meaning of embarrassing mistakes, tough challenges, hurtful setbacks, negative criticism and long slogs into opportunities. These students internalize the questions: what can I learn from this? What can I do to improve for next time?

One vital ingredient in the motivation mix is our beliefs. If we believe our intelligence grows with practice, effort and discipline, we will be more likely to seek challenge and persist in the face of setbacks. If we don't, we'll avoid challenge and give up as soon as we start to struggle. The promise of the growth mindset is that we no longer see tough, challenging work as long or boring: we not only seek challenge, we thrive on it.

Imagine this scenario: you've coached a student debating team all year through practice debates. Your team is strong and aims to win an annual competition. They've even imagined taking the trophy home. In the event, your team does well but is defeated on points. They are devastated. How would you react as their coach?

1. Tell them you thought they were best.

2. Tell them they were robbed of the trophy.

3. Tell them debating isn't that important in the grand scheme of things.

4. Tell them they have the ability and will surely win next time.

5. Tell them they didn't deserve to win.

Which did you choose?

Dweck argues that choices 1–4 don't help us improve. Instead, she recommends 5: tell them they didn't deserve to win. "I know how you feel. It's disappointing to do your best but not win. But you haven't earned it yet. The other teams have practiced harder. If you really want this, it's something you'll have to really work for."[7] Our mindset is a choice we can control.

Choice architecture

Which brings us to choice architecture. Maybe we can redesign the contexts within which students make choices. In their book, *Nudge*, Richard Thaler and Cass Sunstein suggest we can design contexts to help people make better decisions.[8] This has obvious and urgent applications in schools: as teachers and school leaders we are responsible for organizing the contexts around the decisions students make about whether to exert effort in lessons.

One of the greatest design tools a choice architect has is understanding cognitive biases. In addition to all the biases we explored in Chapter 1, it's also worth getting our heads round the status quo bias. Inertia is sticky and most people tend to stick with the default option. Even if we don't give them a seating plan, students will sit in the same seats week in, week out. The default option is perceived as the normal choice; deviating from the normal choice requires more effortful deliberation and more responsibility. These powerful forces guide the decisions of those otherwise unsure of what to do. Never underestimate the power of inertia. That power can be harnessed.

Organ donation is an instructive example. There's a huge shortage of organ donors but only about 40 percent of us opt for it. But when potential donors were asked whether they wanted to actively opt out of organ donation, take up increased to 80 percent. Opt outs as default options are powerful because we have such a strong tendency to stick with the way things are. By changing the default setting we can change the way people decide.

The anchoring effect (see Chapter 2) directs and constrains our thinking. Once your mind is hooked by an anchor, it's hard to stray away from it. Combining the promise of the growth mindset with the effects of anchoring, the default option and status quo bias could be a powerful way of increasing students' motivation to exert effort in lessons. The question is, how can we make a growth mindset response to challenge, effort and setbacks the default option?

How would you know when a school has succeeded in developing a growth mindset culture? Maybe when choosing effort and risking setbacks have become the default option for every student. If you were to go into any classroom at any time and find every student on task, on every task, then a school would be on a steady course to achievement. Of course, this is easier said than done. It's much simpler for schools to see developing a growth mindset as desirable for students while maintaining a very fixed approach to confronting bias and changing policies.

Motivation and peer pressure

A casual stroll through any town center on any Friday night will demonstrate just how powerful an influence peer pressure is. The pressure to drink to excess and act foolishly is difficult to avoid; few of us are able to hold firm against the urge to conform.

In schools, peer pressure is just as visceral. Whether it is a force for good or ill depends. Where kids are pressurized into bullying or bystanding, disrupting lessons or disrespecting teachers it can be monstrously damaging. Where it creates a virtuous circle of friendly competition, encouragement, hard work and useful revision it's a huge asset. But beware: if it tips over into unhealthy competition, sleepless nights and agonizing stress over grades it can be equally destructive.

How do we harness the incredible power of peer pressure, especially when it comes to motivation, willpower and self-control?

We run into difficulty when our self-control is tested. As Oscar Wilde said, "I can resist everything except temptation." When choices and consequences are separated, over time it becomes much more difficult to exercise self-control. We know we shouldn't stuff our faces with cream cakes; it takes months for the weight to show. The cost – doing without – is borne immediately, but the benefits are delayed. In the cream cake example, the benefit – remaining slim – is intangible as we never see the alternative. It's so much easier to get the pleasure now and suffer the consequences later. Delaying gratification requires an ability to look into the future and decide what will be best for us in the long term.

This sounds exactly like the decision students face: "Do I make the costly effort to work hard now for some hazy, eventual, potential future? Or do I have fun, fool around and disrupt the lesson, earning street cred now from my peers, which pays off right away?" The options of effort exertion and lesson disruption have opposite reward profiles (see Table 24.2): the first has immediate costs and delayed benefits; the second has instant benefits and delayed costs.

Table 24.2. Disruption/effort

Disruption	
Instant reward	Long run costs
Effort	
Instant costs	Long run rewards

However, as we know from Chapter 2, what appear to be simple, rational incentives can turn out to cause perverse behavior. We need to pay attention to the different aspects of how we think. Rapid, impulsive System 1 (what Thaler and Sunstein refer to as the "myopic Doer") and slow, effortful System 2 (the "far-sighted Planner"). The planner attempts to plan for the long term but has to contend with the doer who needs instant gratification. Efforts at self-control are our planners trying to reign in our doers. As anyone who's made a New Year's resolution knows, this is easier said than done. And the more distant the pay-off, the harder it is for the planner to come out on top: "For example, alarm clocks lead to fierce battles between the Planner and the Doer. Stickk.com is a way planners can constrain their doers by committing to a specific action or habit. It uses peer pressure such as emails to family and friends, group blog. Alarm clocks are external commitment devices people use to solve their self-control problems."[9]

Internal control systems are vital; you still have to overcome the temptation of the snooze button! Behavioral economist Daniel Goldstein says there's a very unequal war being waged between our present and future selves. Our present self is present – it dominates our awareness, while our future self is distant and weak.[10]

For many students, the battle is even more unequal: the present self prefers fun to effort, and so do their 30 peers. Arrayed against this tsunami, weakly voicing the need for effort, like an internal King Cnut, is the feeble future self. And us, their teachers. The temptation to give in to distraction is great indeed. And as we well know, being self-controlled for extended periods of time (such as the school day) takes it out of you.

Given that peer pressure is an ever present reality, how do we turn peer pressure from a negative to a positive influence? Goldstein gives us a clue: external commitment devices like alarm clocks (or, for students, sanctions like detentions) don't always work, so intrinsic commitment is vital.

Making positive peer pressure more visible just might work. Goldstein does this with finance: he makes the future self more powerful by building visual products that let people 'see' the future consequences of their present actions. Why might this work? Behavioral economists have shown in scientific research that the urge for conformity is strong – we prefer to conform rather than face disapproval of the group, and so we do as those around us do. For instance, including a message on tax returns saying "more than 90 percent of people have already complied" increased compliance. So visual, public displays of students' effort could harness the power of peer pressure for effort exertion.

We are hardwired to connect to others. In *The Willpower Instinct*, Kelly McGonigal says, "Our social brains catch willpower failures contagiously through unintentional mimicry, emotion contagion and seeing others give in to temptation. We eat more with others than alone, and spend more when shopping with friends. Rule-breaking is contagious."[11]

We looked at the concept of social proof in Chapter 2. The way those around us behave has an enormous sway over our behavior. But if rule breaking is contagious, so is rule following. If we can establish strong social norms that make it easier to make positive choices, students will deplete less of their ego exerting self-control. Doing 'the right thing' becomes a habit.

Moral psychologist Jonathan Haidt says, "We care more about looking good than being good." He explains further, "People are simultaneously selfish and groupish. We evolved to live in groups, we are designed by natural selection as conditional hive creatures. Groupishness was a key innovation that took us beyond selfishness and into civilization."[12]

Ultimately, external commitment needs to be internalized in student mindsets. What does this mean? The key insight is the difference between automatic System 1 and the reasoned System 2. Haidt's metaphor of the powerful elephant and the reasoning rider can help us to better understand our mental processes: "The rider's inability to control the elephant by force explains many puzzles about our mental life, particularly why we have such trouble with weakness of will. Learning how to train the elephant is the secret of self-improvement."[13]

So, we're ruled by instinct rather than reason, self-control is a habit and behavior is contagious. The key to getting students to learn is understanding what motivates them, and insights from psychology suggest this is less chaotic and confusing than it might first appear.

The question we should be considering is how to design systems and policies that:

- Train students' elephants.

- Tap into students' hivish and chimpish nature.

- Strengthen students' self-control and willpower.

- Empower students' future selves over their present selves.

- Give students' restrained, far-sighted planners control over their impulsive, myopic doers.

- Ensure they choose effort over disruption every lesson, no matter who teaches it.

- Strengthen their weak System 2.

The answer lies in making it easy to learn and socially awkward and undesirable to fool around. We need to apply gentle but firm pressure to encourage students to avoid the behaviors that run counter to their best interests, and then provide rewarding release when they make choices that result in them being best able to learn.[14]

Notes

1   See John Hattie and Gregory Yates, *Visible Learning and the Science of How We Learn* (London: Routledge, 2014) for more detail on this problem area.

2   Graham Nuthall, *The Hidden Lives of Learners* (Wellington: New Zealand Council for Educational Research Press, 2007), p. 24.

3   Ibid. p. 35.

4   Daniel Willingham, *Why Don't Students Like School? A Cognitive Scientist Answers Questions About How the Mind Works and What It Means for the Classroom* (San Francisco, CA: Jossey-Bass, 2009), p. 8.

5   Daniel Kahneman, *Thinking, Fast and Slow* (London: Penguin, 2012), pp. 47–48.

6   Robert Marzano, *The Art and Science of Teaching: A Comprehensive Framework for Effective Instruction* (Alexandria, VA: Association for Supervision & Curriculum Development, 2007), p. 162.

7   Carol Dweck, *Mindset: The New Psychology of Success* (New York: Ballantine, 2007), p. 212.

8   Richard H. Thaler and Cass R. Sunstein, *Nudge: Improving Decisions About Health, Wealth and Happiness* (New Haven, CT: Yale University Press, 2008).

9   Ibid. p. 44.

10 Daniel Goldstein, The Battle Between Your Present and Future Self, *ted. com* [video] (November 2011). Available at: http://www.ted.com/talks/ daniel_goldstein_the_battle_between_your_present_and_future_self.

11 Kelly McGonigal, *The Willpower Instinct: How Self-Control Works, Why It Matters, and What You Can Do To Get More of It* (New York: Avery, 2013), p. 192.

12 Jonathan Haidt, *The Righteous Mind* (London: Penguin, 2012), p. xv.

13 Ibid. p. x.

14 Material in this chapter has been adapted from Joe Kirby's excellent blog, *Pragmatic Education*. Joe Kirby, How Willpower Works: The Science of Self-Control, *Pragmatic Education* (10 May 2014). Available at: https://pragmaticreform.wordpress. com/2014/05/10/willpower/. Joe Kirby, Motivation and Instruction, *Pragmatic Education* (24 May 2014). Available at: https://pragmaticreform.wordpress. com/2014/05/24/motivation-instruction/. Joe Kirby, Motivation and Emotion, *Pragmatic Education* (31 May 2014). Available at: https://pragmaticreform.wordpress. com/2014/05/31/motivation-emotion/. Joe Kirby, Motivation and Peer Pressure, *Pragmatic Education* (14 June 2014). Available at: https://pragmaticreform.wordpress. com/2014/06/14/motivation-peer-pressure/.

Chapter 25
Are schools killing creativity?

Creativity is constraints.

Ken Campbell

With all this emphasis on conformity, obeying rules and preparing children for the treadmill of exams, are schools killing creativity? Creativity guru Sir Ken Robinson certainly thinks so. In his staggeringly popular TED Talk, 'How Schools Kill Creativity,'* he says creativity is as important in education as literacy and should be treated with the same status.[1] Now, we all want children to be creative, but is it something we can actually teach? Well, that rather depends on what it is.

Robinson equates creativity with 'divergent thinking' – the ability to interpret a question in many different ways and to see many different answers to a question. Apparently, NASA test astronauts' capacity for divergent thinking by getting them to think of as many different uses for a paperclip as possible. Most people are able to come up with 10 to 15 uses for a paperclip. People who are good at divergent thinking come up with around 200.

Unfortunately, our capacity for divergent thinking deteriorates with age. A longitudinal study of kindergarten children measured 98 percent of them at genius level in divergent thinking. Five years later, when they were aged 8 to 10 years, those at genius level had dropped to 50 percent. After another five years, the number of divergent thinking geniuses had

....

* With over 30 million views and counting, it's the most popular TED Talk of all time. In it he says you can't be creative unless you're prepared to be wrong, which is lucky for me.

fallen further still. Robinson argues that the main intervention that these children have had is education, a conveyor belt education that tells them, "There's only one answer. It's at the back. And don't look. That's called cheating."[2] Schools are killing creativity.

As a remedy, Robinson argues that we should value the arts more highly and find ways to foster creativity in those subjects where it doesn't necessarily appear naturally. We should do this because creativity is increasingly important in a world where jobs that don't require creativity have disappeared or been outsourced to other countries where people do them more cheaply. Far from having to teach kids to be creative, all we have to do is stop teaching them *not* to be. Robinson defines creativity as "the process of having original ideas that have value".[3] This process, he tells us, is distinct from imagination. We can imagine loads of stuff without actually creating anything worthwhile. It's not creative to come up with ridiculous, impractical nonsense; it's creative to work within boundaries. Children's imaginations are already pretty vast and the younger the child, the greater the depth of their imagination. We don't need to teach this, it just is.

But however useful it might be to see all this stuff that no one else sees, the point is that for it to be useful ideas have to, eventually, converge. They have to make sense and they have to be practical. Without clear knowledge of forms and rules creativity loses cohesion, and we end up with a kitchen sink soup of ideas where everything has been thrown into the pot with little regard for recipe, structure or purpose.

This is as true of mathematics, art, music, science and engineering as it is of writing. It's the 'having worth' bit that's important here. Writing down lots of interesting numbers but leaving out all the pesky calculations is futile. Similarly, twanging randomly at guitar strings may well give vent to your feelings but is in no way to be considered music. One could perhaps argue that daubing paint randomly on canvas worked for Jackson Pollock, but I (and perhaps he) might argue that he went through a rigorous process of experimentation before arriving at a new and beautiful form.

And that's the point: creativity requires form. In order to write a sonnet you have to understand the rules of the sonnet form. And in order to play with the form, to experiment with the rules and, yes, to break them, you still need to know what those rules are. If you don't know how a sentence operates, how can you truly be creative in the way you construct your sentences? Just having ideas and tossing them at the page simply isn't good enough. Providing a clear, comprehensible framework for how to structure these ideas will help students to have a greater ability to process their ideas into a form which 'has worth'.

There are, however, some pretty unhelpful myths out there. Consider this oft-quoted advice from sci-fi writer Ray Bradbury: "Don't think. Thinking is the enemy of creativity. It's self-conscious, and anything self-conscious is lousy. You can't try to do things. You simply must do things." But that seems nonsensical. If you don't think, and think hard, you'll never learn anything. It's only possible to 'simply do things' after lots and lots of practice. Once you've passed through the thresholds to expertise then spontaneity is straightforward – maybe then Bradbury's advice makes sense. But as we've seen, there's no reliable shortcut to expertise, and thinking hard is the only sure fire way to get there.

Dilbert cartoonist Scott Adams is more helpful. He says, "Creativity is allowing yourself to make mistakes. Art is knowing which ones to keep." Acknowledging that creativity is a process and that we make mistakes along the way is much more honest. Only through making mistakes do we start to understand which ideas are worthwhile. Robinson agrees. He says the problem is that schools make children afraid to take risks and make mistakes. And to that extent, he may be right.

More interestingly (and contrary to most other creativity gurus), the poet T. S. Eliot is widely quoted as having said, "Anxiety is the hand maiden of creativity." If we're not stressed, if we're content with just aimlessly plucking ideas from the underdeveloped jumble of an undisciplined mind, we're unlikely to come up with much of value.

If we really want children to be more creative here are three suggestions. Firstly, we must feed their imaginations. We need to teach them stuff before we can expect them to question and criticize. We need to show them how ideas coalesce into something useful before they can start making their own connections.

Secondly, if we want students to be free, they need to have something to be free from. Therefore we need to give them rules. Constraints force creativity: too much freedom stifles it.

If you doubt this, try the following exercise:

1. Find a friend and chat about anything you like for three minutes.

2. Repeat the process but this time you're not allowed to use any words containing the letter *e*.*

Which one was more difficult? Which forced you to be more creative? It is by coping with difficulty and by overcoming adversity that we become creative.

And that brings us to the third suggestion: as well as all the other benefits, making learning harder might make students more creative. By expecting students to struggle, we create the conditions for them to accept the frustrations of liminality and grasp new ways of thinking.

Teachers are routinely encouraged to 'be more creative' and to teach students to think creatively. But actually, does anyone *really* want that? Do we *really* want teachers to do things that no other teachers are doing? Do we *really* want students to put the information we give them together in ways that are mistaken? I think what is actually meant is that teachers should 'do' creativity in an approved, safe way and that students ... well, students should pass exams.

Notes

1   Ken Robinson, How Schools Kill Creativity [video], *ted.com* (February 2006). Available at: http://www.ted.com/talks/ken_robinson_says_schools_kill_creativity?language=en.
2   Ibid.
3   Ken Robinson, *The Element: How Finding Your Passion Changes Everything* (London: Penguin, 2009), p. 67.

....

*   In 1969, French novelist Georges Perec wrote *La Disparition*, a 300 page novel in which he managed to avoid using any words containing the letter e (except for those in his name).

Conclusion:
The cult of outstanding

It is a truism that almost any sect, cult, or religion will legislate its creed
into law if it acquires the political power to do so.

Robert A. Heinlein

I'm convinced that as a result of some of the mistakes I've outlined in this
book, we have unwittingly, but actively, undermined students' ability to
learn. Understandably, this runs smack up against the sunk cost fallacy
and is not a popular message. Many very influential people have got a
lot invested in the belief that the pedagogical methodologies popularly
understood to result in 'outstanding' lessons are the right way to teach.
In fact, it may well be easier for a rich man to pass through the eye of a
needle than for an evaluator, an education consultant or a school leader
to admit that they've been wrong.

If nothing else, I hope that by reviewing some of our brain's limitations I
have persuaded you to accept that you are more than capable of making
mistakes and convincing yourself that all is well.

I hope too that you are convinced by some of the alternatives I've presented. Let's remind ourselves of the threshold concepts of the book:

- **We are all victims of cognitive bias:** We make decisions on
  emotional grounds and then justify and rationalize our choices after
  the fact. An awareness of how and why we make mistakes can help
  us to see that dogmatic certainty often stems from very twisted
  roots.

- **Learning is invisible:** Students *may* have learned something in a
  lesson, but this can only be inferred from their performance. Any

attempt to judge lessons on what students can do during the lesson is misguided.

- **Current performance is a poor indication of learning:** And worse, improving performance may actually prevent learning. When we design lessons that boost students' performance, the net result is that we are delaying the likelihood that they will learn. Conversely, "Conditions that induce the most errors during acquisition are often the very conditions that lead to the most learning!"[1]

- **Learning is liminal:** The boundary between working memory and long-term memory is what decides whether information becomes stored. Being aware of organizing threshold concepts helps to focus on the most troublesome and transformative areas of the curriculum.

- **Forgetting boosts remembering:** Forgetting is an important precondition for strengthening our ability to retrieve stored information. Allowing ourselves to forget, and then struggling to retrieve, makes it more likely that we will remember in the long term.

- **Learning should be hard:** Making the process of learning more difficult can make it easier for students to forget, and therefore to learn.

- **Experts and novices are different:** We only become experts by first having been novices. Novices must first grasp the threshold concepts of a subject – there's no shortcut to expertise.

We've examined the idea that good lessons are ones in which the students are visibly engaged and 'getting it' and found it wanting. Learning is a lot more mysterious than that, and any attempt to define teaching quality that fails to accommodate the essential chaos of how we learn is misguided at best.

Until July 2014, Ofsted's criteria for outstanding teaching and learning included the following:

- Sustained and rapid progress.

- Consistently high expectations.

- Excellent subject knowledge.

- Systematic, accurate assessment.

- Well-judged, imaginative teaching strategies.

- Sharply focused and timely support.

- Enthusiasm, participation and commitment.

- Resilience, confidence and independence.

- Frequent and consistently high quality feedback.

- Engagement, courtesy, collaboration and cooperation.

While each of these areas make sense on a superficial level, once you've passed through the thresholds, they no longer seem quite so useful.

In one of the most unlikely but fortuitous pieces of happenstance, Ofsted's national director for schools, Sean Harford, had been reading some of my thoughts on education and got in touch to ask me whether I'd be willing to help redraft the *Inspection Handbook*. I'm privileged and proud to report that I have been able to substantially influence the 'quality of teaching' section so as to take account of the material discussed in this book.

It would be the most appalling hubris to claim too much of the credit for this, but the fact that Ofsted agreed that individual lessons should not be graded is a triumph of rational argument over cognitive bias. That the leaders of Ofsted were able to make this change speaks very well of them. Perhaps the contribution of which I feel most proud is this: "When observing teaching, evaluators should be 'looking at' and reflecting on the effectiveness of what is being done to promote learning, not 'looking for' specific or particular things."[2]

That said, the idea that teaching can and should be judged as outstanding by someone who may have very little understanding of the extent to which their judgement is informed by cognitive bias, who lacks an understanding of the difference between performance and learning, and who may not accept or understand that continued and linear progress is unrealistic, is alarming. As long as teaching is judged in this way, teachers will be compelled to do things which are not in children's best interests.

Let's consider some of the mistakes made in the name of the cult of outstanding.

Progress

If we do something really quickly is it likely to last? I contend that rapid and sustained progress are mutually exclusive: they cancel each other out. You can have one or the other. We have to choose, and I'd strongly recommend sustained progress. The problem is that the route to sustained progress is deeply counter-intuitive. We're all a lot more comfortable with the idea of making rapid progress because it 'feels right'. But there's a significant body of research which suggests that slowing performance and increasing the errors made during instruction has a significant impact on our ability to retain and transfer skills and knowledge. Simply put, we learn better by struggling. But this is not what happens in an outstanding lesson where students are expected to demonstrate rapid progress and not look confused as they grapple with challenging concepts.

This has now been successfully challenged. Although the word 'rapid' has been excised from the *Inspection Handbook*, and there's an explicit acknowledgement that learning happens over time, a belief in the myth of progress persists. As we saw in Chapter 6, it's unrealistic to expect students to make continuous progress without pause or relapse. We're not only contending with the chaos of liminality, there's also motivation to consider – what if students have off days? It's impossible for evaluators to ever really know if students' progress is sustained.

High expectations

On the face of it you'd think I would have little to argue against here. And on the face of it you'd be right. But consistently high expectations of what? If our expectation as teachers is that students perform to a high level only in our lessons then we may well be guilty of engineering a situation which makes it harder for them to retain and transfer what we're teaching. This leads to a culture where it becomes routine for students not to remember or be able to apply the basics. Consider this: in a 11th grade English lesson, we read an article about Barack Obama taking a 5 percent pay cut to show support for the plight of the US economy. We decided to award him a nicely rounded salary of $150,000 and calculate what this 5 percent reduction might represent. I was appalled when the class, which contained some very bright mathematicians, notably failed to work out what is, even for me, a pretty simple sum. I'm fairly sure the same thing goes on when students that I know for a fact can spell and paragraph accurately in my lessons, suddenly lose this ability in, say, geography or science.

Excellent subject knowledge

Having expert subject knowledge is highly desirable and likely to result in students making significant gains in their learning. But beware the curse of knowledge. The more you know, the more difficult it may be to put it across to someone without sufficient background knowledge. Once we've passed through a threshold, it's almost impossible to put ourselves in the position of someone who has not yet grasped a tricky concept. Physicist Eric Mazur suggests that the better we know something, the harder it can be to teach it.[3] It therefore pays teachers to develop pedagogical content knowledge – an understanding of the likely mistakes and misconceptions students are likely to make in a given subject. If these mistakes are anticipated and headed off before they become ingrained then a great deal of harm is avoided. This is where a working knowledge of your subject's threshold concepts could be so invaluable. That said, having great subject knowledge is a necessary but not sufficient condition for teaching. In other words, if you don't know your stuff, your kids ain't gonna get very far.

Systematic, accurate assessment

Again, this seems obvious doesn't it? How can systematic and accurate assessment be a bad thing? The short answer is that it can't. But the problem is that very little assessment is accurate and systematic in the right way. Most grade schemes are highly subjective and do little to encourage accuracy. As Tim Oates says, "Even a well-crafted statement of what you need to get an A grade can be loaded with subjectivity – even in subjects such as science. It's genuinely hard to know how difficult a specific exam is."[4]

The slippery nature of words like 'effectively' makes assessment meaningless. What, for instance, is the difference between 'confident' and 'sophisticated'? Deciding that sophisticated is better than confident is arbitrary. We can only get a glimpse of what this might mean from comparing grade schemes to exemplar responses. As a result, our assessment is much more inaccurate and vague than we care to admit.

Well-judged, imaginative teaching strategies

Of course, well-judged teaching strategies are brilliant. If, however, teachers believe they should be improving students' current performance then it's highly unlikely that the strategies selected will be well-judged. It's certainly very rare for teaching to be judged outstanding if students are still struggling by the end of a lesson; this is more often viewed as being inadequate. But if sustained progress is our goal then neat resolutions and slick performances may well undermine our aim.

And what do we really mean by 'imaginative'? No one actually wants teachers to imagine something so creative that we're not sure what they're up to. What is the point of concocting new ways to teach when there are perfectly good ways of teaching that have been developed and passed down over decades, if not centuries? Often, what is meant is 'conforming to a fairly narrow set of expectations of what constitutes good teaching'. We would do much better to expect teachers to justify their practice and ask them for the evidence base that led them to choosing a particular way of working. That is not to say that everything a teacher does can or should be provable by research evidence – sometimes it's more than good enough to say that trial and error has convinced us that what we're doing is in the best interests of the children we teach. In the first instance, it should be assumed that teachers are professionals who have made informed choices.

Sharply focused and timely support

Providing effective support is, of course, highly desirable, but too much support will create learned helplessness. Also, we often support students because we're obsessed with improving their performance. But there's nothing inherently wrong with struggle; in fact, it's often essential for information to make its way from working to long-term memory. So why are we so squeamish about children being stuck? We'd do better sometimes to plan to celebrate what's hard and damn what comes easily. There's a toxic trend in our society to dismiss hard work as the preserve of idiots and fools. It's in our language: 'Hard luck!', 'Easy does it!' All this sharply focused support may well be eroding the confidence and resilience we so desire in our students. The point of scaffolding is that it must be removed, otherwise students will become dependent on it.

Often, the problem with so-called outstanding teaching is that it rarely devotes the time necessary for effective explanations or modeling (see below) for fear that the teacher will be accused of talking for too long.

Enthusiasm, participation and commitment

Enthusiasm, participation and commitment, along with engagement, are the very stuff of Robert Coe's "poor proxies for learning" (page 155). These things are lovely and certainly sociably desirable, but they tell us little about the quality of students' learning.

It's relatively well-known that doodling can increase your retention, and in the past I've taught children whose apparent attention in lessons is minimal and yet they learn.[5] As mentioned in Chapter 3, one boy

I shepherded through GCSEs spent two years building piles of erasers only to get an A! Certainly we should insist on good behavior; the alternative is horrible. But we must be informed and honest enough to acknowledge that observation feedback like, "That boy at the back was off-task for 3 minutes", is utterly meaningless.

But still, we all know how crucial engagement is, don't we? Well, according to some recent research into students' achievement in PISA math scores, there is some very surprising correlational evidence that suggests "the relationship of achievement to student engagement is not clear cut, with some evidence pointing toward a weak positive relationship and other evidence indicating a modest negative relationship".[6] Of course, this shouldn't be taken to mean that engagement and intrinsic motivation are actually bad for attainment, but serious doubts may be cast on policy measures which seek to boost student engagement in the belief that results will improve. Suitably cautious, Loveless says, "PISA provides, at best, weak evidence that raising student motivation is associated with achievement gains. Boosting motivation may even produce declines in achievement."[7]

Resilience, confidence and independence

I'm all for students being resilient, confident and independent. Who wouldn't be? Resilience is fine; students keep on doing things despite setbacks. Confidence is unreliable because it's easy to be confident and wrong (as 'experts' often are); uncertainty can be a good thing. The problem here is that we've got ourselves into the perfectly understandable muddle of believing that independent learning will result in independence. It doesn't. Independent learning actually makes students more dependent. If we really value independence and want our students to be confident and resilient then we're much better off teaching them. This process can be broken down into four stages of the teaching sequence (as explained in Chapter 10):

1. **Explaining:** You can't think about what you don't know, so if we want our students to do anything interesting or creative we must give them the vocabulary and background knowledge required to explore a subject. If students are going to be able to work and

think independently then they'll need you to carefully explain the context in which the topic is rooted.

2. **Modeling**: No one is ever going to get good at anything unless they go through the process of deconstructing high-quality examples and then 'seeing' the expert thought processes which go into creating an expert example. We learn poorly from watching experts perform. Instead, we need their performance deconstructed and broken down into chunks that can be thoroughly examined. The road to hell is paved with vague success criteria.

3. **Scaffolding**: Once students have had new concepts explained and had great examples modeled then they're ready to have a go. Our job is to make sure that everyone is challenged to do something they will find difficult and help them to deal with the frustration of not being able to get it. And then, to prevent students becoming dependent on it, support needs to be withdrawn as quickly as is possible.

4. **Practicing**: Students are now ready to work independently. Our role is to be aware that practice doesn't make perfect; practice makes permanent. We must be vigilant about the mistakes students are likely to make and prevent them becoming embedded.

Frequent and consistently high-quality feedback

Yet again this appears entirely desirable. That is, until we examine the staggering weight of research which suggests that delaying and reducing feedback, while having a negative impact on short-term performance gains, tends to boost long-term retention and transfer. This leads us, inevitably, down a rabbit hole of trying to determine exactly what 'high-quality' feedback might be. Is it high-quality if it visibly supports students' performance in the classroom? Or is it high-quality if it means that they're more likely to pass an exam? This issue is that one of these is easy to check for during an observation and the other isn't. Guess which we tend to prefer?

As we saw in Chapter 17, frequent feedback might actually be undermining students' efforts to learn. As Soderstrom and Bjork tell us, "Numerous studies – some of them dating back decades – have shown that frequent and immediate feedback can, contrary to intuition, degrade learning."[8]

Engagement, courtesy, collaboration and cooperation

No right thinking teacher would object to politeness except to say that it has very little bearing on learning. Collaboration and cooperation betray a preference for groupwork. As discussed in Chapter 3, there's a time and a place for groupwork: it fits best into the scaffolding phase of teaching. But the idea that all lessons should contain collaborative or cooperative learning is preposterous. Also in Chapter 3, we unpicked the idea that lessons should be fun and engaging. Certainly no one would actively seek to make lessons dull, but the objective of engagement for engagement's sake is a slippery slope.

....

It's become abundantly clear to me that what might appear to be passive may well conceal a vigorous and seismic inner turmoil that heralds real learning. So the next time you think you've seen an outstanding lesson, think again. There's no such thing!

And while we're at it, the concept that teaching can or should be judged as outstanding is highly dubious. We can certainly have good teaching – it's the preserve of those teachers who get consistent and startling results, where students really learn. The received wisdom on outstanding lessons actively obstructs outstanding teaching. Teachers have routinely been encouraged to boost students' short-term performance at the cost of real learning. We all need the humility to accept that our preferences and biases are just that: ours. They do not lead to better learning. And further, it is my considered opinion that the pursuit of outstanding has done more to damage education than any of the more obvious absurdities we've had to put up with over the years.

The burden placed on schools and teachers to prove themselves outstanding is absurd. Former evaluator Colin Richards argues that Ofsted are asking the impossible: "A reasonable criterion for a 'good' school ('Teachers have high expectations') becomes an unreasonable one for an 'outstanding' school ('*All* teachers have consistently high expectations of *all* students'). For each of the seven criteria, what is reasonable and possible for a 'good' school is rendered unreasonable and impossible for an 'outstanding' one – and not just impossible for the teachers, but for evaluators too."[9]

That Ofsted are officially distancing themselves from some of the more deluded facets of the outstanding jamboree can only be good news. But that still leaves us with a situation where very many evaluators and school leaders have got where they are on the strength of their ability to dance the rapid progress jig. Will they be able to admit the possibility that they were hoodwinked by the cult of outstanding? As the cliché goes, it takes time to turn a tanker. Some of the more entrenched thinking in schools continues to result in teachers believing good teaching equates with demonstrating progress.

Before we all get too overexcited, I'm not proposing a free-for-all where we all do whatever the hell we please and damn the consequences. Schools and teachers must be accountable. But it does raise some interesting questions about what we value. Is the ability to deliver outstanding lessons more important than getting great results? Who would we be more likely to promote or put on notice? Which type of teacher is more likely to lead a school, and what are they likely to train their staff to do?

It seems obvious that we tend to value what we're good at, and consequently most schools are led by teachers who have proved themselves able to teach 'outstanding' lessons. Teachers who teach lessons like lesson 1 (see Chapter 20) get promoted. They become advanced skills teachers and senior leaders in charge of teaching and learning and then train others how to do what they do.

And it's equally clear that we tend to be suspicious of what we don't understand, and are likely to dismiss it as dangerous and aberrant. Teachers who fail to conform to narrow expectations get put on notice. They are marginalized, ignored and, ultimately, if they fail to put on the required show, forced out.

The increased focus on quality assurance and teachers' accountability might actually be generating a lack of quality. Somewhere along the line it seems to have become an unquestioned assumption that teachers are useless slackers who, left to their own devices, would slop cheap coffee over the students' books and do the barest minimum in lessons.

Certainly when I was a student in the 1980s there were some teachers like that. My history teacher 'taught' the wrong GCSE syllabus and the entire class failed. He shrugged his shoulders and nothing happened. I had an English teacher whose classroom was next door to the staffroom. After he'd set some work he'd slope off to smoke his pipe. If we got too rowdy, he'd pound on the wall for us to shut up. There were certainly some incredible excesses back in the 'bad old days' before Ofsted was a gleam in Chris Woodhead's eye. But there were also some wonderful eccentrics and many, perhaps most, of them are long gone. I worked with a fabulous old boy who'd taught at the school for over 30 years. He could recite vast tracts of Shakespeare, Keats and Donne, and had a quotation for every occasion. He'd taught the students' parents, sometimes grandparents, and was a much loved member of the community. When the school failed an inspection, he was put under intolerable pressure to change the way he taught despite his excellent results. He went from confident pomp to incompetence in less than a year and gratefully accepted the offer of early retirement.

The argument usually goes that although the accountability measures we take for granted in schools take their toll, they are necessary. Without the lists of non-negotiables it would be a free-for-all. But I just don't think that's true. Few teachers are in it for the money or the social standing. Almost all decide to teach because they want to make a difference. They're passionate. They care. There may be some bad apples, but why should we allow them to spoil the whole barrel? After a book review a few years ago in which 'ordinary' teachers were invited to participate, I remember one angry member of staff saying to another, "You're the reason management don't trust us!"

Of course, it's unfair to blame school leaders entirely. They, in turn, are held in contempt by those who hold them to account and treated with the same disregard and lack of trust. They're rightly afraid of losing their jobs, and who can blame them? Naturally, there are many schools which are led with compassion and courage and where teachers are trusted.

It's not naive to believe that there might be a better way; there are wonderful models of school leadership out there that prove it can be done. You see, while it may be true that the quality of an education system cannot exceed the quality of its teachers, it's extremely unlikely for the quality of teaching to exceed the quality of school leadership. It's ludicrously easy for bad leaders to destroy good teachers.

An insidious culture of fear and suspicion has become endemic, and it's doing much more harm than good. Why *should* teachers be expected to give up so much of their home and family lives to fulfil the requirements of their job? We work ever longer hours, but is this really desirable or even necessary? It doesn't seem that teachers in other European countries have the same weight of workload expectations. Are their students suffering?

The solution? Trust that teachers will, when happy and supported, do the right thing. If teachers are struggling to grade their work, consider what could be done to help them. The unspoken expectation that they take ever more work home is untenable. Be clear: if they have too much grading to cope with then this is, in part, the school's fault and responsibility. If teachers are struggling to maintain acceptable standards of behavior, make sure proper systems are in place and don't make them feel guilty for using them. If there are teachers who are not doing the right thing, rather than making everyone else suffer, deal with the problem at its source. Collective punishment, for that's what a lot of accountability measures effectively are, violates the Geneva Convention.

And if someone somewhere does the wrong thing occasionally, so what? Barring grosser excesses that endanger students' health and well-being, why not forgive and forget? Flogging teachers might improve outcomes over the short term, but this cannot be a sustainable or efficient way to run a school over the longer term. If it's true that improving teaching is the best route to long-term success, trusting teachers might be the best way to get there. Accountability processes will not improve teaching and learning. They just won't. Take a risk. Trust your staff. As rear admiral Grace Murray Hopper once said, "Go ahead and do it. It's much easier to apologize after something's been done than to get permission ahead of time."

So, to be absolutely clear, I am not, repeat not, advocating ignoring what goes on in teachers' classrooms and focusing solely on examination results. All I suggest is that we think a little more and jerk our knees a little less. We understand a hell of a lot less than we think.

Before making a decision that will affect the lives of teachers or students, ask yourself, what if everything you know about education is wrong? What then?

Notes

1   Nicholas C. Soderstrom and Robert A. Bjork, Learning versus Performance, in Dana Dunn (ed.), *Oxford Bibliographies Online: Psychology* (New York: Oxford University Press, 2013). Available at: http://bjorklab.psych.ucla.edu/pubs/Soderstrom_Bjork_Learning_versus_Performance.pdf, p. 2.

2   Ofsted, *School Inspection Handbook* (January 2015). Ref: 120101. Available at: https://www.gov.uk/government/publications/school-inspection-handbook, p. 58.

3   Eric Mazur, Confessions of a Converted Lecturer [video] (12 November 2009). Available at: https://www.youtube.com/watch?v=WwslBPj8Ggl.

4   Tim Oates, How Our Exam System Really Functions, *School House* (n.d.). Available at: http://www.schoolhousemagazine.co.uk/education/examinations/how-our-exam-system-really-functions.

5   Annett Schmeck, Richard E. Mayer, Maria Opfermann, Vanessa Pfeiffer and Detlev Leutner, Drawing Pictures During Learning from Scientific Text: Testing the Generative Drawing Effect and the Prognostic Drawing Effect, *Contemporary Educational Psychology* 39(4) (2014): 275–286.

6   Tom Loveless, *How Well Are American Students Learning? The 2015 Brown Center Report on American Education.* Available at: http://www.ewa.org/sites/main/files/file-attachments/brown_ctr_2015_v2.pdf.

7   Ibid.

8   Soderstrom and Bjork, Learning versus Performance, p. 23.

9   Colin Richards, Ofsted's Criteria for 'Outstanding Teaching' Are Outstanding Nonsense, and Here's Why, *TES* (7 January 2015). Available at: https://news.tes.co.uk/b/opinion/2015/01/07/ofsted-s-criteria-for-outstanding-teaching-are-outstanding-nonsense-and-here-s-why.aspx#.VK9c1ayKxhJ.facebook.

Appendix 1
Data by numbers

Jack Marwood

If you torture data sufficiently, it will confess to almost anything.

Fred Menger

We live in an era of Big Data. This is worth noting, since those relatively new to teaching may be surprised how little we used to know about schools. Until 1992, those not actually working in a given English secondary school had no way of finding out basic information about measures of achievement such as, say, the average exam results of 16-year-olds in a particular secondary school.[1] Likewise, no one outside of an English elementary school had access to any published data before 1996. There was simply no data publicly available to anyone outside of a school.

This changed through a combination of politics and computing power. The era of the personal computer has enabled huge amounts of data to be collected, disseminated and dissected. Governments have taken advantage of this, requiring schools to create and collect large amounts of information of considerably variable quality. Schools, particularly at secondary level, often employ specific data managers. Elsewhere this role is fulfilled by teachers or their managers. Modern schools are awash with a veritable ocean of data.

What data about schools is publicly available?

The simple answer is 'a great deal': from 'number of students' to 'percentage of children with English not as a first language', to 'average gross salary of all full-time qualified teachers' in a school via 'average point score' and more. And this is just the information published online by the government on its School Performance Tables website.[2] There are, in fact, over 500 separate items of information available on every elementary school in England. At secondary level, there are over 1,000 fields of data for every school available for members of the public to download. While the relevance of much of this data for those outside the school is unclear, it has been made available regardless of its reliability or utility.

Schools collect and analyze a huge amount of data every year. This includes fairly obvious measures such as the number of students enrolled, the gender split, the number of children who are known to be eligible for free school meals and the percentage 'stability' (i.e. the number of children who are still in the school in January having started the school year in the previous September). Beyond these measures, we also have 'school deprivation indicators', 'percentage of students from minority ethnic groups' (with 18 different ethnic groups tracked) and 'language not or not believed to be English' and 12 different categories of special educational need. Schools also collect attendance data, recording both the total number of sessions missed and tracking 'persistent absentees' who miss more than 15 percent of school sessions.

School dashboards

As well as the exhaustive information available on the School Performance Tables website, there is currently summary data available on Ofsted's School Data Dashboards[3] and Governor Dashboards.[4] The School Data Dashboard shows a school's test results as well as information on progress, attendance, closing the gap and school context. In many ways this information mirrors the School Performance Tables, with some minor but important variations. The main difference is that the current School Data Dashboard includes average data on 'similar schools' with which a given school is compared. It also presents information in quintiles to enable comparisons to be made with other schools.

Governor Dashboards are specifically for school governors and are not publicly available, although you can find examples online. These are designed to help governors with the following questions:

- How does attainment and student progress compare to the national average?

- How are we performing in different subjects?

- Do we have any underperforming students?

- How might the context of our school affect our performance?

- How does student attendance compare to the national average?

- What are the strengths and weaknesses of our school?

The dashboard is a four page summary of a school, with information on student results (with measures of absolute attainment and relative progress), headline performance with future projections and overview data on the last three years. There is also a breakdown of Key Stage 2 performance in key subject areas and a graph of the progress performance of different groups, along with a breakdown of the most recent 6th grade/11th grade classes by various groupings and absence data.

The National Student Database

All of this publicly available information is held in the National Student Database (NPD). The NPD is based on a school 'census' undertaken each semester. Key stage attainment records, including Early Years Foundation Stage profile records, are also incorporated into the NPD, along with a history of schools attended by any given child.

NPD information is made available to schools via a flexible, interactive database known as Reporting and Analysis for Improvement through school Self-Evaluation Online (RAISEonline) which allows schools to analyze data by a large number of variables.[5] RAISEonline also collates the attainment data which schools collect and submit to central government.

RAISEonline in elementary schools

For an elementary school, summary reports are typically 60 pages long and include data from the 1st grade phonics screening check (which is broken down by gender, FSM (free school meals), English as a first language, SEN (special education needs), ethnic group and term of birth) and the follow-up 2nd grade phonics screening check, Key Stage 1 attainment in reading, writing and mathematics (broken down by eight different categories including term of birth) and Key Stage 2 attainment (in nine categories but not term of birth).

It also includes data on 'progress measures value added' for mathematics, reading, writing and English overall, broken down into ethnic background, gender, FSM, prior attainment, whether enrolled for all of 5th grade and 6th grade, whether first language is English and category of SEN. There are also breakdowns of 'expected progress' in reading, writing and mathematics, and for each measure in eight different categories once again, but with no term of birth information.

Following all this information, there is also 'closing the gaps with student premium at Key Stage 2' data in which the achievement of children receiving FSM are compared with those who are not, and a 'closing the gap trend' which collates the previous three years' FSM vs. non-FSM data. The report finishes with a graph showing 'actual KS2 score' against 'expected KS2 score'.

RAISEonline in secondary schools

For a secondary school, summary reports are around 80 pages long and include prior attainment data ('average fine score at KS2' and also a breakdown by three ability bands) and attainment at Key Stage 4, beginning with the percentage of students achieving five or more A* to C (including English and mathematics) at GCSE and equivalent over the previous three years, then a 'best 8 subjects' measure (again over three years), then English, mathematics and all other subjects.

The Key Stage 4 information for 5+ A* to C (including equivalents), English, 'basics', GCSE only 5+ A* to C and 5+ A* to G is broken down by gender, FSM, English as a first language, SEN and ethnicity group. There are also detailed breakdowns for various subject groupings (languages, science, humanities).

The report also includes data over three years on 'progress measures value added' for best eight, English, mathematics, science, languages and humanities overall, then broken down into ethnic backgrounds, gender, FSM, prior attainment, whether enrolled for all of 10th grade and 11th grade, whether first language is English and category of SEN. There are also detailed breakdowns of 'value added' for the latest results in English, mathematics, science, languages and humanities, followed by 'expected progress' breakdowns in English and mathematics for each measure in eight different categories once again, but with no term of birth information.

Following all this information, there is also 'closing the gaps with student premium at Key Stage 4' in which the achievement of children receiving FSM are compared with those who are not, and a 'closing the gap trend' which collates the previous three years' FSM vs. non-FSM data. The report finishes with a graph showing 'actual KS4 score' against 'expected KS4 score'.

Looking back and looking forward

The School Performance Tables, Ofsted School Data Dashboards, Governor Dashboards and RAISEonline are all reviews of performance, and give information about the historic performance of schools. Within schools, there is a need to look forward and to make educated guesses about the future progress of children, in a process known universally as 'target setting'. The primary dataset behind this is provided by the Fischer Family Trust (FFT).*

The FFT is best known for providing 'estimates', which are designed to be used when setting targets for children. These estimates would suggest that, based on a mixture of prior attainment, age, context, gender and ethnicity, a child might be expected to achieve a given range of levels at Key Stage 2 or GCSE grades in the future. There's a bit more to it, but that's it in summary.

Don't forget the commercial data consultants, corporations and international comparison industry

As well as all of this, there are many external companies which will take school data and perform any number of complicated analyses to help a school become 'data aware'. This is in addition to various providers of management information systems specifically created for schools. Increasingly, large conglomerates are entering education data management, with well-known names such as Capita and Serco joining those who specialize in the education sector such as RM plc and TASC Software Solutions.

Education data management has become such big business, it now has its own business community serviced by websites such as edugeek.net, annual international conferences (organized by, for example, organizations such as the International Society for Technology in Education (ISTE) and the International Working Group on Educational Data Mining) and publications such as *EdTech* and the *Journal of Educational Data Mining*.

....

*   The FFT dataset was called FFTlive until 2014 when it was due to be renamed and relaunched as FFTaspire. Either way, the FFT dataset does two things: look back and look forward. Most of the ways the FFT allows schools to look back mimics RAISEonline. The dataset allows schools to look forward using complicated analysis of the results of children across the country to estimate future grades both at Key Stage 2 and Key Stage 4 (which has confusingly crept into the dashboards described above).

Further to the development of education data analysis at a national level, there are also international organizations such as the OECD which have become hugely important within the political education area. The OECD's Program for International Student Assessment (PISA) has had a considerable impact on politicians, claiming as it does to be able to compare the relative educational performance of students at international level. In addition, the US Department of Education's National Center for Education Statistics has published the Trends in International Mathematics and Science Study (TIMSS) every four years since 1995, as well as the Progress in International Reading Literacy Study (PIRLS) which began in 2001.

In summary

There is a huge amount of information which is generated both within schools, by and for government departments, by external data consultants and corporations and by multinational agencies. This data is becoming increasingly embedded within our school system and is becoming a significant driver of thinking about education. The thinking behind education data is, however, flawed on multiple levels and is – in the main – completely wrong.

What's wrong with education data?

The data isn't data

Just about all of the internal progress tracking data and external test data which is used in English education could actually be more correctly described as cargo cult data* – that is to say, it has the appearance of real, measurable data, without fulfilling any of the requirements of being

....

*   Cargo cult science is the term popularized by Richard Feynman in his 1985 book, *Surely You're Joking, Mr Feynman!*, referring to activity which has the trappings of real science but which lacks the rigor expected of real science.

statistically valid, approximately measured, error accepting countable data from which one could reasonably draw inferences. The fundamental problem with education data is that it cannot be subjected to close statistical scrutiny.

Teacher assessments can't be used to track progress

Of course, teachers assess children all the time in the sense that they check what children know through what they can do. Each subject has a broad range of knowledge, skills and understanding which a child will be introduced to and required to think about, will practice repeatedly and be encouraged to remember and use in their schooling. But slapping a number on this assessment makes no real sense; numbers obscure the specific assessment a teacher will have made of the child's current position. The broad range of formative assessments cannot meaningfully be reduced to a single figure. For the last 20 years, teachers have increasingly been expected to turn their assessments into progress tracking data to be collated and analyzed. This tracking data – often subject to all kinds of fudges in schools – is treated as if it were meaningful. It isn't.

External tests can't be used to measure educational achievement

The field of psychometrics is concerned with the objective measurement of various aspects of the human mind. A sub-branch of the field is the objective measurement of educational achievement. Teacher, physicist and psychometrician Noel Wilson has set out the key issues which have been demonstrated to actively prevent anyone from objectively measuring educational knowledge with any degree of accuracy.

In brief, any measurement of anything which is continuous and equally spaced (such as time or length) has to be measured using a specified standard unit, and this will necessarily involve a degree of error. The units have to be defined as a standard, and the standard has to be completely accurate by definition. So a centimeter is a centimeter because we say so; it is a *definition* and not a *measurement*. Additionally, when measuring a

378

distance, for example, a measuring tool such as a ruler, tape measure or micrometer – some kind of instrument – has to be used. Whatever the instrument measures will introduce an element of error.

In attempting to measure educational knowledge, the standards are not standard and the measurements are not accurate. What is the 'unit of education'? There are other errors which enter the fray. The interference effect says that 'any measuring instrument distorts the field it is intended to measure'. This means that the specific content of any test itself affects the grade anyone taking the test is awarded. Uncontrollable boundary conditions mean that humans respond to tests in unimagined ways. Giving the test is an artificial situation and is not a true indicator of knowledge, just as a wind tunnel test of a car cannot accurately test the actual performance on any given road on any given day or in any set of weather conditions: "Perception and conception, and hence response, to 'identical' situations invariably differ, as the variables that affect such reactions – attention, mood, focus, metabolic rate, tiredness, visualizations, imagination, memory, habit, divergence, growth etc. – come into play."[6]

Wilson goes further into the problems inherent in trying to measure educational ability. He concludes that "tests have so many independent sources of invalidity that they do not measure anything in particular, nor do they place people in any particular order of anything".[7] In summary, tests don't measure anything objectively, and they ignore huge errors inherent in any system which tries to rank people in order of merit. Knowledge isn't measurable on a continuous, linear scale.

This means that externally assessed grades are effectively guesses. The vagaries of designing and grading written tests of a student's ability mean that the guesses are often wrong, and simply offer a snapshot of a student's actual knowledge, skills and understanding of a given subject rather than their 'true score'. On a different day, with a different test, a student is highly likely to get a completely different grade and quite likely to be awarded a different grade entirely.

As noted above, the situation in those school years which are not externally assessed – any year other than 6th, 11th and 13th grade – is equally murky. Schools have vast systems for tracking data, and most teachers have to submit assessments each semester for the children they teach.

These assessments are turned into numbers on a theoretical continuous linear scale and fed into central data tracking systems, before being used in a variety of dubious ways. Most elementary schools undertake controlled assessments of some sort, which are then usually moderated in some way in-house. The end result is a strange system of give and take, in which children are recorded in a way which aims for a 'Goldilocks' level of progress, neither too much or too little, regardless of what the child might have actually learned during any given year. This effectively renders in-school tracking a gigantic compromise which is more likely to obscure children's actual educational achievement than shed light on their path through school.

Surely someone is aware that tests and assessments are not accurate?

The problems with testing are fairly well understood within education, although this may come as a surprise to many teachers. For example, Lord Bew noted in his 2011 report on Key Stage 2 testing:

> It is generally accepted that any test or examination, however well constructed, will always include a degree of measurement error. We understand that, as with all tests where students are categorized, the level thresholds in Key Stage 2 tests mean that one grade can make the difference between one level and the next. That grade could be lost or gained through a student mis-reading an instruction in the test or making a fortunate choice in a multiple-choice question, or through slight variations in grading practice. These differences will be highly significant for the individual student.[8]

Lord Bew also noted that Dylan Wiliam has suggested that 32 percent of students could be given the wrong national curriculum level. Wiliam observed, "we must be aware that the results of even the best tests can be wildly inaccurate for individual students, and that high-stakes decisions should never be based on the results of individual tests".[9]

How is this data used?

Assessment data, used to track students internally in schools, forms the basis upon which decisions are made regarding groups within classrooms, the focus of additional teaching (often in small 'intervention' groups or, more rarely, in one-to-one sessions), the classes in which particular teachers should be placed and so on.

Assessment data is also used to judge the 'effectiveness' of schools. Elementary schools are judged on progress across key stages, typically from Key Stage 1 (students aged 7) to Key Stage 2 (aged 11). Secondary schools are judged across Key Stage 2 to 4 (ages 11–16).

This introduces immediate problems, since secondary schools are not responsible for Key Stage 2 results, which are widely held to be hopelessly inaccurate because of the distorting effect of teaching to the test in the last year of elementary school. Students' schools are typically very small, with an average of 24 children in each Key Stage 2 class. If there are a few children who struggle in a class or, alternatively, who find learning very easy, then a school can find itself being lauded or damned based on very small amounts of dubious 'data'.

There are other problems. Children often move school and assessment data is regularly lost when this happens. There are also issues with the limited number of data points within key stages, particularly at Key Stage 1, which does not cater very well for tracking more able children. Subjects are lumped together into average point scores, which hides any particular strengths or weaknesses the children might have. Elementary children are only assessed in two areas – English and math – ignoring all other subject areas entirely. Comparing classes across different school years is pointless, since the children in any given class are simply too diverse.

All in all, gathering dubious data across wide age ranges, across different schools and across quite different classes means that it is almost impossible to use this data to decide whether a school is any good or not. This inconvenient truth is simply ignored by government evaluators who want to know how good a school is. However, evaluators still use such data to inform their judgements.

There are additional problems with this. Firstly, the evaluators clearly do not understand the data with which they are presented. Secondly, school data is analyzed centrally using statistical procedures designed to extrapolate from a sample to a population. But because schools are not randomly selected samples of the population, this kind of analysis is invalid, and thus any conclusion will give a false impression of some schools being 'good' and others 'bad'. Finally, because school evaluators have access to this dubious data prior to entering schools to inspect them, they cannot help but be biased by their preconceived notions of the school's effectiveness; their judgements thus suffer from the halo effect (see Chapter 2) and this influences many of the assessments evaluators make.

In England and Wales, all school data is presented centrally using RAISE-online. Because this uses standard statistical techniques, which assume that a given sample is truly representative of a wider population, this gives the RAISEonline data analysis a false sense of validity. The use of standard statistical techniques – calculating statistical significance and confidence intervals to 'test' how a school compares to the national population – is not valid for a number of reasons. Firstly, no given school can be said to be drawn from the wider population because families and their children are clustered geographically and demographically. Secondly, even if the data could be regarded as a sample of the population, it isn't valid to treat it as such. It would have to be regarded as a clustered subsection of the complete population data which has been collected, and if that were the case, statistical techniques for sample data simply aren't valid.

Despite these obvious problems, RAISEonline sails merrily on, coloring certain items of data green and blue, comparing school data to national means as if it were a random sample of an unknown population and generally creating a completely misleading impression of any given school. When we make assumptions based on such data, we delude ourselves. So, given the inaccuracy of assessment 'data', and the invalid analysis it presents, there is simply no point in drawing any worthwhile conclusions from RAISEonline.

The fundamentally flawed assumptions in performance tables

Performance tables in England use measures of 'added value'. Value added is a concept familiar to us all in value added tax (VAT) and its origin in economics. Since the rise of big education data, value added has come to mean the difference which a school or teacher makes to a children's test results. There are many, many problems with this, but this is not considered when data is crunched into performance tables.

The 'similar schools' comparison

A given school's 'performance' is compared to the performance of 'similar schools' in a way which is eye-wateringly convoluted and, ultimately, entirely meaningless. It doesn't tell anyone anything, and is an utter waste of everyone's time.

Essentially, at elementary level a big list is made of all the average point scores (APS) at Key Stage 1 for all the children in a school's Key Stage 2. You have to ignore the fact that this has just produced mean averages of three different numbers to create an APS, and introduced huge statistical errors into the following calculations. Each child's APS is fed into an equation based on one year's 6th grade results. This produces a graph which has actual APS (whatever that measures) on one axis and a number on the other axis.

The number produced in this way is supposed to be a particular student's 'estimated probability of achieving level 4 or above' in reading, writing and math – the 'modeled' 'student level' based on the child's prior attainment. These numbers are taken (ignoring their now vastly larger statistical errors once again) and a mean average of all the estimates of probability of children in the school's Key Stage 2 getting level 4 or above in Key Stage 2 is calculated. This is a 'school level' estimate of the likelihood of getting level 4 or above at the end of Key Stage 2.

The school performance tables website then simply produces a list of the 62 schools which sit immediately above and below a given school's 'school level' estimate. These schools are, according to the government, similar to a given school. The list may as well be chosen randomly for all that this tells you. In fact, to all intents and purposes the list *is* random, as a look at any school's 'similar schools' will show you. There is no regular pattern for schools in general; the data crunching delivers exactly what you would expect if it were random. If this method of selecting schools showed any kind of non-random distribution of school results at Key Stage 2 it might be of interest, but there is simply nothing there. Some schools get higher estimated average point scores and some don't. That's it. The 'similar schools' are not similar and to suggest so is entirely misleading.

At this point, however, the schools on a given school's list of similar schools are then ranked by the actual 'percentage achieving level 4 or above in reading, writing and math results for each school, and the given school is shown as *x* out of 125. Which means absolutely nothing to anyone.

Random is as random does

Other than for headline data on 'percentage achieving level 4 or above in reading, writing and math, the performance tables only give data for a single year. This is not terribly helpful for parents using this data to select a school for a 4-year-old as the child isn't going to take Key Stage 2 assessments for another eight years. Maybe a bit more data might be useful.

Except it wouldn't because, for most schools, the data varies with the class, not the quality of teaching. The only exception is for schools with consistent results of 100 percent, but this is more likely to be due to the students, not the teaching in isolation.

For the 42 other measures of student performance, there is only one year's results. This is because a set of results tells you nothing about anything other than a given group of 6th grade students, because there's no trend from year to year.

Here is Seaside Primary School in North Yorkshire, a fairly typical two-form entry school. These are the percentages of children achieving level 4 or above in reading, writing and math:

2013: 77%

2012: 70%

2011: 58%

2010: 69%

2009: 77%

2008: 76%

There is no pattern. Unless a school consistently records 100 percent, there never is a pattern for any school, in any historical data. This is because the data is based on children's results, and children are complicated and individual, and the school population in any given school is statistically too small to make meaningful generalizations.

The lack of a trend may be why the data isn't presented over a number of years, because anyone looking at the data would realize that it is random. As any financial advertisement will tell you in the small print, past performance is no guarantee of future success. Long-term trends in something as complex as educational outcomes are – unless you mess with the data by, you know, making the tests easier, selecting by ability or dis-applying certain children from assessment, or simply not reporting stuff – always random.

What should we be doing?

The statistical measures used to judge schools are invalid; simply using mathematical calculations on flawed data can never tell us what we want to know. The way we track progress falls into many of the traps described in Chapter 2. We can't get into children's heads to find out what they are really learning. We can ask children to write things down, but this isn't the same as tracking their progress. It is pretty much the source of all progress tracking data, however, and because of the myth of linear progress, it is regularly fudged in schools in order to smooth out any wrinkles in a child's progress.

High stakes written tests can only indicate how well children can answer (or be taught to answer) a written test. If progress is tracked against 'teacher assessment', data is likely to be hugely compromised by in-school fudges, the effects of targets and many other distortions. The end result is that much of the progress tracking data used to judge learning, schools and teachers is simply junk.

What actual data can we collect and analyze?

The truth is, not very much. Children's learning and progress is too complicated to be reduced to a few numbers. While tests only assess test taking, it is possible to track the acquisition of certain kinds of fundamental knowledge which is vital for students to make progress in education. For example, their knowledge of number bonds and times tables, since this is simply testing recall of factual information which is clear and unambiguous. It might also be worth keeping an eye on students' knowledge of the alphabet, phonemes and graphemes, and punctuation marks for those who have yet to master writing. It's hard to track such progress in a meaningful numerical way, let alone trying to measure those things which are much more complicated core concepts. However, monitoring progress is possible, and teachers can track whether students are using certain key concepts correctly. But this does not mean it is possible to assign numbers to this in the way that most schools currently employ.

Beyond this, it's clearly possible to record indicators of children's progress against what you *think* they should have learned based on your teaching. My guess is that, currently, this is what most teachers actually do, even if the data then ends up being used as cargo cult data. For example England's national curriculum levels can be quite useful as indicators. Yes, using levels is hugely subjective and susceptible to all kinds of biases, and we almost certainly under-record some children and over-record others. As long as no one tries to abuse this information with the widely misunderstood techniques often used to summarize actual data (a forlorn hope in most cases), I have no problem with it, and find it useful.

It's probably worth testing how well children can answer questions in external written tests on which they will be judged. Depending on the context, it's probably worth spending some time developing the ability to score highly in these tests, since teachers are judged by the results of the children in their charge. All that can be hoped is that this doesn't put children off education long before they have completed their time in school.

Age within a class is highly important but is completely ignored by most schools. This should be tracked, as it is actual data – a child's age is a very good, robust measurement – and it does affect what a child can do. Too often, high ability groups are simply the older children in a class, with lower ability groups made up of the younger children. The middle of the school year – March 2 – should be central to every teacher's understanding of the relative abilities of the children in a class. This is data worth using.

What if I'm wrong?

For now, it doesn't really matter whether I'm right or if I'm wrong, as the relentless march of non-data shows no signs of slowing down, much less stopping. The United States has shown some quite unacceptable use of data-driven education, with individual teachers being hired or fired based on the results of the children they teach; the use of value added measures (VAM) has reached startling proportions. Since England seems to follow behind the United States in many areas of modern life, we may yet see that nightmare introduced here. In the United States, VAM has driven many committed teachers out of education, and it is likely that it would have the same result were it to become commonplace on this side of the Atlantic.

It could be argued that, regardless of the fundamental flaws psychometricians have identified in any test of ability, the use of test non-data has shone a light on schools, and has made it possible to identify schools which are failing, coasting or thriving as measured by test results. This argument suggests that, even if the data isn't quite accurate, it's still a good idea to keep the pressure on schools to focus on student achievement as measured by written tests. And who knows, maybe the use of flawed measures which don't really test what many people think they test is a good idea. As long as you can sort the world into winners and losers, the fact that such a distinction is flawed, and therefore unfair, is not that important. All do not get prizes, and that keeps teachers on their toes.

Maybe it doesn't matter that the wrong kind of statistical analysis has been used, and the problems I've highlighted with this juggernaut can be ignored. It might be that the convoluted mechanisms used to compare schools against not-in-the-least similar schools don't matter, as long as some schools rise to the pressure placed on them. What if the non-existent trends in the 'value' schools 'add' to children are important in some way?

Maybe I am wrong to feel that schools are judged unfairly by the use of dubious made up data. It could be that questioning the other pressures on English education are more important, and the issues being raised by those in and around education in our more connected world need to be dealt with first. Misuse of voodoo data could be halfway up the flawed foundations of the way we look at education; there could be more fundamental issues to address.

But for now, the abuse of 'data' places an intolerable burden on teachers, on schools and – most importantly – on children; it really needs to be addressed urgently. When a 6-year-old can only tell you which 'level' they are, and the glory of expanding young minds is reduced to plotting numbers on a chart, we might have to accept that we've gone down the wrong road. We need to reverse, and quickly.

Notes

1   Jodie Reed and Joe Hallgarten, Time to Say Goodbye? The Future of School Performance Tables (December 2003). Available at: http://www.leeds.ac.uk/educol/documents/00003500.htm.
2   See http://www.education.gov.uk/schools/performance/.
3   See http://dashboard.ofsted.gov.uk.
4   See http://www.fft.org.uk/fft-live/governor-dashboard.aspx.
5   See https://www.raiseonline.org.
6   Noel Wilson, Educational Standards and the Problem of Error, Educational Policy Analysis Archives 6(10) (1998): 95.
7   Ibid. 12.

8   Lord Bew, *Independent Review of Key Stage 2 Testing, Assessment and Accountability: Final Report* (June 2011). Available at: http://www.educationengland.org.uk/documents/pdfs/2011-bew-report-ks2tests.pdf, p. 55.

9   Dylan Wiliam, Reliability, Validity, and All That Jazz, *Education 3–13* 29(3) (2001): 17–21. Available at: http://eprints.ioe.ac.uk/1156/2/Wiliam2001Reliability3long.pdf, 3.

Appendix 2
Five myths about intelligence

Andrew Sabisky

Education is bedevilled by cargo cult science, but the amount of folklore that has built up around the topic of intelligence is exceptional. Differential psychology – the science that investigates the nature and causes of differences between individuals in their cognition – is perhaps unique in one unhappy respect. Certainly I can think of no other psychological arena of investigation where mainstream science and popular understanding have so spectacularly diverged. This is an attempt to bridge that gulf.

Myth 1: Multiple intelligences

It is an article of faith in many educational circles that it is not useful to speak of a general intelligence, an all-purpose cognitive engine, but instead to speak of multiple intelligences. According to this view, promoted by Howard Gardner, there is a range of separate intelligences. He lists logical-spatial intelligence, verbal intelligence, musical intelligence, mathematical intelligence, bodily-kinaesthetic intelligence and even, in later works, naturalistic and spiritual intelligences. There are two main criticisms to be made of Gardner's work: the first is that it is conceptually confused and the second is that it is empirically false.

The first criticism is relatively unimportant but still worth pointing out. In almost the entirety of human history prior to Gardner, intelligence was taken to be a property of the mind. A popular synonym for intelligence is *cognitive ability*. The clue is in the name: cognitive ability clearly refers to *cognitive processes*, and these, by definition, are properties of the brain. It therefore seems highly unusual to speak of bodily-kinaesthetic ability as an 'intelligence' when such ability is clearly more related to the body than the brain. It obviously doesn't hurt to be an intelligent (in the conventional sense) soccer player, but far more important is your athletic ability: your stamina, your passing skill, your sprinting speed and your shooting prowess. It is, of course, entirely up to Gardner whether or not he wishes to arbitrarily redefine words to suit his purpose; I would not deny that it is his prerogative to do so. It is not clear that the rest of us benefit by following suit.

Of course, such a criticism only applies clearly to one of Gardner's multiple intelligences; the others do not appear to be obviously dependent on physical skill. So what should we make of Gardner's empirical claims? How well have they stood up to testing? It is clear that a key tenet of his model is that the intelligences are separate. This means that they are uncorrelated. The assumption is that possessing above average verbal gifts makes you no more or less likely to have above average mathematical gifts. Is this, in fact, what we find when we put the hypothesis to the test? To answer this question fully, we will need to travel to the turn of the 20th century and the birth of the intelligence test.

Throughout the 19th century, most commentators on mental abilities assumed they were independent – a school of thought called 'faculty psychology'. Such a model remained untested until an English psychologist, Charles Spearman, found that boys' grades in school subjects were highly correlated; the boys who excelled at math were likely to be better than average in English and Latin. Spearman developed a novel statistical technique called factor analysis to analyze his data and proposed that one common factor, g, explained most of the variance in a battery of mental tests, but that each subtest also had its own specific variance (Spearman called this non-shared variation s factor). Spearman's original finding has since been modified by later analyses and the factors derived from analyses of mental tests are best thought to fit into a pyramidal structure, with g at the top (see Figure A2.1). The finding that all mental tests positively inter-correlate is probably the most replicated result in all of psychology, and factor analysis is now an extremely popular statistical tool used widely across the social and biological sciences.

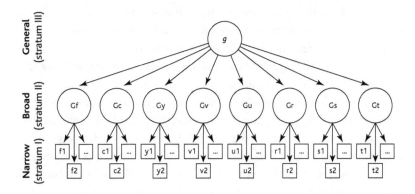

Figure A2.1. Carroll's three stratum model of human intelligence
Source: Creative Commons, Timothy Bates (University of Edinburgh).

It has proved impossible to devise a battery of mental tests that does not produce a *g* factor solution as the best fit to the data, though psychometricians have spent decades trying. Even test batteries that are explicitly designed not to measure *g* always yield a *g* that correlates highly with the *g* extracted from conventional IQ tests.[1] In such batteries, the *g* factor normally accounts for about 50 percent of the variance. We can now measure *g* with very high reliability (at 0.9 or above).* Naturally, the implication is that some common biological factor underpins performance across all cognitive tasks. A substantial body of data supports this interpretation, both on the genetic[2] and neurological level.[3] The *g* factor accounts for nearly all of the predictive validity of IQ tests, a topic more fully discussed below, and is most highly correlated with such phenomena as brain size, brain glucose uptake, reaction time, average evoked potentials and inbreeding depression.[4] G does not appear to be a chimerical statistical artefact, as has sometimes been alleged by Stephen J. Gould and others, but a biological reality fundamental to cognition.[5]

....

*   It is worth noting that the test–retest reliability of IQ tests is far higher than the test–retest reliability of many medical tests administered by skilled physicians (see Jensen's *The G Factor*, p. 50). Despite popular perception, we can measure some psychological phenomena with far greater accuracy than we can their physiological counterparts.

To return to Gardner, his model of mental abilities is entirely contrary to the evidence. Gardner is himself opposed to measurement, and has offered no operationalizations of his theories which could allow them to be put to the test. Consequently his arguments are largely unfalsifiable. Insofar as they are testable, however, they are among the most consistently rejected ideas in the history of psychology. The extraordinary thing was that the Gardner model of uncorrelated mental abilities that do not yield a g factor was in fact not novel to him; it lay at the core of 19th century faculty psychology, and was still in some form adhered to in the 20th century. The g factor solution only triumphed, in the teeth of great opposition, because of the overwhelming mass of data supporting it. Gardner was at least half a century out of date. His ideas can perhaps best be thought of as the return from the grave of one of psychology's many 'undead theories' – zombie notions that persevere in some quarters long after they have lost widespread support.[6]

Myth 2: IQ tests only measure the ability to take an IQ test

Of all the criticisms made against intelligence testing, this is surely the most misleading. IQ tests predict academic achievement extremely well. This is perhaps unsurprising, given that the original purpose of the first tests, created by Alfred Binet, was to identify children who were likely to struggle in mainstream education.* But the predictive power of IQ tests goes far beyond the academic sphere. IQ predicts income, probability of divorce, probability of welfare dependency and job performance.[7] The more complex the job, the better performance on it can be predicted by IQ, but even performance on low-skilled jobs is predictable by IQ to some extent. The US military does not generally accept recruits with an IQ below 85 because they know that such recruits are much harder to train. In addition, the training does not stick as well as it does for higher-IQ recruits, and such recruits are also more likely to die in combat.[8] Intelligence also predicts an array of health related outcomes:

---

* According to Deary and colleagues in 'Intelligence and Educational Achievement', the correlation between IQ measured at age 11 and GCSE scores at age 16 is 0.81, in a sample of 70,000.

all-cause mortality, obesity, cancer rates and sperm quality.[9] The correlations between IQ and these outcomes may not be entirely mediated by individual differences in health-related behaviors; they may arise in part because the IQ test taps into some kind of fundamental neurobiological integrity of the organism.[10] Further evidence in favor of this view is that IQ correlates with brain size at about 0.4,[11] and also with a wide range of elementary cognitive tasks, such as reaction and inspection time. Most reaction time tasks are so straightforward that 10-year-old children perform at near flawless rates; they are all some variant of 'light goes off, push a button as fast as you can'. Yet the general factor of speed of response computed from a battery of these tests correlates highly with the g factor derived from conventional IQ tests; chronometric g and psychometric g appear to be very similar, if not entirely isomorphic.[12]

In conclusion, the high-predictive validity of IQ tests demonstrates that the construct they measure is of vast importance in today's world. The old rumor that they do not measure anything of relevance was never justified.

Myth 3: IQ tests don't measure intelligence

This is less a misconception and more a vacuous, hollow debate. The everyday English word 'intelligence' is scientifically meaningless and the understanding of what it means varies from person to person, just as is the case for most other abstract nouns in common usage. Consequently, the debate as to whether or not IQ tests measure intelligence is empty because a definition of intelligence that completely satisfies everyone can never be agreed upon. That the construct that IQ tests measure is usually called 'intelligence' is an unfortunate accident of history that most differential psychologists probably regret. You can call the construct intelligence, g, general mental ability, cognitive ability or Kim Kardashian's Left Fake Eyelash – it matters not a whit. They are all perfectly satisfactory shorthands so long as they are understood by everyone to mean a very general capacity for learning that predicts academic achievement and a wide range of life outcomes, as reviewed above. Whether or not everyone agrees that this construct can be perfectly identified with the everyday meaning of intelligence is irrelevant: the only concern is if the construct has sufficient predictive validity to be of great scientific and practical importance. As shown, it does.*

Myth 4: The family environment is the most important influence on IQ

At the core of this myth lies the tiniest kernel of truth overlain with a web of misunderstanding and outright lie. It is reinforced by a regular diet of newspaper articles reporting on studies showing correlations between childhood IQ/vocabulary/academic achievement and number of books in the family, parental vocabulary, parental income and so on. The problem with all these correlational studies is that there is a vast, unobserved, yet perfectly obvious genetic confound that sociologists and educational researchers persistently refuse to wrap their heads around.

Assume for a moment a genetic contribution to individual differences in IQ. Now, IQ is closely correlated with vocabulary: in fact, the vocabulary subtest in popular intelligence test batteries is one of the most highly correlated with the g factor.[13] If parents, for genetic reasons, have low IQs, they will have smaller than average vocabularies. These genes will be passed on to their children. Consequently, if parental vocabulary size is closely correlated with child vocabulary size, we should not assume that this is due to the detrimental effect of the environment that the parents provide, unless we have somehow controlled for the genotypes that the parents and their offspring share but that we cannot ordinarily observe. Of course, much the same may be said for number of books in the home: genetically smarter parents are likely to read and own more books, and they pass those genes down to their children. In fact, I strongly suspect that number of books in the home is a much better measure of parental IQ than parental income!

But income itself, of course, is correlated with IQ. This is unsurprising; the more intelligent perform better at their jobs,[14] and are more likely

----

* In 1980, Jensen argued that the construct measured by IQ tests closely approximated our everyday conception of intelligence; by 1998, he had changed his mind slightly and argued that the whole debate is unresolvable and not worth discussing. I largely concur with this latter position.

to be attracted to mentally taxing, higher-paying jobs. Assume again a genetic contribution to variation in intelligence. If this were so, we would in fact expect genetic differences to emerge between different classes of socioeconomic status (SES) in very short order. It should not be surprising when, *on average,** middle class children tend to outperform working class children, assuming that the job marketplace is vaguely meritocratic and that higher intelligence results in higher income (both assumptions that appear to be largely validated by the empirical data).[15]

Thus far I have asked you to assume a genetic contribution to variation in intelligence. How to test if this is so? We could check if the IQs of adopted children more closely track the IQs of their biological parents than the IQs of their adoptive parents and siblings. We could also check whether the IQs of identical twins are more closely correlated than the IQs of non-identical twins, because identical twins are almost 100 percent genetically similar (near-clones), whereas non-identical twins are only as genetically similar as full siblings (50 percent). These two approaches are the basic methods of the field of behavior genetics, and have produced a vast literature covering the contributions of genes and environments to all kinds of traits, from IQ to personality traits such as extraversion and conscientiousness to illnesses such as schizophrenia.**

What is not often appreciated is that behavior genetic methods give us useful information about environmental as well as genetic effects. Identical twin pairs share all their genes and a familial environment; their similarity is, therefore, the sum of genetic and shared environmental influences on variation of the trait in question. Any differences between identical twin pairs must be non-genetic in origin and, crucially, arise from environments that are unique to each twin – that is, environmental influences that originate *outside the family*. What behavior geneticists

---

* In 2014, Trzaskowski et al. found that the correlation between IQ and SES is approximately a low but significant 0.3 – this explains substantial disparities in group means but also the poor validity of SES as a predictor of IQ (absent any other information) on the individual level.

** Many excellent and readable introductions to behavior genetics have been written that discuss the findings of the field, its core assumptions and its methodological issues, and their resolution more fully than I have the space for here. Among them are Jensen's 'How Much Can We Boost IQ and Scholastic Achievement', Miele's *Intelligence, Race, and Genetics*, and Sesardic's *Making Sense of Heritability*. Plomin et al.'s *Behavioral Genetics* is a more specialist text.

have found is that environmental influences on traits are, by adulthood, almost entirely non-shared in origin; the familial environment, while it has some importance in childhood, does not contribute to variation in adult outcomes. In the long run, sibling pairs (as well as parents and their offspring) resemble each other because of their shared genes, not their shared experiences. This pattern holds true not just for IQ but for almost every trait you can imagine. As shared environmental influence goes to zero, heritability – the statistic that gives us the percentage of genetic variance on the trait in question – usually rises with age. For intelligence, we find heritability coefficients of well under 50 percent in early childhood, but by adolescence and adulthood these rise to 70–80 percent, and even higher figures have been reported for the g factor. It is common to find heritabilities of about 50 percent or higher for most behavioral traits; a range of figures are given in Table A2.1.

Table A2.1. Heritability factors

Trait/outcome	Heritability	Source
IQ (general intelligence)	50–80%	The literature is vast: Plomin et al. (1994) is a good start
GCSE scores (core subjects)	58%	Shakeshaft et al. (2013)
Conscientiousness	75%	Riemann et al. (1997)
Bullying (at age 10)	61%	Ball et al. (2008)
Altruism	56%	Rushton et al. (1986)
Alcoholism	50%	
Autistic traits (at age 8)	64–92% (depending on diagnostic cut-off)	Ronald et al. (2006)
ADHD	70–80% (consensus estimate)	Martin et al. (2002)
Obesity	40–75% (consensus estimate)	O'Rahilly and Farooqi (2008)
Time spent watching TV	30–45%	Plomin et al. (1990)
Smoking initiation	44%	Vink et al. (2005)
Nicotine dependence	75%	Vink et al. (2005)
Political conservatism	About 40–60%	Martin et al. (1986); Bouchard et al. (2003)
Conduct disorder (age 11–18)	53%	Gelhorn et al. (2005)

It is important at this point to think about what heritability is and is not. It is not a percentage of the total contribution of genes to your personal IQ. It is not, in fact, a meaningful question to ask how genes and environments have contributed to an individual phenotype because the process of development within individuals is incredibly complex. It is, however, meaningful to ask about the contributions of genes and environments to variation within a population, and even to make probabilistic statements about the contributions of genes and environments to why one person within that population is smarter than another. (If the heritability of IQ is high for today's Western world, it is likely that Stephen Hawking is smarter than I because he has better genes, not because he benefited from a superior environment.) This should make us realize that heritability is not some fixed constant, like the speed of light, but a fluctuating statistic that varies according to societal conditions.

Imagine we lived in a world where half the population, through no merit of their own, lived in the lap of idle luxury and the other half, through no fault of their own, in the most grinding, dreadful poverty you can imagine: children grow up with no formal education, primitive technology, malnutrition and iodine deficiency are rampant, along with crime, infectious diseases and so on. In such a world, if you were to measure the whole population, differences in outcomes and traits would be largely due to the environment because your environment, in this scenario, (a) determines your outcomes, and (b) will significantly shape your core traits (via such mechanisms as malnutrition and disease impairing intelligence).

Genetic factors, in our anti-meritocracy, would not significantly influence individual differences. Now, what would happen if we were to equalize these environments? Let's imagine our anti-meritocracy became a communist utopia where all experience very similar upbringings. In the absence of significant environmental variation between individuals, most differences between individuals must be down to genes.

If environments across the population are fairly equal, heritability will be high; if they are very unequal, heritability will be low. High heritability in today's developed world can be taken as an indicator that attempts to achieve equality of opportunity have been tolerably successful and that everyone is getting a fair shot at success within the limitations of their genotype; non-genetic familial factors are not playing an unduly important role in trait development and behavioral outcomes. That is not, of course, to say that a more meritocratic world could not be achieved.

It is also vital to remember that heritability coefficients give a snapshot of the world as it is and are mostly uninformative about the world as it could be. Suppose we find fairly high heritability of classroom behavior, as we do.[16] This does not imply that the degree of classroom misbehavior is under strong genetic influence, simply that the position of individuals within the distribution is. In a world with better behavior policy, although the kids with the genotypes that incline them most towards classroom delinquency are still likely to be the worst behaved, there is every reason to expect that they would only be mildly annoying pains in the backside, rather than absolutely out of control tearaways. This argument holds true for academic achievement as well – so, yes, teaching is absolutely worth it! It's a wonderful thing to increase the amount of knowledge in the world and to produce a better educated society; just don't expect individual and group differences in academic achievement to go away anytime soon.*

If at this point you are wondering what the point of parenting is – well, I can't help you there. Just make sure you choose a partner with a good genotype to have kids with, and all shall, probabilistically speaking, be well.**

Twin studies are vulnerable to a number of criticisms, not all well-founded,[17] but it is a strength of behavior genetics that adoption studies converge on similar conclusions; the correlation between the IQs of adopted children and their adoptive parents is often significant in childhood, but by adulthood it typically goes to near-zero.[18]

....

*   High heritability constrains the possible effect of changes within the existing range of environments. But what about some completely novel environment? Some wonder drug? Electrical brain stimulation? There is no reason why such entirely new techniques could not remove achievement gaps – again, heritability statistics only capture a snapshot of the world as it is now. This is not the stuff of science fiction; such techniques and their application are the most exciting products in development of the new field called educational neuroscience.

**   This is partly hyperbole. If you want to have a good relationship with your children, of course it matters how you parent them. If you want your children to be happy and fulfilled throughout childhood and adolescence, parenting matters. But looking for long-term effects of parenting is a struggle; the vast majority of parenting seems to be good enough beyond a (fairly low) threshold.

In summary, the kernel of truth mentioned in the first paragraph of this section is that family environments do have some influence on trait variation at young ages, though even here substantial heritability coefficients are the norm. In the long run, however, the family environment has minimal, if any, impact on variation in IQ – or indeed on variation in any trait – among the population.*

Myth 5: IQ tests are biased against non-white, non-middle class people

The test bias allegation is frequently made, not just against IQ tests but against any standardized test whose scores show sex, race or class differences. The assumption is taken for granted that all groups are exactly equal in their ability and that any differences between them result from biased tests. I have already shown that this is not a reasonable prior belief in terms of social class. I will now argue that the evidence does not support test bias as a source of differences in test scores.

Firstly, some facts. Most studies report no non-trivial sex differences in full scale IQ.[19] The shape of the distributions, however, appears to differ significantly; the male distribution is considerably more spread out. In practical terms, this means that even if the means of the sexes are in fact identical, we should expect to find significantly more male geniuses and

---

* It is sometimes argued – indeed, it is sometimes stated as fact – that the heritability of IQ decreases with SES. Hanscombe et al. did not find this interaction in the UK in their very large sample for 'Socioeconomic Status (SES) and Children's Intelligence (IQ)' (around 8,000 twin pairs), though it has replicated somewhat better in the US. It is hard to come to definite conclusions on this matter since the statistical power required to accurately detect GxE (genetic and environment) interactions is very high, far higher than it is to detect main effects; this makes false positives and false negatives more likely. The most frequently cited study in this field – Turkheimer et al.'s 'Socioeconomic Status Modifies Heritability of IQ in Young Children' – is severely crippled by this issue. It is also very difficult to recruit and retain large numbers of twin pairs from the lowest percentiles of the SES distribution. My own view is that some modification of heritability by SES is almost inevitable, but I suspect that in today's Britain such modification only occurs when a certain threshold is reached, and that threshold is only found in the very poorest households. Brain development appears to be far more robust than it is popularly given credit for, and may even be immune to such insults as in utero famine and maternal crack cocaine use according to Hurt et al.'s 1997 article on the subject and Flynn's book, *What is Intelligence?*

significantly more male dullards.[20] Why greater male variability arises is unknown.

Ethnic differences in IQ are much larger and of far more serious social importance. Assuming a white gentile norm of 100 (standard deviation 15), black African-Americans average a score around 85, Hispanics around 93 and Asian-Americans (usually of Far Eastern extraction) score around 105. Ashkenazi Jews score higher still (between 110–115).[21] These differences are not unique to IQ tests but are well-replicated in other test batteries such as the SAT, GRE (General Test), job application tests and those administered by the army.[22] It has proved impossible to devise a test battery with good predictive validity that does not give rise to substantial ethnic score gaps, and industrial and organizational psychologists have spent a very long time trying.[23] *

By far the most studied of these ethnic differences is the black-white difference in IQ, largely because the United States has a substantial black population with a very long history of educational underachievement. It emerges at around the age of 3 and remains stable thereafter.[24] Scholars of the hereditarian[25] and environmentalist[26] camps have been arguing over its aetiology for at least the past 40 years. I am not going to stoke the flames of that debate here, but merely demonstrate that whatever the actual origin(s) of ethnic differences in IQ, test bias is not among them.

To begin with, it is vital to clearly define test bias. Bias is not a reflection of how well the phenotype accords with the genotype. A Romanian orphan who has a low IQ because she has suffered from continual severe malnourishment and other forms of deprivation still has real cognitive deficits. The test is not biased just because in the case of our Romanian orphan the phenotype (IQ) is probably not a good reflection of the underlying genotype. Tests can only attempt to measure reality, and they are not biased if, in other worlds, things would have been different. Bias, properly defined, is a question of predictive validity and measurement invariance.

Predictive validity is easy to discuss. The point of intelligence testing is to allow prediction of real-world achievement: at school, at work, on the

----

*   The tests that best predict job performance also discriminate the most against non-Asian ethnic minorities, and especially blacks. The dilemma that this gives rise to is known in industrial-organizational psychology as the *diversity-validity trade-off*.

battleground. If IQ tests gave below average scores to group X yet group X learned mathematics, English and Latin at the same rate and with the same proficiency as other students, then we have good reason to suspect that the tests are poor measures of the true ability of group X and are inherently biased, for some reason, against members of group X. Just the opposite is, in fact, found in the case of most ethnic differences in IQ and academic achievement; for non-Asian minorities, the tests tend to very slightly over-predict their later performance and marginally under-predict that of whites and Asians.[27] This is not some novel finding but has been replicated very well across samples and considerable timespans.*

Measurement invariance is shorthand for, 'Is the same latent construct being assessed by the same tests across different groups?' If members of group X have completely different item pass rates from members of group A, we may conclude that the test is measuring something different in groups X and A. Imagine a series of matrix reasoning problems that have been designed to get progressively harder. We test this hypothesis on group A and find that, in accordance with our prediction, the later items in the test battery have lower pass rates. When testing group X, however, we find that the earlier items in the test have lower pass rates and that group X do better on the later items. Something has clearly gone wrong; we cannot make valid comparisons between groups A and X with regards to the construct we are trying to measure because the necessary condition of measurement invariance has been violated. We can, thankfully, test for measurement invariance using a technique called multigroup confirmatory factor analysis (MGCFA). When MGCFA is applied to ethnic group differences, the assumption of measurement invariance is generally upheld.[28] **

In summary, a large literature strongly rejects the notion of endemic bias against minority groups implicit to IQ tests. This does not mean

....

* The minor over-prediction by IQ tests of non-Asian minority performance is just a meaningless statistical artefact produced by the common regression model – it should not be taken to imply that minority performance on these later measures is artificially depressed by some unknown factor. The same effect arises when comparing the prediction of weight by height for men and women.

** Note that this is not true for class differences (that is, the Flynn effect). This strongly implies that within class racial-ethnic differences and within race class differences are separate phenomena; one does not tell us anything about the aetiology of the other.

that IQ tests are never biased: it is clear that giving verbal IQ tests to certain groups (recent immigrants and the deaf) leads to substantial underestimation of their true intellectual competence.[29] In such cases, the inadequacy of the verbal IQ tests is normally very obvious because the groups in question score much higher on non-verbal IQ tests such as Raven's matrices. When there are no gross disparities in linguistic exposure, the evidence reviewed shows that group differences in both verbal and non-verbal IQ scores reflect real differences in ability and are not artefacts of test bias. This is also the conclusion of the American Psychological Association.[30]

Practical implications for education

Some persons assume that discussing such impolite subjects as IQ and genetics in an educational context means that one is going to argue for a return to grammar schools or for greater setting within comprehensive education. Nothing could be further from the truth. The debates over grammars and ability setting are largely separate arguments. Ability setting either works or it does not. That debate is a purely empirical affair with almost no relevance to the validity of intelligence testing. Grammar schools either have beneficial effects on society or they do not. Again, this is an empirical matter and one of little relevance. The immediate practical implications of the scholarly literature reviewed above are more modest and also of more relevance to the everyday concerns of teachers, senior management, Ofsted and governments.

Firstly, schools and teachers should not be judged on the basis of raw test scores. Such scores are largely the products of their students' IQs and those IQs are, in turn, largely due to variations in DNA.[31] As a friend of mine, an excellent math teacher, once aptly put it, "All we're doing at GCSE is measuring g." This is an overstatement but is rooted in truth, though far better measures of g than GCSEs are available. Due to local variability and historical demographic trends, schools will vary somewhat in their intakes' quantities of g. Within the school, there will be far greater variability in g, and even with no ability setting random chance will mean that some teachers wind up teaching classes with a below average mean IQ. Poor results from such classes should not be laid at the door of the teacher. It is necessary to look at long-term trends and not short-term results when evaluating teacher performance. More broadly, it is critical to think coherently about what our public examinations are actually for. Do we want to assess the intellectual ability of our students? Such tests are certainly of great value to universities and even more to many employers. Or do we want to assess the competence of our teachers by making sure that our students have in fact learned, with some reasonable proficiency, a core stock of knowledge that we value as a society? There is nothing wrong with either aim, but it is asking a great deal to say that the same test should achieve both ends.

Secondly, schools should not be judged according to the extent to which they are closing various achievement gaps, contrary to the latest Ofsted guidance. It is not a coherent prior belief to expect that, in a meritocratic society, the various social classes will not differ somewhat in their mean IQs and innate capability for academic achievement. A powerful body of literature implies that schools will not be able to produce equitable outcomes, and common sense and prior experience both suggest that encouraging them to try will only result in rampant gaming of the system and an unhealthy focus on the few at the expense of the many, as occurred for years in the case of students on the critical C/D grade borderline at GCSE. It is better to encourage schools to aim for higher achievement across the entire distributions of income and ability.

Thirdly, it is necessary to cast a skeptical eye over observational studies that, with no built in genetic control, make sweeping claims of causal relations between parental and child vocabulary size, or parental income and child school readiness, or number of books in the parental home and offspring academic achievement. There are always unobserved genetic confounds at play that neither goodwill nor multiple regression can wish away. The usual policy recommendations stemming from this kind of study are ever greater investment in a more academically structured pre-kindergarten sector. It would be uncharitable to suggest that the people making these recommendations often have something of a vested interest in seeing them come to reality. Rather, I prefer to argue that it is honorable naivety that leads to such proposals, along with an overly optimistic view of the literature on pre-school intervention. The rather more dismal reality should give us pause.[32]

Fourthly, tests that produce score disparities along racial and socio-economic lines should not be prematurely judged as biased. Bias is a question of predictive validity and measurement invariance, and it is these questions that must be resolved. Between group differences in mean achievement are uninformative with regards to assessing test bias. There are, in fact, powerful reasons to think that some such disparities are the natural products of an unbiased test. This has relevance for the debate over the admissions procedures of the remaining grammar schools, and also applies to the occasional controversies over the ethnic and socioeconomic make-up of gifted and talented programs. This latter debate has heretofore been largely an American issue; with the establishment, on the Russian model, of UK's first specialist math schools, it may arise in the UK with greater frequency.

Lastly, there is a robust finding that some aspects of cognitive decline begin at young ages, with fluid IQ (roughly defined as the ability to solve novel problems) reaching its peak around the middle of the third decade of life, and declining thereafter. This is accompanied by a decline in the size of the brain, although vocabulary and knowledge clearly continue to expand.[33] It is surely no coincidence that many of the eminent mathematicians and scientists of history achieved their greatest feats at young ages; the early Nobel Prizes in physics, chemistry and medicine were largely given to those under 40, though over the course of the 20th century the ages of prizewinners have risen.[34] The chess performance of grandmasters peaks in the early thirties.[35] If we want our brightest minds to solve our scientific, technological and social problems, we need their talents to be utilized while their brains are at their innovative peak. Instead, we squander their talents in a laughably unproductive and protracted education system. The top percentiles of IQ coast through their GCSEs and A levels, accumulating piles of A*s with minimal effort, quite often becoming bored and disaffected in the process. Matters do not improve in the first few years at university on many courses. We are insufficiently unambitious in our goals. For the cognitive elite, A level material can and should be completed by age 15–16 or younger, and after this a fairly broad curriculum covering more advanced mathematics, statistics and literature should be covered, with options for specialization in modern and ancient languages, evolutionary theory, probability, psychometrics and so on.

Conclusion

Large, permanent individual differences in talent are a fact of life and are not going to go away for the foreseeable future. To a very great extent, these differences are due to variations in the innate qualities of persons and are not the result of manipulable differences in environments. Despite the scientific consensus as to these truths, teachers and governments have largely ignored or misunderstood them. In defence of teachers, I strongly suspect that this is largely due to the scientific illiteracy of the people running initial teacher training (ITT). Even at the Institute of Education, my alma mater, the ITT department is largely severed from the psychology and human development faculty, much to the frustration of the latter. Consequently, myths such as learning styles and multiple intelligences still infect ITT, even at universities such as Edinburgh, home of some of the Anglosphere's leading differential psychologists. This has led to some serious policy missteps with negative consequences for everyday classroom practice. It is hoped that wider knowledge of the truth of human variation and its aetiology will lead to a more autonomous, skilled and evidence aware teaching profession. In the long run, there is no other way to improve the quality of education in this country.

Acknowledgements

Parts of this chapter were adapted from a talk on behavior genetics delivered at researchED 2014. I am grateful to Rosalind Arden, Jan de Ruiter, Stuart Ritchie and Michael Story for their work on editing the drafts of the present chapter, and to Anna for her eternal love and devoted proofreading. The greatest thanks are due to David Didau for asking me to contribute to his book. David and I met by chance at the Wellington Festival of Education 2014, and fell to talking about intelligence and the genetics of education. Within an hour he had asked me to write what eventually became this Appendix. I have never given him a personality test, but can confidently state that he would score exceptionally highly on the openness to experience factor. It is a rare gift in an educator – the world needs more like him.

Notes

1 Arthur R. Jensen, *The G Factor: The Science of Mental Ability* (Westport, CT: Praeger, 1998), p. 117.
2 Maciej Trzaskowski, Nicholas G. Shakeshaft and Robert Plomin, Intelligence Indexes Generalist Genes for Cognitive Abilities, *Intelligence* 41(5) (2013): 560–565.
3 Ian J. Deary, Lars Penke and Wendy Johnson, The Neuroscience of Human Intelligence Differences, *Nature Reviews Neuroscience* 11(3) (2010): 201–211.
4 Jensen, *The G Factor*, ch. 6.
5 Thomas J. Bouchard, Genes, Evolution and Intelligence, *Behavior Genetics* 44(6) (2014): 549–557.
6 Christopher J. Ferguson and Moritz Heene, A Vast Graveyard of Undead Theories: Publication Bias and Psychological Science's Aversion to the Null, *Perspectives on Psychological Science* 7(6) (2012): 555–561.
7 Linda S. Gottfredson, G, Jobs and Life, in Helmuth Nyborg (ed.), *The Scientific Study of General Intelligence: A Tribute to Arthur R. Jensen* (Oxford: Elsevier Science/Pergamon, 2003), pp. 293–342; Frank L. Schmidt and John Hunter, General Mental Ability in the World of Work: Occupational Attainment and Job Performance, *Journal of Personality and Social Psychology* 86(1) (2004): 162–173; Richard J. Herrnstein and Charles Murray, *Bell Curve: Intelligence and Class Structure in American Life* (New York: Simon & Schuster, 2010).
8 Janice H. Laurence and Peter F. Ramsberger, *Low-Aptitude Men in the Military: Who Profits, Who Pays?* (New York: Praeger, 1991); Linda S. Gottfredson, Why G Matters: The Complexity of Everyday Life, *Intelligence* 24(1) (1997): 79–132.
9 Ian J. Deary and Geoff Der, Reaction Time Explains IQ's Association with Death, *Psychological Science* 16(1) (2005): 64–69; Rosalind Arden, Linda S. Gottfredson and Geoffrey Miller, Does a Fitness Factor Contribute to the Association Between Intelligence and Health Outcomes? Evidence from Medical Abnormality Counts Among 3654 US Veterans, *Intelligence* 37(6) (2009): 581–591; Shira Goldberg, Nomi Werbeloff, Eyal Fruchter, Shirly Portuguese, Michael Davidson and Mark Weiser, IQ and Obesity in Adolescence: A Population-Based, Cross-Sectional Study, *Pediatric Obesity* 9(6) (2014): 419–426.
10 Deary and Der, Reaction Time Explains IQ's Association with Death.
11 J. Philippe Rushton and C. Davison Ankney, Whole Brain Size and General Mental Ability: A Review, *International Journal of Neuroscience* 119(5) (2009): 692–732.
12 Arthur R. Jensen, *Clocking the Mind: Mental Chronometry and Individual Differences* (Oxford: Elsevier, 2006).
13 Jensen, *The G Factor*, p. 156.
14 Frank L. Schmidt and John Hunter, General Mental Ability in the World of Work: Occupational Attainment and Job Performance, *Journal of Personality and Social Psychology* 86(1) (2004): 162–173.
15 Jensen, *The G Factor*, pp. 564–568.
16 Essi Viding, Alice P. Jones, Paul J. Frick, Terrie E. Moffitt and Robert Plomin, Heritability of Antisocial Behaviour at 9: Do Callous-Unemotional Traits Matter?, *Developmental Science* 11(1) (2008): 17–22.
17 Neven Sesardic, *Making Sense of Heritability* (Cambridge: Cambridge University Press, 2005).
18 Robert Plomin, David W. Fulker, Robin Corley and John C. DeFries, Nature, Nurture, and Cognitive Development from 1 to 16 years: A Parent-Offspring Adoption Study, *Psychological Science* 8(6) (1997): 442–447; Kevin M. Beaver, Joseph A. Schwartz, Mohammed Said Al-Ghamdi, Ahmed Nezar Kobeisy, Curtis S. Dunkel and Dimitri

van der Linden, A Closer Look at the Role of Parenting-Related Influences on Verbal Intelligence Over the Life Course: Results from an Adoption-Based Research Design, *Intelligence* 46 (2014): 179–187.

19 Jensen, *The G Factor*, p. 541; Wendy Johnson, Andrew Carothers and Ian J. Deary, Sex Differences in Variability in General Intelligence: A New Look at the Old Question, *Perspectives on Psychological Science* 3(6) (2008): 518–531; but see also Paul Irwing, Sex Differences in *G*: An Analysis of the US Standardization Sample of the WAIS-III, *Personality and Individual Differences* 53(2) (2012): 126–131.

20 Johnson et al., Sex Differences in Variability in General Intelligence.

21 Herrnstein and Murray, *Bell Curve*; J. Philippe Rushton and Arthur R. Jensen, Thirty Years of Research on Race Differences in Cognitive Ability, *Psychology, Public Policy, and Law* 11(2) (2005): 235–294.

22 Philip L. Roth, Craig A. Bevier, Philip Bobko, Fred S. Switzer III and Peggy Tyler, Ethnic Group Differences in Cognitive Ability in Employment and Educational Settings: A Meta-Analysis, *Personnel Psychology* 54(2) (2001): 297–330.

23 Amy L. Wax, Disparate Impact Realism, *William and Mary Law Review* 53(2) (2011): 621; Juan M. Madera and JeAnna Abbott, The Diversity-Validity Dilemma Implications from the Ricci v. DeStefano US Supreme Court Case, *Cornell Hospitality Quarterly* 53(1) (2012): 31–39.

24 Jensen, *The G Factor*.

25 Rushton and Jensen, Thirty Years of Research on Race Differences.

26 William T. Dickens and James R. Flynn, Heritability Estimates versus Large Environmental Effects: The IQ Paradox Resolved, *Psychological Review* 108(2) (2001): 346.

27 Arthur R. Jensen, *Bias in Mental Testing* (New York: Free Press, 1980); Leonard Ramist, Charles Lewis and Laura McCamley-Jenkins, *Student Group Differences in Predicting College Grades: Sex, Language and Ethnic Group* (New York: The College Board, 1994); Howard Wainer and Lisa M. Brown, Three Statistical Paradoxes in the Interpretation of Group Differences: Illustrated with Medical School Admission and Licensing Data, *Handbook of Statistics* 26 (2007): 893–918.

28 Conor V. Dolan and Ellen L. Hamaker, Investigating Black-White Differences in Psychometric IQ: Multi-Group Confirmatory Factor Analyses of the WISC-R and K-ABC and a Critique of the Method of Correlated Vectors, in Frank Columbus (ed.), *Advances in Psychological Research* (Huntington, NY: Nova Science Publishers, 2001), pp. 31–59; Jelte M. Wicherts, Conor V. Dolan, David J. Hessen, Paul Oosterveld, G. Caroline M. van Baal, Dorret I. Boomsma and Mark M. Span, Are Intelligence Tests Measurement Invariant Over Time? Investigating the Nature of the Flynn Effect, *Intelligence* 32(5) (2004): 509–537.

29 Arthur R. Jensen, *Bias in Mental Testing* (New York: Free Press, 1980); Jeffrey P. Braden, *Deafness, Deprivation, and IQ* (New York: Springer, 1994).

30 Ulric Neisser, Gwyneth Boodoo, Thomas J. Bouchard, A. Wade Boykin, Nathan Brody, Stephen J. Ceci, Diane F. Halpern, John C. Loehlin, Robert Perloff, Robert J. Sternberg and Susana Urbina, Intelligence: Knowns and Unknowns, *American Psychologist* 51(2) (1996): 77.

31 Nicholas G. Shakeshaft, Maciej Trzaskowski, Andrew McMillan, Kaili Rimfeld, Eva Krapohl, Claire M. A. Haworth, Philip S. Dale and Robert Plomin, Strong Genetic Influence on a UK Nationwide Test of Educational Achievement at the End of Compulsory Education at Age 16, *PLOS ONE* 8(12) (2013): e80341.

32 Alfred A. Baumeister and Verne R. Bacharach, Early Generic Educational Intervention Has No Enduring Effect on Intelligence and Does Not Prevent Mental Retardation: The Infant Health and Development Program, *Intelligence* 28(3) (2000): 161–192.

33 Arthur R. Jensen, *Clocking the Mind: Mental Chronometry and Individual Differences* (Oxford: Elsevier, 2006), ch. 6.

34 Benjamin F. Jones and Bruce A. Weinberg, Age Dynamics in Scientific Creativity, *Proceedings of the National Academy of Sciences* 108(47) (2011): 18910–18914.

35 Geoffroy Berthelot, Stéphane Len, Philippe Hellard, Muriel Tafflet, Marion Guillaume, Jean-Claude Vollmer, Bruno Gager, Laurent Quinquis, Andy Marc and Jean-François Toussaint, Exponential Growth Combined with Exponential Decline Explains Lifetime Performance Evolution in Individual and Human Species, *Age* 34(4) (2012): 1001–1009.

Bibliography

Books

Adey, Philip and Justin Dillon (eds) (2012). *Bad Education: Debunking Myths in Education* (Buckingham: Open University Press).

Ariely, Dan (2009). *Predictably Irrational: The Hidden Forces That Shape Our Decisions* (London: HarperCollins).

Arthus, Maurice (1943). *Philosophy of Scientific Investigation* (Baltimore, MD: Johns Hopkins Press).

Baines, Ed (2012). Grouping Pupils By Ability In Schools. In P. Adey and J. Dillon (eds), *Bad Education: Debunking Myths in Education* (Buckingham: Open University Press), pp. 37–55.

Beadle, Phil (2010). *How to Teach* (Carmarthen: Crown House Publishing).

Benjamin, Aaron S. (ed.) (2011). *Successful Remembering and Successful Forgetting: A Festschrift in Honor of Robert A. Bjork* (New York: Psychology Press).

Bjork, Robert A. (1994). Memory and Metamemory Considerations in the Training of Human Beings. In J. Metcalfe and A. Shimamura (eds), *Metacognition: Knowing About Knowing* (Cambridge, MA: MIT Press), pp. 185–205.

Bjork, Robert A. (1999). Assessing Our Own Competence: Heuristics and Illusions. In D. Gopher and A. Koriat (eds), *Attention and Performance XVII. Cognitive Regulation of Performance: Interaction of Theory and Application* (Cambridge, MA: MIT Press), pp. 435–459.

Bjork, Robert A. (2011). On the Symbiosis of Learning, Remembering, and Forgetting. In A. S. Benjamin (ed.), *Successful Remembering and Successful Forgetting: A Festschrift in Honor of Robert A. Bjork* (London: Psychology Press), pp. 1–22.

Blatchford, Peter (2012). Class Size: Is Small Better? In P. Adey and J. Dillon (eds), *Bad Education: Debunking Myths in Education* (Buckingham: Open University Press), pp. 57–76.

Braden, Jeffrey P. (1994). *Deafness, Deprivation, and IQ* (New York: Springer).

Brown, Peter C., Henry L. Roediger and Mark A. McDaniel (2014). *Make It Stick: The Science of Successful Learning* (Cambridge, MA: Harvard University Press).

Buonomano, Dean (2011). *Brain Bugs: How the Brain's Flaws Shape Our Lives* (New York: W.W. Norton & Co.).

Carey, Benedict (2014). *How We Learn: The Surprising Truth About When, Where, and Why It Happens* (London: Random House).

Chabris, Christopher and Daniel Simons (2010). *The Invisible Gorilla* (London: HarperCollins).

Christodoulou, Daisy (2014). *Seven Myths About Education* (London: Routledge).

Cialdini, Robert (2007). *Influence: The Psychology of Persuasion* (New York: Harper Business).

Coffield, Frank (2012). Learning Styles: Unreliable, Invalid and Impractical And Yet Still Widely Used. In P. Adey and J. Dillon (eds), *Bad Education: Debunking Myths in Education* (Buckingham: Open University Press), pp. 215–230.

Dale, Edgar (1948). *Audio-Visual Methods in Teaching* (New York: Dryden Press).

Dawkins, Richard (2006). *The Selfish Gene*, new edn (Oxford: Oxford University Press).

De Bruyckere, Pedro, Paul A. Kirschner and Casper D. Hulshof (2015). *Urban Myths about Learning and Education* (London: Academic Press).

Delisle, James (2014). *Dumbing Down America: The War On Our Nation's Brightest Young Minds (and What We Can Do to Fight Back)* (Waco, TX: Prufrock Press Inc.).

Dennett, Daniel (1993). *Consciousness Explained* (London: Penguin).

Didau, David (2014). *The Secret of Literacy* (Carmarthen: Independent Thinking Press).

Dobelli, Rolf (2013). *The Art of Thinking Clearly* (London: Scepter).

Dolan, Conor V. and Ellen L. Hamaker (2001). Investigating Black-White Differences in Psychometric IQ: Multi-Group Confirmatory Factor Analyses of the WISC-R and K-ABC and a Critique of the Method of Correlated Vectors. In F. Columbus (ed.), *Advances in Psychological Research*, Vol. 6 (Huntington, NY: Nova Science Publishers), pp. 31–59.

Donovan, M. Suzanne, John D. Bransford and James W. Pellegrino (eds) (2001). *How People Learn Bridging Research and Practice* (Washington, DC: National Academy Press).

Druckman, Daniel and Robert A. Bjork (eds) (1991). *In the Mind's Eye: Enhancing Human Performance* (Washington, DC: National Academy Press).

Dweck, Carol (2007). *Mindset: The New Psychology of Success* (New York: Ballantine).

Egan, Kieran (2002). *Getting It Wrong from the Beginning: Our Progressive Inheritance from Herbert Spencer, John Dewey, and Jean Piaget* (New Haven, CT: Yale University Press).

Festinger, Leon (1957). *A Theory of Cognitive Dissonance* (Stanford, CA: Stanford University Press).

Festinger, Leon, Henry Riecken and Stanley Schachter (2009). *When Prophecy Fails: A Social and Psychological Study of a Modern Group That Predicted the Destruction of the World* (Eastford, CT: Martino Fine Books).

Feynman, Richard (1985). *Surely You're Joking, Mr Feynman!* (New York: W.W. Norton & Co.).

Flynn, James R. (2007). *What is Intelligence? Beyond the Flynn Effect* (Cambridge: Cambridge University Press).

Foster, Jonathan K. (2009). *Memory: A Very Short Introduction* (Oxford: Oxford University Press).

Franken, Al (1998). *Rush Limbaugh is a Big Fat Idiot* (New York: Bantam Doubleday Dell).

Gates, Arthur I. (1917). *Recitation as a Factor in Memorizing* (New York: Science Press).

Gawande, Atul (2011). *The Checklist Manifesto: How to Get Things Right* (London: Profile Books).

Gladwell, Malcom (2013). *David and Goliath: Misfits and the Art of Battling Giants* (London: Penguin).

Goldacre, Ben (2009). *Bad Science* (London: HarperCollins).

Gottfredson, Linda S. (2003). G, Jobs and Life. In H. Nyborg (ed.), *The Scientific Study of General Intelligence: A Tribute to Arthur R. Jensen* (Oxford: Elsevier Science/Pergamon), pp. 293–342.

Gregory, Richard L. (2009). *Seeing Through Illusions* (Oxford: Oxford University Press).

Haidt, Jonathan (2012). *The Righteous Mind* (London: Penguin).

Harvey, Jerry B. (1996). *The Abilene Paradox and Other Meditations on Management* (San Francisco, CA: Jossey-Bass).

Hattie, John (2008). *Visible Learning: A Synthesis of Over 800 Meta-Analyses Relating to Achievement* (Abingdon: Routledge).

Hattie, John (2011). *Visible Learning for Teachers: Maximizing Impact on Learning* (London: Routledge).

Hattie, John and Gregory Yates (2014). Using Feedback to Promote Learning. In V. A. Benassi, C. E. Overson and C. M. Hakala (eds), *Applying Science of Learning in Education: Infusing Psychological Science into the Curriculum* (Washington, DC: American Psychological Association), pp. 45–58.

Hattie, John and Gregory Yates (2014). *Visible Learning and the Science of How We Learn* (London: Routledge).

Heath, Chip and Dan Heath (2007). *Made to Stick: Why Some Ideas Take Hold and Others Come Unstuck* (London: Arrow Books).

Heath, Chip and Dan Heath (2011). *Switch: How to Change Things When Change is Hard* (New York: Random House).

Herrnstein, Richard J. and Charles Murray (2010). *Bell Curve: Intelligence and Class Structure in American Life* (New York: Simon & Schuster).

Hirsch Jr, E. D. (2007). *The Knowledge Deficit: Closing the Shocking Education Gap for American Children* (Boston, MA and New York: Houghton Mifflin).

Hitchens, Christopher (2002). *Letters to a Young Contrarian* (New York: Basic Books).

Jensen, Arthur R. (1980). *Bias in Mental Testing* (New York: Free Press).

Jensen, Arthur R. (1998). *The G Factor: The Science of Mental Ability* (Westport, CT: Praeger).

Jensen, Arthur R. (2006). *Clocking the Mind: Mental Chronometry and Individual Differences* (Oxford: Elsevier).

Kahneman, Daniel (2012). *Thinking, Fast and Slow* (London: Penguin).

Kerr, Hugo (n.d.). *The Cognitive Psychology of Literacy Teaching: Reading, Writing, Spelling, Dyslexia (& a Bit Besides)*. Available at: http://www.hugokerr.info/book.pdf.

Keynes, John Maynard (1936). Concluding Notes on the Social Philosophy Towards Which the General Theory Might Lead. In *The General Theory of Employment, Interest and Money* (Basingstoke: Palgrave Macmillan). Available at: https://www.marxists.org/reference/subject/economics/keynes/general-theory/ch24.htm.

Knight, Oliver and David Benson (2013). *Creating Outstanding Classrooms: A Whole-School Approach* (Abingdon and New York: Routledge).

Lagemann, Ellen Condliffe (2000). *An Elusive Science: The Troubling History of Education Research* (Chicago, IL: Chicago University Press).

Lakatos, Imre and Alan Musgrave (eds) (1970). *Criticism and the Growth of Knowledge* (Cambridge: Cambridge University Press).

Laurence, Janice H. and Peter F. Ramsberger (1991). *Low-Aptitude Men in the Military: Who Profits, Who Pays?* (New York: Praeger).

Lederer, Richard (1987). *Anguished English: An Anthology of Accidental Assaults Upon Our Language* (Charleston, SC: Wyrick).

Lee, Chee Ha and Slava Kalyuga (2014). Expertise Reversal Effect and its Instructional Implications. In V. A. Benassi, C. E. Overson and C. M. Hakala (eds), *Applying Science of Learning in Education: Infusing Psychological Science into the Curriculum* (Washington, DC: American Psychological Association), pp. 31–44.

Leiberman, Matthew D. (2013). *Social: Why Our Brains Are Wired to Connect* (Oxford: Oxford University Press).

Lemov, Doug (2010). *Teach Like a Champion: 49 Techniques That Put Students on the Path to College* (San Francisco, CA: Jossey-Bass).

Levitt, Steven D. and Stephen J. Dubner (2014). *Think Like a Freak* (New York: Allen Lane).

Lilienfeld, Scott O., Steven J. Lynn, John Ruscio and Barry L. Beyerstein (2010). *50 Great Myths of Popular Psychology* (Oxford: Wiley-Blackwell).

Marzano, Robert (2007). *The Art and Science of Teaching: A Comprehensive Framework for Effective Instruction* (Alexandria, VA: Association for Supervision & Curriculum Development).

Marzano, Robert, Debra Pickering and Jane Pollock (2003). *Classroom Instruction That Works: Research Based Strategies for Increasing Student Achievement* (Alexandria, VA: Association for Supervision and Curriculum Development).

McGonigal, Kelly (2013). *The Willpower Instinct: How Self-Control Works, Why It Matters, and What You Can Do to Get More of It* (New York: Avery).

McGuiness, Diane (2006). *Early Reading Instruction: What Science Really Tells Us About How to Teach Reading* (Cambridge, MA: MIT Press).

McRaney, David (2013). *You Can Beat Your Brain: How to Turn Your Enemies Into Friends, How to Make Better Decisions, and Other Ways to Be Less Dumb* (New York: Gotham Books).

Meyer, Jan and Ray Land (eds) (2006). *Overcoming Barriers to Student Understanding: Threshold Concepts and Troublesome Knowledge* (London and New York: Routledge).

Meyer, Jan, Ray Land and Caroline Bailie (eds) (2010). *Threshold Concepts and Transformational Learning* (Rotterdam: Sense Publishers).

Meyer, Jan, Ray Land and Peter Davies (2006). Implications of Threshold Concepts for Course Design and Evaluation. In J. Meyer and R. Land (eds), *Overcoming Barriers to Student Understanding: Threshold Concepts and Troublesome Knowledge* (London and New York: Routledge), pp. 195–206.

Miele, Frank (2002). *Intelligence, Race, and Genetics: Conversations with Arthur R. Jensen* (Boulder, CO: Westview Press).

Morley, John (1908). *On Compromise* (London: Macmillan and Co.). Available at: http://www.gutenberg.org/files/11557/11557-h/11557-h.htm.

Nichols, Ralph G. and Thomas R. Lewis (1954). *Listening and Speaking: A Guide to Effective Oral Communication* (Dubuque, IA: W.C. Brown).

Nuthall, Graham (2007). *The Hidden Lives of Learners* (Wellington: New Zealand Council for Educational Research Press).

Oakeshott, Michael (1962). The Voice of Poetry in the Conversation of Mankind. In *Rationalism in Politics and Other Essays* (London: Methuen), pp. 197–247.

O'Hear, Anthony (ed.) (1996). *Karl Popper, Philosophy and Problems* (Cambridge: Cambridge University Press).

Peal, Robert (2014). *Progressively Worse: The Burden of Bad Ideas in British Schools* (London: Civitas).

Perkins, David (2006). Constructivism and Troublesome Knowledge. In J. Meyer and R. Land (eds), *Overcoming Barriers to Student Understanding: Threshold Concepts and Troublesome Knowledge* (London and New York: Routledge), pp. 33–47.

Perkins, David (2010). *Making Learning Whole: How Seven Principles of Teaching Can Transform Education* (San Francisco, CA: Jossey-Bass).

Pinker, Stephen (1998). *How the Mind Works* (London: Penguin).

Plato (1881). *The Theaetetus of Plato*, tr. Benjamin Hall Kennedy (Cambridge: Cambridge University Press).

Plomin, Robert, John C. DeFries, Gerald E. McClearn and Peter McGuffin (2001). *Behavioral Genetics*, 4th edn (New York: Freeman).

Polanyi, Michael (1958). *Personal Knowledge: Towards a Post-Critical Philosophy* (London: Routledge & Kegan Paul).

Poling, Judson (2003). *Do Science and the Bible Conflict?* (Great Rapids, MI: Zondervan).

Ramist, Leonard, Charles Lewis and Laura McCamley-Jenkins (1994). *Student Group Differences in Predicting College Grades: Sex, Language and Ethnic Group* (New York: The College Board).

Robinson, Ken (2009). *The Element: How Finding Your Passion Changes Everything* (London: Penguin).

Robinson, Ken (2011). *Out of Their Minds: Learning to be Creative* (Chichester: Capstone).

Robinson, Martin (2013). *Trivium 21c: Preparing Young People for the Future with Lessons from the Past* (Carmarthen: Independent Thinking Press).

Roediger III, Henry L., Adam L. Putnam and Megan A. Smith (2011). Ten Benefits of Testing and their Application to Educational Practice. In J. P. Mestre and B. H. Ross (eds), *Psychology of Learning and Motivation*, Vol. 55: *Cognition in Education* (San Diego, CA: Academic Press).

Russell, Bertrand (1919). *Proposed Roads to Freedom: Socialism, Anarchism and Syndicalism* (New York: H. Holt).

Russell, Bertrand (1958). On the Value of Scepticism. In *The Will to Doubt* (New York: Philosophical Library). Available at: http://www.positiveatheism.org/hist/russell4.htm.

Russell, Bertrand (1998). The Triumph of Stupidity. In *Mortals and Others*, Vol. II: *American Essays, 1931–1935* (New York: Psychology Press). Available at: http://russell-j.com/0583TS.HTM.

Salkind, Neil J. and Kristin Rasmussen (eds) (2008). *Encyclopedia of Educational Psychology*, Vol. 1 (Thousand Oaks, CA: Sage).

Saul, Richard (2014). *ADHD Does Not Exist: The Truth About Attention Deficit and Hyperactivity Disorder* (New York: HarperCollins).

Schneider, Frank, Jamie Gruman and Larry Coutts (2012). *Applied Social Psychology*, 2nd edn (Thousand Oaks, CA: Sage).

Schopenhauer, A. (1831). *The Art of Being Right: 38 Ways to Win an Argument* (PDF generated using the open source mwlib toolkit: http://code.pediapress.com/).

Schulz, Kathryn (2011). *Being Wrong: Adventures in the Margin of Error* (London: Portobello Books).

Sennett, Richard (2009). *The Craftsman* (London: Penguin).

Sesardic, Neven (2005). *Making Sense of Heritability* (Cambridge: Cambridge University Press).

Shermer, Michael (2008). *Why People Believe Weird Things: Pseudoscience, Superstition, and Other Confusions of Our Time* (London: Souvenir Press).

Shermer, Michael (2011). *The Believing Brain* (London: Robinson).

Shulman, Lee S. (2004). *The Wisdom of Practice: Essays on Teaching, Learning, and Learning to Teach* (San Francisco, CA: Jossey-Bass).

Siegler, Robert (1998). *Emerging Minds: The Process of Change in Children's Thinking* (Oxford and New York: Oxford University Press).

Silver, Nate (2012). *The Signal and the Noise: The Art and Science of Prediction* (London and New York: Penguin).

Slavin, Robert (2006). *Educational Psychology: Theory and Practice*, 8th edn (Boston, MA: Pearson/Allen & Bacon).

Slavin, Robert (2010). Cooperative Learning: What Makes Groupwork Work? In H. Dumont, D. Istance and F. Benavides (eds), *The Nature of Learning: Using Research to Inspire Practice* (Paris: OECD).

Slavin, Robert, Eric Hurley and Anne Chamberlain (2003). Cooperative Learning and Achievement. In W. M. Reynolds and G. J. Miller (eds), *Handbook of Psychology*, Vol. 7: *Educational Psychology* (Hoboken, NJ: Wiley), pp. 177–198.

Soderstrom, Nicholas C. and Robert A. Bjork (2013). Learning versus Performance. In D. Dunn (ed.), *Oxford Bibliographies Online: Psychology* (New York: Oxford University Press). Available at: http://bjorklab.psych.ucla.edu/pubs/Soderstrom_Bjork_Learning_versus_Performance.pdf.

Taleb, Nassim Nicholas (2007). *The Black Swan: The Impact of the Highly Improbable* (London: Penguin).

Tavris, Carol and Elliot Aronson (2007). *Mistakes Were Made (But Not By Me): Why We Justify Foolish Beliefs, Bad Decisions and Hurtful Acts* (Orlando, FL: Harcourt Books).

Thaler, Richard H. and Cass R. Sunstein (2008). *Nudge: Improving Decisions About Health, Wealth and Happiness* (New Haven, CT: Yale University Press).

Tulving, Endel and Fergus Craik (eds) (2005). *The Oxford Handbook of Memory* (New York: Oxford University Press).

von Glasersfeld, Ernst (1987). Learning as a Constructive Activity. In C. Janvier (ed.), *Problems of Representation in the Teaching and Learning of Mathematics* (Hillsdale, NJ: Lawrence Erlbaum Associates), pp. 3–17.

Vygotsky, Lev Semenovich (1978). *Mind in Society: The Development of Higher Psychological Processes*, ed. Michael Cole (Cambridge, MA: Harvard University Press).

White, John (2005). *Howard Gardner: The Myth of Multiple Intelligences* (London: Institute of Education, University of London).

Wiliam, Dylan (2010). An Integrative Summary of the Research Literature and Implications for a New Theory of Formative Assessment. In H. L. Andrade and G. J. Cizek (eds), *Handbook of Formative Assessment* (New York: Taylor & Francis), pp. 18–40.

Wiliam, Dylan (2011). *Embedded Formative Assessment* (Bloomington, IN: Solution Tree Press).

Willingham, Daniel (2009). *Why Don't Students Like School? A Cognitive Scientist Answers Questions About How the Mind Works and What It Means for the Classroom* (San Francisco, CA: Jossey-Bass).

Willingham, Daniel (2012). *When Can You Trust the Experts? How to Tell Good Science from Bad in Education* (San Francisco, CA: Jossey-Bass).

Wittgenstein, Ludwig (1953). *Philosophical Investigations*, tr. G. E. M. Anscombe (Oxford: Basil Blackwell).

Articles

Abikoff, Howard, Mary Courtney, William E. Pelham and Harold S. Koplewicz (1993). Teachers' Ratings of Disruptive Behaviors: The Influence of Halo Effects, *Journal of Abnormal Child Psychology* 21(5): 519–533.

Anderson, Barton L. and Jonathan Winawer (2005). Image Segmentation and Lightness Perception, *Nature* 434: 79–83. Available at: http://www.psych.usyd.edu.au/staff/barta/lab/AndersonWinawer.pdf.

Arden, Rosalind, Linda S. Gottfredson and Geoffrey Miller (2009). Does a Fitness Factor Contribute to the Association Between Intelligence and Health Outcomes? Evidence from Medical Abnormality Counts Among 3654 US Veterans, *Intelligence* 37(6): 581–591.

Arden, Rosalind, Linda S. Gottfredson, Geoffrey Miller and Arand Pierce (2009). Intelligence and Semen Quality Are Positively Correlated, *Intelligence* 37(3): 277–282.

Ashman, Greg (2014). Your Own Personal PISA – What Does the TALIS Show Us?, *ResearchED*. Available at: http://www.workingoutwhatworks.com/en-GB/Magazine/2014/10/Your_own_personal_PISA.

Bahrick, Harry P., Lorraine E. Bahrick, Audrey S. Bahrick and Phyllis E. Bahrick (1993). Maintenance of Foreign Language Vocabulary and the Spacing Effect, *Psychological Science* 4(5): 316–321.

Ball, Harriet A., Louise Arseneault, Alan Taylor, Barbara Maughan, Avshalom Caspi and Terrie E. Moffitt (2008). Genetic and Environmental Influences on Victims, Bullies, and Bully-Victims in Childhood, *Journal of Child Psychology and Psychiatry and Allied Disciplines* 49(1): 104–112.

Barnett, Susan and Stephen Ceci (2002). When and Where Do We Apply What We Learn? A Taxonomy for Far Transfer, *Psychological Bulletin* 128(4): 612–637.

Baumeister, Alfred A. and Verne R. Bacharach (2000). Early Generic Educational Intervention Has No Enduring Effect on Intelligence and Does Not Prevent Mental Retardation: The Infant Health and Development Program, *Intelligence* 28(3): 161–192.

Beaver, Kevin M., Joseph A. Schwartz, Mohammed Said Al-Ghamdi, Ahmed Nezar Kobeisy, Curtis S. Dunkel and Dimitri van der Linden (2014). A Closer Look at the Role of Parenting-Related Influences on Verbal Intelligence Over the Life Course: Results from an Adoption-Based Research Design, *Intelligence* 46: 179–187.

Bergstrøm, Ida Irene (2014). All Boys Are Not Poor School Achievers, And All Girls Are Not Smart Pupils, *KILDEN* (15 December). Available at: http://eng.kilden.forskningsradet.no/c52778/nyhet/vis.html?tid=89729.

Berthelot, Geoffroy, Stéphane Len, Philippe Hellard, Muriel Tafflet, Marion Guillaume, Jean-Claude Vollmer, Bruno Gager, Laurent Quinquis, Andy Marc and Jean-François Toussaint (2012). Exponential Growth Combined with Exponential Decline Explains Lifetime Performance Evolution in Individual and Human Species, *Age* 34(4): 1001–1009.

Biesta, Gert J. J. (2010). Why 'What Works' Still Won't Work: From Evidence-Based Education to Value-Based Education, *Studies in Philosophy and Education* 29(5): 491–503.

Birnbaum, Monica S., Nate Kornell, Elizabeth L. Bjork and Robert A. Bjork (2012). Why Interleaving Enhances Inductive Learning: The Roles of Discrimination and Retrieval, *Memory & Cognition* 41: 392–402. Available at: http://bjorklab.psych.ucla.edu/pubs/Birnbaum_Kornell_EBjork_RBjork_inpress.pdf.

Bjork, Elizabeth L. and Robert A. Bjork (2003). Intentional Forgetting Can Increase, Not Decrease, Residual Influences of To-Be-Forgotten Information, *Journal of Experimental Psychology: Learning, Memory, and Cognition* 29(4): 524–531.

Bjork, Robert A. and Marcia C. Linn (2002). Introducing Desirable Difficulties for Educational Applications in Science. Available at: http://iddeas.psych.ucla.edu/IDDEASproposal.pdf.

Black, Paul J. and Dylan Wiliam (2009). Developing the Theory of Formative Assessment, *Educational Assessment, Evaluation and Accountability* 21(1): 5–31.

Bloom, Benjamin S. (1984). The Search for Methods of Group Instruction as Effective as One-to-One Tutoring, *Educational Leadership* (May): 4–17. Available at: http://www.ascd.org/ASCD/pdf/journals/ed_lead/el_198405_bloom.pdf.

Bonawitz, Elizabeth, Patrick Shafto, Hyowon Gweon, Noah D. Goodman, Elizabeth Spelke and Laura Schulz (2011). The Double-Edged Sword of Pedagogy: Instruction Limits Spontaneous Exploration and Discovery, *Cognition* 120(3): 322–330. Available at: http://cocosci.berkeley.edu/Liz/BonawitzShaftoetalRevised.pdf.

Bouchard, Thomas J. (2014). Genes, Evolution and Intelligence, *Behavior Genetics* 44(6): 549–557.

Bouchard, Thomas J., Nancy L. Segal, Auke Tellegen, Matt McGue, Margaret Keyes and Robert Krueger (2003). Evidence for the Construct Validity and Heritability of the Wilson–Patterson Conservatism Scale: A Reared-Apart Twins Study of Social Attitudes, *Personality and Individual Differences* 34: 959–969.

Bryan, William and Noble Harter (1899). Studies on the Telegraphic Language: The Acquisition of a Hierarchy of Habits, *Psychological Review* 6(4): 345–375.

Butler, Ruth (1987). Task-Involving and Ego-Involving Properties of Evaluation: Effects of Different Feedback Conditions on Motivational Perceptions, Interest, and Performance, *Journal of Educational Psychology* 79(4): 474–482.

Carpenter, Shana K., Miko M. Wilford, Nate Kornell and Kellie M. Mullaney (2013). Appearances Can Be Deceiving: Instructor Fluency Increases Perceptions of Learning Without Increasing Actual Learning, *Psychonomic Bulletin & Review* 20(6): 1350–1356.

Cepeda, Nicholas, Edward Vul, Doug Rohrer, John Wixted and Harold Pashler (2008). Spacing Effects in Learning: A Temporal Ridgeline of Optimal Retention, *Psychological Science* 19: 1095–1102.

Chingos, Matthew M. and Grover J. 'Russ' Whitehurst (2011). Class Size: What Research Says and What It Means for State Policy. Available at: http://www.brookings.edu/research/papers/2011/05/11-class-size-whitehurst-chingos.

Claxton, Guy L. (1995). What Kind of Learning Does Self-Assessment Drive? Developing a 'Nose' for Quality: Comments on Klenowski, *Assessment in Education: Principles, Policy and Practice* 2(3): 339–343.

Cohen, Gillian (1990). Why is it Difficult to Put Names to Faces? *British Journal of Psychology* 81: 287–297.

Cousin, Glynis (2006). An Introduction to Threshold Concepts, *Planet* 17 (December): 4–5. Available at: http://www.et.kent.edu/fpdc-db/files/DD%2002-threshold.pdf.

Crocker, Jennifer, Marc-Andre Olivier and Noah Nuer (2009). Self-Image Goals and Compassionate Goals: Costs and Benefits, *Self and Identity* 8: 251–269.

Deary, Ian J. and Geoff Der (2005). Reaction Time Explains IQ's Association with Death, *Psychological Science* 16(1): 64–69.

Deary, Ian J., Lars Penke and Wendy Johnson (2010). The Neuroscience of Human Intelligence Differences, *Nature Reviews Neuroscience* 11(3): 201–211.

Deary, Ian J., Steve Strand, Pauline Smith and Cres Fernandes (2007). Intelligence and Educational Achievement, *Intelligence* 35(1): 13–21.

Delisle, James (2015). Differentiation Doesn't Work, *Education Week* (6 February). http://www.edweek.org/ew/articles/2015/01/07/differentiation-doesnt-work.html?qs= differentiation+doesn%27t+work.

Dickens, William T. and James R. Flynn (2001). Heritability Estimates versus Large Environmental Effects: The IQ Paradox Resolved, *Psychological Review* 108(2): 346.

Duckworth, Angela Lee, Teri A. Kirby, Eli Tsukayama, Heather Berstein and K. Anders Ericsson (2010). Deliberate Practice Spells Success: Why Grittier Competitors Triumph at the National Spelling Bee, *Social Psychological and Personality Science* 2: 174–181.

Dunlosky, John, Katherine A. Rawson, Elizabeth J. Marsh, Mitchell J. Nathan and Daniel T. Willingham (2013). Improving Students' Learning with Effective Learning Techniques: Promising Directions from Cognitive and Educational Psychology, *Psychological Science in the Public Interest* 14(1): 4–58.

Ferguson, Christopher J. and Moritz Heene (2012). A Vast Graveyard of Undead Theories: Publication Bias and Psychological Science's Aversion to the Null, *Perspectives on Psychological Science* 7(6): 555–561.

Galton, Maurice and Linda Hargreaves (2009). Group Work: Still a Neglected Art?, *Cambridge Journal of Education* 39: 1–6.

Gelhorn, Heather L., Michael C. Stallings, Susan E. Young, Robin P. Corley, Soo Hyun Rhee and John K. Hewitt (2005). Genetic and Environmental Influences on Conduct Disorder: Symptom, Domain and Full-Scale Analyses, *Journal of Child Psychology and Psychiatry and Allied Disciplines* 46(6): 580–591.

Gilbert, Daniel T., George S. Krull and Patrick S. Malone (1990). Unbelieving the Unbelievable: Some Problems in the Rejection of False Information, *Journal of Personality and Social Psychology* 59: 601–613.

Glenn, David (2010). Carol Dweck's Attitude, *Chronicle of Higher Education* (9 May). Available at: http://chronicle.com/article/Carol-Dwecks-Attitude/65405/.

Goldberg, Shira, Nomi Werbeloff, Eyal Fruchter, Shirly Portuguese, Michael Davidson and Mark Weiser (2014). IQ and Obesity in Adolescence: A Population-Based, Cross-Sectional Study, *Pediatric Obesity* 9(6): 419–426.

Gopnik, Alison (2011). Why Preschool Shouldn't Be Like School, *slate.com* (16 March). Available at: http://www.slate.com/articles/double_x/doublex/2011/03/why_ preschool_shouldnt_be_like_school.html?wpsrc=sh_all_tab_tw_bot.

Gottfredson, Linda S. (1997). Why G Matters: The Complexity of Everyday Life, *Intelligence* 24(1): 79–132.

Griffin, Peter (1989). Teaching Takes Place in Time, Learning Takes Place Over Time, *Mathematics Teaching* 126: 12–13.

Haimovitz, Kyla and Jennifer Henderlong Corpus (2011). Effects of Person versus Process Praise on Student Motivation: Stability and Change in Emerging Adulthood, *Educational Psychology* 31(5): 595–609. Available at: http://www.reed.edu/motivation/ docs/Haimovitz_Corpus_AERA.pdf.

Hanscombe, Ken B., Maciej Trzaskowski, Claire M. Haworth, Oliver S. Davis, Philip S. Dale and Robert Plomin (2012). Socioeconomic Status (SES) and Children's Intelligence (IQ): In a UK-Representative Sample SES Moderates the Environmental, Not Genetic, Effect on IQ, *PLOS ONE* 7(2): e30320.

Hanushek, Eric A. (1992). The Trade-Off Between Child Quantity and Quality, *Journal of Political Economy* 100(1): 84–117.

Hattie, John and Helen Timperley (2007). The Power of Feedback, *Review of Educational Research* 77(1): 81–112.

Hurt, Hallam, Elsa Malmud, Laura Betancourt, Nancy L. Brodsky and Joan M. Gianetta (1997). Children with In Utero Cocaine Exposure Do Not Differ from Control Subjects on Intelligence Testing, *Archives of Pediatric and Adolescent Medicine* 151: 1237–1241.

Hyland, Ken and Fiona Hyland (2006). Feedback on Second Language Students' Writing, *Language Teaching* 39(2): 83–101.

Ioannidis, John P. A. (2005). Why Most Published Research Findings Are False, *PLOS Medicine* (30 August). Available at: http://journals.plos.org/plosmedicine/article?id=10.1371/journal.pmed.0020124.

Irwing, Paul (2012). Sex Differences in G: An Analysis of the US Standardization Sample of the WAIS-III, *Personality and Individual Differences* 53(2): 126–131.

Jensen, Arthur R. (1969). How Much Can We Boost IQ and Scholastic Achievement, *Harvard Educational Review* 39(1): 1–123.

Johnson, Wendy, Andrew Carothers and Ian J. Deary (2008). Sex Differences in Variability in General Intelligence: A New Look at the Old Question, *Perspectives on Psychological Science* 3(6): 518–531.

Jones, Benjamin F. and Bruce A. Weinberg (2011). Age Dynamics in Scientific Creativity, *Proceedings of the National Academy of Sciences* 108(47): 18910–18914.

Kamins, Melissa L. and Carol S. Dweck (1999). Person vs. Process Praise and Criticism: Implications for Contingent Self-Worth and Coping, *Developmental Psychology* 35(3): 835–847.

Kerr, Robert and Bernard Booth (1978). Varied Motor Skill Practice is Beneficial for Beginners, *Perceptual and Motor Skills* 46: 395–401.

Kessels, Ursula, Lisa M. Warner, Julia Holle and Bettina Hannover (2008). Threat to Identity Through Positive Feedback About Academic Performance, *Zeitschrift fur Entwicklungspsychologie und Padagogische Psychologie* 40(1): 22–31.

Kirschner, Paul, John Sweller and Richard Clark (2006). Why Minimal Guidance During Instruction Does Not Work: An Analysis of the Failure of Constructivist, Discovery, Problem-Based, Experiential, and Inquiry-Based Teaching, *Educational Psychologist* 41(2): 75–86.

Kluger, Avraham and Angelo DeNisi (1996). The Effects of Feedback Interventions on Performance: A Historical Review, a Meta-Analysis, and a Preliminary Feedback Intervention Theory, *Psychological Bulletin* 119(2): 254–284.

Kornell, Nate, Matthew Jensen Hays and Robert A. Bjork (2009). Unsuccessful Retrieval Attempts Enhance Subsequent Learning, *Journal of Experimental Psychology: Learning, Memory, and Cognition* 35: 989–998.

Kruger, Justin and David Dunning (1999). Unskilled and Unaware of it: How Difficulties in Recognizing One's Own Incompetence Lead to Inflated Self-Assessments, *Journal of Personality and Social Psychology* 77(6): 1121–1134.

Madera, Juan M. and JeAnna Abbott (2012). The Diversity-Validity Dilemma Implications from the Ricci v. DeStefano US Supreme Court Case, *Cornell Hospitality Quarterly* 53(1): 31–39.

Makel, Matthew C. and Jonathan A. Plucker (2014). Facts Are More Important Than Novelty: Replication in the Education Sciences, *Educational Researcher* 43(6): 304–316.

Mansell, Warwick (2008). The Answer to Effective Learning, *TES* (21 November).

Martin, Neilson, Jane Scourfield and Peter McGuffin (2002). Observer Effects and Heritability of Childhood Attention-Deficit Hyperactivity Disorder Symptoms, *British Journal of Psychiatry* 180: 26–265.

Martin, Nicholas G., Lindon J. Eaves, Andrew C. Heath, Rosemary Jardine, Lynn M. Feingold and Hans J. Eysenck (1986). Transmission of Social Attitudes, Proceedings of the National Academy of Sciences 15 (June): 4364–4368.

McWeeny, Kathryn, Andrew Young, Dennis Hay and Andrew Ellis (1987). Putting Names to Faces, *British Journal of Psychology* 78: 143–146.

Merryman, Ashley (2014). Losing Is Good for You, *New York Times* (24 September). Available at: http://www.nytimes.com/2013/09/25/opinion/losing-is-good-for-you.html?_r=2&.

Meyer, Jan and Ray Land (2003). Threshold Concepts and Troublesome Knowledge: Linkages to Ways of Thinking and Practising Within the Disciplines, ETL Project Occasional Report 4 (May). Available at: http://www.etl.tla.ed.ac.uk//docs/ETLreport4.pdf.

Moser, Jason S., Hans S. Schroder, Carrie Heeter, Tim P. Moran and Yu-Hao Lee (2011). Mind Your Errors: Evidence for a Neural Mechanism Linking Growth Mind-Set to Adaptive Posterror Adjustments, *Psychological Science* 22: 1484–1489.

Mullen, Brian, Craig Johnson and Eduardo Salas (1991). Productivity Loss in Brainstorming Groups: A Meta-Analytic Integration, *Basic and Applied Social Psychology* 12: 3–24.

Munro, Geoffrey D. and Peter H. Ditto (1997). Biased Assimilation, Attitude Polarization, and Affect in the Processing of Stereotype-Relevant Scientific Information, *Personality and Social Psychology Bulletin* 23: 636–653.

Mussweiler, Thomas and Fritz Strack (2001). The Semantics of Anchoring, *Organizational Behaviour and Human Decision Processes* 86: 234–255.

Neisser, Ulric, Gwyneth Boodoo, Thomas J. Bouchard, A. Wade Boykin, Nathan Brody, Stephen J. Ceci, Diane F. Halpern, John C. Loehlin, Robert Perloff, Robert J. Sternberg and Susana Urbina (1996). Intelligence: Knowns and Unknowns, *American Psychologist* 51(2): 77.

New York Post (2010). Why Losers Have Delusions of Grandeur (23 May). Available at: http://nypost.com/2010/05/23/why-losers-have-delusions-of-grandeur/.

Nisbett, Richard E. and Timothy D. Wilson (1977). The Halo Effect: Evidence for Unconscious Alteration of Judgments, *Journal of Personality and Social Psychology* 35(4): 250–256.

Nuthall, Graham (2005). The Cultural Myths and Realities of Classroom Teaching and Learning: A Personal Journey, *Teachers College Record* 107(5): 895–934.

O'Rahilly, Stephen and Sadaf Farooqi (2008). Human Obesity: A Heritable Neurobehavioral Disorder That is Highly Sensitive to Environmental Conditions, *Diabetes* 57(11): 2905–2910.

Oates, Tim (n.d.). How Our Exam System Really Functions, *School House*. Available at: http://www.schoolhousemagazine.co.uk/education/examinations/how-our-exam-system-really-functions.

Oates, Tim (2014). Why Textbooks Count: A Policy Paper (November). Available at: http://www.cambridgeassessment.org.uk/Images/181744-why-textbooks-count-tim-oates.pdf.

Ohlsson, Stellan (2009). Resubsumption: A Possible Mechanism for Conceptual Change and Belief Revision, *Educational Psychologist* 44(1): 20–40.

Pashler, Harold, Mark McDaniel, Doug Rohrer and Robert A. Bjork (2008). Learning Styles: Concepts and Evidence, *Psychological Science in the Public Interest* 9(3): 105–119. Available at: http://www.psychologicalscience.org/journals/pspi/PSPI_9_3.pdf.

Perkins, David. (1999). The Many Faces of Constructivism, *Educational Leadership* 57(3): 6–11.

Plomin, Robert, Robin Corley, John C. Defries and David W. Fulker (1990). Individual Differences in Television Viewing in Early Childhood: Nature As Well As Nurture, *Psychological Science* 1(6): 371–377.

Plomin, Robert, David W. Fulker, Robin Corley and John C. DeFries (1997). Nature, Nurture, and Cognitive Development from 1 to 16 years: A Parent-Offspring Adoption Study, *Psychological Science* 8(6): 442–447.

Plomin, Robert, Nancy L. Pedersen, Paul Lichtenstein and Gerald E. McClearn (1994). Variety and Stability in Cognitive Abilities Are Largely Genetic in Origin, *Behavior Genetics* 24(3): 207–215.

Potts, Rosalind and David R. Shanks (2014). The Benefit of Generating Errors During Learning, *Journal of Experimental Psychology: General* 143(2): 644–667.

Pronin, Emily, Daniel Lin and Lee Ross (2013). The Bias Blind Spot: Perceptions of Bias in Self versus Others, *Personality and Social Psychology Bulletin* 28: 369–381.

Reed, Jodie and Joe Hallgarten (2003). Time to Say Goodbye? The Future of School Performance Tables (December). Available at: http://www.leeds.ac.uk/educol/documents/00003500.htm.

Richards, Colin (2015). Ofsted's Criteria for 'Outstanding Teaching' Are Outstanding Nonsense, and Here's Why, *TES* (7 January). Available at: https://news.tes.co.uk/b/opinion/2015/01/07/ofsted-s-criteria-for-outstanding-teaching-are-outstanding-nonsense-and-here-s-why.aspx#.VK9c1ayKxhJ.facebook.

Richland, Lindsey E., Nate Kornell and Liche Sean Kao (2009). The Pretesting Effect: Do Unsuccessful Retrieval Attempts Enhance Learning?, *Journal of Experimental Psychology: Applied* 15(3): 243–257.

Riemann, Rainer, Alois Angleitner and Jan Strelau (1997). Genetic and Environmental Influences on Personality: A Study of Twins Reared Together Using the Self- and Peer Report NEO-FFI Scales, *Journal of Personality* 65(3): 449–475.

Rivkin, Steven G., Eric A. Hanushek and John F. Kain (2005). Teachers, Schools, and Academic Achievement, *Econometrica* 73(2): 417–458.

Roediger III, Henry L. and Jeffrey D. Karpicke (2006). The Power of Testing Memory: Basic Research and Implications for Educational Practice, *Perspectives on Psychological Science* 1(3): 181–210.

Rohrer, Doug and Kelli Taylor (2007). The Shuffling of Mathematics Problems Improves Learning, *Instructional Science* 35: 481–498.

Ronald, Angelica, Francesca Happé, Patrick Bolton, Lee M. Butcher, Thomas S. Price, Sally Wheelwright, Simon Baron-Cohen and Robert Plomin (2006). Genetic Heterogeneity Between the Three Components of the Autism Spectrum: A Twin Study, *Journal of the American Academy of Child & Adolescent Psychiatry* 45(6): 691–699.

Rosenshine, Barak (2012). Principles of Instruction: Research-Based Strategies That All Teachers Should Know, *American Educator* 36(1): 12–19.

Rosenthal, Robert and Lenore Jacobson (1968). Pygmalion in the Classroom, *The Urban Review* (September): 16–20. Available at: https://www.uni-muenster.de/imperia/md/content/psyifp/aeechterhoff/sommersemester2012/schluesselstudiendersozialpsychologiea/rosenthal_jacobson_pygmalionclassroom_urbrev1968.pdf.

Roth, Philip L., Craig A. Bevier, Philip Bobko, Fred S. Switzer III and Peggy Tyler (2001). Ethnic Group Differences in Cognitive Ability in Employment and Educational Settings: A Meta-Analysis, *Personnel Psychology* 54(2): 297–330.

Rubie-Davies, Christine M. (2010). Teacher Expectations and Perceptions of Student Attributes: Is There a Relationship?, *British Journal of Educational Psychology* 80: 121–135.

Rushton, J. Philippe and C. Davison Ankney (2009). Whole Brain Size and General Mental Ability: A Review, *International Journal of Neuroscience* 119(5): 692–732.

Rushton, J. Philippe, David W. Fulker, Michael C. Neale, David B. K. Nias and Hans J. Eysenck (1986). Altruism and Aggression: The Heritability of Individual Differences, *Journal of Personality and Social Psychology* 50: 1192–1198.

Rushton, J. Philippe and Arthur R. Jensen (2005). Thirty Years of Research on Race Differences in Cognitive Ability, *Psychology, Public Policy, and Law* 11(2): 235–294.

Schmeck, Annett, Richard Mayer, Maria Opfermann, Vanessa Pfeiffer and Detlev Leutner (2014). Drawing Pictures During Learning from Scientific Text: Testing the Generative Drawing Effect and the Prognostic Drawing Effect, *Contemporary Educational Psychology* 39(4): 275–286.

Schmidt, Frank L. and John Hunter (2004). General Mental Ability in the World of Work: Occupational Attainment and Job Performance, *Journal of Personality and Social Psychology* 86(1): 162–173.

Schwarz, Norbert, Herbert Bless, Fritz Strack, Gisela Klumpp, Helga Rittenauer-Schatka and Annette Simons (1991). Ease of Retrieval as Information: Another Look at the Availability Heuristic, *Journal of Personality and Social Psychology* 61(2): 195–202.

Sedikides, Constantine and Craig Anderson (1992). Causal Explanations of Defection: A Knowledge Structure Approach, *Personality and Social Psychology Bulletin* 18: 420–429.

Senko, Corwin, Chris S. Hulleman and Judith M. Harackiewicz (2011). Achievement Goal Theory at the Crossroads: Old Controversies, Current Challenges, and New Directions, *Educational Psychologist* 46(1): 26–47.

Shakeshaft, Nicholas G., Maciej Trzaskowski, Andrew McMillan, Kaili Rimfeld, Eva Krapohl, Claire M. A. Haworth, Philip S. Dale and Robert Plomin (2013). Strong Genetic Influence on a UK Nationwide Test of Educational Achievement at the End of Compulsory Education at Age 16, *PLOS ONE* 8(12): e80341.

Sherif, Muzafer (1935). A Study of Some Social Factors in Perception, *Archives of Psychology* 27(187): 17–22.

Skipper, Yvonne and Karen Douglas (2011). Is No Praise Good Praise? Effects of Positive Feedback on Children's and University Students' Responses to Subsequent Failures, *British Journal of Educational Psychology* 82(2): 327–339.

Smith, Steven M., Arthur Glenberg and Robert A. Bjork (1978). Environmental Context and Human Memory, *Memory & Cognition* 6(4): 342–353.

Snider, Justin (2011). Rote Memorization: Overrated, or Underrated? *HechingerEd* (11 February). Available at: http://hechingered.org/content/rote-memorization-overrated-or-underrated_3351/.

Spitzer, Herbert F. (1939). Studies in Retention, *Journal of Educational Psychology* 30(9): 641–656.

Staw, Barry (1975). Attribution of the 'Causes' of Performance: A General Alternative Interpretation of Cross-Sectional Research On Organizations, *Organization Behaviour and Human Performance* 13: 414–432.

Stevens, John (2013). Army of Teaching Assistants Faces the Axe as Education Department Attempts to Save Some of the £4billion They Cost Each Year, *Daily Mail* (3 June). Available at: http://www.dailymail.co.uk/news/article-2334853/Army-teaching-assistants-faces-axe-Education-department-attempts-save-4billion-cost-year.html.

Strong, Michael, John Gargani and Ozge Hacifazlioglu (2011). Do We Know a Successful Teacher When We See One? Experiments in the Identification of Effective Teachers, *Journal of Teacher Education* 62(4): 367–382.

Subramony, Deepak, Michael Molenda, Anthony Betrus and Will Thalheimer (2014). The Mythical Retention Chart and the Corruption of Dale's Cone of Experience, *Educational Technology* 54(6): 6–16.

Sweller, John (1988). Cognitive Load During Problem Solving: Effects on Learning, *Cognitive Science* 12(2): 257–285.

Tomlinson, Carol A., Catherine M. Brighton, Holly L. Hertberg, Carolyn M. Callahan, Tonya R. Moon, Kay Brimijoin, Linda A. Conover and Timothy Reynolds (2003). Differentiating Instruction in Response to Student Readiness, Interest, and Learning Profile in Academically Diverse Classrooms: A Review of Literature, *Journal for the Education of the Gifted* 27 (2/3): 119–145.

Trzaskowski, Maciej, Nicole Harlaar, Rosalind Arden, Eva Krapohl, Kaili Rimfeld, Andrew McMillan, Philip S. Dale and Robert Plomin (2014). Genetic Influence on Family Socioeconomic Status and Children's Intelligence, *Intelligence* 42(100): 83–88.

Turkheimer, Eric, Andreana Haley, Mary Waldron, Brian D'Onofrio and Irving I. Gottesman (2003). Socioeconomic Status Modifies Heritability of IQ in Young Children, *Psychological Science* 14(6): 623–628.

Trzaskowski, Maciej, Nicholas G. Shakeshaft and Robert Plomin (2013). Intelligence Indexes Generalist Genes for Cognitive Abilities, *Intelligence* 41(5): 560–565.

Tversky, Amos and Daniel Kahneman (1974). Judgment under Uncertainty: Heuristics and Biases, *Science, New Series* 185(4157): 1124–1131.

Vialle, Wilhelmina J. and Stuart Woodcock (2011). Are We Exacerbating Students' Learning Disabilities? An Investigation of Preservice Teachers' Attributions of the Educational Outcomes of Students with Learning Disabilities. Available at: http://ro.uow.edu.au/cgi/viewcontent.cgi?article=2356&context=edupapers.

Viding, Essi, Alice P. Jones, Paul J. Frick, Terrie E. Moffitt and Robert Plomin (2008). Heritability of Antisocial Behaviour at 9: Do Callous-Unemotional Traits Matter?, *Developmental Science* 11(1): 17–22.

Vink, Jacqueline M., Gonneke Willemsen and Dorret I. Boomsma (2005). Heritability of Smoking Initiation and Nicotine Dependence, *Behavior Genetics* 35(4): 397–406.

Wainer, Howard and Harris L. Zwerling (2006). Evidence That Smaller Schools Do Not Improve Students' Achievement, *Phi Delta Kappan* 88: 300–303.

Wainer, Howard and Lisa M. Brown (2007). Three Statistical Paradoxes in the Interpretation of Group Differences: Illustrated with Medical School Admission and Licensing Data, *Handbook of Statistics* 26: 893–918.

Wax, Amy L. (2011). Disparate Impact Realism, *William and Mary Law Review* 53(2): 621.

Wedge, Marilyn (2012). Why French Kids Don't Have ADHD, *Psychology Today* (8 March). Available at: http://www.psychologytoday.com/blog/suffer-the-children/201203/why-french-kids-dont-have-adhd.

Wicherts, Jelte M., Conor V. Dolan, David J. Hessen, Paul Oosterveld, G. Caroline M. van Baal, Dorret I. Boomsma and Mark M. Span (2004). Are Intelligence Tests Measurement Invariant Over Time? Investigating the Nature of the Flynn Effect, *Intelligence* 32(5): 509–537.

Wieman, Carl (2014). The Similarities Between Research in Education and Research in the Hard Sciences, *Educational Researcher* 43(1): 12–14.

Wiliam, Dylan (2001). Reliability, Validity, And All That Jazz, *Education 3–13* 29(3): 17–21. Available at: http://eprints.ioe.ac.uk/1156/2/Wiliam2001Reliability3long.pdf.

Willingham, Daniel (2002). Inflexible Knowledge: The First Step to Expertise, *American Educator* 26(4): 31–33. Available at: http://www.aft.org/periodical/american-educator/winter-2002/ask-cognitive-scientist.

Willingham, Daniel (2007). Critical Thinking: Why Is It So Hard to Teach? *American Educator* (Summer): 8–18. Available at: http://www.aft.org/sites/default/files/periodicals/Crit_Thinking.pdf.

Willingham, Daniel (2014). Draft Bill of Research Rights for Educators, *Real Clear Education* (10 July). Available at: http://www.realcleareducation.com/articles/2014/07/10/a_draft_bill_of_rights_for_educators.html.

Wilson, Noel (1998). Educational Standards and the Problem of Error, *Educational Policy Analysis Archives* 6(10).

Wozniak, Piotr (n.d.). General Principles of SuperMemo. Available at: http://www.supermemo.com/english/princip.htm.

Zajonc, Robert B. (1980). Feeling and Thinking: Preferences Need No Inferences, *American Psychologist* 35: 151–175.

Reports

Barber, Michael and Mona Mourshed (2007). *How the World's Best Performing Education Systems Come Out on Top* (New York: McKinsey & Co.) Available at: http://mckinseyonsociety.com/downloads/reports/Education/Worlds_School_Systems_Final.pdf.

Bew, P. (Lord Bew) (2011). *Independent Review of Key Stage 2 Testing, Assessment and Accountability: Final Report* (June). Available at: http://www.educationengland.org.uk/documents/pdfs/2011-bew-report-ks2tests.pdf.

Bill and Melinda Gates Foundation (2013). *Ensuring Fair and Reliable Measures of Effective Teaching: Culminating Findings from the MET Project's Three-Year Study*. Available at: http://metproject.org/downloads/MET_Ensuring_Fair_and_Reliable_Measures_Practitioner_Brief.pdf.

Cisco (2008). *Multimodal Learning Through Media: What the Research Says*. Available at: http://www.cisco.com/web/strategy/docs/education/Multimodal-Learning-Through-Media.pdf.

Coe, Robert, Cesare Aloisi, Steve Higgins and Lee Elliot Major (2014). *What Makes Great Teaching? Review of the Underpinning Research* (London: Sutton Trust). Available at: http://www.suttontrust.com/wp-content/uploads/2014/10/What-makes-great-teaching-FINAL-4.11.14.pdf.

Loveless, Tom (2015). *How Well Are American Students Learning? The 2015 Brown Center Report on American Education*. Available at: http://www.ewa.org/sites/main/files/file-attachments/brown_ctr_2015_v2.pdf.

Mihaly, Kata, Daniel F. McCaffrey, Douglas O. Staiger and J. R. Lockwood (2013). A Composite Estimator of Effective Teaching (8 January). Available at: http://www.metproject.org/downloads/MET_Composite_Estimator_of_Effective_Teaching_Research_Paper.pdf.

Murphy, Richard (2013). *Testing Teachers: What Works Best for Teacher Evaluation and Appraisal* (London: Sutton Trust). Available at: http://www.suttontrust.com/wp-content/uploads/2013/03/MURPHYTEACHEREVALUATION-FINAL.pdf.

Ofsted (2015). *School Inspection Handbook* (January). Ref: 120101. Available at: https://www.gov.uk/government/publications/school-inspection-handbook.

Shechtman, Nicole, Angela H. DeBarger, Carolyn Dornsife, Soren Rosier and Louise Yarnall (2013). *Promoting Grit, Tenacity, and Perseverance: Critical Factors for Success in the 21st Century* (US Department of Education Office of Educational Technology). Available at: http://tech.ed.gov/files/2013/10/OET-Draft-Grit-Report-2-17-13.pdf.

Stuhlman, Megan W., Bridget K. Hamre, Jason T. Downer and Robert C. Pianta (n.d.). *What Should Classroom Observation Measure*, Part 2: *A Practitioner's Guide to Conducting Classroom Observations*. Available at: http://curry.virginia.edu/uploads/resourceLibrary/CASTL_practioner_Part2_single.pdf.

Presentations

Coe, Robert (2002). It's the Effect Size, Stupid: What Effect Size is and Why it is Important. Paper presented at the British Educational Research Association annual conference, Exeter, 12–14 September. Available at: http://www.cem.org/attachments/ebe/ESguide.pdf.

Coe, Robert (2013). Improving Education: A Triumph of Hope Over Experience. Inaugural lecture at Durham University, 18 June. Available at: http://www.cem.org/attachments/publications/ImprovingEducation2013.pdf.

DeBarger, Angela, Carlos Ayala, Jim Minstrell, Pamela Kraus and Tina Stanford (2009). Facet-Based Progressions of Student Understanding in Chemistry. Paper presented at the annual meeting of the American Educational Research Association. Available at: http://chemfacets.sri.com/downloads/ChemFacetsTR1.pdf.

Dweck, Carol (2014). The Power of Believing That You Can Improve, *TED* (December). Available at: https://www.ted.com/talks/carol_dweck_the_power_of_believing_that_you_can_improve/transcript?language=en.

Hirsch Jr, E. D. (1997). Address to the California State Board of Education, 10 April. Available at: http://www.coreknowledge.org/mimik/mimik_uploads/documents/5/AddCASTB.pdf.

Sagan, Carl (1987). Keynote address at the Committee for the Scientific Investigation of Claims of the Paranormal (CSICOP) conference, Pasadena, 3–4 April.

Wiliam, Dylan (2006). Assessment for Learning: Why, What and How. Talk delivered at the Cambridge Assessment Network Conference, University of Cambridge, 15 September.

Wiliam, Dylan (2007). Assessment, Learning and Technology: Prospects at the Periphery of Control. Keynote address to ALT-C, Nottingham, 5 September. Available at: https://www.alt.ac.uk/sites/default/files/assets_editor_uploads/documents/altc2007_dylan_wiliam_keynote_transcript.pdf.

Wiliam, Dylan (2010). Stopping People Doing Good Things. Keynote speech at the SSAT conference, Birmingham, November.

Theses and dissertations

Borg, Elin (2014). Beyond a Dual Understanding of Gender Differences in School Achievement: A Study of the Gender Gap Among Youth in Oslo Secondary Schools. PhD thesis, University of Oslo.

Videos and audio-visuals

Bjork, Robert A. (n.d.). Disassociating Learning from Performance [video]. Available at: http://gocognitive.net/interviews/dissociating-learning-performance.

Bjork, Robert A. (n.d.). The Theory of Disuse and the Role of Forgetting in Human Memory [video]. Available at: http://gocognitive.net/interviews/theory-disuse-and-role-forgetting-human-memory.

Foer, Joshua (2012). Feats of Memory Anyone Can Do [video], *ted.com*. Available at: http://www.ted.com/talks/joshua_foer_feats_of_memory_anyone_can_do?awesm=on.ted.com_Foer&utm_campaign=&utm_medium=on.ted.com-static&utm_source=t.co&utm_content=awesm-publisher.

Goldstein, Daniel (2011). The Battle Between Your Present and Future Self [video], *ted.com* (November). Available at: http://www.ted.com/talks/daniel_goldstein_the_battle_between_your_present_and_future_self.

Harpaz, Yoram (n.d.). Teaching and Learning in a Community of Thinking: Theory and Practice. Available at: http://yoramharpaz.com/presentations/teaching-and-learning-in-cot-en.pdf.

Land, Ray (2011). Threshold Concepts and Troublesome Knowledge [video]. Available at: https://www.youtube.com/watch?v=WR1cXIdWnNU.

Mazur, Eric (2009). Confessions of a Converted Lecturer [video]. Available at: https://www.youtube.com/watch?v=WwslBPj8GgI.

Robinson, Ken (2006). How Schools Kill Creativity [video], *ted.com*. Available at: http://www.ted.com/talks/ken_robinson_says_schools_kill_creativity?language=en.

Robinson, Ken (2008). Changing Paradigms. Speech given at the RSA, 16 June. Available at: https://www.thersa.org/discover/videos/event-videos/2008/06/changing-paradigms/.

Wiliam, Dylan (2012). Every Teacher Can Improve [video] (December). Available at: https://www.youtube.com/watch?t=19&v=eqRcpA5rYTE.

Blogs

Atherton, James S. (2013). Learning As Loss 1, *Doceo*. Available at: http://www.doceo.co.uk/original/learnloss_1.htm.

Bishop, Dorothy (2014). What is Educational Neuroscience? *BishopBlog* (25 January). Available at: http://deevybee.blogspot.co.uk/2014_01_01_archive.html.

Bower, Joe (2013). Let Them Eat Grit: 4 Reasons Why Grit Is Garbage, *For the Love of Learning* (12 December). Available at: www.joebower.org/2013_12_08_archive.html.

Christodoulou, Daisy (2012). Why I Am No Longer a Member of the ATL, *The Wing to Heaven* (4 April). Available at: http://thewingtoheaven.wordpress.com/2012/04/04/why-i-am-no-longer-a-member-of-the-atl/.

Coe, Robert (2014). Classroom Observation: It's Harder Than You Think, *CEM Blog* (9 January). Available at: http://www.cem.org/blog/414/.

Didau, David (2014a). Getting Feedback Right, *The Learning Spy* (10 April). Available at: http://www.learningspy.co.uk/featured/getting-feedback-right/#comment-5452.

Didau, David (2014b). Why AfL Might Be Wrong and What To Do About It, *The Learning Spy* (12 March). Available at: http://www.learningspy.co.uk/myths/afl-might-wrong/.

Fletcher-Wood, Harry (2013). What I Learned from Learning the Periodic Table and Other Thoughts on Memory and Retention of Historical Knowledge and Understanding, *Improving Teaching* (20 November). Available at: http://improvingteaching.co.uk/2013/11/20/what-i-learned-from-learning-the-periodic-table-and-other-thoughts-on-memory-and-retention-of-historical-knowledge-and-understanding/.

Fletcher-Wood, Harry (2014). So Simple, It Doesn't Seem Worth Doing. So Potent, It's A Must: How Can Checklists Improve Teaching?, *Improving Teaching* (14 June). Available at: http://improvingteaching.co.uk/2014/06/14/so-simple-it-doesnt-seem-worth-doing-so-potent-its-a-must-how-can-checklists-improve-teaching/.

Haigh, Gerald (2014). Revisiting Lost Learning, *The Learning Spy* (30 November). Available at: http://www.learningspy.co.uk/learning/revisiting-lost-learning-gerald-haigh/.

Isaksen, Bodil (2015). A Lesson is the Wrong Unit of Time, *Bodil's Blog* (25 January). Available at: http://blog.bodil.co.uk/?p=80.

Kirby, Joe (2014). How Willpower Works: The Science of Self-Control, *Pragmatic Education* (10 May). Available at: https://pragmaticreform.wordpress.com/2014/05/10/willpower/.

Kirby, Joe (2014). Motivation and Instruction, *Pragmatic Education* (24 May). Available at: https://pragmaticreform.wordpress.com/2014/05/24/motivation-instruction/.

Kirby, Joe (2014). Motivation and Emotion, *Pragmatic Education* (31 May). Available at: https://pragmaticreform.wordpress.com/2014/05/31/motivation-emotion/.

Kirby, Joe (2014). Motivation and Peer Pressure, *Pragmatic Education* (14 June). Available at: https://pragmaticreform.wordpress.com/2014/06/14/motivation-peer-pressure/.

Kohn, Alfie (2012). Criticizing (Common Criticisms of) Praise, *Alfie Kohn* (3 February). Available at: http://www.alfiekohn.org/blogs/criticizing-common-criticisms-praise/.

McInerney, Laura (2013). What If Everything You Thought About Education, Was Wrong?, *LKMco* (8 August). Available at: http://www.lkmco.org/article/what-if-everything-you-thought-about-education-was-wrong-08082013.

Old, Andrew (2013). How To Be Bad SMT, *Scenes from the Battleground* (19 October). Available at: http://teachingbattleground.wordpress.com/2013/10/19/how-to-be-bad-smt/.

Paul, Annie Murphy (2014). Making Learning Easier and Making It Harder: Both Are Necessary, *Annie Murphy Paul* (20 March). Available at: http://anniemurphypaul.com/2014/03/making-learning-easier-and-making-it-harder-both-are-necessary/.

Theobald, James (2014). How to Eat 50 Hot Dogs in 12 Minutes (and Why Setting Targets Might Hold Back Progress), *Othmar's Trombone* (18 July). Available at: https://othmarstrombone.wordpress.com/2014/07/18/how-to-eat-50-hot-dogs-in-12-minutes-and-why-setting-targets-may-hold-back-progress/.

Index

The Perfect (Ofsted) English Lesson

David Didau

ISBN: 978-178135052-2

Another from Jackie Beere's 'Perfect' stable, David Didau's simple but effective little book is designed to help bring the best out of all English departments during that all-important Ofsted visit.

Packed full of ideas, strategies and simple yet effective innovations, *The Perfect (Ofsted) English Lesson* is an essential tool in the toolkit of every English department – and not just for the evaluation either! With topics including assessment for learning, progress, the learning environment and planning outstanding lessons, this is the book for every English teacher's desk drawer.

The Secret of Literacy

Making the implicit explicit

David Didau

ISBN: 978-178135127-7

Literacy? That's someone else's job, isn't it? This is a book for all teachers on how to make explicit to students those things we do implicitly.

In the Teachers' Standards it is stated that all teachers must demonstrate an understanding of, and take responsibility for promoting, high standards of literacy, articulacy and the correct use of Standard English, whatever the teacher's specialist subject.

In *The Secret of Literacy* David Didau inspires teachers to embrace the challenge of improving students' life chances through improving their literacy.

Topics include:

- Why literacy is important

- Oracy – improving classroom talk

- How we should teach reading

- How to get students to value writing

- How written feedback and grading can support literacy

Making Kids Cleverer

A manifesto for closing the advantage gap

David Didau

ISBN: 978-178583366-3

The question of whether or not we can get cleverer is a crucial one for this book.

In this wide-ranging inquiry into psychology, sociology, philosophy and cognitive science, David argues that with greater access to culturally accumulated information – taught explicitly within a knowledge-rich curriculum – children are more likely to become cleverer, to think more critically and, subsequently, to live happier, healthier and more secure lives.

Furthermore, by sharing valuable insights into what children truly need to learn during their formative school years, he sets out the numerous practical ways in which policy makers and school leaders can make better choices about organizing schools, and how teachers can communicate the knowledge that will make the most difference to young people as effectively and efficiently as possible.

CPSIA information can be obtained
at www.ICGtesting.com
Printed in the USA
JSHW021723160120
3557JS00001B/1

9 781943 920815